Matplotlib 2.x By Example

Multi-dimensional charts, graphs, and plots in Python

Allen Chi Shing Yu
Claire Yik Lok Chung
Aldrin Kay Yuen Yim

BIRMINGHAM - MUMBAI

Matplotlib 2.x By Example

First published: August 2017

Production reference: 1240817

Published by Packt Publishing Ltd.
Livery Place
35 Livery Street
Birmingham
B3 2PB, UK.
ISBN 978-1-78829-526-0

www.packtpub.com

Credits

Authors
Allen Chi Shing Yu
Claire Yik Lok Chung
Aldrin Kay Yuen Yim

Reviewer
Nikhil Borkar

Commissioning Editor
Sunith Shetty

Acquisition Editor
Tushar Gupta

Content Development Editor
Mayur Pawanikar

Technical Editor
Vivek Arora

Copy Editor
Vikrant Phadkay

Project Coordinator
Nidhi Joshi

Proofreader
Safis Editing

Indexer
Tejal Daruwale Soni

Graphics
Tania Dutta

Production Coordinator
Arvindkumar Gupta

About the Authors

Allen Chi Shing Yu, PhD, is a Chevening Scholar, 2017-18, and an MSc student in computer science at the University of Oxford. He holds a PhD degree in Biochemistry from the Chinese University of Hong Kong, and he has used Python and Matplotlib extensively during his 10 years of experience in the field of bioinformatics and big data analysis. During his research career, Allen has published 12 international scientific research articles and presented at four international conferences, including on-stage presentations at the Congress On the Future of Engineering Software (COFES) 2011, USA, and Genome Informatics 2014, UK. Other research highlights include discovering the novel subtype of Spinocerebellar ataxia (SCA40), identifying the cause of pathogenesis for a family with Spastic paraparesis, leading the gold medalist team in 2011 International Genetically Engineered Machine (iGEM) competition, and co-developing a number of cancer genomics project.

Apart from academic research, Allen is also the co-founder of Codex Genetics Limited, which aims to provide personalized medicine service in Asia through the use of the latest genomics technology. With the financial and business support from the HKSAR Innovation and Technology Commission, Hong Kong Science Park, and the Chinese University of Hong Kong, Codex Genetics has curated and transformed recent advances in cancer and neuro-genomics research into clinically actionable insights.

I wish to thank my fiancée, Dorothy, for her constant love and support, especially during the difficult time in balancing family, work, and life. On behalf of the authors, I would like to thank the wonderful team at Packt Publishing—Mayur, Tushar, Vikrant, Vivek, and the whole editorial team who helped in the creation of this book. Thanks to Tushar's introduction, the authors feel greatly honored to take part in this amazing project. Special thanks and much appreciation to Mayur for guiding the production of this book from the ground up. The authors truly appreciate the comprehensive reviews from Nikhil Borkar. We cannot be thankful enough to the entire Matplotlib and Python community for their hard work in creating open and incredibly useful tools. Last but not least, I would like to express my sincere gratitude to Prof. Ting-Fung Chan, my parents, friends, and colleagues for their guidance in my life and work.

Chevening Scholarships, the UK government's global scholarship programme, are funded by the Foreign and Commonwealth Office (FCO) and partner organisations.

Claire Yik Lok Chung is now a PhD student at the Chinese University of Hong Kong working on Bioinformatics, after receiving her BSc degree in Cell and Molecular Biology. With her passion for scientific research, she joined three labs during her college study, including the synthetic biology lab at the University of Edinburgh. Her current projects include soybean genomic analysis using optical mapping and next-generation sequencing data. Claire started programming 10 years ago, and uses Python and Matplotlib daily to tackle Bioinformatics problems and to bring convenience to life. Being interested in information technology in general, she leads the Campus Network Support Team in college and is constantly keeping up with the latest technological trends by participating in PyCon HK 2016. She is motivated to acquire new skills through self-learning and is keen to share her knowledge and experience. In addition to science, she has developed skills in multilingual translation and graphic design, and found these transferable skills useful at work.

I would like to thank Allen for getting me on board in this exciting authorship journey, and for being a helpful senior, always generous in sharing his experience and insights. It has been a great pleasure to work closely with Allen, Aldrin and the whole editorial team at Packt. I am grateful to everyone along the way that brought my interest in computer to daily practice. I wish to extend my sincere gratitude to my supervisor, Prof. Ting-Fung Chan, my parents, teachers, colleagues, and friends. I would like to make a special mention to my dearest group of high school friends for their unfailing support and source of cheer. I would also like to thank my childhood friend, Eugene, for introducing and provoking me into technological areas. With all the support, I will continue to prove that girls are capable of achieving in the STEM field.

Aldrin Kay Yuen Yim is a PhD student in computational and system biology at Washington University School of Medicine. Before joining the university, his research primarily focused on big data analytics and bioinformatics, which led to multiple discoveries, including a novel major allergen class (designated as Group 24th Major allergen by WHO/IUIS Allergen Nomenclature subcommittee) through a multi-omic approach analysis of dust mites (JACI 2015), as well as the identification of the salt-tolerance gene in soybean through large-scale genomic analysis (Nat. Comm. 2014). He also loves to explore sci-fi ideas and put them into practice, that is, the development of a DNA-based information storage system (iGEM 2010, Frontiers in Bioengineering and Biotechnology 2014). Aldrin's current research interest focuses on neuro development and diseases, such as exploring the heterogeneity of cell types within the nervous system, as well as the gender dimorphism in brain cancers (JCI Insight 2017).

Aldrin is also the founding CEO of Codex Genetics Limited, which is currently servicing two research hospitals and the cancer registry of Hong Kong.

It is not a one-man task to write a book, and I would like to thank Allen and Claire for their invaluable input and effort during the time; the authors also owe a great debt of gratitude to all the editors and reviewers that made this book happened. I also wish to thank my parents for their love and understanding over the years, as well as my best friends, Charles and Angus, for accompanying me through my ups and downs over the past two decades. Last but not least, I also wish to extend my heartfelt thanks to Kimmy for all the love and support in life and moving all the way to Chicago to keep our love alive.

About the Reviewer

Nikhil Borkar holds a CQF designation and a postgraduate degree in quantitative finance. He also holds certified financial crime examiner and certified anti-money laundering professional qualifications. He is a registered research analyst with the securities and Exchange Board of India (SEBI) and has a keen grasp of laws and regulations pertaining to securities and investment. He is currently working as an independent FinTech and legal consultant. Prior to this, he worked with Morgan Stanley Capital International as a Global RFP project manager. He is self-motivated, intellectually curious, and hardworking. He loves to approach problems using a multi-disciplinary, holistic approach. Currently, he is actively working on machine learning, artificial intelligence, and deep learning projects. He has expertise in the following areas:

- Quantitative investing: equities, futures and options, and derivatives engineering
- Econometrics: time series analysis, statistical modeling
- Algorithms: parametric, non-parametric, and ensemble machine learning algorithms
- Code: R programming, Python, Scala, Excel VBA, SQL, and big data ecosystems.
- Data analysis: Quandl and Quantopian
- Strategies: trend following, mean reversion, cointegration, Monte-Carlo srimulations, Value at Risk, Credit Risk Modeling and Credit Rating
- Data visualization : Tableau and Matplotlib

www.PacktPub.com

For support files and downloads related to your book, please visit www.PacktPub.com.

Did you know that Packt offers eBook versions of every book published, with PDF and ePub files available? You can upgrade to the eBook version at www.PacktPub.com and as a print book customer, you are entitled to a discount on the eBook copy. Get in touch with us at service@packtpub.com for more details.

At www.PacktPub.com, you can also read a collection of free technical articles, sign up for a range of free newsletters and receive exclusive discounts and offers on Packt books and eBooks.

https://www.packtpub.com/mapt

Get the most in-demand software skills with Mapt. Mapt gives you full access to all Packt books and video courses, as well as industry-leading tools to help you plan your personal development and advance your career.

Why subscribe?

- Fully searchable across every book published by Packt
- Copy and paste, print, and bookmark content
- On demand and accessible via a web browser

Customer Feedback

Thanks for purchasing this Packt book. At Packt, quality is at the heart of our editorial process. To help us improve, please leave us an honest review on this book's Amazon page at `https://www.amazon.com/dp/1788295269`.

If you'd like to join our team of regular reviewers, you can email us at `customerreviews@packtpub.com`. We award our regular reviewers with free eBooks and videos in exchange for their valuable feedback. Help us be relentless in improving our products!

Table of Contents

Preface

Big data analytics drives innovation in scientific research, digital marketing, policy making, and much more. With the increasing amount of data from sensors, user activities, to APIs and databases, there is a need to visualize data effectively in order to communicate the insights to the target audience.

Matplotlib offers a simple but a powerful plotting library that helps to resolve the complexity in big data visualization, and turns overwhelming data into useful information. The library offers versatile plot types and robust customizations to transform data into persuasive and actionable figures. With the recent introduction of version 2, Matplotlib has further established its pivotal role in Python visualization.

Matplotlib 2.x By Example illustrates the methods and applications of various plot types through real-world examples. It begins by giving readers the basic know-how on how to create and customize plots with Matplotlib. It further covers how to plot different types of economic data in the form of 2D and 3D graphs, which give insights from a deluge of data from public repositories such as Quandl Finance and data.gov. By extending the power of Matplotlib using toolkits such as GeoPandas, Lifelines, Mplot3d, NumPy, Pandas, Plot.ly, Scikit-learn, SciPy, and Seaborn, you will learn how to visualize geographical data on maps, implement interactive charts, and craft professional scientific visualizations from complex datasets. By the end of this book, you will become well-versed with Matplotlib in your day-to-day work and be able to create advanced data visualizations.

What this book covers

In the first part of this book, you will learn the basics of creating a Matplotlib plot:

- `Chapter 1`, *Hello Plotting World!*, covers the basic constituents of a Matplotlib figure, as well as the latest features of Matplotlib version 2
- `Chapter 2`, *Figure Aesthetics*, explains how to in customize the style of components in a Matplotlib figure
- `Chapter 3`, *Figure Layout and Annotations*, explains how to add annotations and subplots, which allow more comprehensive representation of the data

Once we have a solid foundation of the basics of Matplotlib, in part two of this book, you will learn how to mix and match different techniques to create increasingly complex visualizations:

- `Chapter 4`, *Visualizing Online Data*, teaches you how to design intuitive infographics for effective storytelling through the use of real-world datasets.
- `Chapter 5`, *Visualizing Multivariate Data*, gives you an overview of the plot types that are suitable for visualizing datasets with multiple features or dimensions.
- `Chapter 6`, *Adding Interactivity and Animating Plots*, shows you that Matplotlib is not limited to creating static plots. You will learn how to create interactive charts and animations.

Finally, in part three of this book, you will learn some practical considerations and data analysis routines that are relevant to scientific plotting:

- `Chapter 7`, *A Practical Guide to Scientific Plotting*, explains that data visualization is an art that's closely coupled with statistics. As a data scientist, you will learn how to create visualizations that are not only understandable by yourself, but legible to your target audiences.
- `Chapter 8`, *Exploratory Data Analytics and Infographics*, guides you through more advanced topics in geographical infographics and exploratory data analytics.

What you need for this book

These are the prerequisites for this book:

- Basic Python knowledge is expected. Interested readers can refer to *Learning Python* by Fabrizio Romano if they are relatively new to Python programming.
- A working installation of Python 3.4 or later is required. The default Python distribution can be obtained from `https://www.python.org/download/`. Readers may also explore other Python distributions, such as Anaconda (`https://www.continuum.io/downloads`), which provides better package dependency management.
- A Windows 7+, macOS 10.10+, or Linux-based computer with 4 GB RAM or above is recommended.

- The code examples are based on Matplotlib 2.x, Seaborn 0.8.0, Pandas 0.20.3, Numpy 1.13.1, SciPy 0.19.1, pycountry 17.5.14, stockstats 0.2.0, BeautifulSoup4 4.6.0, requests 2.18.4, plotly 2.0.14, scikit-learn 0.19.0, GeoPandas 0.2.1, PIL 1.1.6, and lifelines 0.11.1. Brief instructions for installing these packages are included in the chapters, but readers can refer to the official documentation pages for more details.

Who this book is for

This book aims to help anyone interested in data visualization to get insights from big data with Python and Matplotlib 2.x. Well-visualized data aids analysis and communication regardless of the field. This book will guide Python novices to quickly pick up Matplotlib plotting skills through step-by-step tutorials. Data scientists will learn to prepare high-quality figures for publications. News editors and copywriters will learn how to create intuitive infographics to make their message crisply understandable.

Conventions

In this book, you will find a number of text styles that distinguish between different kinds of information. Here are some examples of these styles and an explanation of their meaning. Code words in text, database table names, folder names, filenames, file extensions, pathnames, dummy URLs, user input, and Twitter handles are shown as follows: "Navigate to the `Applications` folder, and then go into the `Utilities` folder."

A block of code is set as follows:

```
evens = []
with open as f:
    for line in f.readlines():
        evens.append(line.split()[1])
```

Any command-line input or output is written as follows:

```
sudo apt update
sudo apt install Python3 build-essential
```

New terms and **important words** are shown in bold. Words that you see on the screen, for example, in menus or dialog boxes, appear in the text like this: "Select **Markdown** from the drop-down list on the toolbar."

Warnings or important notes appear like this.

Tips and tricks appear like this.

Reader feedback

Feedback from our readers is always welcome. Let us know what you think about this book-what you liked or disliked. Reader feedback is important for us as it helps us develop titles that you will really get the most out of. To send us general feedback, simply email `feedback@packtpub.com`, and mention the book's title in the subject of your message. If there is a topic that you have expertise in and you are interested in either writing or contributing to a book, see our author guide at `www.packtpub.com/authors`.

Customer support

Now that you are the proud owner of a Packt book, we have a number of things to help you to get the most from your purchase.

Downloading the example code

You can download the example code files for this book from your account at `http://www.packtpub.com`. If you purchased this book elsewhere, you can visit `http://www.packtpub.com/support` and register to have the files emailed directly to you. You can download the code files by following these steps:

1. Log in or register to our website using your email address and password.
2. Hover the mouse pointer on the **SUPPORT** tab at the top.
3. Click on **Code Downloads & Errata**.
4. Enter the name of the book in the **Search** box.
5. Select the book for which you're looking to download the code files.
6. Choose from the drop-down menu where you purchased this book from.
7. Click on **Code Download**.

Once the file is downloaded, please make sure that you unzip or extract the folder using the latest version of:

- WinRAR / 7-Zip for Windows
- Zipeg / iZip / UnRarX for Mac
- 7-Zip / PeaZip for Linux

The code bundle for the book is also hosted on GitHub at `https://github.com/PacktPublishing/Matplotlib-2.x-By-Example`. We also have other code bundles from our rich catalog of books and videos available at `https://github.com/PacktPublishing/`. Check them out!

Downloading the color images of this book

We also provide you with a PDF file that has color images of the screenshots/diagrams used in this book. The color images will help you better understand the changes in the output. You can download this file from `https://www.packtpub.com/sites/default/files/downloads/Matplotlib2xByExample_ColorImages.pdf`.

Errata

Although we have taken every care to ensure the accuracy of our content, mistakes do happen. If you find a mistake in one of our books-maybe a mistake in the text or the code-we would be grateful if you could report this to us. By doing so, you can save other readers from frustration and help us improve subsequent versions of this book. If you find any errata, please report them by visiting `http://www.packtpub.com/submit-errata`, selecting your book, clicking on the **Errata Submission Form** link, and entering the details of your errata. Once your errata are verified, your submission will be accepted and the errata will be uploaded to our website or added to any list of existing errata under the Errata section of that title. To view the previously submitted errata, go to `https://www.packtpub.com/books/content/support` and enter the name of the book in the search field. The required information will appear under the **Errata** section.

Piracy

Piracy of copyrighted material on the Internet is an ongoing problem across all media. At Packt, we take the protection of our copyright and licenses very seriously. If you come across any illegal copies of our works in any form on the Internet, please provide us with the location address or website name immediately so that we can pursue a remedy. Please contact us at `copyright@packtpub.com` with a link to the suspected pirated material. We appreciate your help in protecting our authors and our ability to bring you valuable content.

Questions

If you have a problem with any aspect of this book, you can contact us at `questions@packtpub.com`, and we will do our best to address the problem.

1
Hello Plotting World!

To learn programming, we often start with printing the "Hello world!" message. For graphical plots that contain all the elements from data, axes, labels, lines and ticks, how should we begin?

This chapter gives an overview of Matplotlib's functionalities and latest features. We will guide you through the setup of the Matplotlib plotting environment. You will learn to create a simple line graph, view, and save your figures. By the end of this chapter, you will be confident enough to start building your own plots, and be ready to learn about customization and more advanced techniques in the coming sections.

Come and say "Hello!" to the world of plots!

Here is a list of topics covered in this chapter:

- What is Matplotlib?
- Setting up the Python environment
- Installing Matplotlib and its dependencies
- Setting up the Jupyter notebook
- Plotting the first simple line graph
- Loading data into Matplotlib
- Exporting the figure

Hello Matplotlib!

Welcome to the world of Matplotlib 2.0! Follow our simple example in the chapter and draw your first "Hello world" plot.

What is Matplotlib?

Matplotlib is a versatile Python library that generates plots for data visualization. With the numerous plot types and refined styling options available, it works well for creating professional figures for presentations and scientific publications. Matplotlib provides a simple way to produce figures to suit different purposes, from slideshows, high-quality poster printing, and animations to web-based interactive plots. Besides typical 2D plots, basic 3D plotting is also supported.

On the development side, the hierarchical class structure and object-oriented plotting interface of Matplotlib make the plotting process intuitive and systematic. While Matplotlib provides a native graphical user interface for real-time interaction, it can also be easily integrated into popular IPython-based interactive development environments, such as Jupyter notebook and PyCharm.

What's new in Matplotlib 2.0?

Matplotlib 2.0 features many improvements, including the appearance of default styles, image support, and text rendering speed. We have selected a number of important changes to highlight later. The details of all new changes can be found on the documentation site at `http://matplotlib.org/devdocs/users/whats_new.html`.

If you are already using previous versions of Matplotlib, you may want to pay more attention to this section to update your coding habits. If you are totally new to Matplotlib or even Python, you may jump ahead to start using Matplotlib first, and revisit here later.

Changes to the default style

The most prominent change to Matplotlib in version 2.0 is to the default style. You can find the list of changes here: `http://matplotlib.org/devdocs/users/dflt_style_changes.html`. Details of style setting will be covered in `Chapter 2`, *Figure Aesthetics*.

Color cycle

For quick plotting without having to set colors for each data series, Matplotlib uses a list of colors called the default property cycle, whereby each series is assigned one of the default colors in the cycle. In Matplotlib 2.0, the list has been changed from the original red, green, blue, cyan, magenta, yellow, and black, noted as `['b', 'g', 'r', 'c', 'm', 'y', 'k']`, to the current category10 color palette introduced by the Tableau software. As implied by the name, the new palette has 10 distinct colors suitable for categorical display. The list can be accessed by importing Matplotlib and calling `matplotlib.rcParams['axes.prop_cycle']` in Python.

Colormap

Colormaps are useful in showing gradient. The yellow to blue "viridis" colormap is now the default one in Matplotlib 2.0. This perceptually uniform colormap better represents the transition of numerical values visually than the classic "jet" scheme. This is a comparison between two colormaps:

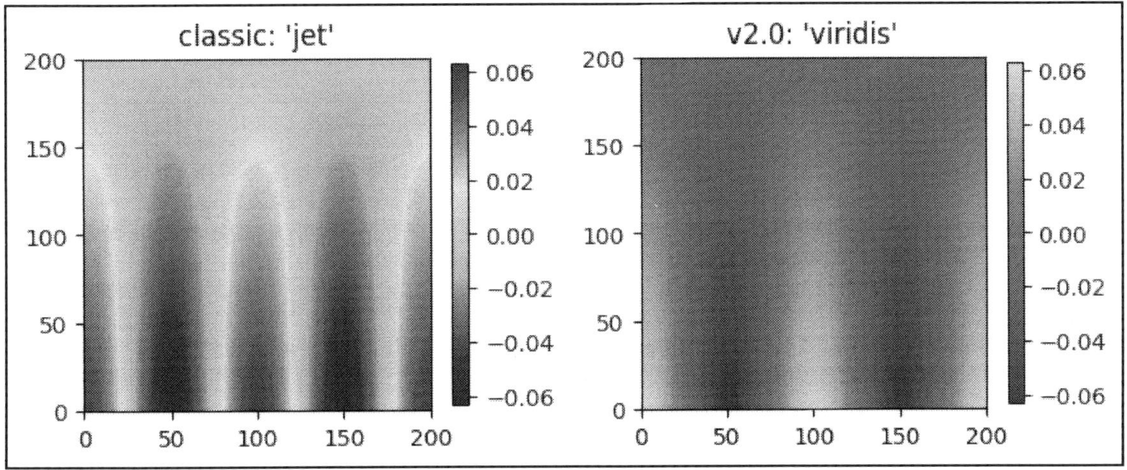

Besides defaulting to a perceptually continuous colormap, qualitative colormaps are now available for grouping values into categories:

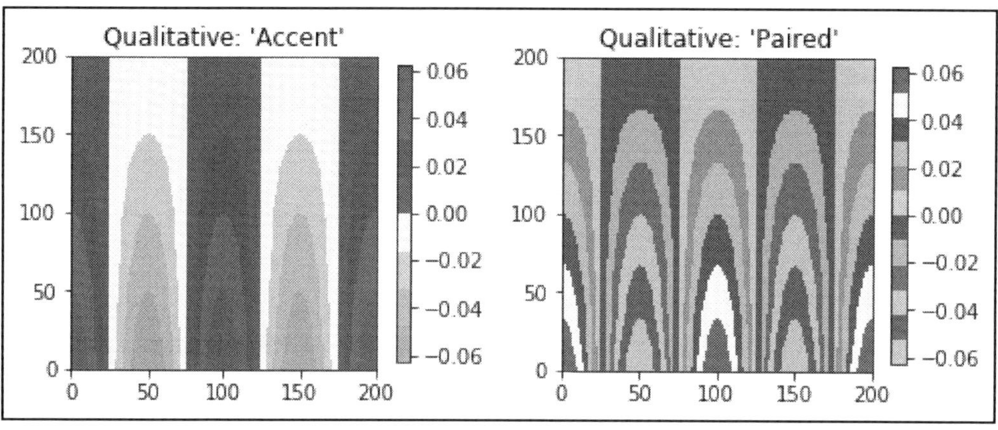

Scatter plot

Points in a scatter plot have a larger default size and no longer have a black edge, giving clearer visuals. Different colors in the default color cycle will be used for each data series if the color is not specified:

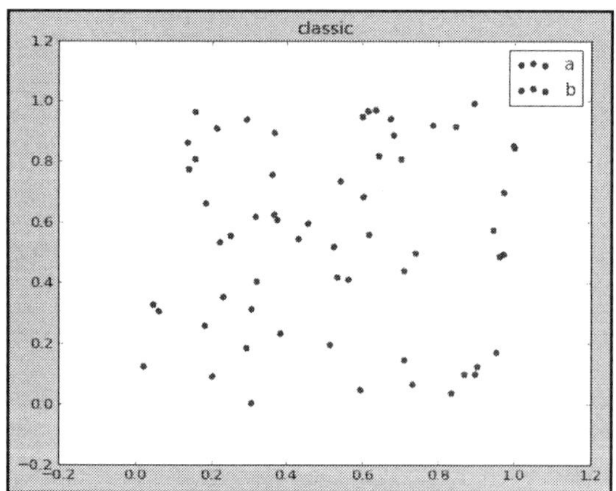

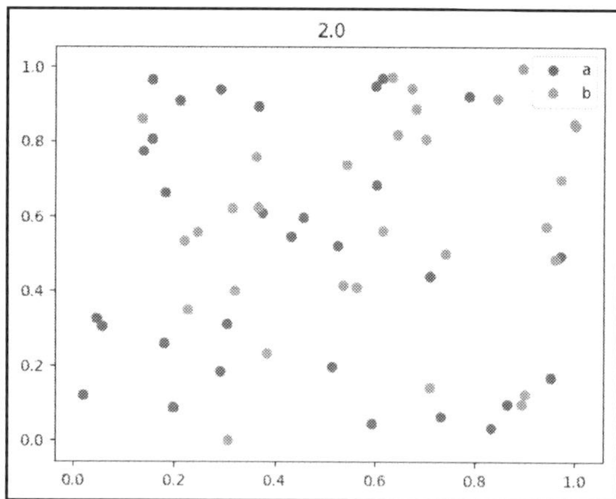

Legend

While previous versions set the legend in the upper-right corner, Matplotlib 2.0 sets the legend location as "best" by default. It automatically avoids overlapping of the legend with the data. The legend box also has rounded corners, lighter edges, and a partially transparent background to keep the focus of the readers on the data. The curve of square numbers in the classic and current default styles demonstrates the case:

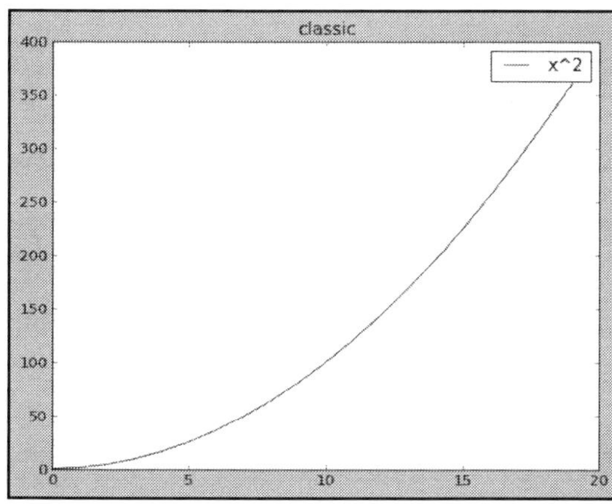

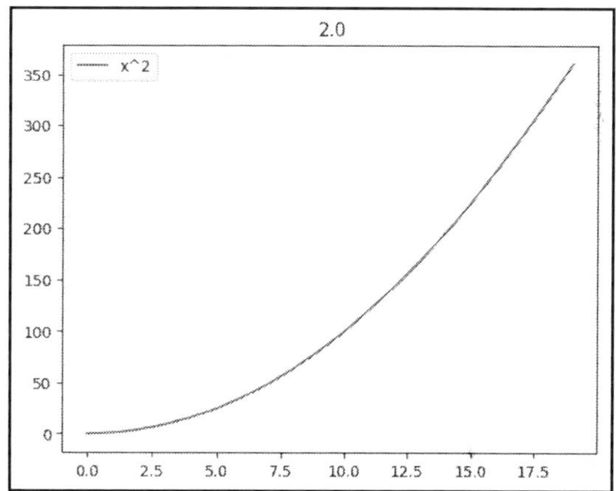

Line style

Dash patterns in line styles can now scale with the line width to display bolder dashes for clarity:

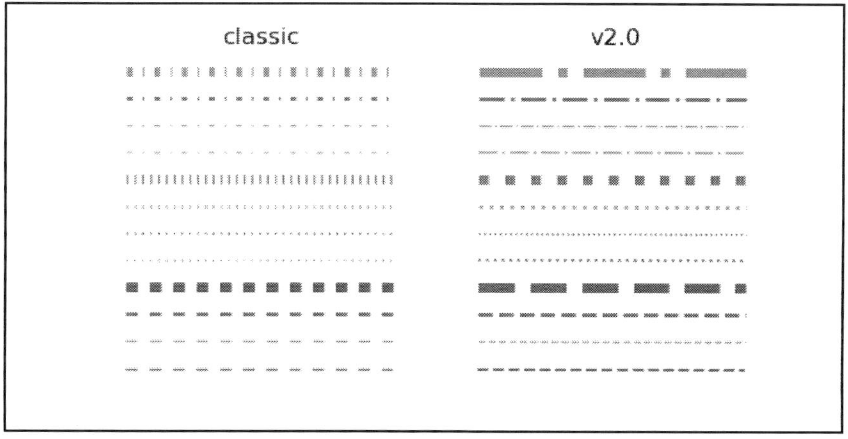

From the documentation (https://matplotlib.org/users/dflt_style_changes.html#plot)

Patch edges and color

Just like the dots in the scatter plot shown before, most filled elements ("artists", which we will explain more in `Chapter 2`, *Figure Aesthetics*) no longer have a black edge by default, making the graphics less cluttered:

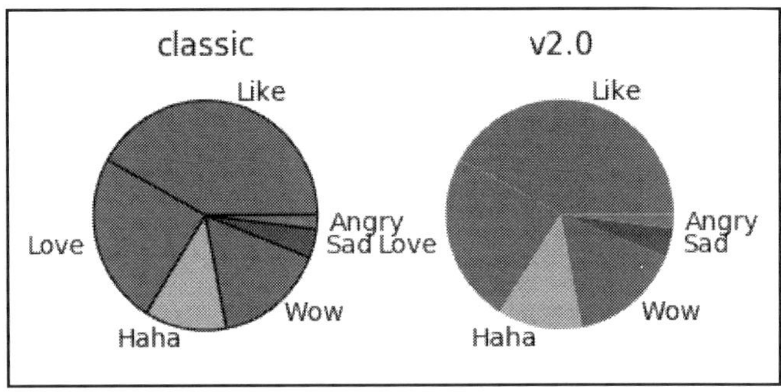

Fonts

The default font is now changed from "Bitstream Vera Sans" to "DejaVu Sans". The current font supports additional international, math, and symbol characters, including emojis.

Improved functionality or performance

Matplotlib 2.0 presents new features that improve the user experience, including speed and output quality as well as resource usage.

Improved color conversion API and RGBA support

The alpha channel, which specifies the degree of transparency, is now fully supported in Matplotlib 2.0.

Improved image support

Matplotlib 2.0 now resamples images with less memory and less data type conversion.

Faster text rendering

It is claimed that the speed of text rendering by the Agg backend is increased by 20%. We will discuss more on backends in `Chapter 6`, *Adding Interactivity and Animating Plots*.

Change in the default animation codec

To generate a video output of animated plots, a more efficient codec, H.264, is now used by default in place of MPEG-4. As H.264 has a higher compression rate, the smaller output file size permits longer video record time and reduces the time and network data needed to load them. Real-time playback of H.264 videos is generally more fluent and in better quality than those encoded in MPEG-4.

Changes in settings

Some of the settings are changed in Matplotlib v2.0 for convenience or consistency, or to avoid unexpected results.

New configuration parameters (rcParams)

New parameters are added, such as `date.autoformatter.year` for date time string formatting.

Style parameter blacklist

Style files are no longer allowed to configure settings unrelated to the style to prevent unexpected consequences. These parameters include the following:

```
'interactive', 'backend', 'backend.qt4', 'webagg.port',
'webagg.port_retries', 'webagg.open_in_browser', 'backend_fallback',
'toolbar', 'timezone', 'datapath', 'figure.max_open_warning',
'savefig.directory', tk.window_focus', 'docstring.hardcopy'
```

Change in Axes property keywords

The Axes properties `axisbg` and `axis_bgcolor` are replaced by `facecolor` to keep the keywords consistent.

Setting up the plotting environment

Matplotlib is a Python package for data visualization. To get ourselves ready for Matplotlib plotting, we need to set up Python, install Matplotlib with its dependencies, as well as prepare a platform to execute and keep our running code. While Matplotlib provides a native GUI interface, we recommend using Jupyter Notebook. It allows us to run our code interactively while keeping the code, output figures, and any notes tidy. We will walk you through the setup procedure in this session.

Setting up Python

Matplotlib 2.0 supports both Python versions 2.7 and 3.4+. In this book, we will demonstrate using Python 3.4+. You can download Python from `http://www.python.org/download/`.

Windows

For Windows, Python is available as an installer or zipped source files. We recommend the executable installer because it offers a hassle-free installation. First, choose the right architecture. Then, simply follow the instructions. Usually, you will go with the default installation, which comes with the Python package manager `pip` and Tkinter standard **GUI** (**Graphical User Interface**) and adds Python to the PATH (important!). In just a few clicks, it's done!

64-bit or 32-bit?

In most cases, you will go for the 64-bit (x86-64) version because it usually gives better performance. Most computers today are built with the 64-bit architecture, which allows more efficient use of system memory (RAM). Going on 64-bit means the processor reads data in larger chunks each time. It also allows more than 3 GB of data to be addressed. In scientific computing, we typically benefit from added RAM to achieve higher speed. Although using a 64-bit version doubles the memory footprint before exceeding the memory limit, it is often required for large data, such as in scientific computing. Of course, if you have a 32-bit computer, 32-bit is your only choice.

Using Python

1. Press Win + *R* on the keyboard to call the **Run** dialog.
2. Type `cmd.exe` in the **Run** dialog to open Command Prompt:

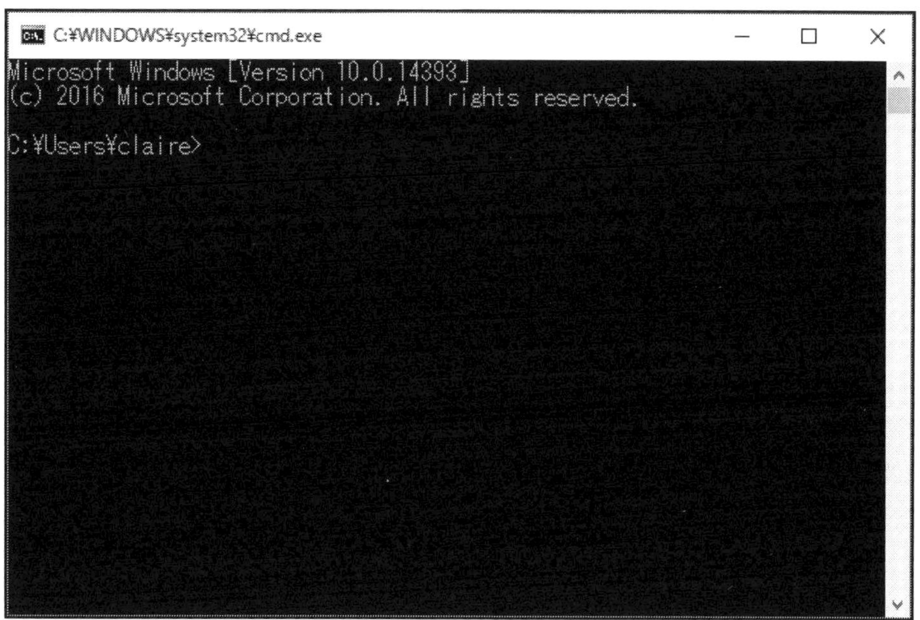

3. In Command Prompt, type `python`.

For brevity, we will refer to both Windows Command Prompt and the Linux or Mac Terminal app as the "terminal" throughout this book.

Some Python packages, such as Numpy and Scipy require Windows C++ compilers to work properly. We can obtain Microsoft Visual C++ compiler for free from the official site: `http://landinghub.visualstudio.com/visual-cpp-build-tools`

As noted in the Python documentation page (`https://wiki.python.org/moin/WindowsCompilers`), a specific C++ compiler version is required for each Python version. Since most codes in this book were tested against Python 3.6, Microsoft Visual C++ 14.0 / Build Tools for Visual Studio 2017 is recommended.

Readers can also check out Anaconda Python (`https://www.continuum.io/downloads/`), which ships with pre-built binaries for many Python packages. According to our experience, the Conda package manager resolves package dependencies in a much nicer way on Windows.

macOS

macOS comes with Python 2.7 installed. To ensure compatibility with the example code in this book, Python 3.4 or above is required, which is available for download from `https://www.python.org/downloads/mac-osx/`. You will be prompted by a graphical installation wizard when you run the downloaded installation package:

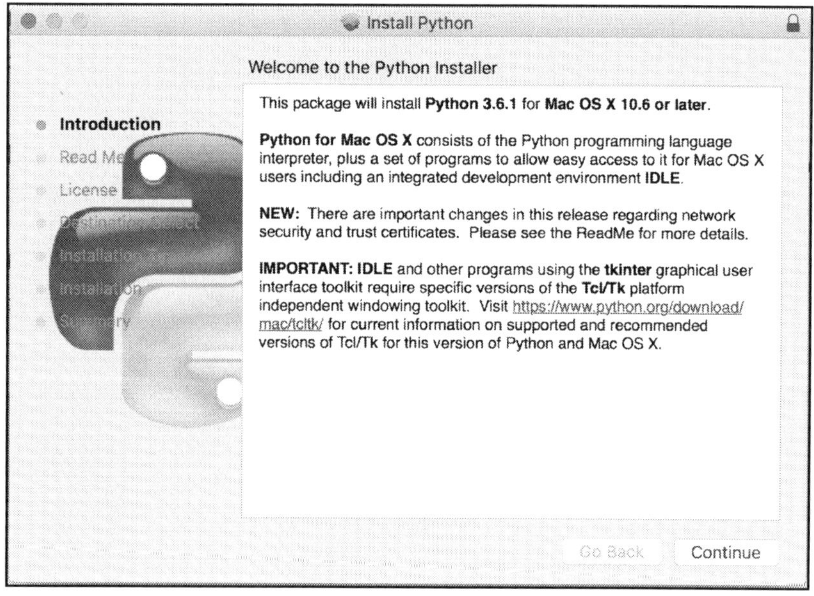

After completing the graphical installation steps, Python 3 can be accessed via these steps:

1. Open the Finder app.
2. Navigate to the `Applications` folder, and then go into the `Utilities` folder.
3. Open the Terminal app.
4. You will be prompted by the following message when you type `python3` in the terminal:

```
Python 3.6.1 (v3.6.1:69c0db5, Mar 21 2017, 18:41:36 [GCC 4.2.1
(Apple Inc. build 5666) (dot 3)] on Darwin
Type "help", "copyright", "credits" or "license" for more
information.
>>>
```

Some Python packages require requires Xcode Command Line Tools to compile properly. Xcode can be obtained from Mac App Store. To install the command line tools, enter the following command in Terminal: `xcode-select --install` and follow the installation prompts.

Linux

Most recent Linux distributions come with Python 3.4+ preinstalled. You can check this out by typing `python3` in the terminal. If Python 3 is installed, you should see the following message, which shows more information about the version:

```
Python 3.4.3 (default, Nov 17 2016, 01:08:31) [GCC 4.8.4] on Linux
Type "help", "copyright", "credits" or "license" for more information.
>>>
```

If Python 3 is not installed, you can install it on a Debian-based OS, such as Ubuntu, by running the following commands in the terminal:

```
sudo apt update
sudo apt install Python3 build-essential
```

The `build-essential` package contains compilers that are useful for building non-pure Python packages. You may need to substitute `apt` with `apt-get` if you have Ubuntu 14.04 or older.

Installing the Matplotlib dependencies

We recommend installing Matplotlib by a Python package manager, which will help you to automatically resolve and install dependencies upon each installation or upgrade of a package. We will demonstrate how to install Matplotlib with `pip`.

Installing the pip Python package manager

`pip` is installed with Python 2>=2.7.9 or Python 3>=3.4 binaries, but you will need to upgrade `pip`.

For the first time, you may do so by downloading `get-pip.py` from `http://bootstrap.pypa.io/get-pip.py`.

Then run this in the terminal:

```
python3 get-pip.py
```

You can then type `pip3` to run `pip` in the terminal.
After `pip` is installed, you may upgrade it by this command:

```
pip3 install -upgrade pip
```

The documentation of `pip` can be found at `http://pip.pypa.io`.

Installing Matplotlib with pip

To install Matplotlib with `pip`, simply type the following:

```
pip3 install matplotlib
```

It will automatically collect and install dependencies such as numpy.

Setting up Jupyter notebook

While Matplotlib offers a native plotting GUI, Jupyter notebook is a good option to execute and organize our code and output. We will soon introduce its advantages and usage.

Why Jupyter notebook?

Jupyter notebook (formerly known as IPython notebook) is an IPython-based interactive computational environment. Unlike the native Python console, code and imported data can easily be reused. There are also markdown functions that allow you to take notes like a real notebook. Code and other content can be separated into blocks (cells) for better organization. In particular, it offers a seamless integration with the `matplotlib` library for plot display.

Jupyter Notebook works as a server-client application and provides a neat web browser interface where you can edit and run your code. While you can run it locally even on a computer without internet access, notebooks on remote servers can be as easily accessed by SSH port forwarding. Multiple notebook instances, local or remote, can be run simultaneously on different network ports.

Here is a screenshot of a running Jupyter Notebook:

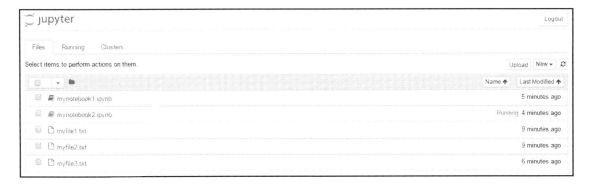

Jupyter notebook provides multiple saving options for easy sharing. There are also features such as auto-complete functions in the code editor that facilitate development.

In addition, Jupyter notebook offers different kernels to be installed for interactive computing with different programming languages. We will skip this for our purposes.

Installing Jupyter notebook

To install Jupyter notebook, simply type this in the terminal:

```
pip3 install jupyter
```

Using Jupyter notebook

Jupyter notebook is easy to use and can be accessed remotely as web pages on client browsers. Here is the basic usage of how to set up a new notebook session, run and save code, and jot down notes with the Markdown format.

Starting a Jupyter notebook session

1. Type `jupyter notebook` in the terminal or Command Prompt.
2. Open your favorite browser.
3. Type in `localhost:8888` as the URL.

To specify the port, such as when running multiple notebook instances on one or more machines, you can do so with the `--port={port number}` option.

For a notebook on remote servers, you can use SSH for port forwarding. Just specify the `-L` option with `{port number}:localhost:{port number}` during connection, as follows:

```
ssh -L 8888:localhost:8888 smith@remoteserver
```

The Jupyter Notebook home page will show up, listing files in your current directory. Notebook files are denoted by a book logo. Running notebooks are marked in green.

Editing and running code

A notebook contains boxes called cells. A new notebook begins with a gray box cell, which is a text area for code editing by default. To insert and edit code:

1. Click inside the gray box.
2. Type in your Python code.
3. Click on the >| play button or press *Shift* + *Enter* to run the current cell and move the cursor to the next cell:

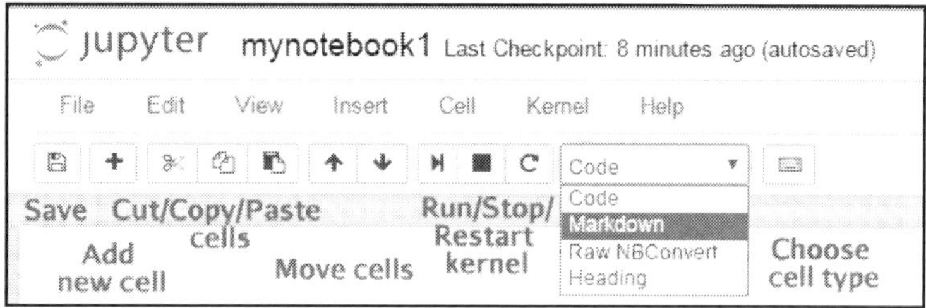

Cells can be run in different orders and rerun multiple times in a session. The output and any warnings or error messages are shown in the output area of each cell under each gray textbox. The number in square brackets on the left shows the order of the cell last run:

```
In [1]: def demo(n):
            for i in range(n):
                print(i)

In [2]: demo(10)

        0
        1
        2
        3
        4
        5
        6
        7
        8
        9

In [3]: demo('xyz')

        ---------------------------------------------------------------------------
        TypeError                                 Traceback (most recent call last)
        <ipython-input-3-db40dbc442aa> in <module>()
        ----> 1 demo('xyz')

        <ipython-input-1-1bacd60b8b94> in demo(n)
              1 def demo(n):
        ----> 2     for i in range(n):
              3         print(i)

        TypeError: range() integer end argument expected, got str.

In [ ]:
```

Once a cell is run, stored namespaces, including functions and variables, are shared throughout the notebook before the kernel restarts.

You can edit the code of any cells while some cells are running. If for any reason you want to interrupt the running kernel, such as to stop a loop that prints out too many messages, you can do so by clicking on the square interrupt button in the toolbar.

Try not to print too much output when using Jupyter Notebook; it may crash your browser. However, long lists will be automatically abbreviated if you print them out.

Jotting down notes in Markdown mode

How do we insert words and style them to organize our notebook?

```
Title: My first notebook
==
# Header 1
## Header 2
- point 1
- point 2

This is <b><i>IMPORTANT</i></b> <br/>
So is **THIS** <br/>
___
```

Here is the way:

1. Select **Markdown** from the drop-down list on the toolbar.
2. Type your notes in the gray box.
3. Click on the >| play button or press *Shift* + *Enter* to display the markdown.

Markdown notation provides a handy way to style without much manual clicking or galore of tags:

Style	**Method**
Headers: H1, H2, H3...	Start the line with a hash #, followed by a space, for example, # xxx, ## xxx, ### xxx.
Title	Two or more equal signs on the next line, same effect as H1.
Emphasis (italic)	*xxx* or _xxx_.
Strong emphasis (bold)	**xxx** or __xxx__.
Unordered list	Start each line with one of the markers: asterisk (*), minus (-), or plus (+). Then follow with a space, for example, * xxx.
Ordered list	Start each line with ordered numbers from 1, followed by a period (.) and a space.
Horizontal rule	Three underscores ___.

A detailed cheatsheet is provided by Adam Pritchard at `https://github.com/adam-p/markdown-here/wiki/Markdown-Cheatsheet`.

Viewing Matplotlib plots

For static figures, type `%matplotlib inline` in a cell. The figure will be displayed in the output area:

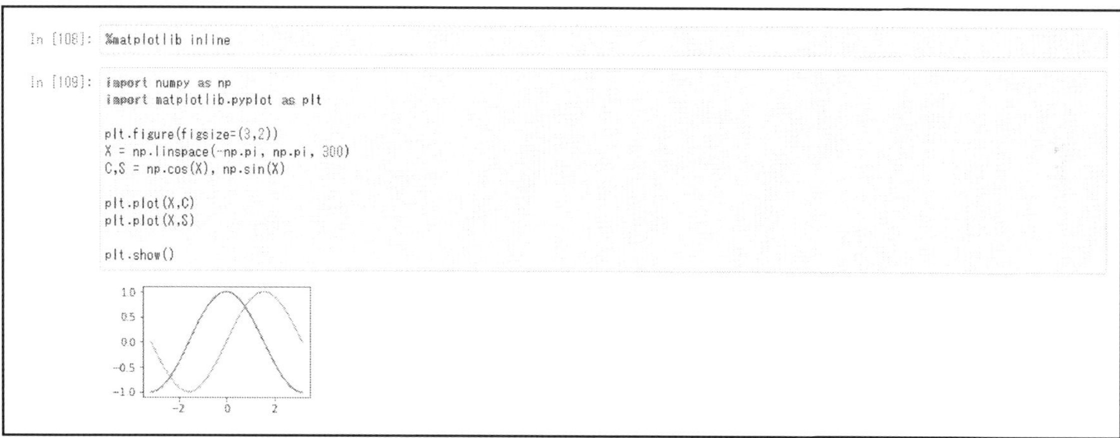

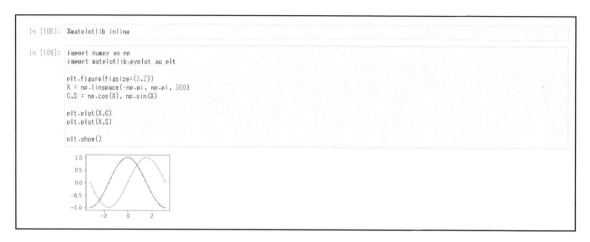

Running `%matplotlib notebook` will embed the Matplotlib interface in the output area.

Real-time interaction such as zooming and panning can be done under this mode. Clicking on the power sign button in the top-right corner will stop the interactive mode. The figure will become static, as in the case of `%matplotlib inline`:

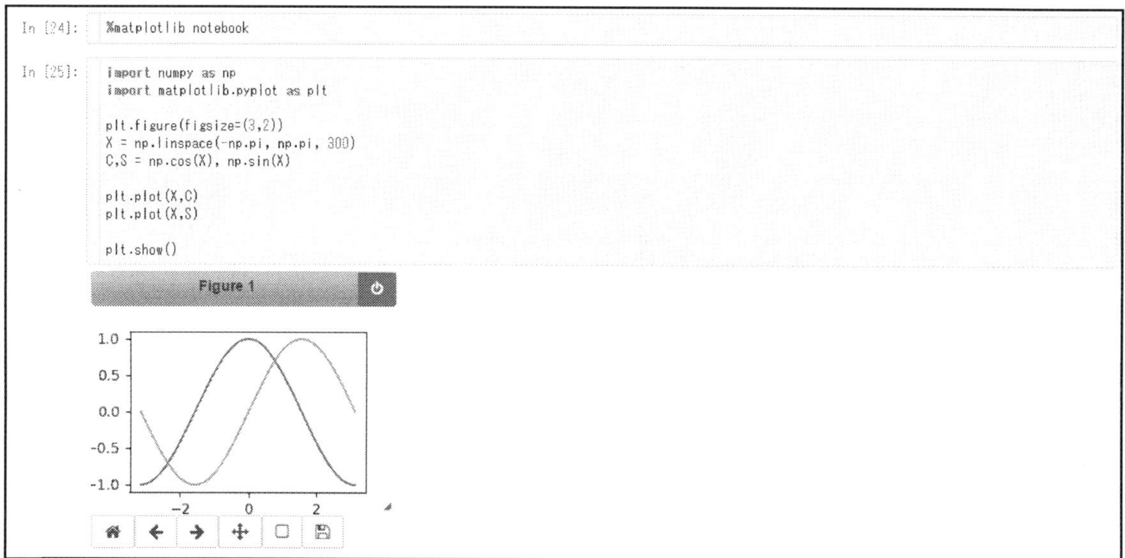

Saving the notebook project

Each notebook project can easily be saved and shared as the standard JSON-based `.ipynb` format (which can be run interactively by Jupyter on another machine), an ordinary `.py` Python script, or a static `.html` web page or `.md` format for viewing. To convert the notebook into Latex or `.pdf` via LaTeX files, Pandoc is required. More advanced users can check out the installation instructions of Pandoc on `http://pandoc.org/installing.html`:

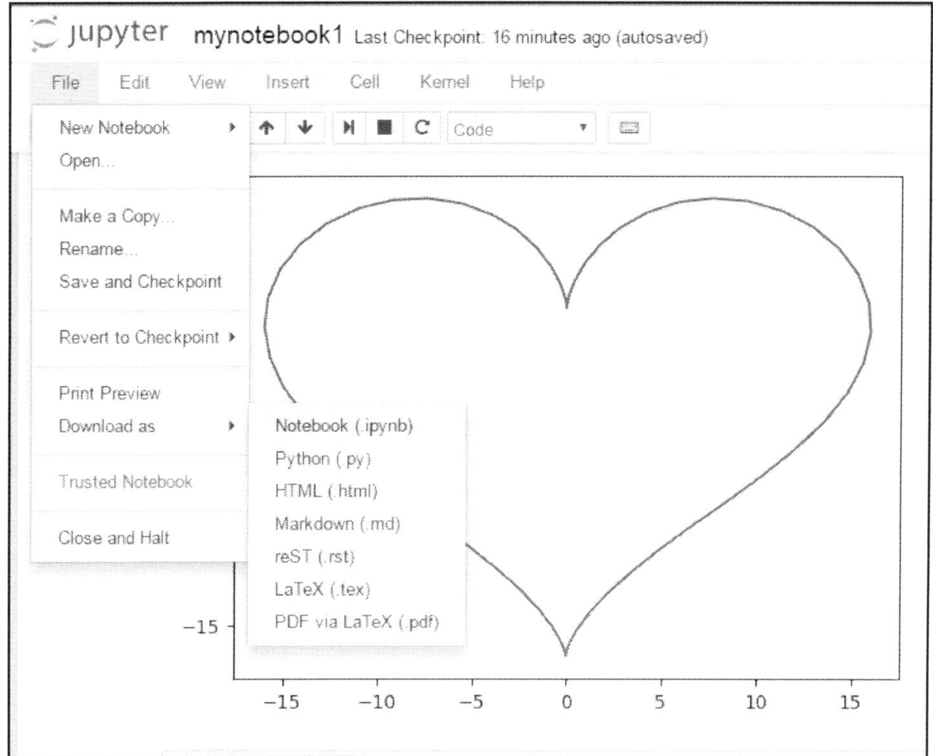

All set to go!

We have now set up the necessary packages and learned the basic usage of our coding environment. Let's start our journey!

Plotting our first graph

We will start with a simple line graph of a curve of squares, that is, $y = x^2$.

Loading data for plotting

To visualize data, we should of course start with "having" some data. While we assume you have some nice data on hand to show, we will briefly show you how to load it in Python for plotting.

Data structures

There are several common data structures we will keep coming across.

List

List is a basic Python data type for storing a collection of values. A list is created by putting element values inside a square bracket. To reuse our list, we can give it a name and store it like this:

```
evens = [2,4,6,8,10]
```

When we want to get a series in a greater range, for instance, to get more data points for our curve of squares to make it smoother, we may use the Python `range()` function:

```
evens = range(2,102,2)
```

This command will give us all even numbers from 2 to 100 (both inclusive) and store it in a list named `evens`.

Numpy array

Very often, we deal with more complex data. If you need a matrix with multiple columns or want to perform mathematical operations over all elements in a collection, then numpy is for you:

```
import numpy as np
```

We abbreviated `numpy` to `np` by convention, keeping our code succinct.

`np.array()` converts a supported data type, a list in this case, into a Numpy array. To produce a numpy array from our `evens` list, we do the following:

```
np.array(evens)
```

pandas dataframe

A pandas dataframe is useful when we have some non-numerical labels or values in our matrix. It does not require homogeneous data, unlike Numpy. Columns can be named. There are also functions such as `melt()` and `pivot_table()` that add convenience in reshaping the table to facilitate analysis and plotting.

To convert a list into a pandas dataframe, we do the following:

```
import pandas as pd
pd.DataFrame(evens)
```

You can also convert a numpy array into a pandas dataframe.

Loading data from files

While all this gives you a refresher of the data structures we will be working on, in real life, instead of inventing data, we read it from data sources. A tab-delimited plaintext file is the simplest and most common type of data input. Imagine we have a file called `evens.txt` containing the aforementioned even numbers. There are two columns. The first column only records unnecessary information. We want to load the data in the second column.

Here is what the dummy text file looks like:

```
abc	2
abc	4
abc	6
abc	8
abc	10
abc	12
abc	14
abc	16
abc	18
abc	20
abc	22
abc	24
abc	26
abc	28
abc	30
abc	32
abc	34
```

The basic Python way

We can initialize an empty list, read the file line by line, split each line, and append the second element to our list:

```
evens = []
with open as f:
    for line in f.readlines():
        evens.append(line.split()[1])
```

Of course, you can also do this in a one-liner:

```
evens = [int(x.split()[1]) for x in
open('evens.txt').readlines()]
```

We are just trying to go step by step, following the Zen of Python: simple is better than complex.

The Numpy way

It is simple when we have a file with only two columns, and only one column to read, but it can get more tedious when we have an extended table containing thousands of columns and rows and we want to convert them into a Numpy matrix later.

Numpy provides a standard one-liner solution:

```
import numpy as np
np.loadtxt('evens.txt',delimiter='\t',usecols=1,dtype=np.int32)
```

The first parameter is the path of the data file. The `delimiter` parameter specifies the string used to separate values, which is a tab here. Because `numpy.loadtxt()` by default separate values separated by any whitespace into columns by default, this argument can be omitted here. We have set it for demonstration.

For `usecols` and `dtype` that specify which columns to read and what data type each column corresponds to, you may pass a single value to each, or a sequence (such as list) for reading multiple columns.

Numpy also by default skips lines starting with #, which typically marks comment or header lines. You may change this behavior by setting the `comment` parameter.

The pandas way

Similar to Numpy, pandas offers an easy way to load text files into a pandas dataframe:

```
import pandas as pd
pd.read_csv(usecols=1)
```

Here the separation can be denoted by either `sep` or `delimiter`, which is set as comma `,` by default (**CSV** stands for **comma-separated values**).

There is a long list of less commonly used options available as to determine how different data formats, data types, and errors should be handled. You may refer to the documentation at `http://pandas.pydata.org/pandas-docs/stable/generated/pandas.read_csv.html`. Besides flat CSV files, Pandas also has other built-in functions for reading other common data formats, such as Excel, JSON, HTML, HDF5, SQL, and Google BigQuery.

To stay focused on data visualization, we will not dig deep into the methods of data cleaning in this book, but this is a survival skill set very helpful in data science. If interested, you can check out resources on data handling with Python.

Importing the Matplotlib pyplot module

The Matplotlib package includes many modules, including artist that controls the aesthetics, and rcParams for setting default values. The Pyplot module is the plotting interface we will mostly deal with, which creates plots of data in an object-oriented manner.

By convention, we use the `plt` abbreviation when importing:

```
import matplotlib.pylot as plt
```

Don't forget to run the Jupyter Notebook cell magic `%matplotlib inline` to embed your figure in the output.

Don't use the pylab module!

The use of the pylab module is now discouraged, and generally replaced by the **object-oriented** (**OO**) interface. While pylab provides some convenience by importing `matplotlib.pyplot` and `numpy` under a single namespace. Many pylab examples are still found online today, but it is much better to call the `Matplotlib.pyplot` and `numpy` modules separately.

Plotting a curve

Plotting a line graph of the list can be as simple as:

```
plt.plot(evens)
```

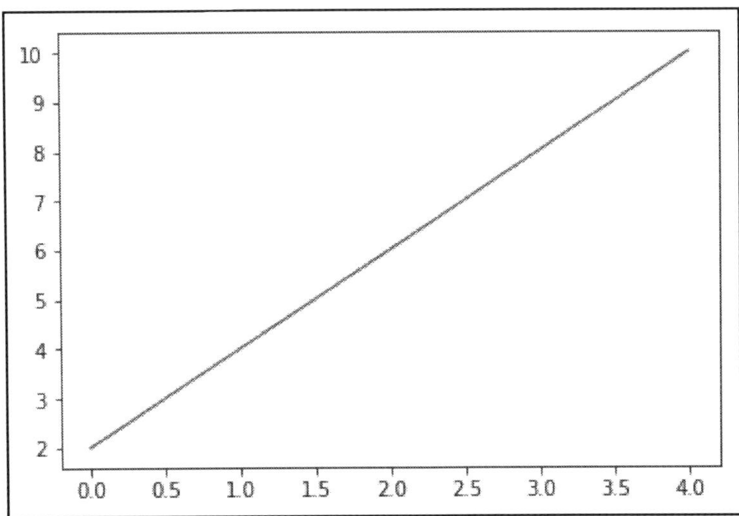

When only one parameter is specified, Pyplot assumes the data we input is on the *y* axis and chooses a scale for the *x* axis automatically.

To plot a graph, call `plt.plot(x,y)` where `x` and `y` are the *x* coordinates and *y* coordinates of data points:

```
plt.plot(evens,evens**2)
```

To label the curve with a legend, we add the label information in the `plot` function:

```
plt.plot(evens,evens**2,label = 'x^2')
plt.legend()
```

Viewing the figure

Now, don't forget to call `plt.show()` to display the figure!

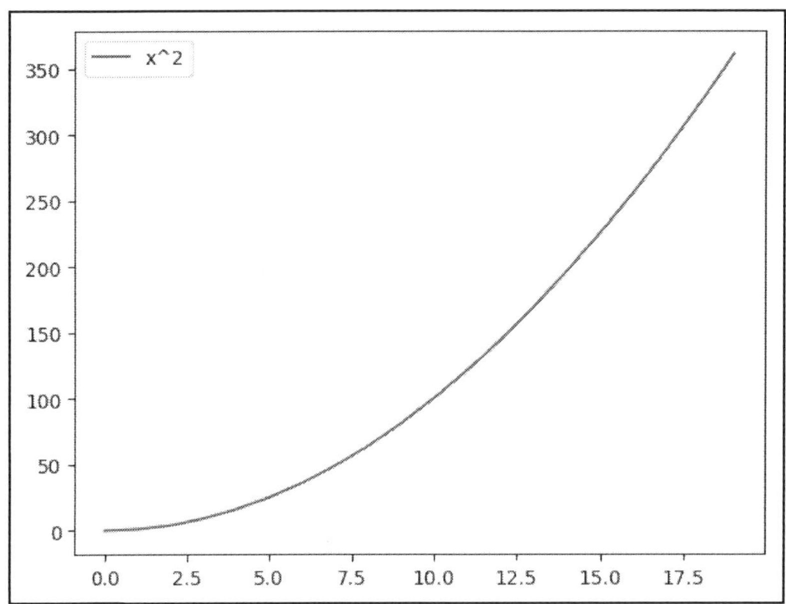

Saving the figure

Now we have drawn our first figure. Let's save our work! Surely we don't want to resort to screen capture. Here is a simple way to do it by calling `pyplot.savefig()`.

If you want to both view the image on screen and save it in file, remember to call `pyplot.savefig()` before `pyplot.show()` to make sure you don't save a blank canvas.

Setting the output format

The `pyplot.savefig()` function takes the path of the output file and automatically outputs it in the specified extension. For example, `pyplot.savefig('output.png')` will generate a PNG image. If no extension is specified, an SVG image will be generated by default. If the specified format is unsupported, let's say `.doc`, a `ValueError` Python exception will be thrown:

```
In [3]: plt.savefig('test.doc')

---------------------------------------------------------------------------
ValueError                                Traceback (most recent call last)
<ipython-input-3-dfc7fc198e20> in <module>()
----> 1 plt.savefig('test.doc')

c:¥users¥claire¥appdata¥local¥programs¥python¥python36¥lib¥site-packages¥matplotlib¥pyplot.py in savefig(*args, **kwargs)
    695 def savefig(*args, **kwargs):
    696     fig = gcf()
--> 697     res = fig.savefig(*args, **kwargs)
    698     fig.canvas.draw_idle()   # need this if 'transparent=True' to reset colors
    699     return res

c:¥users¥claire¥appdata¥local¥programs¥python¥python36¥lib¥site-packages¥matplotlib¥figure.py in savefig(self, *args, **kwargs)
   1570                 self.set_frameon(frameon)
   1571
-> 1572         self.canvas.print_figure(*args, **kwargs)
   1573
   1574         if frameon:

c:¥users¥claire¥appdata¥local¥programs¥python¥python36¥lib¥site-packages¥matplotlib¥backend_bases.py in print_figure(self, filename, dpi, facecolor, edgecolor, orientation, format, **kwargs)
   2143
   2144         # get canvas object and print method for format
-> 2145         canvas = self._get_output_canvas(format)
   2146         print_method = getattr(canvas, 'print_%s' % format)
   2147

c:¥users¥claire¥appdata¥local¥programs¥python¥python36¥lib¥site-packages¥matplotlib¥backend_bases.py in _get_output_canvas(self, format)
   2083         raise ValueError('Format "%s" is not supported.¥n'
   2084                          'Supported formats: '
-> 2085                          '%s.' % (format, ', '.join(formats)))
   2086
   2087     def print_figure(self, filename, dpi=None, facecolor=None, edgecolor=None,

ValueError: Format "doc" is not supported.
Supported formats: eps, pdf, pgf, png, ps, raw, rgba, svg, svgz.
```

PNG (Portable Network Graphics)

Compared to JPEG, another common image file format, PNG, has the advantage of allowing a transparent background. PNG is widely supported by most image viewers and handlers.

PDF (Portable Document Format)

A PDF is a standard document format, which you don't have to worry about the availability of readers. However, most Office software do not support the import of PDF as image.

SVG (Scalable Vector Graphics)

SVG is a vector graphics format that can be scaled without losing details. Hence, better quality can be achieved with a smaller file size. It goes well on the web with HTML5. It may not be supported by some primitive image viewers.

Post (Postscript)

Postscript is a page description language for electronic publishing. It is useful for batch processing images to publish.

The **Gimp Drawing Kit** (**GDK**) raster graphics rendering is deprecated in 2.0, which means image formats such as JPG and TIFF are no longer supported with the default backend. We will discuss the backends later in more detail.

Adjusting the resolution

Resolution measures the details recorded in an image. It determines how much you can enlarge your image without losing details. An image with higher resolution retains high quality at larger dimensions, but also has a bigger file size.

Depending on the purpose, you may want to output your figures at different resolutions. Resolution is measured as the number of color pixel **dot per inch** (**dpi**). You may adjust the resolution of a figure output by specifying the `dpi` parameter in the `pyplot.savefig()` function, for example, by:

```
plt.savefig('output.png',dpi=300)
```

While a higher resolution delivers better image quality, it also means a larger file size and demands more computer resources. Here are some references of how high should you set your image resolution:

- Slideshow presentations: 96 dpi+

Here are some suggestions by Microsoft for graphics resolution for Powerpoint presentations for different screen sizes: `https://support.microsoft.com/en-us/help/827745/how-to-change-the-export-resolution-of-a-powerpoint-slide`:

Screen height (pixel)	Resolution (dpi)
720	96 (default)
750	100
1125	150
1500	200
1875	250
2250	300

- Poster presentation: 300 dpi+
- Web : 72 dpi+ (SVG that can scale responsively is recommended)

Summary

In this chapter, you learned to use Matplotlib to draw a simple line graph. We set up the environment, imported data, and output the figure as an image in different formats.

In the next chapter, you will learn how to customize the appearance of your figure.

2
Figure Aesthetics

Now that you have entered the world of Matplotlib, surely you will want more than plain boring figures that look all the same. This chapter talks about the aesthetics of a figure. We introduce the structure and components of a Matplotlib figure and how to style these details. In this chapter, you will learn how to make a figure stylish, professional, and genuinely yours.

Here are the topics covered in this chapter:

- Basic structure and terminologies of a Matplotlib figure
- Setting colors in Matplotlib
- Adjusting text formats
- Lines and markers
    - Customizing line styles
    - Customizing marker styles
- Grids, ticks, and axes
    - Adding and adjusting grid lines
    - Adjusting tick spacing
    - Customizing tick formatters
    - Adding axes labeling
    - Nonlinear axes
- Title and legends
- Style sheet support

Basic structure of a Matplotlib figure

A basic Matplotlib figure is made up of multiple components common to different plot types. It will be useful to familiarize ourselves with the terminologies, as we will be using them frequently in plotting. To get you up to speed, we have prepared a glossary of these basic objects. For clearer illustration, here is a plot adapted from Matplotlib's official website that nicely highlights the anatomy of a typical Matplotlib figure:

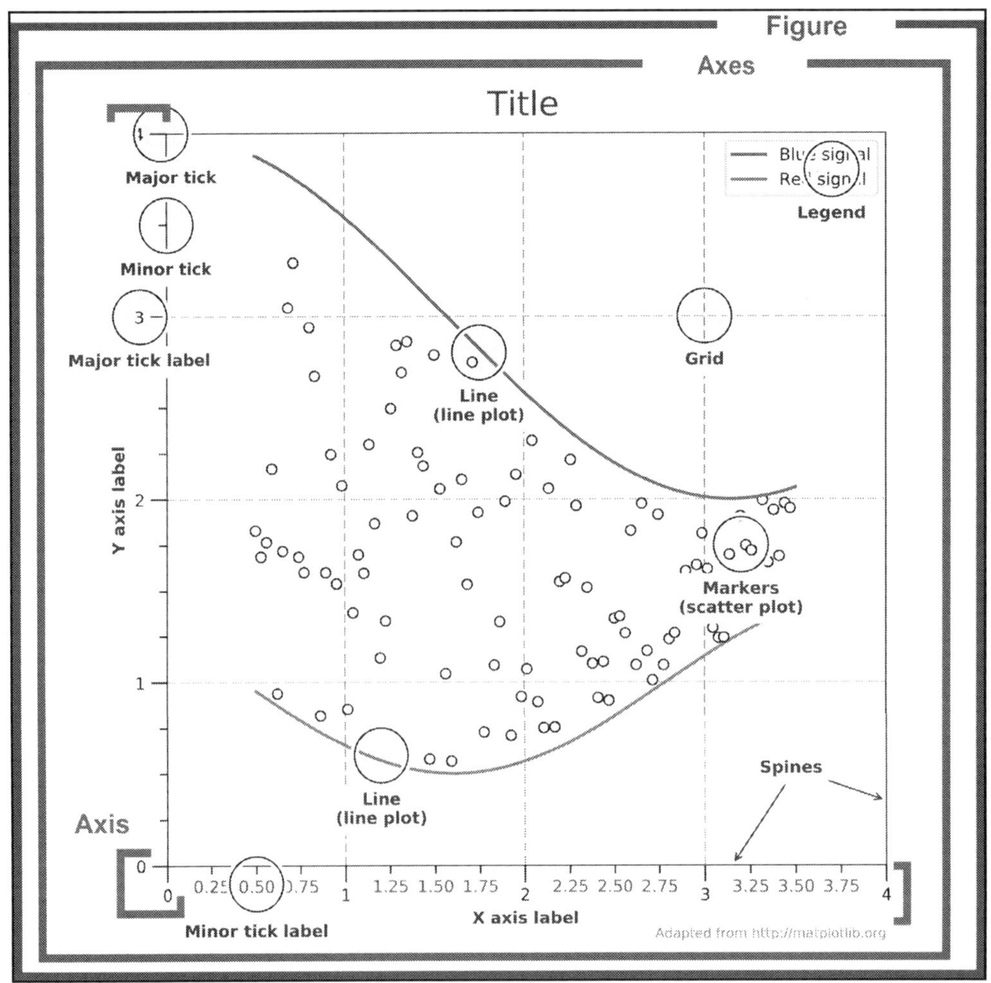

Glossary of objects in a Matplotlib figure

- **Figure**: A figure is the whole plotting area that contains all plot elements. Multiple subplots may be tiled in grid within one figure.
- **Subplot**: A subplot is a subregion in a figure that contains all of the relevant data to be displayed on the same axes. We will demonstrate how to create subplots in `Chapter 3`, *Figure Layout and Annotations*.
- **Axis**: An axis measures the value of a point at a certain position. Most plots contain two axes, *x* (horizontal) and *y* (vertical). Sometimes, multiple axes, each containing one data series, can be overlaid in the same plotting area of a 2D plot. This will be discussed in `Chapter 3`, *Figure Layout and Annotations*. You can also plot a 3D graph using a Matplotlib toolkit package, where the *z* axis will be specified. We will introduce 3D plotting in `Chapter 5`, *Visualizing Multivariate Data*.
- **Axes**: In Matplotlib, the keyword in plural, axes, refers to the combination of axes in a plot. This can be intuitively understood as the data plotting area, as shown in the preceding figure.

Be careful not to confuse axes and axis. While we usually refer to lines where ticks lie on as "axes," in Matplotlib, the plural axes and the singular axis specifically refer to the plotting area and the lines, respectively.

- **Spine**: Spines are the four lines that denote the boundaries of the data area.
- **Grid**: Grids are lines inside the data area that aid the reading of values.
- **Title**: A name of the figure that describes the figure clearly and succinctly.
- **Axis labels**: A word description of each axis. Units should be given if applicable.
- **Ticks**: Ticks are marks of division on a plot axis. We can add major ticks and minor ticks to a figure.
- **Tick labels**: Both major and minor ticks can be labeled. Besides printing the input data values directly, there are also formatters specific for date, logarithmic scale, and so on. We can also use our own defined functions to format the labels.
- **Legend**: A legend has labels of each data series. It usually appears as a box that matches the styles of a data series with the corresponding names.
- **Patches**: Different shapes can be added by `matplotlib.patches`, including rectangles, circles, ellipses, rings, sectors, arrows, wedges, and polygons.

Now that we have understood the basic terms of Matplotlib, let's dive in and start customizing our figure. There are many types of plot APIs available in Matplotlib. They serve as containers for easy conversion of data to graphics. While each plot can look very different, the same kind of elements are controlled by the same class in an object-oriented manner. Lines, markers, and rectangles are the most common elements for data display, such as line plot, scatter plot, and bar chart.

They are controlled by the `lines`, `markers`, and `patches.Rectangle` classes respectively. Patches of different shapes have similar methods for style settings. We will focus on adjusting the style parameters of these three elements in this chapter.

Setting colors in Matplotlib

Many elements in a Matplotlib figure can have their colors specified. There are several ways to do so. You will come across the `color` parameter as a keyword argument for style settings very often in different functions. The alternate abbreviated keyword `c` can often be used. We will first briefly introduce the general rule here.

Single letters for basic built-in colors

There is a list of common colors we can quickly call with single letters:

- `b`: Blue
- `g`: Green
- `r`: Red
- `c`: Cyan
- `m`: Magenta
- `y`: Yellow
- `k`: Black
- `w`: White

Names of standard HTML colors

Examples are `coral`, `gold`, `springgreen`, `deepskyblue`, and `blueviolet`. You can find the full list here: `https://matplotlib.org/examples/color/named_colors.html`.

RGB or RGBA color code

You can parse a tuple of three to four float numbers in the range of 0-1, such as `(0.2,0.4,0.8)` or `(0.2,0.2,0.3,0.8)`. The first three numbers are RGB values that define the amount of red, green, and blue light to mix in the color. The optional fourth number is the alpha value; it determines the degree of transparency.

Hexadecimal color code

You can precisely choose a color from a larger palette by inputting the hex color codes, for example, `'#ff88aa'`. A hex color code is composed of the hexadecimal form of an RGB value, where `ff` stands for the maximum amount of the light. Therefore, you will get pure red, green, blue, black, and white respectively for `'#ff0000'`, `'#00ff00'`, `'#0000ff'`, `'#000000'`, and `'#ffffff'`.

Depth of grayscale

You can specify any value within 0-1 in a string, such as `'0.1'`, `'0.32'`, `'0.5'`, or `'0.75'`. A smaller number gives a darker shade of gray.

Using specific colors in the color cycle

Each style, including the default one, contains a list of colors called the color cycle. By default, one color is used at a time in the order of the cycle before the cycle is reset when we display the figure using `pyplot.show()`. You can choose a specific color in the current color cycle with `C0`, `C1`, `C6`, and so on. Here is a quick example:

```
import matplotlib.pyplot as plt

# Global smartphone sales by operating system in 2009-2016 (in Millions)
# Data were collected from Statista
#
https://www.statista.com/statistics/263445/global-smartphone-sales-by-opera
ting-system-since-2009/
# Data were published by Gartner in Feb 2017

years = list(range(2009,2017))
android = [6.8,67.22,220.67,451.62,761.29,1004.68,1160.21,1271.02]
ios = [24.89,46.6,89.27,130.13,150.79,191.43,225.85,216.07]
microsoft = [15.03,12.38,8.76,16.94,30.71,35.13,26.74,6.94]
```

```
plt.plot(years,android,label='Android')      # color='C0' by default
plt.plot(years,ios,label='iOS')              # color='C1' by default
plt.plot(years,microsoft,label='Microsoft') # color='C2' by default

plt.legend()
plt.show()
```

The preceding code uses colors within the built-in color cycle in default order, that is, `C0`, `C1`, and `C2`:

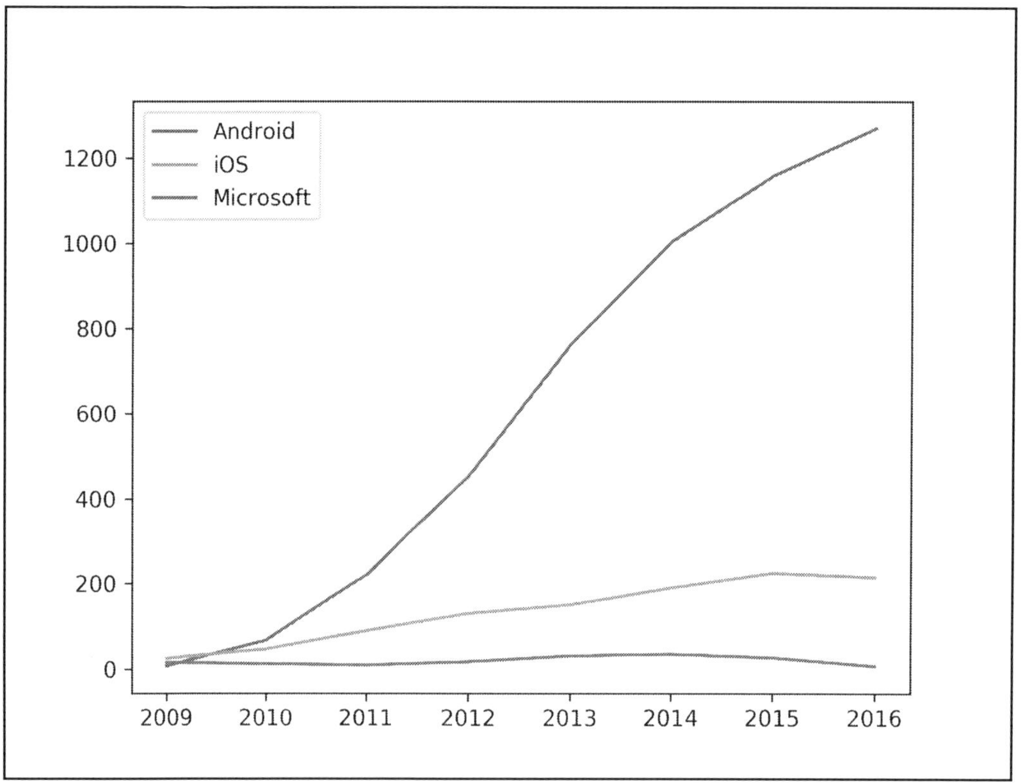

We can use the colors in any order by specifying their respective code, for example, `C0`, `C1`, in each `pyplot.plot()` call:

```
plt.plot(years,android,label='Android',c='C2')
plt.plot(years,ios,label='iOS',c='C0')
plt.plot(years,microsoft,label='Microsoft',c='C1')
```

In this case, we used the third, the second then the first color in the cycle sequentially, giving the following graph:

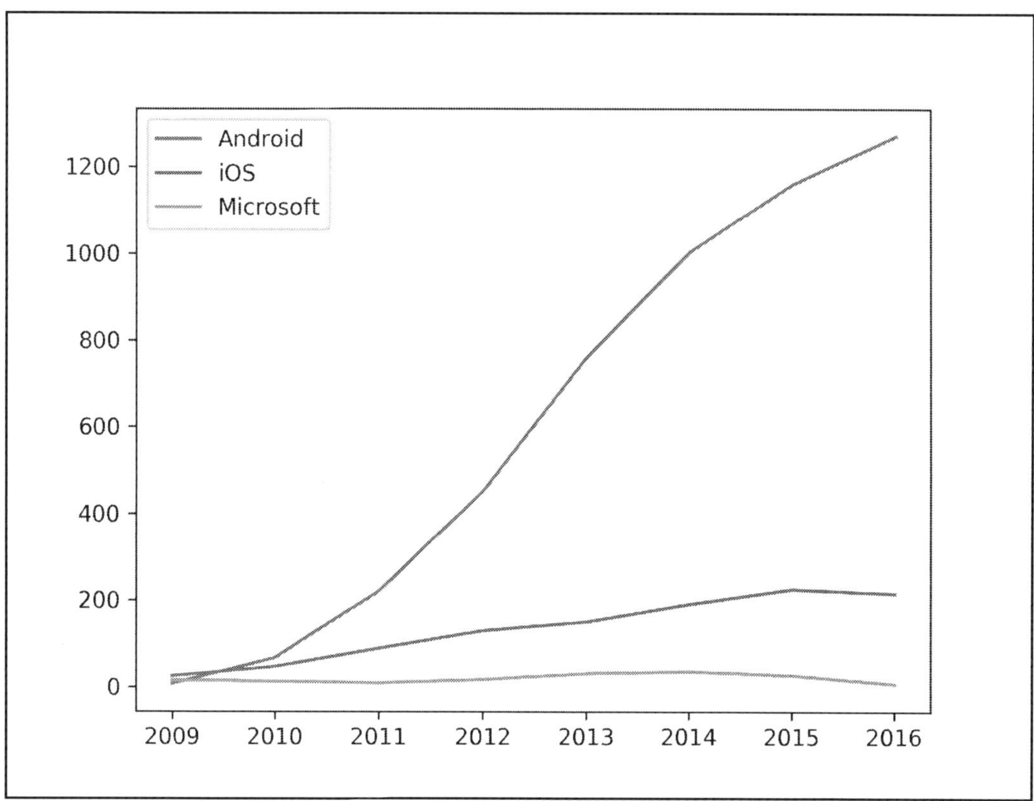

In fact, there is no restriction as to when to use each color. Using consecutive colors in the cycles, with their code as aliases, just speed up color picking to ensure datasets are well distinguished when they are adjacent to each other.

Aesthetic and readability considerations

For good readability, we recommend ample color contrast between background and foreground colors. It is also wise to keep enough contrast between data series for easy recognition. For foreground colors, we generally do not need to set the alpha value to add transparency. When in doubt, you may use or refer to the default color cycle.

For black-and-white printing, it is recommended to combine grayscale colors with different line styles or fill patterns to distinguish between data series. Using grayscale colors has the advantage of ensuring different colors on the resultant printing, since it is possible for two colors, say red and blue, to have very similar hues and appear the same when converted to grayscale.

This is an example where grayscale lines can be displayed distinctively:

```
import numpy as np
import matplotlib.pyplot as plt
import matplotlib as mpl

# Prepare 4 lines with different slopes
x = np.linspace(0,200,100) # Prepare 100 evenly spaced numbers from
#  0 to 200
y1 = x*2
y2 = x*3
y3 = x*4
y4 = x*5

# Set line width to 2 for clarity
mpl.rcParams['lines.linewidth'] = 2

# Drawing the 4 lines
plt.plot(x,y1,label = '2x', c='0')                 # Black solid line
plt.plot(x,y2,label = '3x', c='0.2', ls='--')   # Dark grey dashed line
plt.plot(x,y3,label = '4x', c='0.4', ls='-.')   # Grey dash-dot line
plt.plot(x,y4,label = '5x', c='0.6', ls=':')    # Light grey dotted line

plt.legend()
plt.show()
```

You can see that each line has a distinct pattern and different shade. We can easily match them to the figure legend on the top left for their identities:

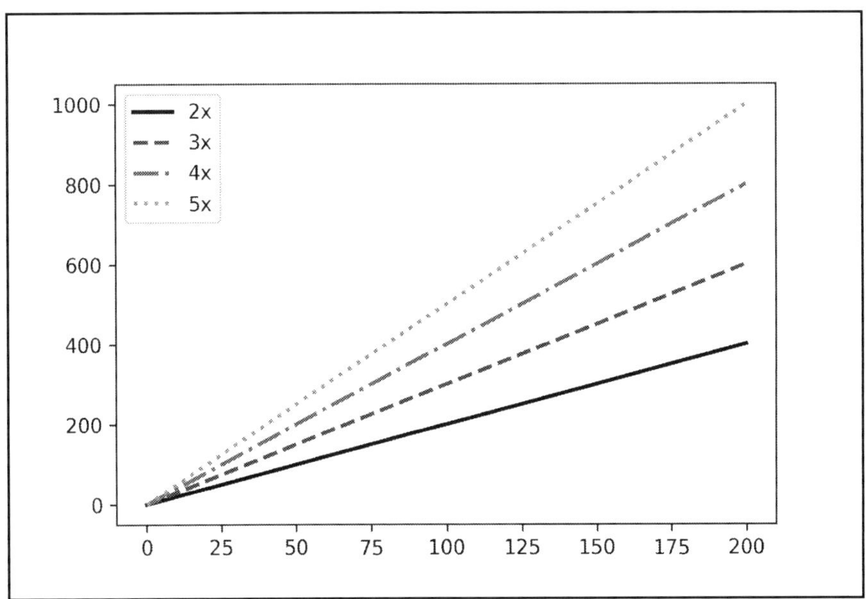

Here is another example of how inappropriate color settings can lead to confusion. We will replace the preceding `plt.plot()` instances with the following:

```
# Draw the 4 lines
# this line is too faint
plt.plot(x,y1,label = '2x', c='0.9')  # light grey
# this line is barely visible
plt.plot(x,y2,label = '3x', c='0.99') # very faint grey line
# these two lines have too little contrast and may be confusing
plt.plot(x,y3,label = '4x', c='0.4')  # grey
plt.plot(x,y4,label = '5x', c='0.45') # slightly lighter grey
```

In this case, the top two lines for `y=4x` and `y=5x` are too close in their grayscale values. Without the aid of different dash patterns, it is difficult to tell which is which. Remember that data is much more complicated in reality!

For the line `y=3x`, it is so faint to be barely visible. This is an extreme case for demonstration and laugh only. Believe me, your readers will not need an eyesight test from plots:

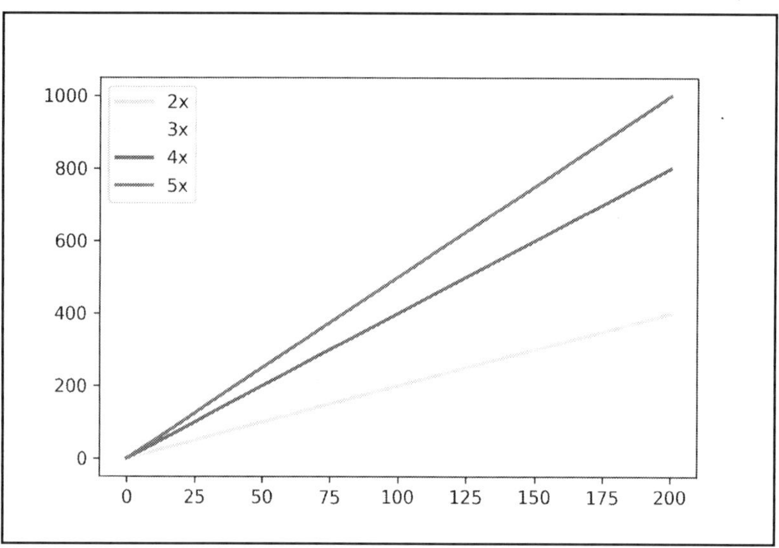

For a target audience with color weaknesses, there are some guidelines to help you create color-blind-friendly graphics, such as `https://www.tableau.com/about/blog/2016/4/examining-data-viz-rules-dont-use-red-green-together-53463`. Matplotlib 2.0 has a `seaborn-colorblind` style sheet that can be easily applied to alter the whole color scheme. There are also 15 color schemes developed by science artist Martin Krzywinski at `http://mkweb.bcgsc.ca/colorblind/` to aid delivering messages to people with varied color vision. Online tools such as `http://www.vischeck.com/vischeck/vischeckImage.php` simulate color-deficient vision experiences. You can upload image files to check how they will be perceived. Another website, `http://www.color-blindness.com/color-name-hue/`, provides instant conversion of a color into corresponding perceived color with hex color codes provided, so you will know your choices in advance.

If you want to set up your own color schemes, here is a list of online tools that may help: `http://learntocodewith.me/posts/color-palette-tools`. You may also look for palette ideas on websites such as `http://www.color-hex.com/color-palettes` and `https://designschool.canva.com/blog/100-color-combinations`.

Adjusting text formats

For an informative figure, we typically have a number of text elements, including the title, labels of axes and ticks, legend, and any additional annotations. We can adjust the font size and font family in the default `rc` settings. These settings are set in a dictionary-like variable, `matplotlib.rcParams`, so you can do `import matplotlib` and define a parameter like this:

```
matplotlib.rcParams['font.size'] = 18
```

Matplotlib also provides functions to alter the settings. The `matplotlib.rc()` changes the parameters one by one, whereas `matplotlib.rcParams.update()` accepts a dictionary input to change multiple settings simultaneously. Let's say we would like to change the font size to 20 and font family to `serif`, then use. We can do so in two ways:

```
matplotlib.rc('font', size=18)
matplotlib.rc('font', family='sans-serif')
```

This is equivalent to the following:

```
matplotlib.rcParams.update({'font.size': 18, 'font.family': 'serif'})
```

Font

Text with well-tuned fonts helps the data speak with good legibility and proper emphasis. While default parameters are generally good enough for us to grasp the impression of data, we routinely need to adjust the font sizes and weight for titles and labels for best presentation. This is especially true when we are customizing the layout, which we will introduce in `Chapter 3`, *Figure Layout and Annotations*. We can achieve this through versatile options of font settings.

Font appearance

The `size`, `style`, `fontweight`, `family`, and `variant` parameters can be set under `font`. They can be set as keyword arguments directly in a text command:

```
plt.xlabel('xlabel',size=20,fontweight='semibold',family='serif',style='ita
lic')
```

Or they can be stored and passed as a dictionary with keys of parameter names in strings and their corresponding values:

```
import matplotlib.pyplot as plt
fontparams = {'size':16,'fontweight':'light',
              'family':'monospace','style':'normal'}

x = [1,2,3]
y = [2,4,6]
plt.plot(x,y)
plt.xlabel('xlabel',size=20,fontweight='semibold',family='serif',style='ita
lic')
plt.ylabel('ylabel',fontparams)
plt.show()
```

The preceding code sets different font families, sizes, weight, and style for the axis labels. You may experiment with these settings with any text in a Matplotlib plot. This discordant setting is unlikely in usual plots. We will discuss more in `Chapter 7`, *A Practical Guide to Scientific Plotting*.

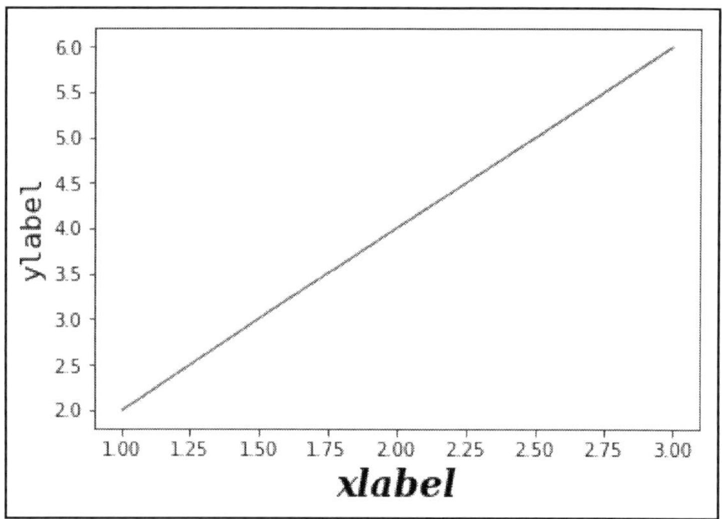

Another alternative method is to use the Matplotlib rc parameter method, such as `matplotlib.rcParams['font.size'] = 20`.

The following are some notes about the available options.

Font size

Floating-point numbers are acceptable for font sizes.

Font style

A text can have `'normal'`, `'italic'`, or `'oblique'` style.

Font weight

You can **bold** a text by setting `fontweight='bold'`. Other font weights are `'light'`, `'normal'`, `'medium'`, `'semibold'`, `'heavy'`, and `'black'`.

Font family

There are five major generic font families in Matplotlib:

- `'serif'`: Serifs are small decorative flourishes attached to stroke ends of characters. Fonts such as Times New Roman, Century, Garamond, and Palatino are serif fonts.
- `'sans-serif'`: This means without serif. Fonts such as Helvetica, Arial, Calibri, and DejaVu Sans are sans-serif.
- `'monospace'`: Monospace fonts have characters of the same width. They are usually used for code.
- `'cursive'`: Cursive features connected brush strokes, usually in *italic*, that give a sense of classical elegance.
- `'fantasy'`: Decorative fonts that look funny.

For scientific publication and usual presentation, we generally use `'sans-serif'`. Special font types may help to deliver messages in infographics. We will discuss more on scientific plotting and infographics in later chapters. You can also installed font families that are installed on your own computer.

The options we listed are the most commonly used text properties settings. A full list of options can be found at `http://matplotlib.org/users/text_props.html`.

Checking available fonts in system

To check the readily usable fonts installed in the system, Matplotlib provides a one-line solution with the `font_manager` class:

```
from matplotlib.font_manager import findSystemFonts
findSystemFonts(fontpaths=None, fontext='ttf')
```

Following is a screenshot showing how the paths of your installed fonts will be output as a list of strings:

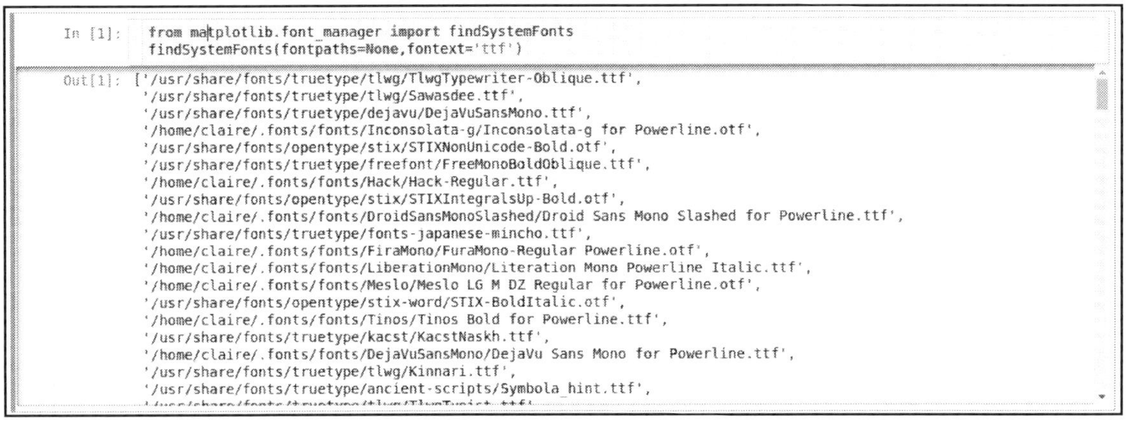

```
In [1]:  from matplotlib.font_manager import findSystemFonts
         findSystemFonts(fontpaths=None,fontext='ttf')

Out[1]: ['/usr/share/fonts/truetype/tlwg/TlwgTypewriter-Oblique.ttf',
         '/usr/share/fonts/truetype/tlwg/Sawasdee.ttf',
         '/usr/share/fonts/truetype/dejavu/DejaVuSansMono.ttf',
         '/home/claire/.fonts/fonts/Inconsolata-g/Inconsolata-g for Powerline.otf',
         '/usr/share/fonts/opentype/stix/STIXNonUnicode-Bold.otf',
         '/usr/share/fonts/truetype/freefont/FreeMonoBoldOblique.ttf',
         '/home/claire/.fonts/fonts/Hack/Hack-Regular.ttf',
         '/usr/share/fonts/opentype/stix/STIXIntegralsUp-Bold.otf',
         '/home/claire/.fonts/fonts/DroidSansMonoSlashed/Droid Sans Mono Slashed for Powerline.ttf',
         '/usr/share/fonts/truetype/fonts-japanese-mincho.ttf',
         '/home/claire/.fonts/fonts/FiraMono/FuraMono-Regular Powerline.otf',
         '/home/claire/.fonts/fonts/LiberationMono/Literation Mono Powerline Italic.ttf',
         '/home/claire/.fonts/fonts/Meslo/Meslo LG M DZ Regular for Powerline.otf',
         '/usr/share/fonts/opentype/stix-word/STIX-BoldItalic.otf',
         '/home/claire/.fonts/fonts/Tinos/Tinos Bold for Powerline.ttf',
         '/usr/share/fonts/truetype/kacst/KacstNaskh.ttf',
         '/home/claire/.fonts/fonts/DejaVuSansMono/DejaVu Sans Mono for Powerline.ttf',
         '/usr/share/fonts/truetype/tlwg/Kinnari.ttf',
         '/usr/share/fonts/truetype/ancient-scripts/Symbola_hint.ttf',
```

You can input custom directories in the font paths and specify other font file extensions such as `'otf'` for `fontext`. When the `fontext` parameter is not set, any font in the directories will be listed.

LaTeX support

LaTeX is useful for scientific publications. The LaTeX and Tex languages provide a neat shortcut to print mathematical formulas with various symbols, Greek characters, and complex layouts. If you are not already familiar with the LaTeX mathematics notation, you can find a detailed manual here here:
`https://en.wikibooks.org/wiki/LaTeX/Mathematics`.

The LaTeX mathematics notations are well supported in Matplotlib. You can use the dollar sign shorthand, `$..$`, to denote the LaTeX text strings. As LaTeX text often contains backslashes, which is an escape character in Python, we need to add `r` before a quoted string to mark it as a raw string:

```
import numpy as np
import matplotlib.pyplot as plt

# Prepare a curve of square numbers
x = np.linspace(0,200,100) # Prepare 100 evenly spaced numbers from
# 0 to 200
y1 = x # Prepare an array of y equals to x squared
y2 = x+20

# Plot a curve of square numbers
plt.plot(x,y1,label = '$x$')
plt.plot(x,y2,label = r'$x^2+\alpha$')

plt.legend()
plt.show()
```

With the LaTeX code, the `2` in squared `x` has been put in superscript and the Greek alphabet alpha appears. It is a quick and nice way to add formulas to plots as annotations:

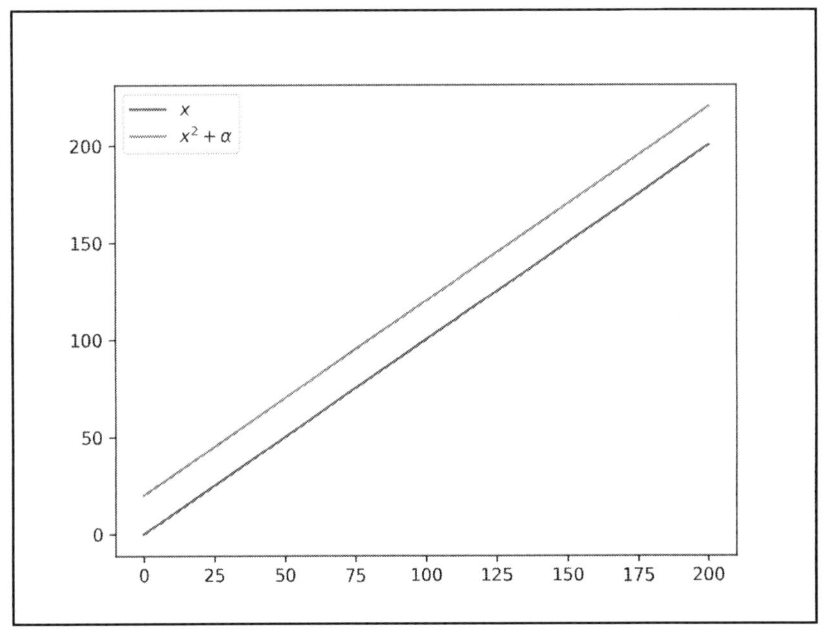

If we have LaTeX installed, we can choose to let external LaTeX engine to render the text elements:

```
matplotlib.rc('text', usetex='false')
```

Customizing lines and markers

Lines and markers are key components found among various plots. Many times, we may want to customize their appearance to better distinguish different datasets or for better or more consistent styling. Whereas markers are mainly used to show data, such as line plots and scatter plots, lines are involved in various components, such as grids, axes, and box outlines. Like text properties, we can easily apply similar settings for different line or marker objects with the same method.

Lines

Most lines in Matplotlib are drawn with the `lines` class, including the ones that display the data and those setting area boundaries. Their style can be adjusted by altering parameters in `lines.Line2D`. We usually set `color`, `linestyle`, and `linewidth` as keyword arguments. These can be written in shorthand as `c`, `ls`, and `lw` respectively. In the case of simple line graphs, we learned in `Chapter 1`, *Hello Plotting World!* that these parameters can be parsed to the `plt.plot()` function:

```
import numpy as np
import matplotlib.pyplot as plt

# Prepare a curve of square numbers
x = np.linspace(0,200,100) # Prepare 100 evenly spaced numbers from
# 0 to 200
y = x**2                   # Prepare an array of y equals to x squared

# Plot a curve of square numbers
plt.plot(x,y,label = '$x^2$',c='burlywood',ls=('dashed'),lw=2)

plt.legend()
plt.show()
```

With the preceding keyword arguments for line color, style, and weight, you get a woody dashed curve:

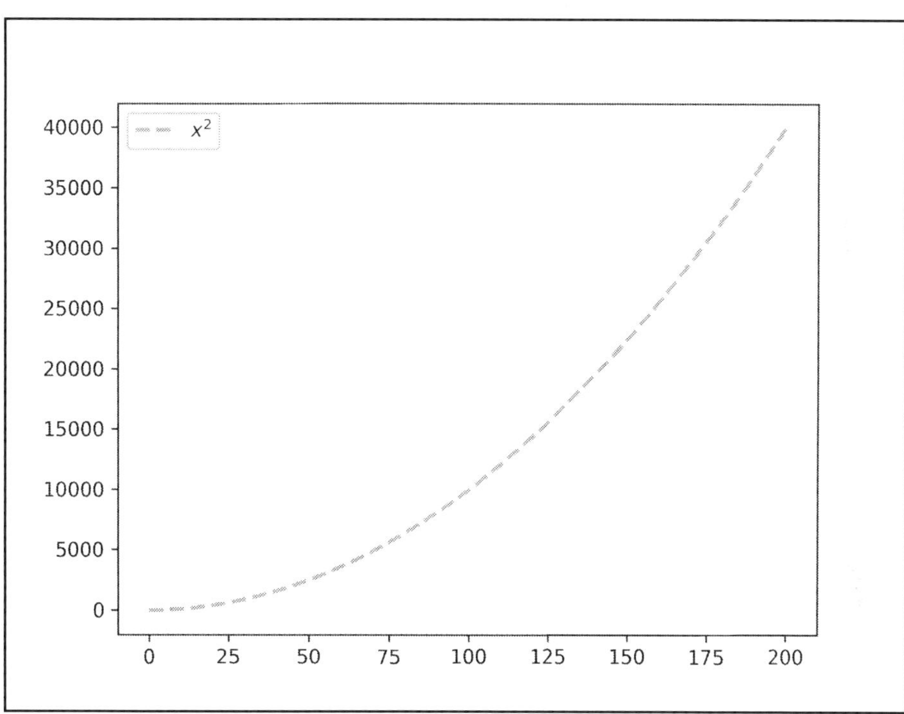

Choosing dash patterns

Whether a line will appear solid or with dashes is set by the keyword argument `linestyle`. There are a few simple patterns that can be set by the `linestyle` name or the corresponding shorthand. We can also define our own dash pattern:

- `'solid'` or `'-'`: Simple solid line (default)
- `'dashed'` or `'--'`: Dash strokes with equal spacing
- `'dashdot'` or `'-.'`: Alternate dashes and dots
- `'None'`, `' '`, or `''`: No lines
- `(offset, on-off-dash-seq)`: Customized dashes; we will demonstrate in the following advanced example

Setting capstyle of dashes

The cap of dashes can be rounded by setting the `dash_capstyle` parameter if we want to create a softer image such as in promotion:

```
import numpy as np
import matplotlib.pyplot as plt

# Prepare 6 lines
x = np.linspace(0,200,100)
y1 = x*0.5
y2 = x
y3 = x*2
y4 = x*3
y5 = x*4
y6 = x*5

# Plot lines with different dash cap styles
plt.plot(x,y1,label = '0.5x', lw=5, ls=':',dash_capstyle='butt')
plt.plot(x,y2,label = 'x', lw=5, ls='--',dash_capstyle='butt')
plt.plot(x,y3,label = '2x', lw=5, ls=':',dash_capstyle='projecting')
plt.plot(x,y4,label = '3x', lw=5, ls='--',dash_capstyle='projecting')
plt.plot(x,y5,label = '4x', lw=5, ls=':',dash_capstyle='round')
plt.plot(x,y6,label = '5x', lw=5, ls='--',dash_capstyle='round')

plt.show()
```

Looking closely, you can see that the top two lines are made up of rounded dashes. The middle two lines with `projecting` capstyle have closer spaced dashes than the lower two with `butt` one, given the same default spacing:

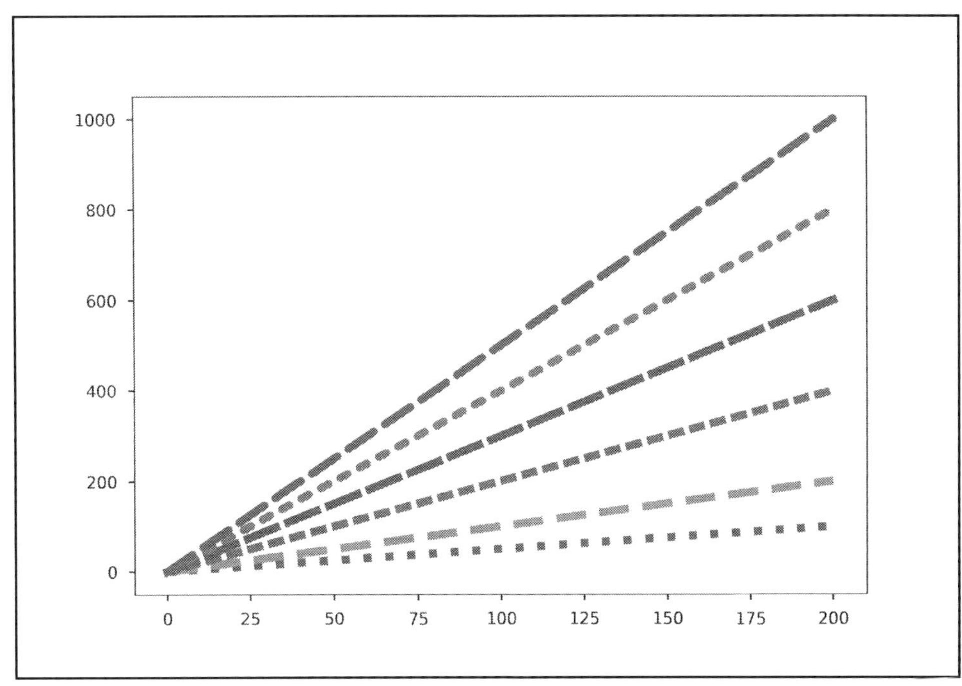

Advanced example

We can design our own dash pattern in the `linestyle` argument. Offset can be set to adjust where to start the dashes. For example, when the two ends of a line fall on spaces, we can shift the dashes so that the line would not be truncated.

The on-off-dash-seq refers to the lengths of a dash. It is a tuple of alternate lengths of dash and space. For instance, tuple `(0, (5,3,1,3,1,3))` creates a dash-dot-dot pattern, with each 5-pt dash and 1-pt dot separated by 3-pt spaces. Keeping the dashes or dots equally spaced generally has a better visual appeal.

Moreover, the same parameter can be set once and for all by calling `matplotlib.rcparams`. The settings changed by this method will only be reset after calling `matplotlib.rcdefaults()`:

```
import numpy as np
import matplotlib.pyplot as plt
import matplotlib as mpl

# Prepare 4 lines
x = np.linspace(0,200,100)
y1 = x*2
```

```
y2 = x*3
y3 = x*4
y5 = x*5

# Set the linewidth to 2 for all lines
mpl.rcParams['lines.linewidth'] = 2

# Plot lines with different line styles
# evenly spaced 1pt dots separated by 1pt space
plt.plot(x,y1,label = '2x', ls=(0,(1,1)))
# 5pt dash followed by two 1pt dots, each separated by 3pt space
plt.plot(x,y2,label = '3x', ls=(0,(5,3,1,3,1,3)))
# 5pt dashes evenly separated by 3pt space, offset by 3
plt.plot(x,y3,label = '4x', ls=(3,(5,5)))
# 5pt dash followed by 1pt dot, offset by 2
plt.plot(x,y4,label = '5x', ls=(2,(5,2,1,2)))

plt.show()
```

The on-off-dash-seq option allows us to custom-make more complex dash patterns:

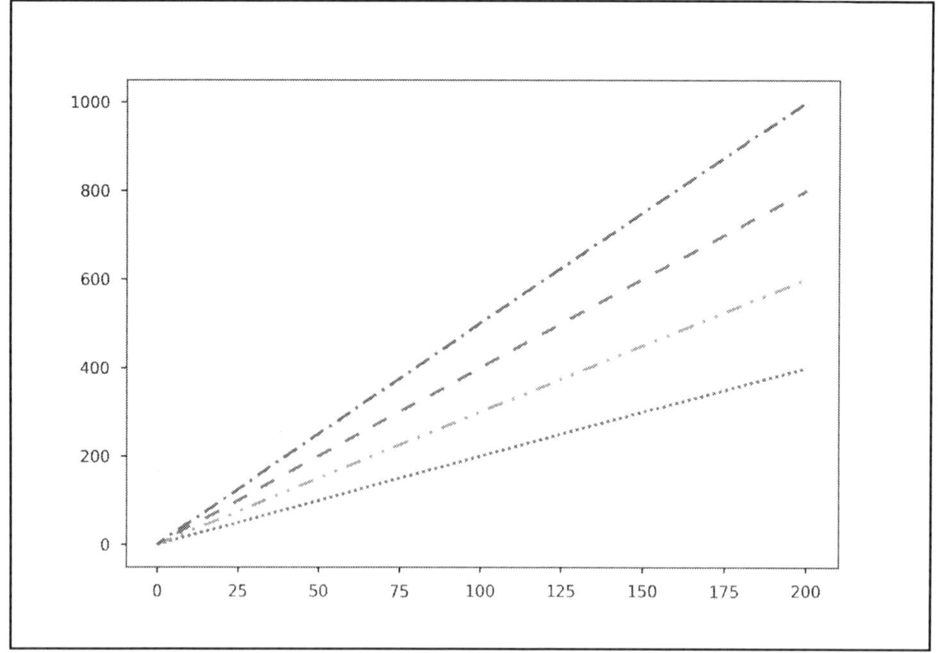

Markers

A marker is another type of important component for illustrating data, for example, in scatter plots, swarm plots, and time series plots.

Choosing markers

There are two groups of markers, unfilled `markers` and `filled_markers`.

The full set of available markers can be found by calling `Line2D.markers`, which will output a dictionary of symbols and their corresponding marker style names. A subset of filled markers that gives more visual weight is under `Line2D.filled_markers`.

Here are some of the most typical markers:

- `'o'`: Circle
- `'x'`: Cross
- `'+'`: Plus sign
- `'P'`: Filled plus sign
- `'D'`: Filled diamond
- `'s'`: Square
- `'^'`: Triangle

Here is a scatter plot of random numbers to illustrate the various marker types:

```
import numpy as np
import matplotlib.pyplot as plt
from matplotlib.lines import Line2D

# Prepare 100 random numbers to plot
x = np.random.rand(100)
y = np.random.rand(100)
# Prepare 100 random numbers within the range of the number of
# available markers as index
# Each random number will serve as the choice of marker of the
# corresponding coordinates
markerindex = np.random.randint(0, len(Line2D.markers), 100)

# Plot all kinds of available markers at random coordinates
# for each type of marker, plot a point at the above generated
# random coordinates with the marker type
for k, m in enumerate(Line2D.markers):
    i = (markerindex == k)
```

```
    plt.scatter(x[i], y[i], marker=m)

plt.show()
```

The different markers suit different densities of data for better distinction of each point:

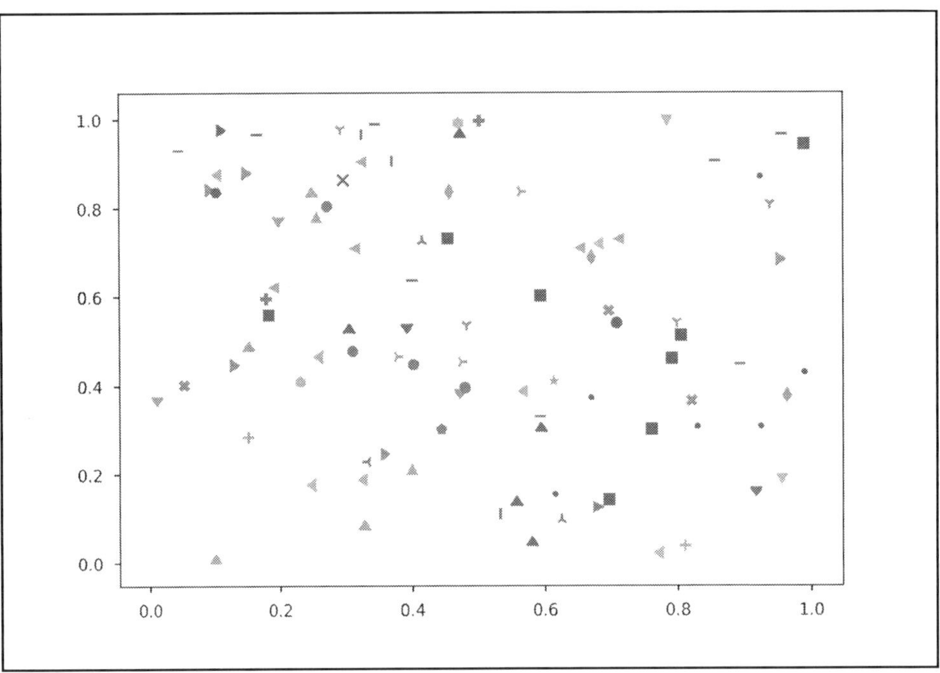

Adjusting marker sizes

We often want to change the marker sizes so as to make them clearer to read from a slideshow. Sometimes we need to adjust the markers to have a different numerical value of `markersize` to:

```
import numpy as np
import matplotlib.pyplot as plt
import matplotlib.ticker as ticker

# Prepare 5 lines
x = np.linspace(0,20,10)
y1 = x
y2 = x*2
y3 = x*3
y4 = x*4
```

```
y5 = x*5


# Plot lines with different marker sizes
plt.plot(x,y1,label = 'x', lw=2, marker='s', ms=10)  # square size 10
plt.plot(x,y2,label = '2x', lw=2, marker='^', ms=12) # triangle size 12
plt.plot(x,y3,label = '3x', lw=2, marker='o', ms=10) # circle size 10
plt.plot(x,y4,label = '4x', lw=2, marker='D', ms=8)  # diamond size 8
plt.plot(x,y5,label = '5x', lw=2, marker='P', ms=12) # filled plus sign
# size 12

# get current axes and store it to ax
ax = plt.gca()
plt.show()
```

After tuning the marker sizes, the different series look quite balanced:

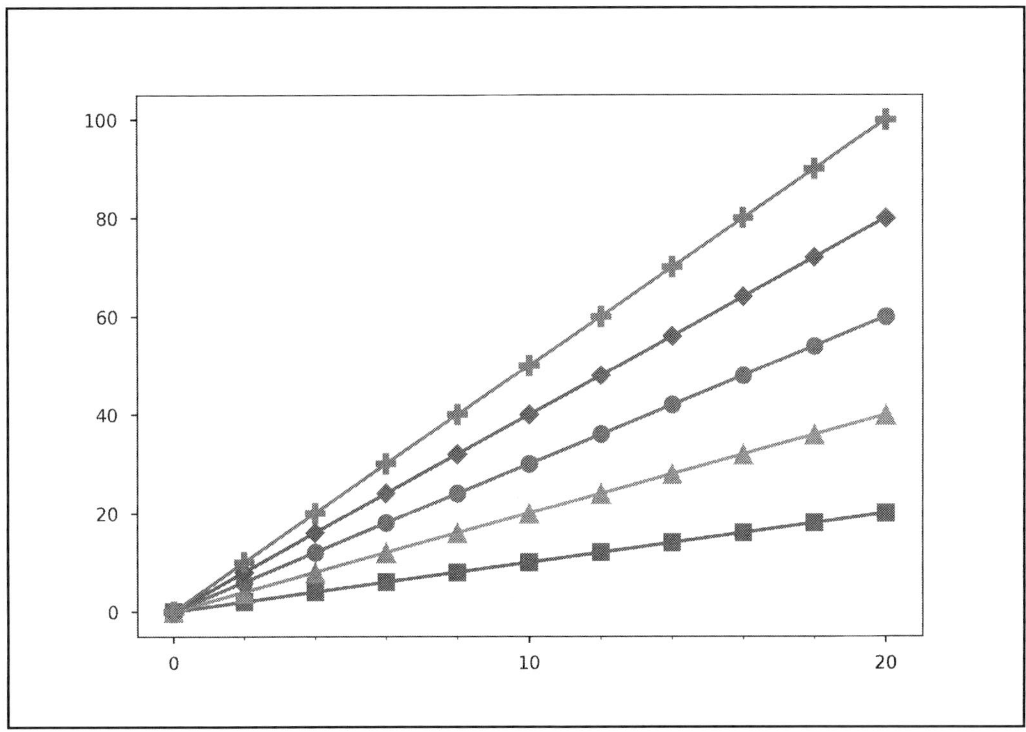

If all markers are set to have the same `markersize` value, the diamonds and squares may look heavier:

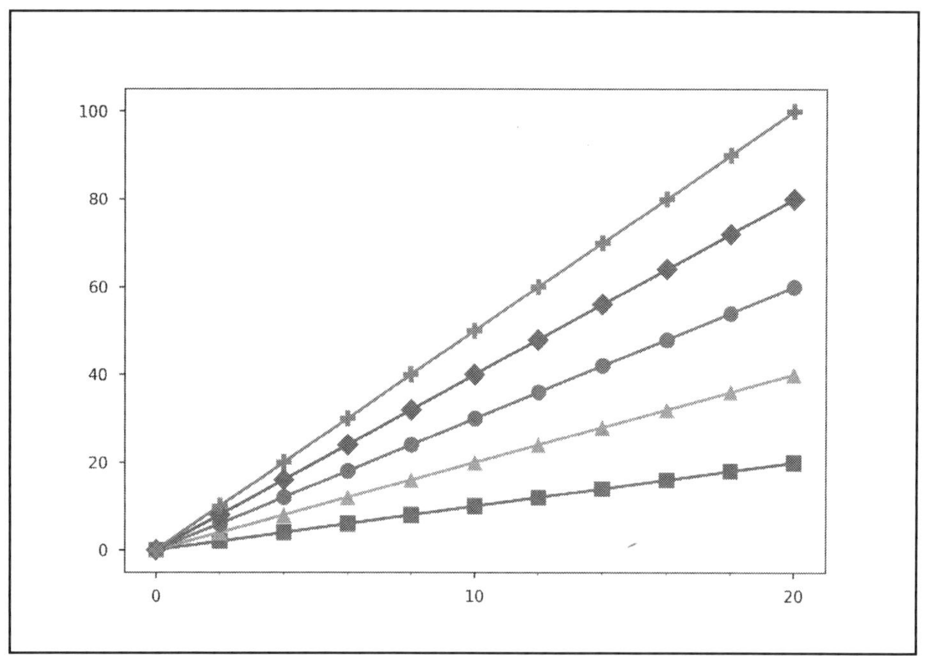

The most common marker styles can also be specified as positional arguments in `pyplot.plot()`. `pyplot.plot(x,y,'^')` is equivalent to `pyplot.plot(x,y,marker='^')`. Note that positional arguments must be put before keyword arguments.

Customizing grids, ticks, and axes

Lines of grids, ticks, and axes help us to visually locate and measure the data values. Their distribution and style determine whether they make good visual aids for the plot or clutter the figure. We will demonstrate the basic methods here.

Grids

Sometimes it may not be easy to tell the coordinates of any point in the plot. Grid lines extend from axis tick marks and help us estimate the value at a certain position.

Adding grids

Grids can be added by calling `pyplot.grid()`. By default, grid lines will be added at major tick marks. As in other line features, `pyplot.grid()` takes in parameters such as `linewidth` (`lw`), `linestyle` (`ls`), and color (`c`):

```
import numpy as np
import matplotlib.pyplot as plt

# Prepare 100 evenly spaced numbers from 0 to 200
evens = np.linspace(0,200,100)

# Plot a square curve
plt.plot(evens,evens**2,label = 'x^2')

# Adding grid lines
plt.grid()

plt.legend()
plt.show()
```

Here you see the default grid lines extending from axis ticks:

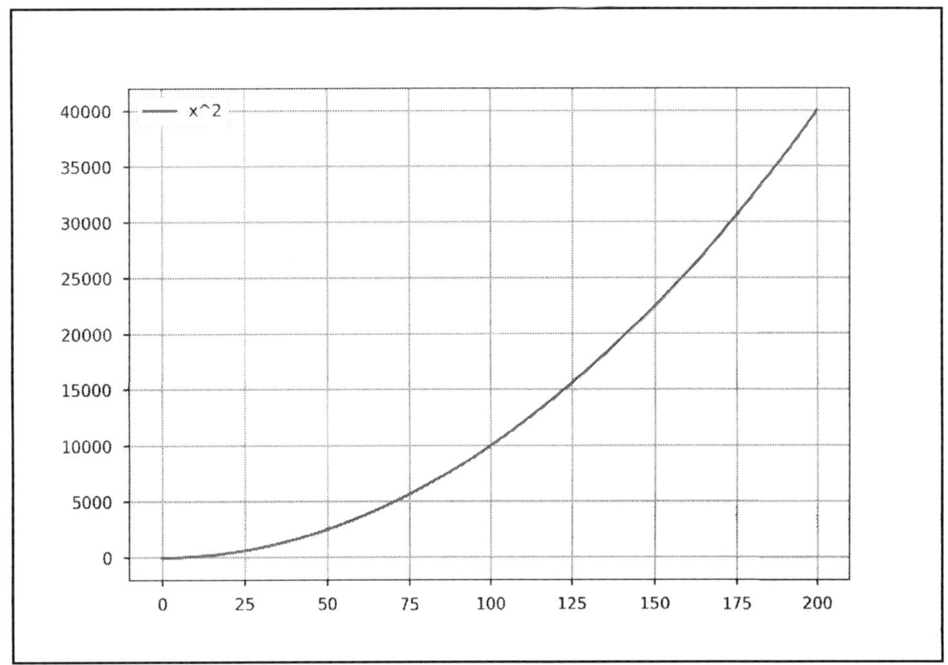

In the preceding example, while the grid lines help us locate the coordinates in different locations, they have also added much clutter and that distracts our focus from the data. We can alleviate this problem by using a lighter hue that matches the tone of the data color. You will get the following figure by substituting `pyplot.grid()` in the previous code block with `pyplot.grid(color='lightblue', linestyle='-.', linewidth=0.6)`:

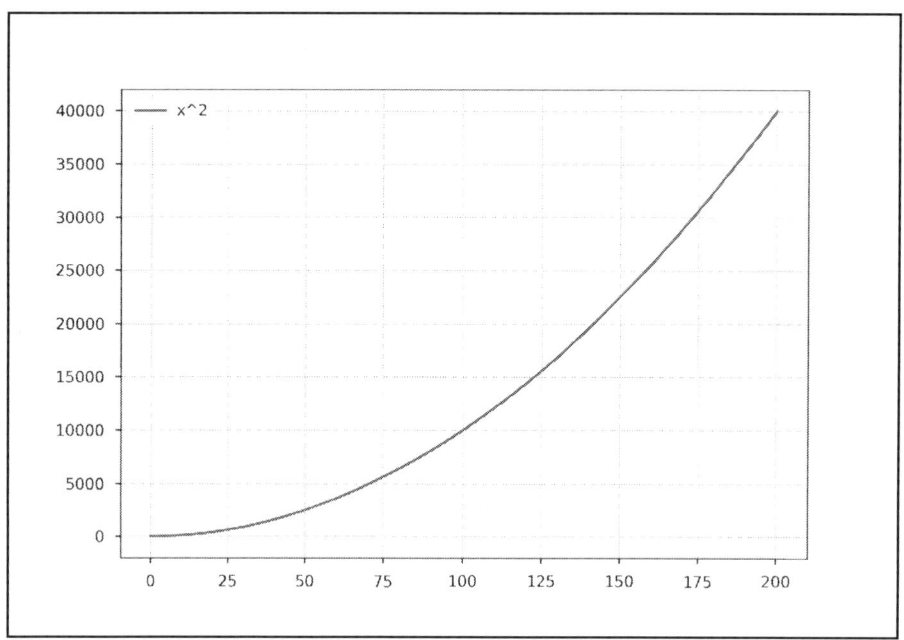

Ticks

Ticks are dividers on an axis that help readers locate the coordinates. Tick labels allow estimation of values or, sometimes, labeling of a data series as in bar charts and box plots.

Adjusting tick spacing

Tick spacing can be adjusted by calling the locator methods:

```
ax.xaxis.set_major_locator( xmajorLocator )
ax.xaxis.set_minor_locator( xminorLocator )
ax.yaxis.set_major_locator( ymajorLocator )
ax.yaxis.set_minor_locator( yminorLocator )
```

Here, `ax` refers to `axes` in a Matplotlib figure.

Since `set_major_locator()` or `set_minor_locator()` cannot be called from the pyplot interface but requires an axis, we call `pyplot.gca()` to get the current axes. We can also store a figure and axes as variables at initiation, which is especially useful when we want multiple axes. The method will be introduced in a later part of this chapter.

Removing ticks

- `NullLocator`: No ticks

Drawing ticks in multiples

- Spacing ticks in multiples of a given number is the most intuitive way. This can be done by using `MultipleLocator` space ticks in multiples of a given value.

Automatic tick settings

- `MaxNLocator`: This finds the maximum number of ticks that will display nicely
- `AutoLocator`: `MaxNLocator` with simple defaults
- `AutoMinorLocator`: Adds minor ticks uniformly when the axis is linear

Setting ticks by the number of data points

- `IndexLocator`: Sets ticks by `index (x = range(len(y))`

Set scaling of ticks by mathematical functions

- `LinearLocator`: Linear scale
- `LogLocator`: Log scale
- `SymmetricalLogLocator`: Symmetrical log scale, log with a range of linearity
- `LogitLocator`: Logit scaling

Locating ticks by datetime

There is a series of locators dedicated to displaying date and time:

- `MinuteLocator`: Locate minutes
- `HourLocator`: Locate hours
- `DayLocator`: Locate days of the month
- `WeekdayLocator`: Locate days of the week
- `MonthLocator`: Locate months, for example, 8 for August
- `YearLocator`: Locate years that in multiples
- `RRuleLocator`: Locate using `matplotlib.dates.rrulewrapper`
    - The `rrulewrapper` is a simple wrapper around a `dateutil.rrule` (`dateutil`) that allows almost arbitrary date tick specifications
- `AutoDateLocator`: On autoscale, this class picks the best `MultipleDateLocator` to set the view limits and the tick locations

Customizing tick formats

Tick formatters control the style of tick labels. They can be called to set the major and minor tick formats on the x and y axes as follows:

```
ax.xaxis.set_major_formatter( xmajorFormatter )
ax.xaxis.set_minor_formatter( xminorFormatter )
ax.yaxis.set_major_formatter( ymajorFormatter )
ax.yaxis.set_minor_formatter( yminorFormatter )
```

Removing tick labels

- `NullFormatter`: No tick labels

Fixing labels

- `FixedFormatter`: Labels are set manually

Setting labels with strings

- `IndexFormatter`: Take labels from a list of strings
- `StrMethodFormatter`: Use the `string` format method

Setting labels with user-defined functions

- `FuncFormatter`: Labels are set by a user-defined function

Formatting axes by numerical values

- `ScalarFormatter`: The format string is automatically selected for scalars by default

The following formatters set values for log axes:

- `LogFormatter`: Basic log axis
- `LogFormatterExponent`: Log axis using `exponent = log_base(value)`
- `LogFormatterMathtext`: Log axis using `exponent = log_base(value)` using Math text
- `LogFormatterSciNotation`: Log axis with scientific notation
- `LogitFormatter` Probability formatter

Setting label sizes

The font size of tick labels can be set by the keyword argument `labelsize` in `axes.axis.set_tick_params()`. Note that Matplotlib 2.0 supports unicode symbols such as emojis by default:

```
import matplotlib.pyplot as plt

# Facebook emoji copied from http://emojipedia.org/facebook/

tick_labels = ['❤','😆','😮','😢','😡']

y = [24,12,16,2,1]
x = range(5)
plt.bar(x, y, tick_label=tick_labels, align='center',facecolor='#3b5998')
```

```
# Get the current axes
ax = plt.gca()
# Set label size
ax.xaxis.set_tick_params(labelsize=20)

plt.tight_layout()
plt.show()
```

Hmm... Do your posts get such a mixed reaction too?

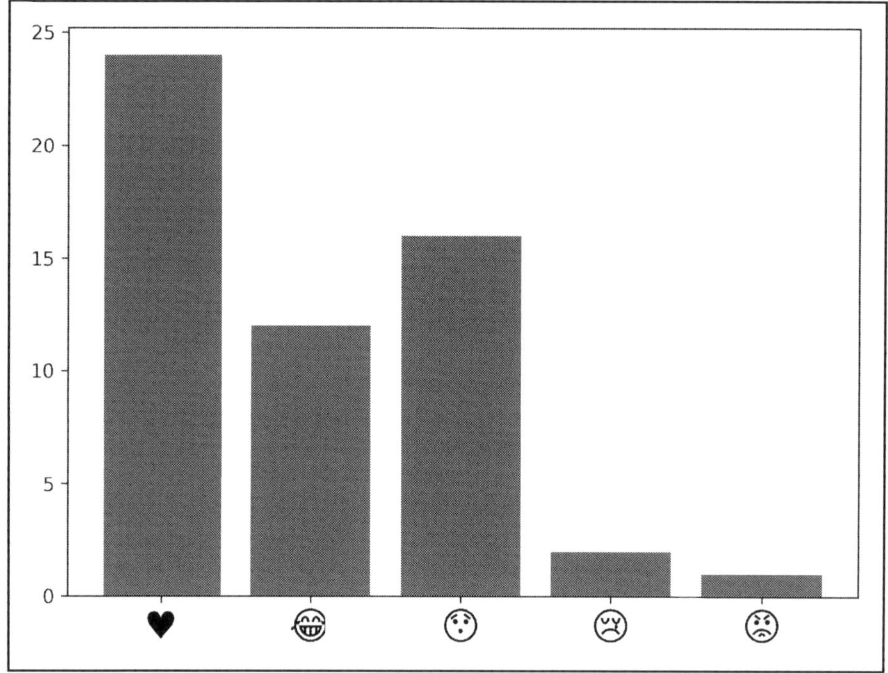

Trying out the ticker locator and formatter

To demonstrate the ticker locator and formatter, here we use Netflix subscriber data as an example. Business performance is often measured seasonally. Television shows are even more "seasonal". Can we better show it in the timeline?

```
import numpy as np
import matplotlib.pyplot as plt
import matplotlib.ticker as ticker

"""
Number for Netflix streaming subscribers from 2012-2017
```

```
Data were obtained from Statista on
https://www.statista.com/statistics/250934/quarterly-number-of-netflix-stre
aming-subscribers-worldwide/ on May 10, 2017. The data were originally
published by Netflix in April 2017.
"""

# Prepare the data set
x = range(2011,2018)
y = [26.48,27.56,29.41,33.27,36.32,37.55,40.28,44.35,
48.36,50.05,53.06,57.39,62.27,65.55,69.17,74.76,81.5,
83.18,86.74,93.8,98.75] # quarterly subscriber count in millions

# Plot lines with different line styles
plt.plot(y,'^',label = 'Netflix subscribers',ls='-')

# get current axes and store it to ax
ax = plt.gca()

# set ticks in multiples for both labels
ax.xaxis.set_major_locator(ticker.MultipleLocator(4)) # set major marks
# every 4 quarters, ie once a year
ax.xaxis.set_minor_locator(ticker.MultipleLocator(1)) # set minor marks
# for each quarter
ax.yaxis.set_major_locator(ticker.MultipleLocator(10)) #
ax.yaxis.set_minor_locator(ticker.MultipleLocator(2))

# label the start of each year by FixedFormatter
ax.get_xaxis().set_major_formatter(ticker.FixedFormatter(x))

plt.legend()
plt.show()
```

From this plot, we see that Netflix has a pretty linear growth of subscribers from the year 2012 to 2017. We can tell the seasonal growth better after formatting the x axis in a quarterly manner. In 2016, Netflix was doing better in the latter half of the year. Any TV shows you watched in each season?

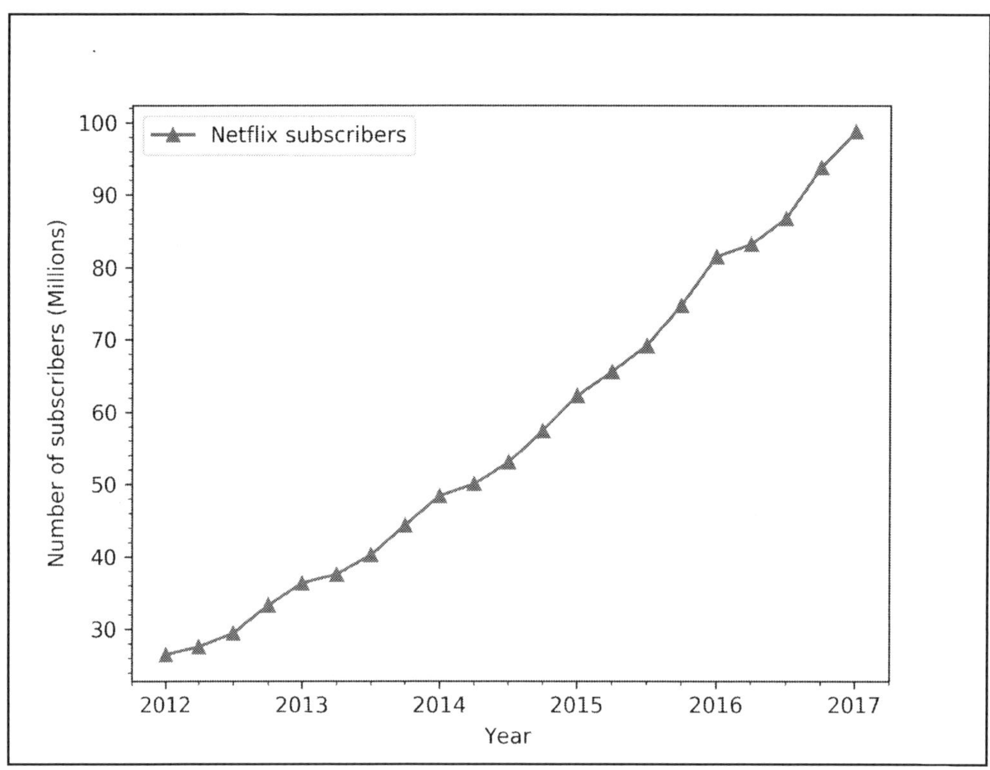

Rotating tick labels

A figure can get too crowded or some tick labels may get skipped when we have too many tick labels or if the label strings are too long. We can solve this by rotating the ticks, for example, by `pyplot.xticks(rotation=60)`:

```
import matplotlib.pyplot as plt
import numpy as np
import matplotlib as mpl

mpl.style.use('seaborn')

techs = ['Google Adsense','DoubleClick.Net','Facebook Custom
```

```
Audiences','Google Publisher Tag', 'App Nexus']
y_pos = np.arange(len(techs))

# Number of websites using the advertising technologies
# Data were quoted from builtwith.com on May 8th 2017
websites = [14409195,1821385,948344,176310,283766]
plt.bar(y_pos, websites, align='center', alpha=0.5)

# set x-axis tick rotation
plt.xticks(y_pos, techs, rotation=25)
plt.ylabel('Live site count')
plt.title('Online advertising technologies usage')

plt.show()
```

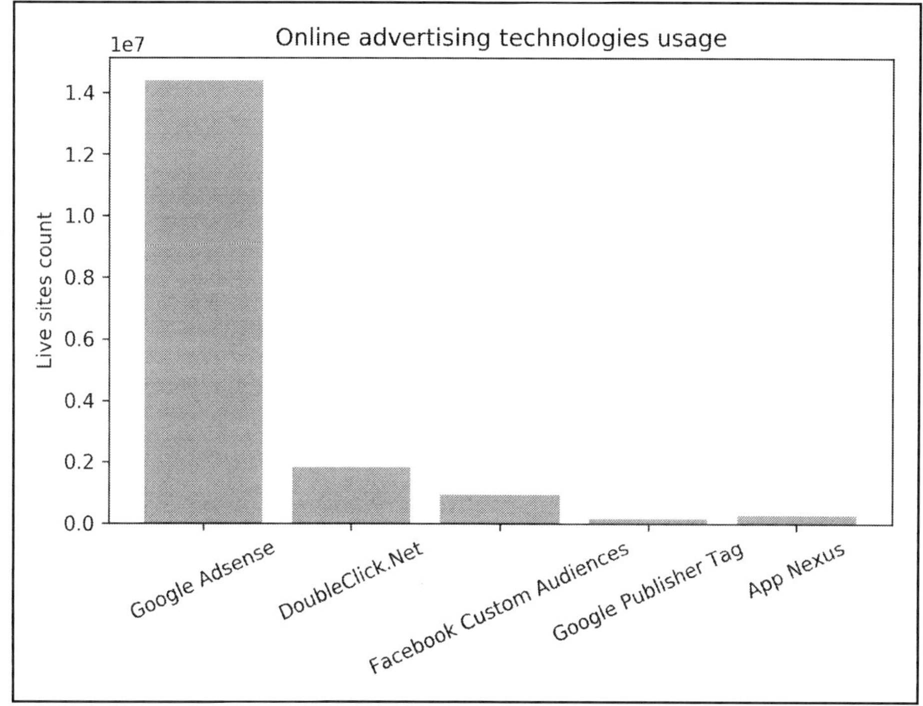

Use `pyplot.tight_layout()` to avoid image clipping.

Using rotated labels can sometimes result in image clipping, as follows, if you save the figure by `pyplot.savefig()`. You can call `pyplot.tight_layout()` before `pyplot.savefig()` to ensure a complete image output.

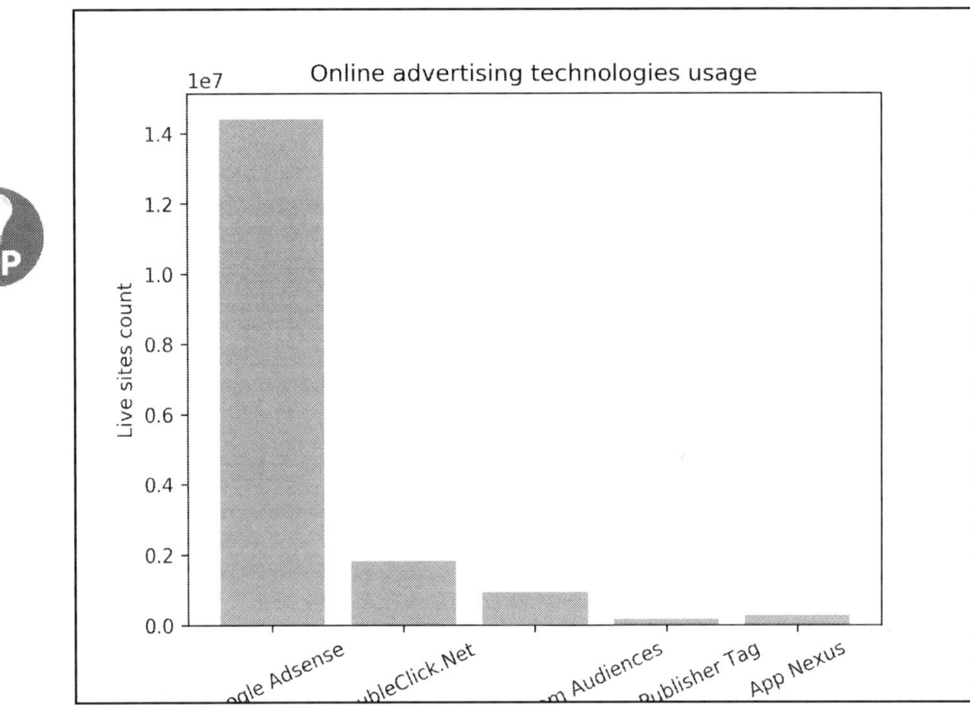

Axes

A basic plot consists of two axes: x and y. As we can see from previous examples, Matplotlib handles linear scaling automatically by inferring from data. Depending on the data's nature, we can also manually set the scale and limits of display. We will introduce a nonlinear axis here.

Nonlinear axis

A nonlinear axis, or nonuniform axis, is useful in two major scenarios:

- Sometimes a few extreme data points that deviate a lot from the rest of the data can result in misleading charts. These outliers skew a chart towards large values, while the area for representing smaller values becomes compressed. A nonlinear axis can help better represent values that span several orders of magnitude.
- In the fields of finance or science, it is common to come across nonlinear measurements, such as compound interest, growth rate, earthquake strength, sound loudness, and light intensity. By switching to a nonlinear axis, equal percentage changes can be represented as the same linear distance on a scale. This allows a clearer representation of growth or decline.

Matplotlib supports three types of nonlinear axes, namely logarithmic (log), symmetrical logarithmic (symlog), and logit scales. The scale of the *x* or *y* axis can be easily changed via `pyplot.xscale()` or `pyplot.yscale()`, respectively. If you are working with the `axes` class instead of the `pyplot` class, you will need `axes.set_xscale()` or `axes.set_yscale()`. The `axes` class will be discussed in `Chapter 3`, *Figure Layout and Annotations*. Let us show you more details of each of these nonlinear axes with examples:

```
import numpy as np
import matplotlib.pyplot as plt

# Prepare 100 evenly spaced numbers from 0 to 200
x = np.linspace(0, 200, 100)
y = x * 2

plt.figure()
plt.plot(x,y)

# Plot an outlier point
plt.plot([100], [100000], 'o')

plt.xlabel('x')
plt.ylabel('y')
plt.show()
```

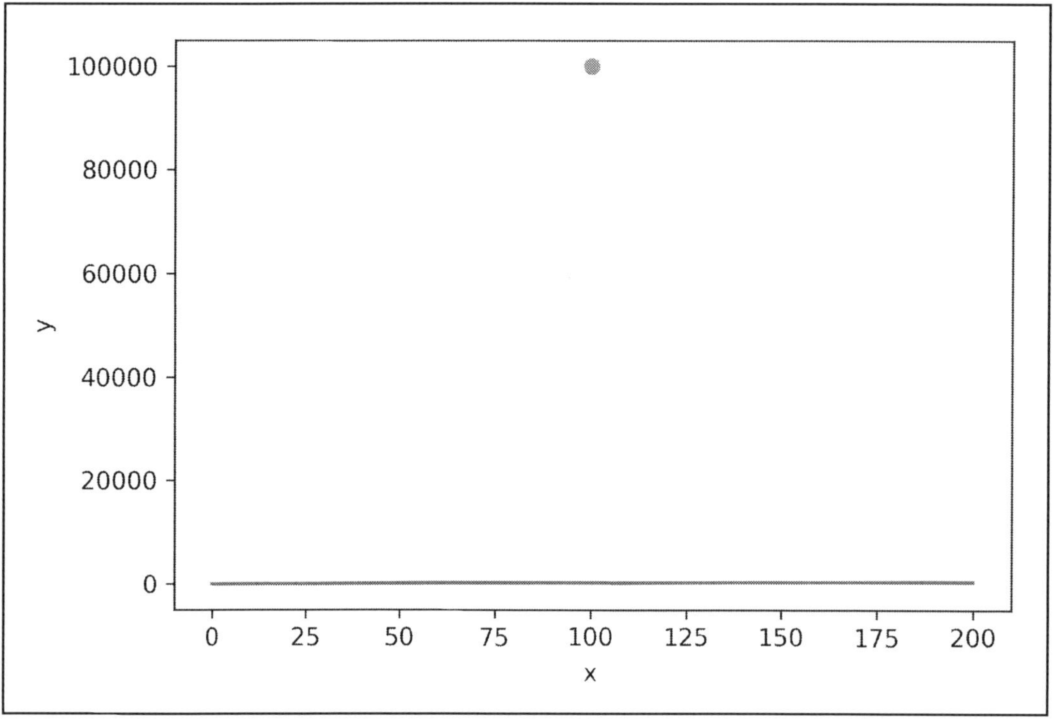

Logarithmic scale

As you can see from the previous example, the line appears to be completely flat due to the presence of a single outlier point.

A logarithmic scale is one of the most widely used nonlinear scales. Suppose there is a series of values, where each value equals the previous value multiplied by a constant factor; they can be represented by equidistant ticks on the logarithmic scale. Therefore, the distance from 1 to 2 is equivalent to that from 2 to 4, or 4 to 8.

Matplotlib uses base 10 as the default for logarithmic scale. As a quick reminder of math, log corresponds to the exponent. For example, $log_{10}(100) = log_{10}(10^2) = 2$.

This can be done by calling `pyplot.yscale()` before `pyplot.show()`:

```
#Change y-axis to log10 scale
plt.yscale('log')
```

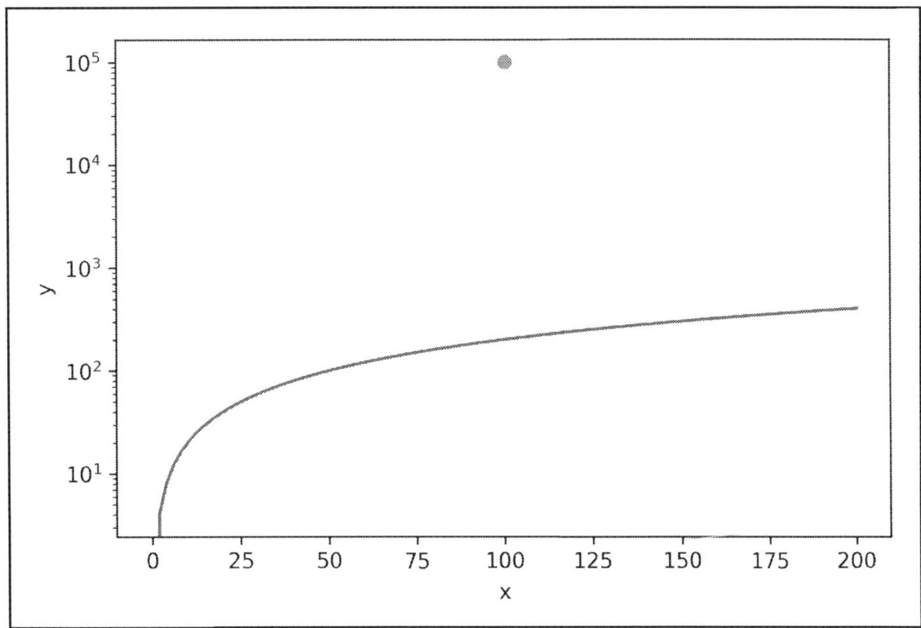

After switching to the use of $\log_{10}$ scale on the *y* axis, we can clearly observe the full range of `y` values, from the order of 10^0 to 10^2.

Changing the base of the log scale

While a log base of 10 is common, we might need to use other bases when the data has a larger or smaller range. The base of the log scale can be adjusted by using the two keyword arguments, `basex` or `basey`, in `pyplot.xscale()` and `pyplot.yscale()` respectively. In the following example, a $\log_2$ scale is used on the *y* axis.

This time, we add `basey=2` in our `pyplot.yscale()` call:

```
plt.yscale('log', basey=2)
```

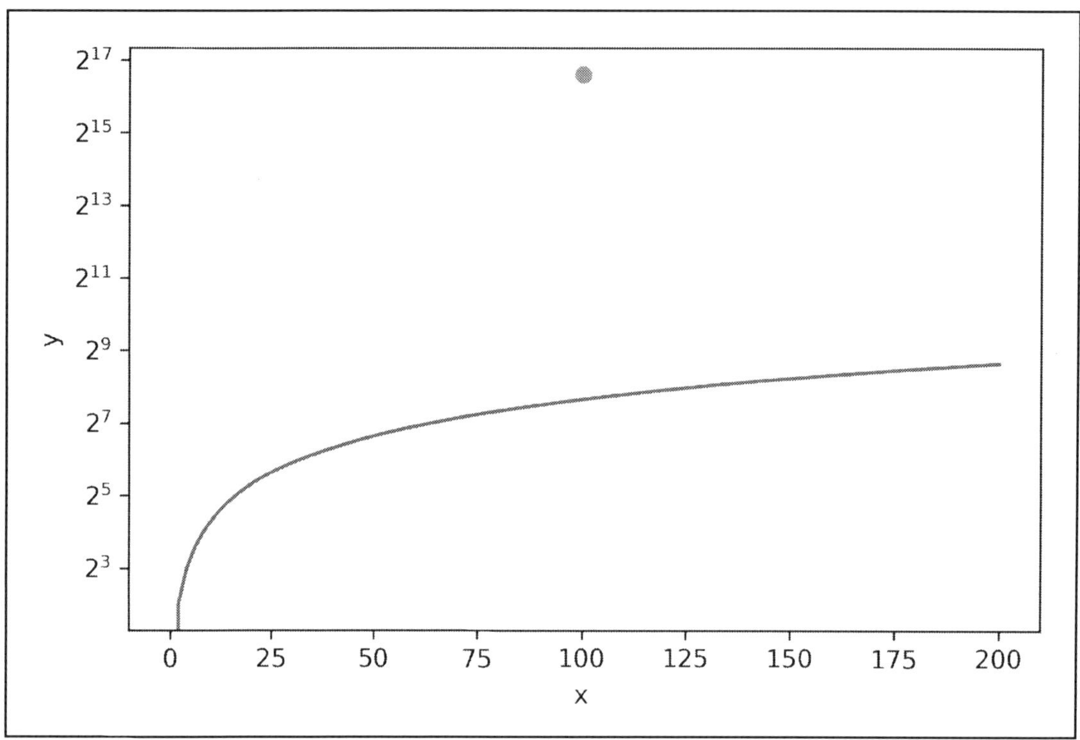

Advanced example

Alternatively, `pyplot.loglog()` can be used to make a plot with log scaling on both the *x* and y axes instead of specifying the scale after running `pyplot.plot()`. In the following complete example, we are going to combine the use of tick formatters to display the *y* axis in natural log scale, as well as the use of keyword argument `basex` to display the *x* axis in $\log_2$ scale:

```
import numpy as np
import matplotlib.pyplot as plt
from matplotlib.ticker import FuncFormatter

def ticks(y, pos):
    """ Method that formats the axis labels to natural log scale
    """
    # Use Python string formatter to limit the number of decimal places
```

```
    # for float values.
    # The precision of the formatted float value can be specified using
    # a full stop, followed
    # by the number of decimal places you would like to include.
    #
    # Latex notation is denoted by $$ in Matplotlib.
    # The outer double curly braces {{ }} will be escaped by
    # Python to {}, while the innermost
    # curly braces contains the actual Python float format string.
    # As an example, 7.389 will
    # be converted to $e^{2}$ in latex notation.
    return r'$e^{{{:.0f}}}$'.format(np.log(y))


x = np.linspace(0, 200, 100)
y = x * 2
plt.figure()

# The two keyword arguments, basex and basey, can be specified together in
plt.loglog().
# Note: natural log scale is used on the y axis by supplying numpy.e to
# basey
plt.loglog(x,y, basex=2, basey=np.e)

# Plot an outlier point
plt.plot([100], [100000], 'o')

# Get the current axes in this plot
ax = plt.gca()
# Apply the tick formatter to the y-axis
ax.yaxis.set_major_formatter(FuncFormatter(ticks))

plt.xlabel('x')
plt.ylabel('y')

plt.show()
```

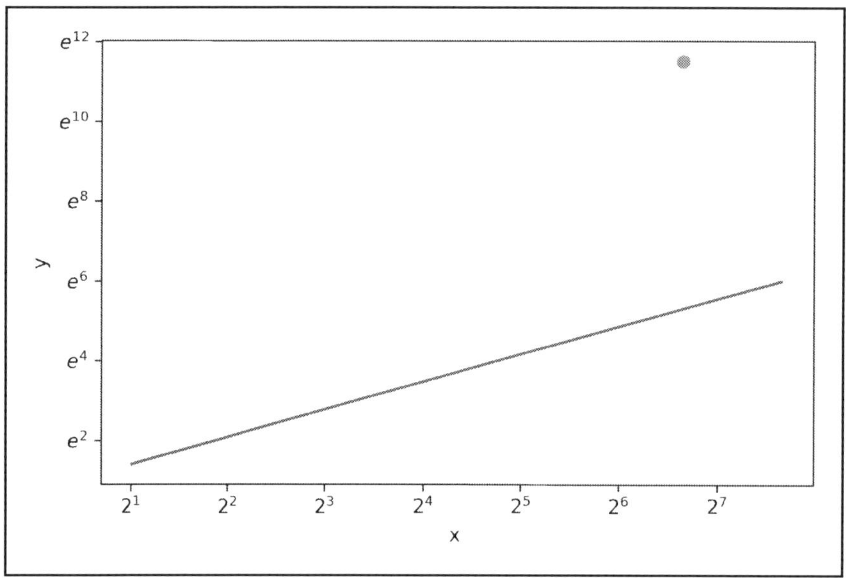

Symmetrical logarithmic scale

The logarithmic scale described in the previous section supports positive numbers only. Suppose $y = ab$, where a is positive; y must be also positive if b equals to any real number (positive, negative, whole numbers, and decimal numbers). When y approaches zero, the limit of the base a logarithm of y is minus infinity. Meanwhile, the base a logarithm of a negative number is undefined. If we try to supply non-positive numbers (≤0) to `numpy.log()`, we see the following errors:

```
import numpy as np
np.log(0)
# Output: -inf

np.log(-1)
# Output: nan
```

Matplotlib provides three ways to address non-positive numbers in a logarithmic scale.

Firstly, Matplotlib can mask non-positive values as invalid. This is equivalent to specifying the keyword arguments nonposx='mask' or nonposy='mask' in `plt.xscale()`, `plt.yscale()`, or `plt.loglog()`.

Secondly, by specifying `nonposx='clip'` or `nonposy='clip'` instead, any non-positive values in x or y will be clipped to a very small positive number (1e-300).

Finally, we can also use the symmetrical logarithmic scale (symlog). Symlog is similar to the log scale, but it allows you to define a range of linearity near the zero point of the axis, as defined by the `linthreshx` or `linthreshy` arguments, without driving the range of the axes to infinity. The `linscalex` and `linscaley` arguments control the relative scale of linear region versus the logarithmic range. Let's begin with a simple graph with linear-scaled axes and then compare the results from the three methods for handling non-positive numbers:

```
import numpy as np
import matplotlib.pyplot as plt

# Prepare 100 evenly spaced numbers from -200 to 200
x = np.linspace(-200, 200, 100)
y = x * 2

# Setup subplot with 3 rows and 2 columns, with shared x-axis.
# More details about subplots will be discussed in Chapter 3.
f, axarr = plt.subplots(nrows=3, ncols=2, figsize=(8,10), sharex=True)

# Linear scale
axarr[0, 0].plot(x, y)
axarr[0, 0].plot([-200,200], [10,10])

# Horizontal line (y=10)
axarr[0, 0].set_title('Linear scale')

# Log scale, mask non-positive numbers
axarr[0, 1].plot(x,y)
axarr[0, 1].plot([-200,200], [10,10])
axarr[0, 1].set_title('Log scale, nonposy=mask')
axarr[0, 1].set_yscale('log', nonposy='mask')
# Note: axes object requires set_yscale instead of yscale method.

# Log scale, clip non-positive numbers
axarr[1, 0].plot(x,y)
axarr[1, 0].plot([-200,200], [10,10])
axarr[1, 0].set_title('Log scale, nonposy=clip')
axarr[1, 0].set_yscale('log', nonposy='clip')

# Symlog scale
axarr[1, 1].plot(x,y)
axarr[1, 1].plot([-200,200], [10,10])
axarr[1, 1].set_title('Symlog scale')
axarr[1, 1].set_yscale('symlog')
```

```
# Symlog scale, expand the linear range to -50,50 (default=None)
axarr[2, 0].plot(x,y)
axarr[2, 0].plot([-200,200], [10,10])
axarr[2, 0].set_title('Symlog scale, linthreshy=50')
axarr[2, 0].set_yscale('symlog', linthreshy=50)# Symlog scale, expand the
# linear scale to 3 (default=1)
# The linear region is expanded, while the log region is compressed.
axarr[2, 1].plot(x,y)
axarr[2, 1].plot([-200,200], [10,10])
axarr[2, 1].set_title('Symlog scale, linscaley=3')
axarr[2, 1].set_yscale('symlog', linscaley=3)
plt.show()
```

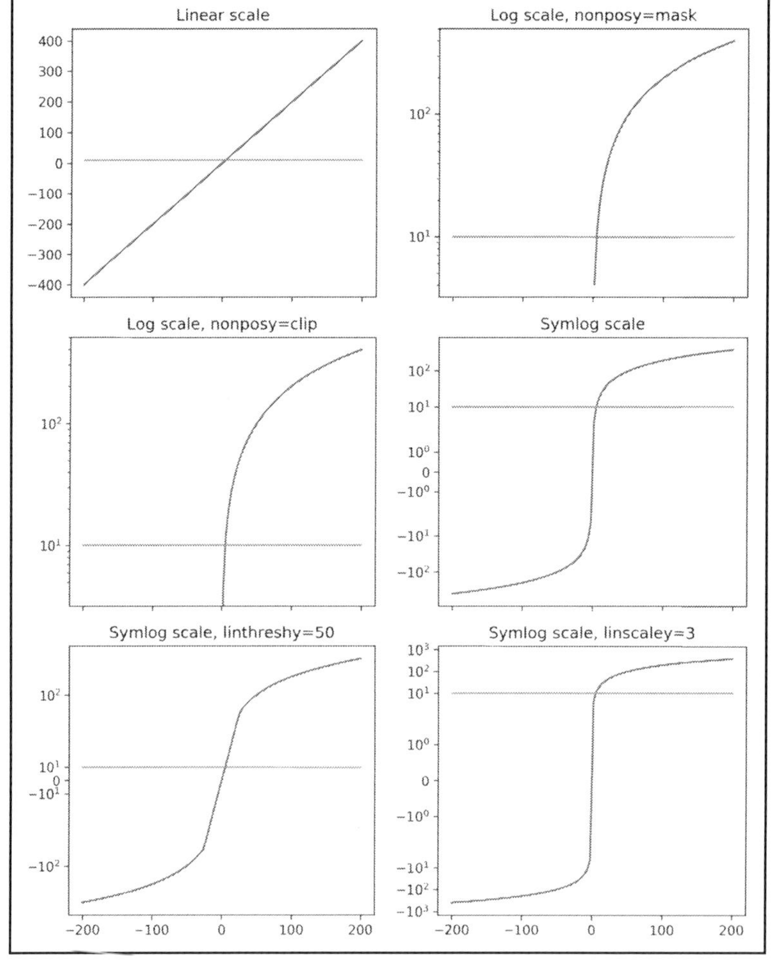

Logit scale

Values within the range of 0 to 1, such as probability and proportion, are often transformed using the logit function. The logit function is given by the following formula:

$$logit(p)=log(p/(1-p))$$

This transformation function has a sigmoidal shape, and it demonstrates symmetry for very small and very large values. The region around 0.5 is almost linear.

For the extreme values of 0 and 1, *logit(p)* cannot be determined. Like the log scale, we can specify the keyword argument `nonpos` to `mask` or `clip` to handle values beyond 0 and 1:

```
import numpy as np
import matplotlib.pyplot as plt

# Prepare 1000 sorted random numbers from the normal distribution
np.random.seed(1)
y = np.random.normal(0.5, 0.1, 1000)
y.sort()
x = np.arange(len(y))

plt.figure()
plt.plot(x,y)

# Transform x-axis to logit scale
plt.yscale('logit')
plt.show()
```

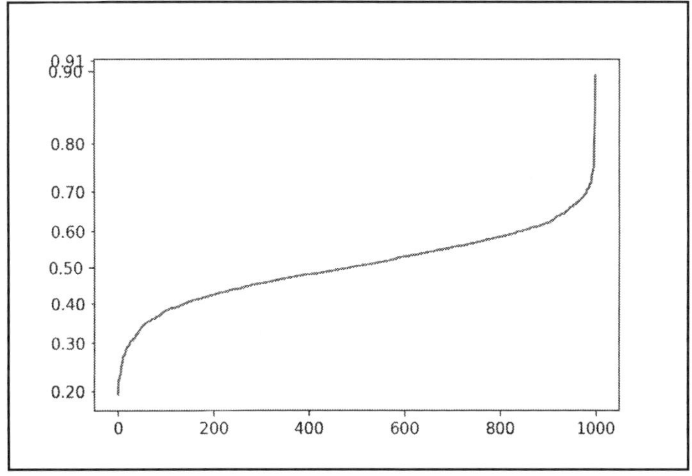

To plot variables with different units on the same chart, we can plot multiple axes that share the x axis by calling the `pyplot.twinx` method. As an alternative, `pyplot.twiny` can generate multiple axes that share the y axis. For those who are working with the `axes` object, `twinx` and `twiny` are also exposed as Python methods in `matplotlib.axes.Axes`. We can assign independent labels and tick formatters to each axis. More elaborate examples will be introduced in `Chapter 4`, *Visualizing Online Data.*

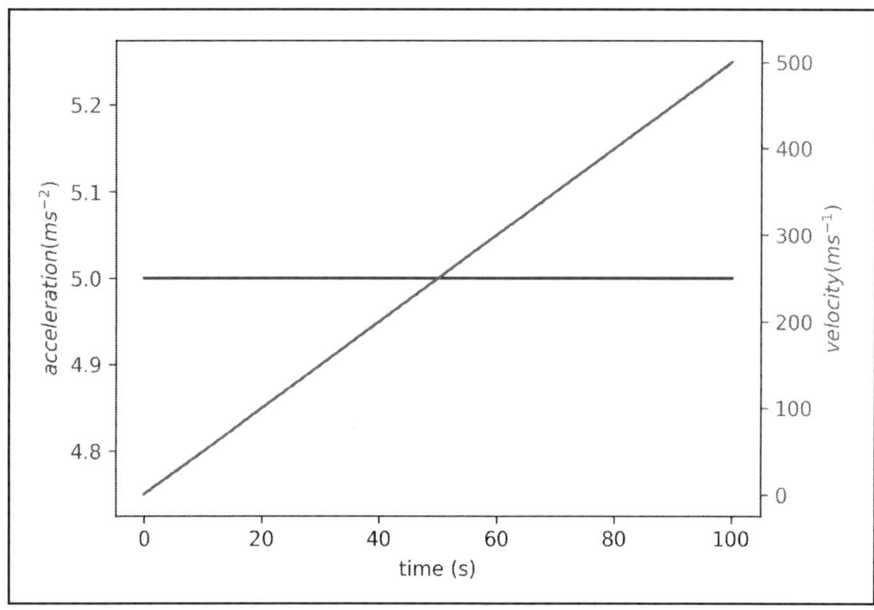

Using style sheets

We have learned to set the style details step by step so far. The `matplotlib.style` module provides a handy way to apply a predefined global style to the whole figure. There are a number of built-in style sheets coming along the `matplotlib` package. You can call `matplotlib.style.available` to check them out:

```
In [27]: import matplotlib as mpl
         mpl.style.available

Out[27]: ['bmh',
          'classic',
          'dark_background',
          'fivethirtyeight',
          'ggplot',
          'grayscale',
          'seaborn-bright',
          'seaborn-colorblind',
          'seaborn-dark-palette',
          'seaborn-dark',
          'seaborn-darkgrid',
          'seaborn-deep',
          'seaborn-muted',
          'seaborn-notebook',
          'seaborn-paper',
          'seaborn-pastel',
          'seaborn-poster',
          'seaborn-talk',
          'seaborn-ticks',
```

The function returns a list of built-in style sheets, including `classic`, `seaborn`, and `ggplot`. Classic refers to the Matplotlib style before version 2.0. Seaborn is a popular package built on top of Matplotlib that offers some special plotting APIs and themes for generating aesthetically attractive statistical figures. In Matplotlib 2.0, we can easily work on the styling natively for simple plot types, without importing an extra module. Multiple style sheets for different purposes are available. The `ggplot` style emulates `ggplot_`, a popular plotting package in R that features vibrant colors on a gray data area with white lines.

Applying a style sheet

Using a style is as simple as calling `pyplot.style.use()`. This function takes in style sheets within the Matplotlib package, as well as local paths and URL. Let's now try with one of the built-in style sheets, `'bmh'`:

```
import matplotlib.pyplot as plt
import numpy as np
import matplotlib as mpl

# set the style as 'bmh'
mpl.style.use('bmh')

months = ['JAN','FEB','MAR','APR','MAY','JUN','JUL','AUG','SEP','OCT',
'NOV','DEC']
y_pos = np.arange(len(months))
# 2016 Hong Kong monthly mean temperature
# Data were quoted from Hong Kong Observatory data on May 8th 2017
# http://www.hko.gov.hk/wxinfo/pastwx/2016/ywx2016.htm
meantemp = [16.,15.5,17.5,23.6,26.7,29.4,29.8,28.4,27.9,26.8,22.3,19.6]
```

```
plt.bar(y_pos, meantemp, align='center', alpha=0.5)
plt.xticks(y_pos, months)
plt.ylabel('Temperature (ºC)')
plt.title('Hong Kong 2016 monthly mean temperature')

plt.show()
```

The name `'bmh'` may not sound familiar to everyone. This is actually a style adapted from a book *Bayesian Methods for Hackers* by Cameron Davidson Pilon. Whether or not you relate to it immediately, this style features a clean layout with modest color scheme and well-adjusted fonts, and is therefore a fair choice for univariate exploratory data like this case.

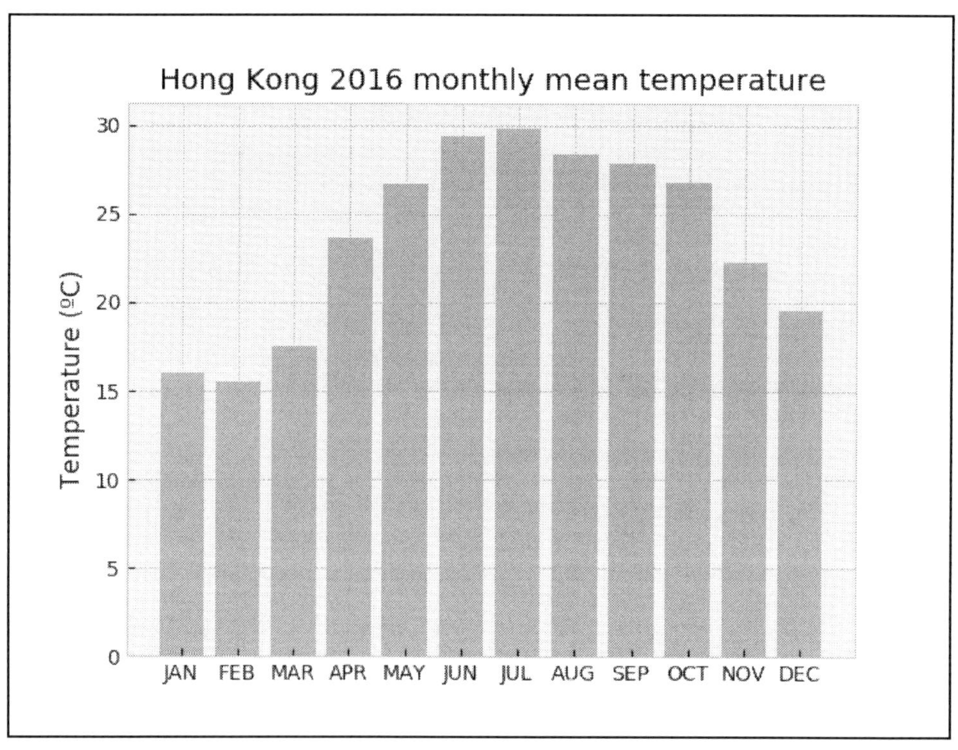

Resetting to default styles

The effects remain after changing styles with the `matplotlib.style` or `matplotlib.rcParams` method, even for a new graph. To revert to default styling, call `pyplot.rcdefaults()` to reset the Matplotlib parameters.

Customizing a style sheet

You can compose a style sheet to store and reuse your own style. For the specifications of a Matplotlib style sheet file, you can have a look at the documentation page at `http://matplotlib.org/users/customizing.html`.

Title and legend

Title and legend are pieces of text that facilitate quick comprehension of the data context. Although a title is not required or recommended, sometimes, such as in inline figures of many scientific publications, adding a title for your plot often helps make the message clear, especially when your figure is not accompanied by explanatory text. For plots with multiple datasets, it is a good practice to keep a data legend with a distinct color or pattern code labeled with the corresponding identities.

Adding a title to your figure

The title of a figure can be set by `pyplot.title()` or `axes.set_title()`. Text properties can be supplied as keyword arguments.

Adding a legend

Adding a legend of data labels in Matplotlib is as simple as setting `label='yourlabel'` when plotting and adding `pyplot.legend()` before `pyplot.show()`. By default, Matplotlib finds the "best" location to prevent the legend from overlapping with data. You may also specify a location using `pyplot.legend(loc='3', **kwargs)`, where text properties can be assigned as keyword arguments:

Location String	Location Code
'best'	0
'upper right'	1
'upper left'	2
'lower left'	3
'lower right'	4
'right'	5
'center left'	6
'center right'	7
'lower center'	8
'upper center'	9
'center'	10

Test your skills

Now that we have gone through each style setting one by one, it's your showtime to combine all the techniques!

```
import matplotlib.pyplot as plt; plt.rcdefaults()
import numpy as np
import matplotlib as mpl

mpl.style.use('seaborn-darkgrid')

# 2001-2015 per genome sequencing cost in USD
# Adapted from NIH National Human Genome Research Institute figures
# genome.gov/sequencingcosts
# Data were quoted from builtwith.com on May 8th 2017
# Seasonal data were averaged by year for simplicity
```

```
# Prepare the data
years = list(range(2001,2016))
y_pos = np.arange(len(years))
seqcost = [95263071.92,70175437.42,61448421.50,53751684.08,
40157554.23,28780376.21,\
20442576.14,19934345.74,18519312.16,17534969.56,16159699.44,
16180224.10,\
13801124.19,12585658.90,11732534.52,11455315.22,10474556.36,
9408738.91,\
9047002.97,8927342.14,7147571.39,3063819.99,1352982.23,752079.90,
342502.06,\
232735.44,154713.60,108065.14,70333.33,46774.27,31512.04,31124.96,
29091.73,\
20962.78,16712.01,10496.93,7743.44,7666.22,5901.29,5984.72,6618.35,
5671.35,\
5826.26,5550.26,5096.08,4008.11,4920.50,4904.85,5730.89,3969.84,4210.79,
1363.24,1245.00]

# Plot the data
plt.plot(seqcost,marker='D',ms=3,color='navy',\
label='Genome sequencing cost') # Set the data label
plt.xticks(y_pos, years)

# Set logarithmic scale on y-axis
plt.yscale('log')
plt.title('2001-2015 per Genome Sequencing Cost',color='darkblue',
fontweight='semibold')

# Place the legend
plt.legend()

# Get current axes
ax = plt.gca()

# Set ticks in multiples for x-axis
ax.xaxis.set_major_locator(ticker.MultipleLocator(4))
ax.xaxis.set_minor_locator(ticker.MultipleLocator(1))

# label the start of each year by FixedFormatter
ax.get_xaxis().set_major_formatter(ticker.FixedFormatter(years))

# Label the axes
ax.set_xlabel('Year')
ax.set_ylabel('Per Genome Sequencing Cost (USD)')

ax.xaxis.set_tick_params(labelsize=10)

plt.show()
```

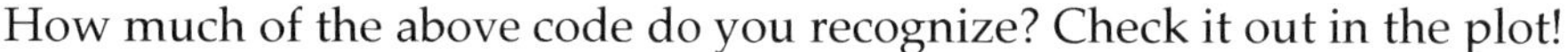

How much of the above code do you recognize? Check it out in the plot!

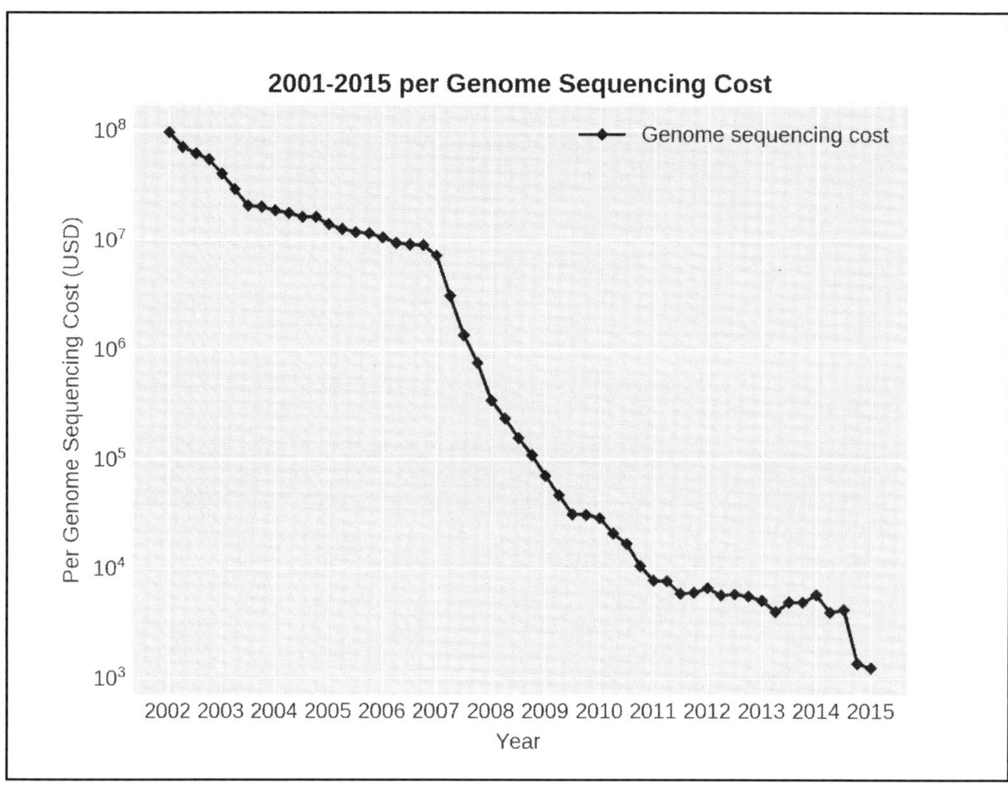

Summary

In this chapter, you learned how to set the styles, including colors, sizes, and shapes, of various elements in a Matplotlib plot. Now you are also aware of some stylistic considerations for a refined figure.

In the next chapter, we will continue to discuss the appearance of plots, moving our focus to the layout and annotation.

3

Figure Layout and Annotations

A picture is worth a thousand words. Photographers and painters need to plan their picture composition, and so do data graphics designers. Layout is an important aspect of creating an appealing figure.

Sometimes, your story weighs more than a thousand words to be told via a single figure. We often see a group of relevant plots lying adjacently to deliver a message in multiple aspects.

Just as you may quote some particular phrases in a book paragraph or comment your code for easier comprehension, it is also likely that we need extra annotation to point out areas of emphasis in plots. Now we have mastered the basic techniques to adjust the look and feel in a single plot, in this chapter, we will go through the following topics:

- Layout:
    - Adjusting the size of the figure
    - Modifying or removing spines
    - Multiple plots within the same figure
    - Adding subplots
    - Adding inset plots
    - Adjusting margins
- Annotations:
    - Adding basic annotations
    - Adding a textbox
    - Adding shapes

Adjusting the layout

Figure layout, including the size and location of plots, directs the focus of our readers. A figure with good layout facilitates data presentation in a logical flow. It is thus important to familiarize ourselves with layout settings when plotting. Let's learn how to assign proper sizes, positions, and spacing to our plots.

Adjusting the size of the figure

Depending on where you want to put your figure, you may want to adjust the size and layout. Instead of manually stretching your image output afterward, which takes extra effort and can distort the text. You can set the height and width directly by calling `pyplot.figure(figsize=())`. As briefly mentioned in `Chapter 2`, *Figure Aesthetics*, the figure module contains all the plot elements. The `figsize` setting controls the overall size in inches and aspect ratio of the figure. This is also useful when we want to show a larger plot directly in a notebook, without having to export it in a high-resolution image.

Here is an example of setting the figure size and aspect. We set equal aspect with `plt.figure(figsize=(12,12))` to keep the pie chart a circle instead of a compressed ellipse:

```
import matplotlib.pyplot as plt

# Median Annual earnings ratio for full-time, year-round workers in US by
# gender 2015
# http://www.aauw.org/research/the-simple-truth-about-the-gender-pay-gap/

# Prepare the data
m = 51212.
f = 40742.
m_perc = m/(m+f)
f_perc = f/(m+f)

# Set the colors and labels
colors = ['navy','lightcoral']
labels = ["Male","Female"]

# Set the figure container box to be a square
# to keep our pie chart a circle but not an elipse
plt.figure(figsize=(12,12))

# Draw the pie chart
# In a matplotlib pie chart, patches, texts and autotexts control the
# sectors, data labels and value labels respectively
```

```
patches, texts, autotexts =
plt.pie([m_perc,f_perc],labels=labels,autopct='%1.1f%%',\
         explode=[0,0.05], startangle=0,colors=colors)

plt.title('Median Annual Earnings Ratio for Full-Time, Year-Round Workers
in the US by Gender in 2015',fontsize=20)

# Format the text labels
for text in texts+autotexts:
    text.set_fontsize(20)
    text.set_fontweight('bold')

for text in autotexts:
    text.set_color('white')

# Show the figure
plt.show()
```

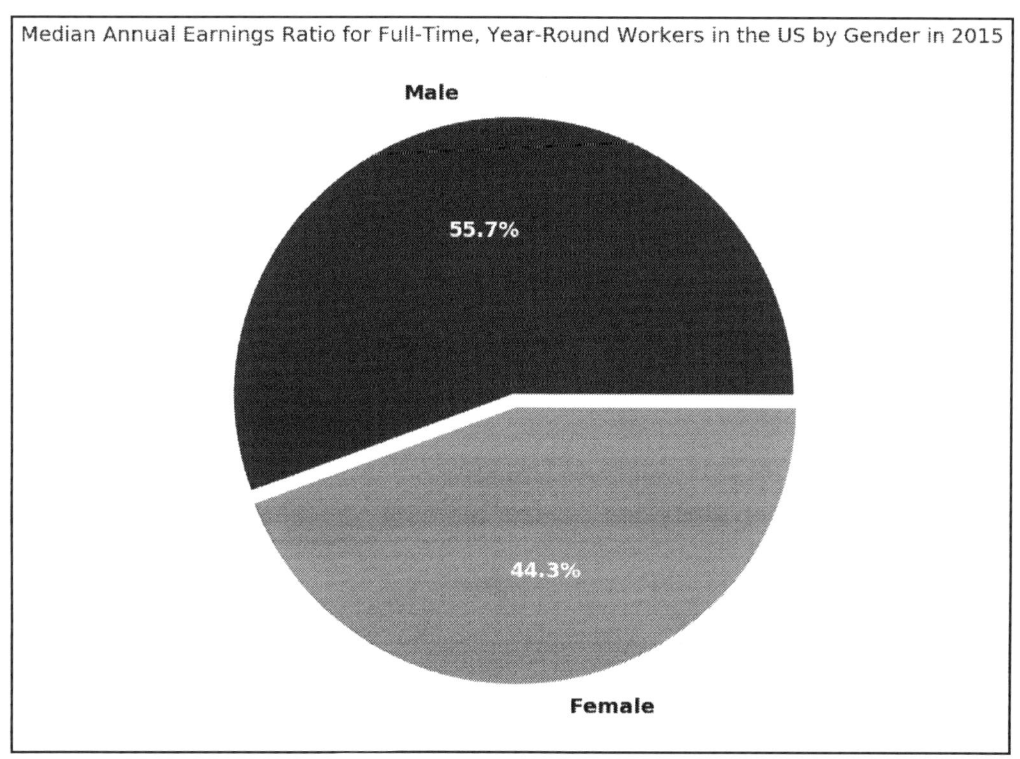

Alternatively, for cases where only the aspect matters and not the size, you can use `ax.set_aspect(1)` to set equal aspect after defining the axes.

Adjusting spines

Matplotlib figures have four spines, which enclose the plot data area by default. We may prefer to style or remove them to suit different purposes. Sometimes, we would like to follow certain conventions. For instance, it is common for biologists to publish their western blot or other analysis results in black and white with thick lines and two spines only. While the trend is slowly changing, this style is still adopted by many journal papers. We will discuss this a bit deeper in `Chapter 7`, *A Practical Guide to Scientific Plotting*. Meanwhile, users such as news editors and marketing speakers may also find it too boring to have black lines surrounding their graphics. Let's jump in and learn to how to adjust or remove spines.

Spine properties can be set by calling different functions under `set_linewidth()` and `set_edgecolor()` under `axis.spines`.

To remove unnecessary spines, let's say the right spine, we can use `axis.spines['right'].set_visible(False)`.

Here is a social neuroscience article published in the Nature journal in 2017. The study reported that the UBE3A gene and seizures synergize to affect sociability. To illustrate the spine styling, we adopted the published source data to remake a figure in the paper with adaptations. We tuned the spine line widths and removed the top and right spines. We will leave the lines and text annotation showing statistical significance until later in the chapter:

```
import numpy as np
import matplotlib.pyplot as plt
import matplotlib.ticker as ticker

"""
Data from Figure 2b
Autism gene Ube3a and seizures impair sociability by repressing VTA Cbln1.
Krishnan V et al., Nature. 2017 Mar 23;543(7646):507-512.
doi: 10.1038/nature21678.
https://www.nature.com/nature/journal/v543/n7646/fig_tab/nature21678_F2.htm
l
"""
# Prepare the data
saline_social = [123,96,111,85,74,115,74,91]
saline_opposite = [24,12,20,25,53,19,29,28]
```

```
ptz_social = [39,20,32,43,61,82,46,64,57,71]
ptz_opposite = [40,70,40,71,24,8,27,30,29,13]

n = 2
xloc = np.arange(2)
y1 = [np.mean(saline_social),np.mean(ptz_social)]
y2 = [np.mean(saline_opposite),np.mean(ptz_opposite)]
# Filling zeroes to draw positive error bars only
yerr1 = [(0,0),[np.std(saline_social),np.std(saline_opposite)]]
yerr2 = [(0,0),[np.std(ptz_social),np.std(ptz_opposite)]]

# Set the figure
fig = plt.figure(figsize=(3,5))

# Set the bar widths and locations
width = 0.3

# Draw the bar chart
plt.bar(xloc, y1, width=width, align='center', color='black',
label='Social')
plt.bar(xloc+width, y2, width=width, edgecolor='black', facecolor='white',
align='center', linewidth=3, label='Opposite')

# Format errorbars. More details will be covered in scientific plotting
# chapter.
plt.errorbar(xloc, y1, yerr=yerr1, ls='none', lw=3, color='black',
capsize=8, capthick=3, xlolims=True)
plt.errorbar(xloc+width, y2, yerr=yerr2, ls='none', lw=3, color='black',
capsize=8, capthick=3,xlolims=False)

# Get current axes and store it to ax
ax = plt.gca()

# Format the spines
ax.spines['left'].set_linewidth(3)
ax.spines['bottom'].set_linewidth(3)
ax.spines['right'].set_visible(False)
ax.spines['top'].set_visible(False)

# Format the axes
ax.xaxis.set_tick_params(width=3)
ax.yaxis.set_tick_params(width=3)
ax.yaxis.set_major_locator(ticker.MultipleLocator(50))
labels = ['Saline','PTZ']
plt.xticks(range(2), labels, fontsize=16, rotation=30)
plt.yticks(fontsize=16)
plt.ylabel('Sniffing time (s)', fontsize=18)
plt.ylim(0,150)
```

```
# Add a legend
plt.legend(loc='upper center',fontsize=18,frameon=False)

# Show the figure
plt.show()
```

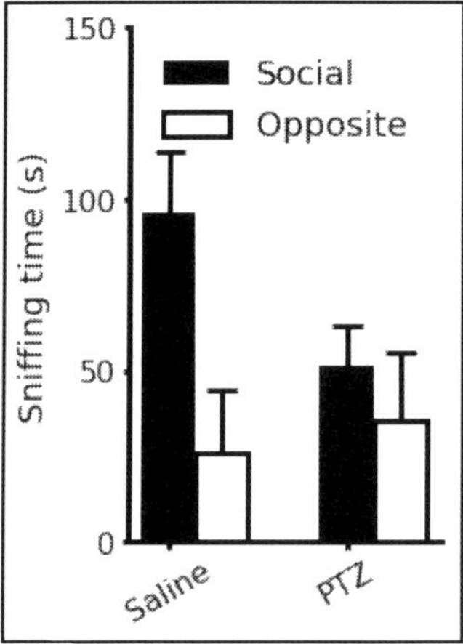

Adding subplots

There are frequent occasions when it is preferable to have different plots aligned in the same figure. For example, when you have groups of relevant data, such as a series of different analysis on the same data or a baseline control experiment data to align with, you may want to show them in subplots of the same figure. There are a few ways to add subplots in Matplotlib, demonstrated as follows.

Adding subplots using pyplot.subplot

A basic method to add subplots is to use the `pyplot.subplot(nrows, ncols, plot_number)` function. For `nrows * ncols < 10`, we can omit the commas as shorthand. For example, "111" denotes the first subplot in a 1 x 1 grid, "132" denotes the second subplot in a 1 x 3 grid. When we plot axes with `pyplot`, a figure and a subplot are generated implicitly, so it is optional to call `pyplot.figure(1)` and `pyplot.subplot(111)`:

```
import numpy as np
import matplotlib.pyplot as plt
```

```
# Prepare the data
y = np.arange(200)

# Draw the plots
ax1 = plt.subplot(121) # Create the first subplot (on left)
plt.plot(-y) # Plot on ax1
ax2 = plt.subplot(122) # Create the second subplot
plt.plot(y) # Plot on ax2

# Show the figure
plt.show()
```

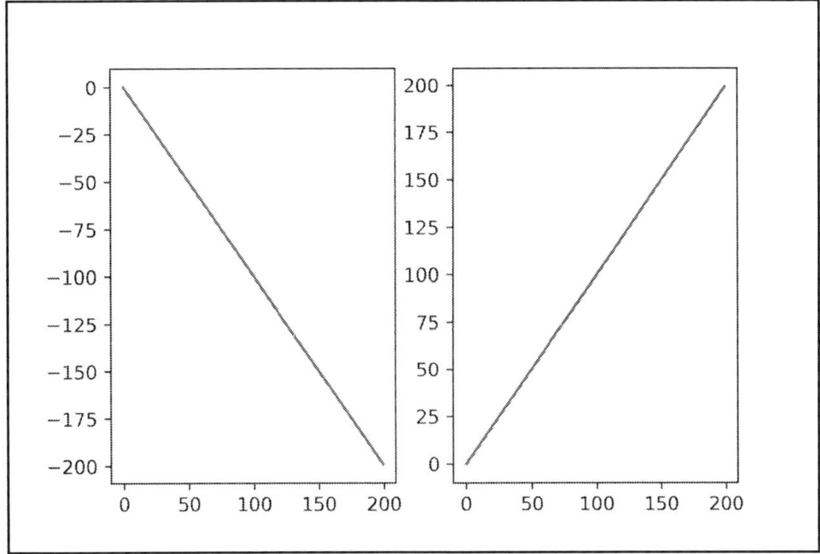

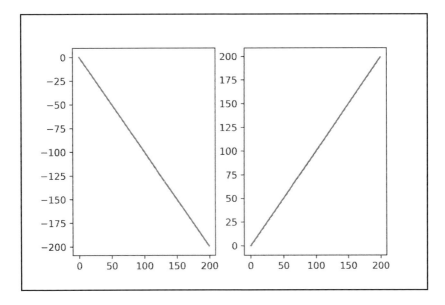

The subplots must be created in the order of the plot number parameter. For instance, calling `plt.plot(122)` before `plt.plot(121)` will result in a ValueError exception.

Using pyplot.subplots() to specify handles

While a figure with one subplot is automatically generated whenever we plot axes, sometimes we would like to get more control over the figure and axes by storing them into variables. There is a more convenient way to do this. We can call `fig, ax = plt.subplots()`, which is equivalent to `fig = plt.figure(); ax = fig.add_subplot(111)`. It returns a tuple that corresponds to the figure and axis objects:

```
import matplotlib.pyplot as plt
import numpy as np

# Draw 2x2 subplots and assign them to axes variables
fig, axarr = plt.subplots(2,2)

# Prepare data
x1 = np.linspace(5,5)
x2 = np.linspace(0,10)
y1 = x2
y2 = 10-x2

# Plot the data to respective subplots
axarr[0,0].plot(x2,y1)
axarr[0,1].plot(x2,y2)
axarr[1,0].plot(x1,y2)
axarr[1,1].plot(x1,y1)

# Show the figure
plt.show()
```

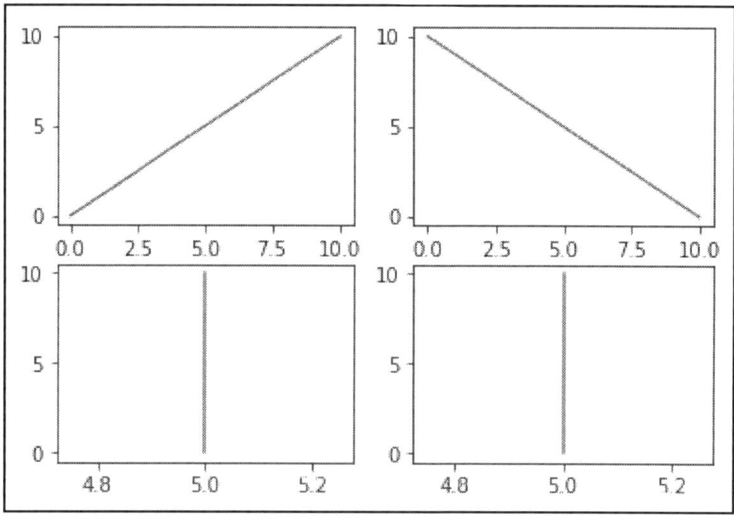

You may probably think that this looks somewhat imbalanced, with the column gap much wider than the separation between the rows. We can rectify this by adjusting the subplot margins, introduced next.

Sharing axes between subplots

We can specify shared x and/or y axes in the `pyplot.subplots` function. For instance, if we set `sharex` and `sharey` to `True` in the preceding example as `fig, axarr = plt.subplots(2,2,sharex=True,sharey=True)`, we will get the following figure:

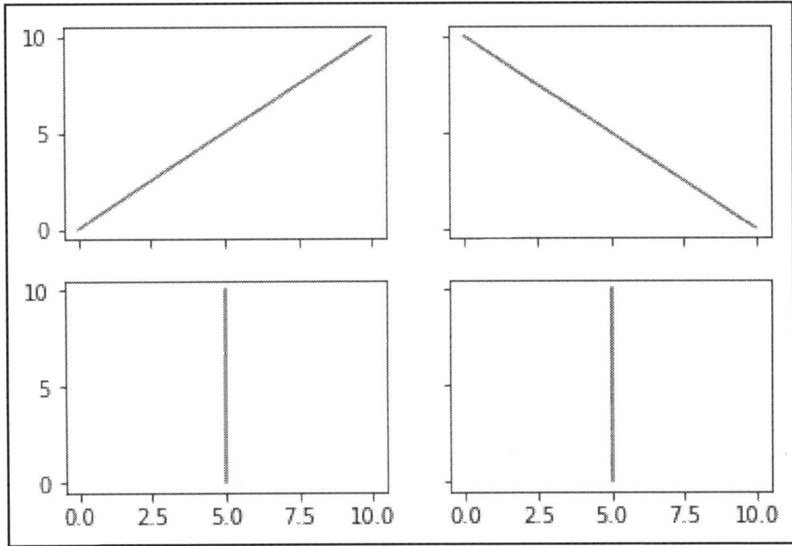

Adjusting margins

Besides the overall figure size, we can also adjust the subplot axes (plot area) to fit the inner layout. There are several ways to do this.

Setting dimensions when adding subplot axes with figure.add_axes

We can set the subplot size by parsing the dimension parameters to `fig.add_axes` when defining the axes:

```
plt.figure()
ax = fig.add_axes([left, bottom, width, height])
```

This will be further showcased in the inset plot section.

Modifying subplot axes dimensions via pyplot.subplots_adjust

Alternatively, we can adjust the subplot dimensions after defining the axes:

```
fig, ax = plt.subplots()
plt.subplots_adjust(left=0.1, right=0.9, top=0.9, bottom=0.1)
```

Aligning subplots with pyplot.tight_layout

When we have a group of subplots, depending on various layout concerns (including how much information we are showing on each axis), we may want to adjust the gap sizes between different subplots. In general, we would often like to align subplots with minimum white space. Matplotlib provides a function, `pyplot.tight_layout()`, for this purpose.

If we replace the `plt.show()` in the previous example of 2 x 2 subplots with `plt.tight_layout()`, the gap between columns will narrow. This can be further customized by parsing the parameters `pad`, `w_pad`, `h_pad` into `tight_layout()`, which corresponds to the padding between the figure edge and edges of subplots, and the height and the width between adjacent subplots. The padding values are relative to the font size.

All gaps will be removed if we change `plt.show()` in the example to `plt.tight_layout(pad=0, w_pad=-1, h_pad=-1)`:

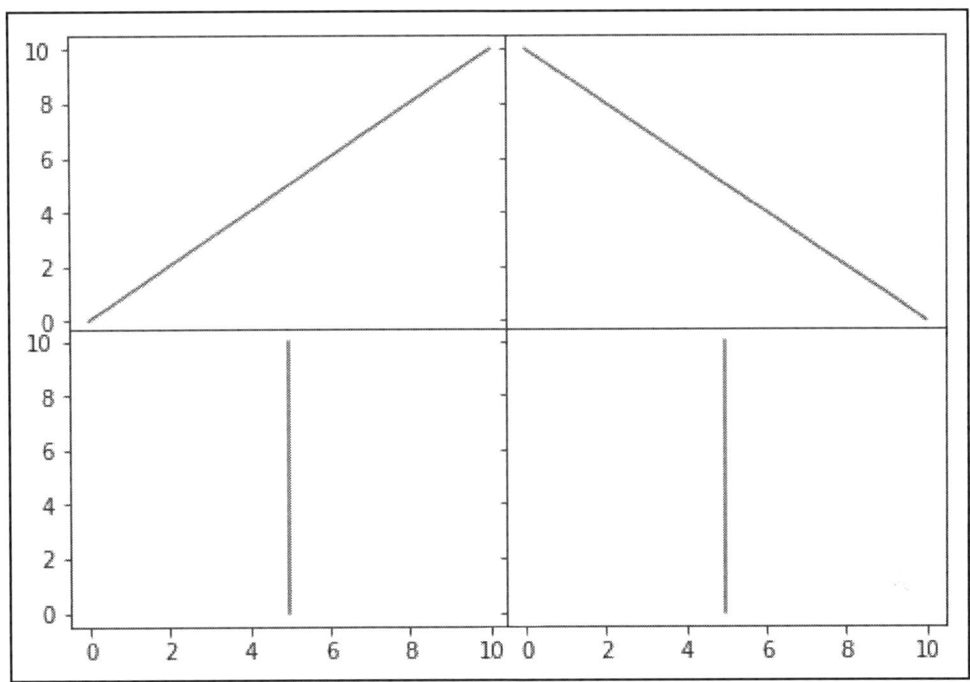

Auto-aligning figure elements with pyplot.tight_layout

Besides adjusting the spacing between subplots, the `tight_layout` module is also helpful in automatically aligning other elements within a figure, without adjusting sizes by trial and error. It considers axis labels, tick labels, axis titles, and offset boxes anchored to axes to align them.

Stacking subplots of different dimensions with subplot2grid

When we want to group plots of different dimensions, `pyplot.subplot2grid` proves useful by allowing a subplot to span across multiple rows and columns:

```
ax1 = plt.subplot2grid((3, 3), (0, 0))
ax2 = plt.subplot2grid((3, 3), (1, 0))
ax3 = plt.subplot2grid((3, 3), (0, 2), rowspan=3)
ax4 = plt.subplot2grid((3, 3), (2, 0), colspan=2)
ax5 = plt.subplot2grid((3, 3), (0, 1), rowspan=2)
```

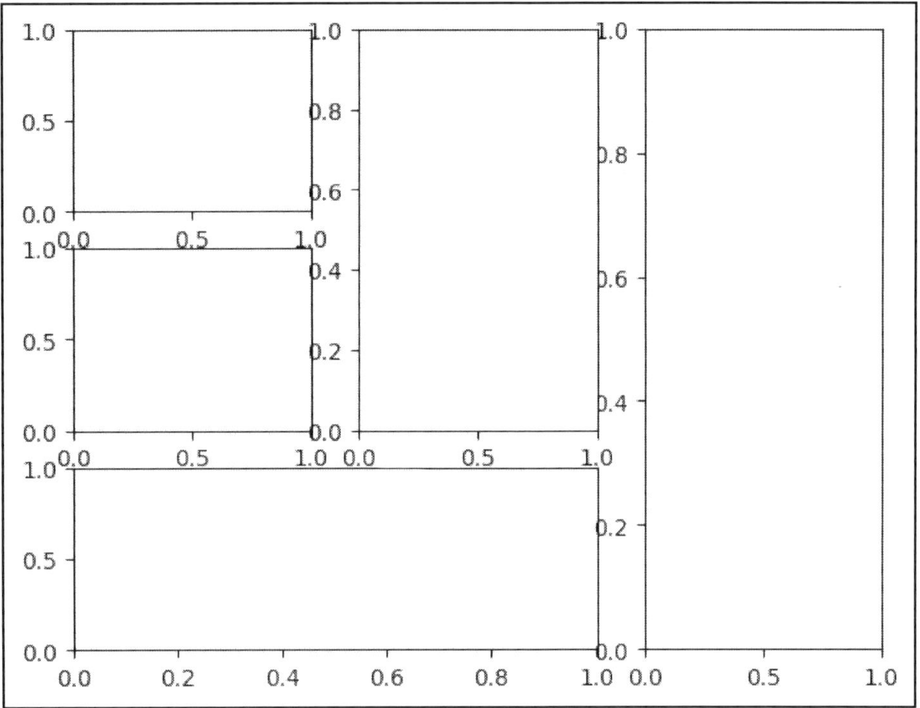

Drawing inset plots

While aligning relevant plots side by side, we also have the option to embed a smaller plot in the main figure to visualize data of a different scope. Typically, we use the main figure to give an overall idea of our major message and support it with other perspectives or zoom into a focus via minor figures.

Drawing a basic inset plot

We can draw an inset plot by calling `figure.add_axes()`. The dimension can be set by these parameters--`[left, bottom, width, height]`:

```
import matplotlib.pyplot as plt
import numpy as np

x = np.linspace(0,10,1000)
y2 = np.sin(x**2)
y1 = x**2

# Initiate a figure with subplot axes
fig, ax1 = plt.subplots()

# Set the inset plot dimensions
left, bottom, width, height = [0.22, 0.45, 0.3, 0.35]
ax2 = fig.add_axes([left, bottom, width, height])

# Draw the plots
ax1.plot(x,y1)
ax2.plot(x,y2)

# Show the figure
plt.show()
```

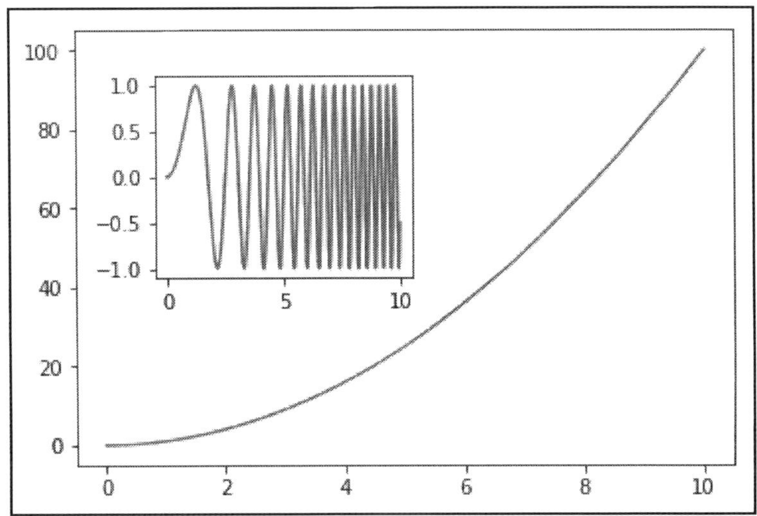

Plot the data after axis and tick formatting for the inset plot axes!

To avoid conflicts with the settings left over from the main plot, such as the tick locations, it is recommended to plot the data after formatting and scaling the ticks and axes.

Using inset_axes

The native Matplotlib method we just described gives good flexibility to adjust the position of the inset axes. When we want to set a quick location, `inset_axes` may be a good start. There are a number of predefined locations you may select with the keyword argument `loc` without the hassle of specifying the exact coordinates by trial and error. It can be set by the strings or integer index of the corresponding positions:

```
'upper right'  : 1,
'upper left'   : 2,
'lower left'   : 3,
'lower right'  : 4,
'right'        : 5,
'center left'  : 6,
'center right' : 7,
'lower center' : 8,
'upper center' : 9,
'center'       : 10
```

To use this method, we first import the module:

```
from mpl_toolkits.axes_grid1.inset_locator import inset_axes
```

Here is an example of embedding inset axes `ax2` of 6.5-inch width and 45% height of the container `parent_bbox`. The inset axes lie on the right within the `ax1` axes:

```
ax2 = inset_axes(ax1, width=6.5, height=45%, loc=5)
```

Now, let's try to plot a real figure with the `inset_axes` function. Up next is a figure showing the number of arrivals to the USA in 2016 from January to October. We draw the count from the top 10 countries with a bar chart, and we put a pie chart to show the share of arrivals from different world regions (Canada and Mexico excluded):

```
import matplotlib.pyplot as plt
from mpl_toolkits.axes_grid1.inset_locator import inset_axes
"""
Data from ITA National Travel & Tourism Office of US
I-94 Program: 2016 Monthly Arrivals Data
http://travel.trade.gov/view/m-2016-I-001/index.asp
```

```
"""
# Prepare the data
top10_arrivals_countries = ['CANADA','MEXICO','UNITED\nKINGDOM',\
                            'JAPAN','CHINA','GERMANY','SOUTH\nKOREA',\
                            'FRANCE','BRAZIL','INDIA']
top10_arrivals_values = [13.428347, 12.255948, 3.019111, 2.352919,\
                         2.098333, 1.322882, 1.282097, 1.127868,\
                         1.109066, 0.874016]
arrivals_countries = ['WESTERN\nEUROPE','ASIA','SOUTH\nAMERICA',\
                      'OCEANIA','CARIBBEAN','MIDDLE\nEAST',\
                      'CENTRAL\nAMERICA','EASTERN\nEUROPE','AFRICA']
arrivals_percent = [36.2,30.8,13.9,4.3,4.1,3.8,2.8,2.6,1.5]

# Set up the figure and the main subplot
fig, ax1 = plt.subplots(figsize=(20,12))

# Draw the bar plot
rects1 = ax1.bar(range(10),top10_arrivals_values,
align='center',color='#3b5998')

# Set spines to be invisible
for spine in ax1.spines.values():
    spine.set_visible(False)

# Format ticks and labels
plt.xticks(range(10),top10_arrivals_countries,fontsize=18)
for tic in ax1.xaxis.get_major_ticks():
    tic.tick1On = tic.tick2On = False
plt.yticks(fontsize=18)
plt.xlabel('Top 10 tourist generating countries',fontsize=24,
fontweight='semibold')
plt.ylabel('Arrivals (Million)',fontsize=24,fontweight='semibold')

# Prepare the inset axes
ax2 = inset_axes(ax1, width=6.5, height=6.5, loc=5)

# Store the pie chart sectors, sample labels and value labels
# Set the properties
explode = (0.08, 0.08, 0.05, 0.05,0.05,0.05,0.05,0.05,0.05)
patches, texts, autotexts = ax2.pie(arrivals_percent, \
                                    labels=arrivals_countries,\
                                    autopct='%1.1f%%', \
                                    shadow=True, startangle=180,\
                                    explode=explode, \
                                    counterclock=False, \
                                    pctdistance=0.72)

# Set properties of text in pie chart
```

```
for text in texts+autotexts:
    text.set_fontsize(16)
    text.set_fontweight('semibold')

# Add a super title to all the subplots
plt.suptitle('Non-Resident Arrivals to the US in 2016 (by Aug) by
Regions',fontsize=36,color='navy',fontweight='bold')

# Show the figure
plt.show()
```

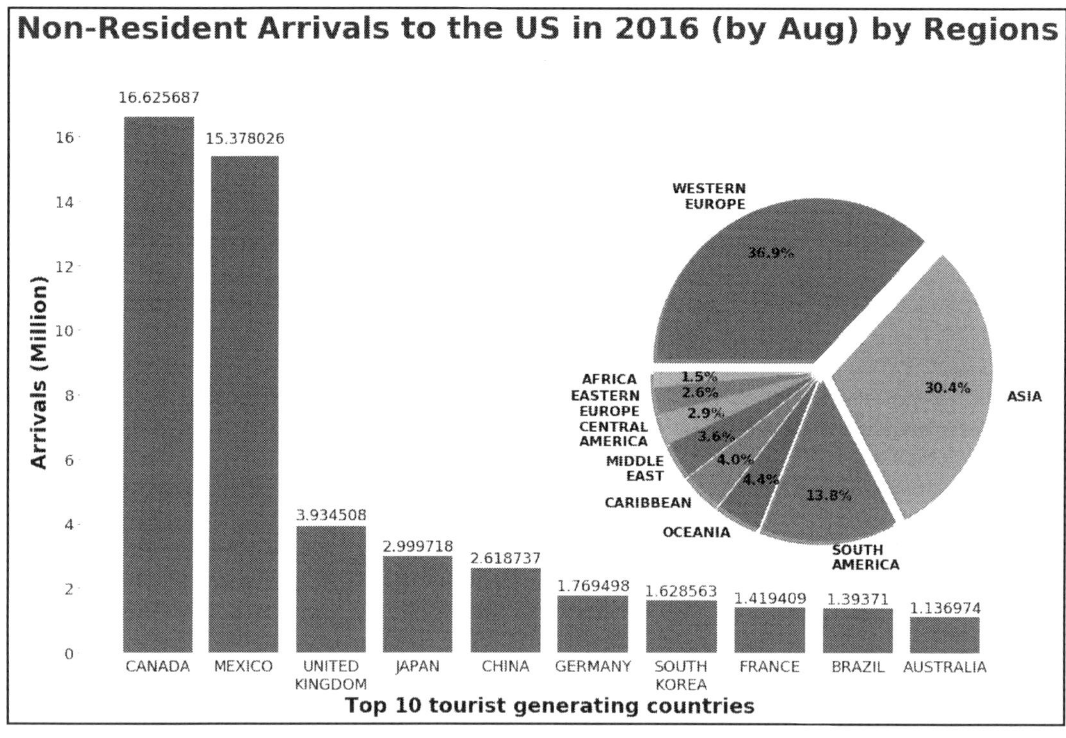

Annotations

To give further explanation or guide readers to focus on certain remarkable details, annotations can be added to a figure. Matplotlib offers several modules to add text, arrows, and shapes that can be exploited.

Adding text annotations

Annotations can be added easily by specifying the desired locations through some built-in functions in Matplotlib.

Adding text and arrows with axis.annotate

Matplotlib has an `axis.annotate` function that draws an arrow extending across specified *x* and *y* coordinates and adds a text label if a string is input. The target coordinates of the pointed location and text label are assigned by the `xy` and `xytext` parameters in tuples, respectively. Here is an example of drawing the basic demand-supply curves we learn in high school economics:

```
import matplotlib.pyplot as plt
import numpy as np

# create 1000 equally spaced points between -10 and 10
x = np.linspace(0, 10)

# Prepare the data
y1 = x
y2 = 10-x

# Plot the data
fig, ax = plt.subplots()
plt.plot(x,y1,label='Supply')
plt.plot(x,y2,label='Demand')

# Annotate the equilibrium point with arrow and text
ax.annotate("Equilibrium", xy=(5,5), xytext=(4,2), \
            fontsize=12, fontweight='semibold',\
            arrowprops=dict(linewidth=2, arrowstyle="->"))

# Label the axes
plt.xlabel('Quantity',fontsize=12,fontweight='semibold')
plt.ylabel('Price',fontsize=12,fontweight='semibold')
```

```
# Style the plot to a common demand-supply graph
ax.spines['top'].set_visible(False)
ax.spines['right'].set_visible(False)
ax.xaxis.set_major_locator(plt.NullLocator())
ax.yaxis.set_major_locator(plt.NullLocator())

plt.legend()
plt.show()
```

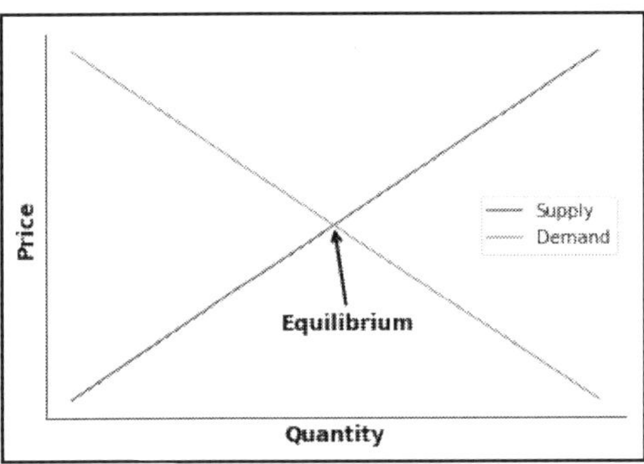

Adding a textbox with axis.text

Instead of drawing an extra legend with `pyplot.legend()`, we can add textboxes using `text()` to directly label the curves. Up next is a figure generated by replacing `pyplot.legend()` with the following two lines of code. Text styling introduced in `Chapter 2`, *Figure Aesthetics* applies here:

```
ax.text(9, 9.6, "Supply", ha="center", va="center", size=16,
rotation=33,color='C0')
ax.text(9, 1.5, "Demand", ha="center", va="center", size=16,
rotation=-33,color='C1')
```

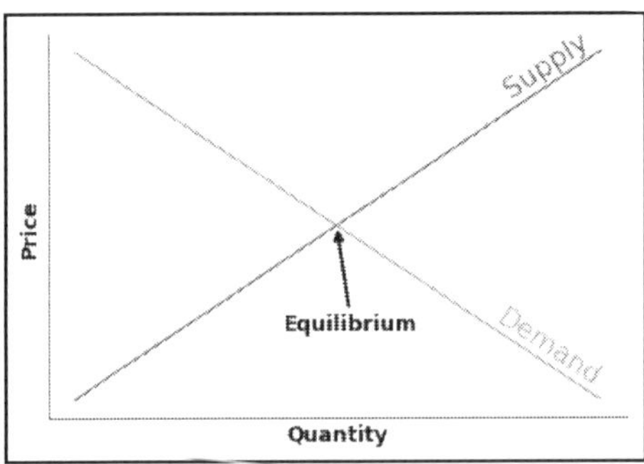

Adding arrows

Here is another way to add arrows, which are more sophisticated than the single line we draw with `pyplot.annotate()`.

Using the previous demand-supply example, substituting the annotation by `pyplot.annotate()` with the following code block will yield the blue arrow textbox as shown:

```
# Annotate the equilibrium point with arrow and text
bbox_props = dict(boxstyle="rarrow", fc=(0.8, 0.9, 0.9), ec="b", lw=2)
t = ax.text(2,5, "Equilibrium", ha="center", va="center", rotation=0,
            size=12,bbox=bbox_props)
bb = t.get_bbox_patch()
bb.set_boxstyle("rarrow", pad=0.6)
```

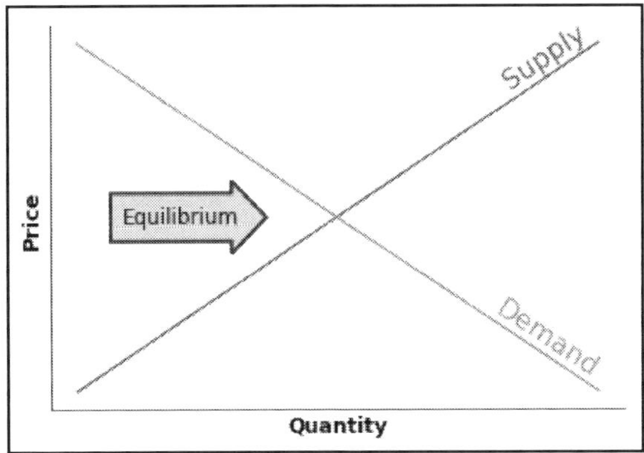

Labeling data values on a bar chart

Sometimes we would prefer more exact values than guess between ticks on axes. To automatically retrieve and label data values on a bar graph, we can define our own function to put text above each bar. Essentially, the `pyplot.bar()` function creates a list of rectangles with assigned dimensions. What we do is collect these dimensions to determine the location of the text to be added.

We are recycling the previous non-resident arrivals figure. We can add the following code block of the value-labeling function and call it after defining `ax1.bar()` to add value labels above each bar:

```
# Prepare the bar value labelling function
def autolabel(rects):
```

```
        """
        Attach a text label above each bar displaying its height
        Adapted from http://matplotlib.org/examples/api/barchart_demo.html
        """
        for rect in rects:
            height = rect.get_height()
            ax1.text(rect.get_x() + rect.get_width()/2., 1.02*height,
            "{:,}".format(int(height)),
            ha='center', va='bottom',fontsize=18)

    autolabel(rects1)
```

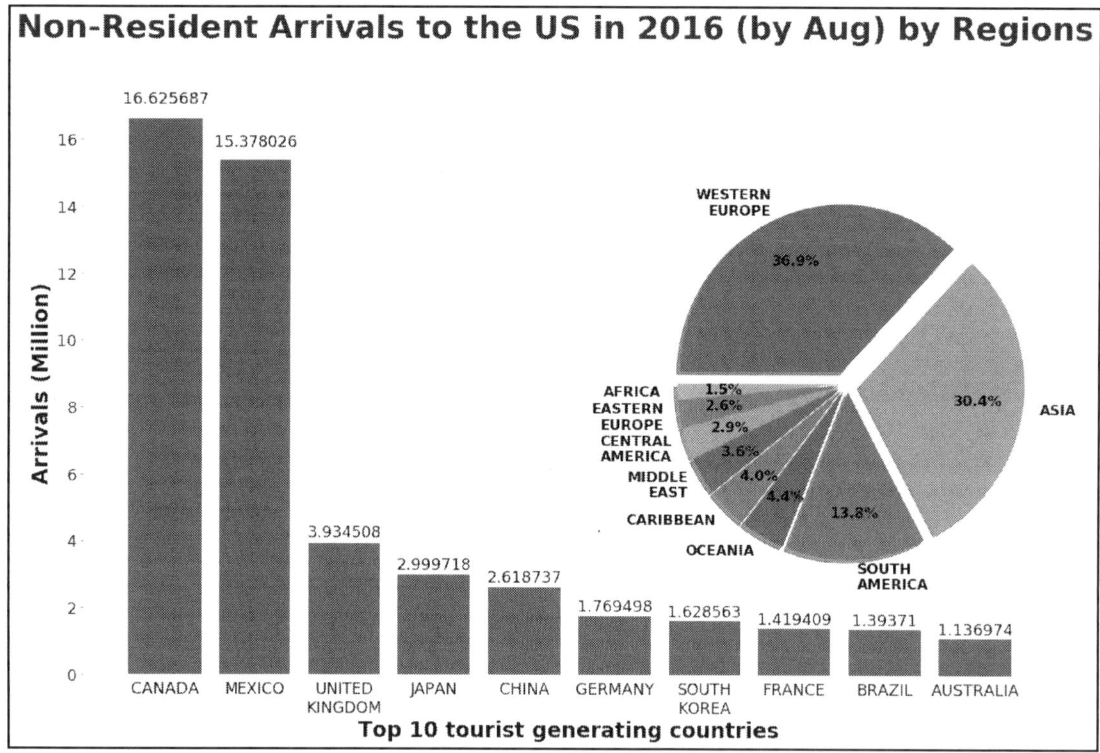

Adding graphical annotations

Whereas text offers extra information, shapes help to spotlight interesting areas for readers to focus on.

Adding shapes

We have introduced ways to put arrows before. The `patches` class in Matplotlib defines a number of other shapes, including `Circle`, `Ellipse`, `Wedge`, and `Polygon`. Various relevant shapes, including sectors and rings, can also be drawn. For demonstration purposes, we draw a cartoon with different patches to locate the different shapes and vertex coordinates intuitively:

```
import numpy as np
from matplotlib.patches import Circle, Wedge, Polygon, Ellipse
from matplotlib.collections import PatchCollection
import matplotlib.pyplot as plt

fig, ax = plt.subplots()
patches = []

# Full and ring sectors drawn by Wedge((x,y),r,deg1,deg2)
leftstripe = Wedge((.46, .5), .15, 90,100) # Full sector by default
midstripe = Wedge((.5,.5), .15, 85,95)
rightstripe = Wedge((.54,.5), .15, 80,90)
lefteye = Wedge((.36, .46), .06, 0, 360, width=0.03) # Ring sector drawn
# when width <1
righteye = Wedge((.63, .46), .06, 0, 360, width=0.03)
nose = Wedge((.5, .32), .08, 75,105, width=0.03)
mouthleft = Wedge((.44, .4), .08, 240,320, width=0.01)
mouthright = Wedge((.56, .4), .08, 220,300, width=0.01)
patches += [leftstripe,midstripe,rightstripe,lefteye,righteye,nose,
mouthleft,mouthright]

# Circles
leftiris = Circle((.36,.46),0.04)
rightiris = Circle((.63,.46),0.04)
patches += [leftiris,rightiris]

# Polygons drawn by passing coordinates of vertices
leftear = Polygon([[.2,.6],[.3,.8],[.4,.64]], True)
rightear = Polygon([[.6,.64],[.7,.8],[.8,.6]], True)
topleftwhisker = Polygon([[.01,.4],[.18,.38],[.17,.42]], True)
bottomleftwhisker = Polygon([[.01,.3],[.18,.32],[.2,.28]], True)
toprightwhisker = Polygon([[.99,.41],[.82,.39],[.82,.43]], True)
bottomrightwhisker = Polygon([[.99,.31],[.82,.33],[.81,.29]], True)
patches+=[leftear,rightear,topleftwhisker,bottomleftwhisker,toprightwhisker
,bottomrightwhisker]

# Ellipse drawn by Ellipse((x,y),width,height)
body = Ellipse((0.5,-0.18),0.6,0.8)
patches.append(body)
```

```
# Draw the patches
colors = 100*np.random.rand(len(patches)) # set random colors
p = PatchCollection(patches, alpha=0.4)
p.set_array(np.array(colors))
ax.add_collection(p)

# Show the figure
plt.show()
```

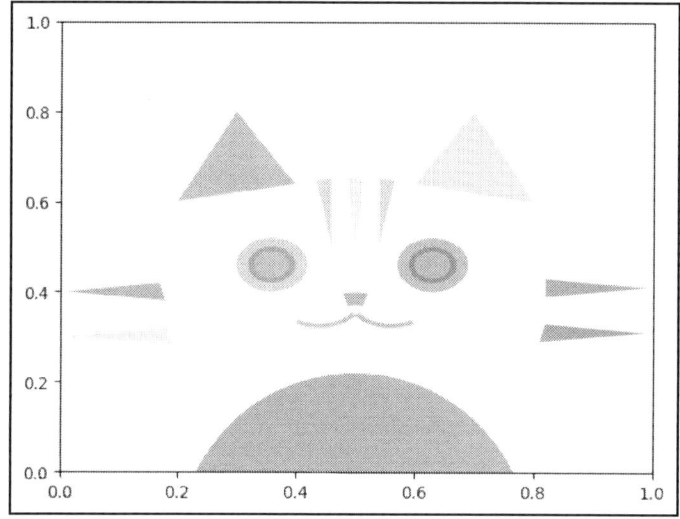

Adding image annotations

Adding images can sometimes be a more intuitive and attractive way to add annotations. We can place images in a `AnnotationBbox`, which is a container for annotations. Versatile settings allow easy pointing from the box to target.

There are a few steps in adding image annotations.

Firstly, we obtain the image, either by fetching it online or by saving it locally.

To get an online image, we use the `urllib` package:

```
import urllib
img_fetch = urllib.request.urlopen(url)
```

Then, we then call `pyplot.imread(img_fetch, format)` to read the image. For local images, put the path at the first argument. Common formats such as JPG and PNG are supported.

Next, we open an image box using `imagebox = OffsetImage(img, zoom)`, where `zoom` is a ratio for specifying the size of image.

After that, we set the axes to place the image box by `imagebox.image.axes = ax`.

We then put the image box into an `AnnotationBbox` container as in the following example. `(x1,y1)` specifies the target coordinates pointed by arrows, whereas `(x2,y2)` sets the position of the box. `xycoords` and `boxcoords` can generally be kept as the default value: `data`. Padding and arrow styles can be adjusted as well:

```
ab = AnnotationBbox(imagebox, (x1,y1),
 xybox=(x2,y2),
 xycoords='data',
 boxcoords='data',
 pad=0.5,
 arrowprops=dict(
 arrowstyle="->",
 connectionstyle="angle,angleA=90,angleB=0,rad=3")
 )
```

Finally, we add the `AnnotationBbox` to the preferred axes via `ax.add_artist(ab)`:

Challenge yourself!

In this final example of `Chapter 3`, *Figure Layout and Annotations*, besides image annotation, we also combine multiple techniques covered in previous chapters from figure styling to subplot layout for revision. Do you recognize their usage?

```
import matplotlib as mpl
import matplotlib.pyplot as plt
import numpy as np
from matplotlib.offsetbox import (OffsetImage,AnnotationBbox)
import urllib

"""
List of all Nobel laureate by age
https://www.nobelprize.org/nobel_prizes/lists/age.html
Plot adapted from "Why are Nobel Prize winners getting older?" by Will
Dahlgreen on BBC news
http://www.bbc.com/news/science-environment-37578899
"""
```

```
mpl.style.use('seaborn')
# A dictionary with the six fields as keys and tuples of years and ages of
award received is prepared
# Data can be downloaded from our Github repository
# Prizes = {'Peace': [(2014, 17), (1976, 32), (2011, 32), ...,
'Chemistry':...}

# Prepare the subplots
fig, axarr = plt.subplots(2,3,sharex=True,sharey=True)
plt.subplots_adjust(left=0, right=1, top=1.5, bottom=0)

# For each nobel prize field, plot the data to
for i,prize in enumerate(['Physics','Chemistry','Physiology or
Medicine','Economics','Literature','Peace']):
    years = [x[0] for x in prizes[prize]]
    ages  = [x[1] for x in prizes[prize]]
    a = int(i/3)  # subplot row index
    b = i%3       # subplot column index
    axarr[a,b].scatter(years,ages,s=2.5)
    axarr[a,b].plot(years, np.poly1d(np.polyfit(years, ages,
2))(years),linewidth=2) # Plot the trendline, can be taken as is for now
    axarr[a,b].set_xlabel(prize,fontsize=16)

# Annotate with photo of the youngest Nobel laureate
img_fetch =
urllib.request.urlopen("https://www.nobelprize.org/nobel_prizes/peace/laure
ates/2014/yousafzai_postcard.jpg") # fetch the online image
img = plt.imread(img_fetch, format='jpg')
imagebox = OffsetImage(img, zoom=0.2)
imagebox.image.axes = axarr[1,2]
ab1 = AnnotationBbox(imagebox, (2014,16),
                    xybox=(1920,28),
                    xycoords='data',
                    boxcoords='data',
                    pad=0.5,
                    arrowprops=dict(
                    arrowstyle="->",
                    connectionstyle="angle,angleA=90,angleB=0,rad=3")
                    )
axarr[1,2].add_artist(ab1)

# Annotate with photo of the oldest Nobel laureate
img_fetch = urllib.request.urlopen("http://www.nobelprize.org/
nobel_prizes/economic-sciences/laureates/2007/hurwicz_postcard.jpg")
img = plt.imread(img_fetch, format='jpg')
imagebox = OffsetImage(img, zoom=0.2)
imagebox.image.axes = axarr[1,2]
ab2 = AnnotationBbox(imagebox, (2007,89),
```

```
                    xybox=(1930,60),
                    xycoords='data',
                    boxcoords='data',
                    pad=0.5,
                    arrowprops=dict(
                    arrowstyle="->",
                    connectionstyle="angle,angleA=90,angleB=0,rad=3")
                    )

# Show the figure
plt.show()
```

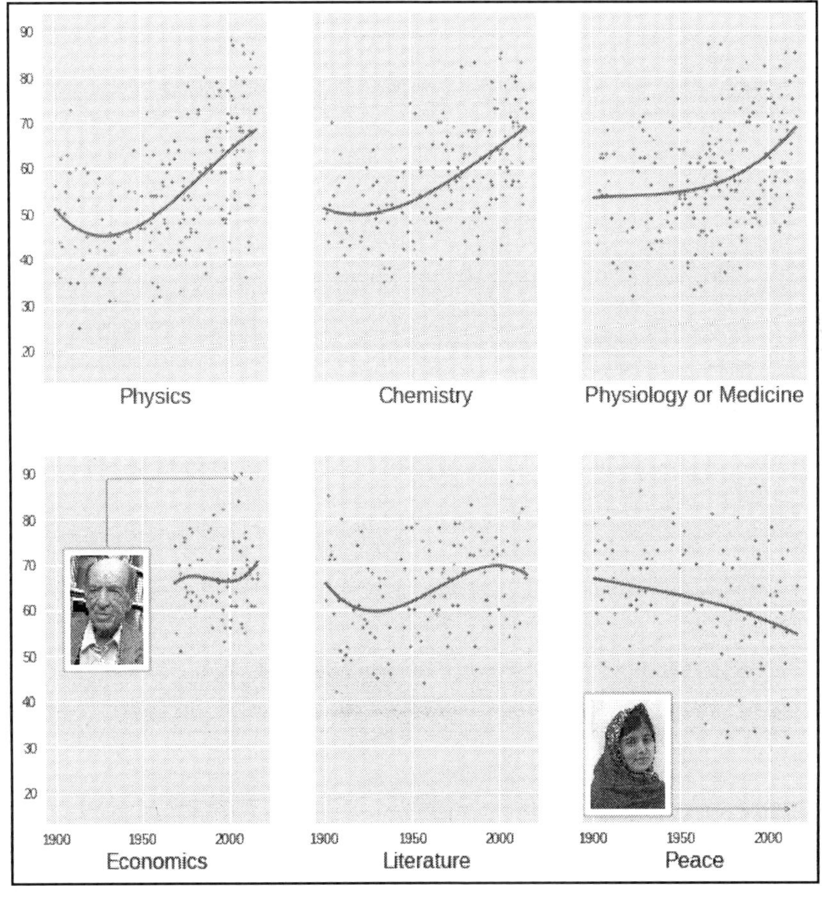

`AnnotationBbox` can also be used with `TextArea` and `DrawingArea` to hold the relevant content, in a similar way as with `OffsetImage`. Since we have covered how to add text and patches without `AnnotationBbox`, the usage should be easily comprehensible. You may refer to a demo case at `https://matplotlib.org/examples/pylab_examples/demo_annotation_box.html` for more details.

Summary

In this chapter, you learned multiple ways to align subplots to group relevant data, fine-tune the layout, and add extra annotations. Over the session, you equipped yourself with a basic understanding of each component in a common Matplotlib figure, and the know-how needed to adjust them.

Congratulations! You are now all ready to go for more real data exploration!

4
Visualizing Online Data

At this point, we have already covered the basics of creating and customizing plots using Matplotlib. In this chapter, we begin the journey of understanding more advanced Matplotlib usage through examples in specialized topics.

When considering the visualization of a concept, the following important factors have to be considered carefully:

- Source of the data
- Filtering and data processing
- Choosing the right plot type for the data:
    - Visualizing the trend of data:
        - Line chart, area chart, and stacked area chart
    - Visualizing univariate distribution:
        - Bar chart, histogram, and kernel density estimation
    - Visualizing bivariate distribution:
        - Scatter plot, KDE density chart, and hexbin chart
    - Visualizing categorical data:
        - Categorical scatter plot, box plot, swarm plot, violin plot
- Adjusting figure aesthetics for effective storytelling

We will cover these topics via the use of demographic and financial data. First, we will discuss typical data formats when we fetch data from the **Application Programming Interface** (**API**). Next, we will explore how we can integrate Matplotlib 2.0 with other Python packages such as Pandas, Scipy, and Seaborn for the visualization of different data types. All source codes in this chapter can be found at `https://github.com/PacktPublishing/Matplotlib-2.x-By-Example/`.

Typical API data formats

Many websites offer their data via an API, which bridges applications via standardized architecture. While we are not going to cover the details of using APIs here as site-specific documentation is usually available online; we will show you the three most common data formats as used in many APIs.

CSV

CSV (**Comma-Separated Values**) is one of the oldest file formats, which was introduced long before the internet even existed. However, it is now becoming deprecated as other advanced formats, such as JSON and XML, are gaining popularity. As the name suggests, data values are separated by commas. The preinstalled `csv` package and the `pandas` package contain classes to read and write data in CSV format. This CSV example defines a population table with two countries:

```
Country,Time,Sex,Age,Value
United Kingdom,1950,Male,0-4,2238.735
United States of America,1950,Male,0-4,8812.309
```

JSON

JSON (**JavaScript Object Notation**) is gaining popularity these days due to its efficiency and simplicity. JSON allows the specification of number, string, Boolean, array, and object. Python provides the default `json` package for parsing JSON. Alternatively, the `pandas.read_json` class can be used to import JSON as a Pandas dataframe. The preceding population table can be represented as JSON in the following example:

```
{
 "population": [
 {
 "Country": "United Kingdom",
```

```
 "Time": 1950,
 "Sex", "Male",
 "Age", "0-4",
 "Value",2238.735
 },{
 "Country": "United States of America",
 "Time": 1950,
 "Sex", "Male",
 "Age", "0-4",
 "Value",8812.309
 },
 ]
}
```

XML

XML (**eXtensible Markup Language**) is the Swiss Army knife of data formats, and it has become the default container for Microsoft Office, Apple iWork, XHTML, SVG, and more. XML's versatility comes with a price, as it makes XML verbose and slower. There are several ways to parse XML in Python, but `xml.etree.ElementTree` is recommended due to its Pythonic interface, backed by an efficient C backend. We are not going to cover XML parsing in this book, but good tutorials exist elsewhere (such as `http://eli.thegreenplace.net/2012/03/15/processing-xml-in-python-with-elementtree`).

As an example, the same population table can be transformed into XML:

```
<?xml version='1.0' encoding='utf-8'?>
<populations>
 <population>
 <Country>United Kingdom</Country>
 <Time>1950</Time>
 <Sex>Male</Sex>
 <Age>0-4</Age>
 <Value>2238.735</Value>
 </population>
 <population>
 <Country>United States of America</Country>
 <Time>1950</Time>
 <Sex>Male</Sex>
 <Age>0-4</Age>
 <Value>8812.309</Value>
 </population>
</populations>
```

Introducing pandas

Beside NumPy and SciPy, pandas is one of the most common scientific computing libraries for Python. Its authors aim to make pandas the most powerful and flexible open source data analysis and manipulation tool available in any language, and in fact they are almost achieving that goal. Its powerful and efficient library is a perfect match for data scientists. Like other Python packages, Pandas can easily be installed via PyPI:

```
pip install pandas
```

First introduced in version 1.5, Matplotlib supports the use of pandas DataFrame as the input in various plotting classes. Unlike the simpler examples in previous chapters, where Python lists were supplied as the source of data, Pandas DataFrame is a powerful two-dimensional labeled data structure that supports indexing, querying, grouping, merging, and some other common relational database operations. DataFrame is similar to spreadsheets in the sense that each row of the DataFrame contains different variables of an instance, while each column contains a vector of a specific variable across all instances.

pandas DataFrame supports heterogeneous data types, such as string, integer, and float. By default, rows are indexed sequentially and columns are composed of pandas Series. Optional row labels or column labels can be specified through the index and columns attributes.

Importing online population data in the CSV format

Let's begin by looking at the steps to import an online CSV file as a pandas DataFrame. In this example, we are going to use the annual population summary published by the Department of Economic and Social Affairs, United Nations, in 2015. Projected population figures towards 2100 were also included in the dataset:

```
import numpy as np # Python scientific computing package
import pandas as pd # Python data analysis package

# URL for Annual Population by Age and Sex - Department of Economic
# and Social Affairs, United Nations
source =
"https://github.com/PacktPublishing/Matplotlib-2.x-By-Example/blob/master/W
PP2015_DB04_Population_Annual.zip"

# Pandas support both local or online files
data = pd.read_csv(source, header=0, compression='zip', encoding='latin_1')
```

```
# Show the first five rows of the DataFrame
data.head()
```

The expected output of the code is shown here:

LocID	Location	VarID	Variant	Time	MidPeriod	SexID	Sex	AgeGrp	AgeGrpStart	AgeGrpSpan	Value	
0	4	Afghanistan	2	Medium	1950	1950.5	1	Male	0-4	0	5	630.044
1	4	Afghanistan	2	Medium	1950	1950.5	1	Male	5-9	5	5	516.205
2	4	Afghanistan	2	Medium	1950	1950.5	1	Male	10-14	10	5	461.378
3	4	Afghanistan	2	Medium	1950	1950.5	1	Male	15-19	15	5	414.368
4	4	Afghanistan	2	Medium	1950	1950.5	1	Male	20-24	20	5	374.110

The `pandas.read_csv` class is extremely versatile, supporting column headers, custom delimiters, various compressed formats (for example, `.gzip`, `.bz2`, `.zip`, and `.xz`), different text encodings, and much more. Readers can consult the documentation page (`http://pandas.pydata.org/pandas-docs/stable/generated/pandas.read_csv.html`) for more information.

By calling the `.head()` function of the Pandas DataFrame object, we can quickly observe the first five rows of the data.

As we progress through this chapter, we are going to integrate this population dataset with other datasets in Quandl. However, Quandl uses three-letter country codes (ISO 3166 alpha-3) to denote geographical locations; therefore we need to reformat the location names accordingly.

The `pycountry` package is an excellent choice for conversion of country names according to ISO 3166 standards. Similarly, `pycountry` can be installed through PyPI:

```
pip install pycountry
```

Continuing the previous code example, we are going to add a new `country` column to the dataframe:

```
from pycountry import countries


def get_alpha_3(location):
    """Convert full country name to three letter code (ISO 3166 alpha-3)

    Args:
        location: Full location name
    Returns:
```

```
        three letter code or None if not found"""

    try:
        return countries.get(name=location).alpha_3
    except:
        return None

# Add a new country column to the dataframe
population_df['country'] = population_df['Location'].apply(lambda x:
get_alpha_3(x))
population_df.head()
```

The expected output of the code is shown here:

-	LocID	Location	VarID	Variant	Time	MidPeriod	SexID	Sex	AgeGrp	AgeGrpStart	AgeGrpSpan	Value	country
0	4	Afghanistan	2	Medium	1950	1950.5	1	Male	0-4	0	5	630.044	AFG
1	4	Afghanistan	2	Medium	1950	1950.5	1	Male	5-9	5	5	516.205	AFG
2	4	Afghanistan	2	Medium	1950	1950.5	1	Male	10-14	10	5	461.378	AFG
3	4	Afghanistan	2	Medium	1950	1950.5	1	Male	15-19	15	5	414.368	AFG
4	4	Afghanistan	2	Medium	1950	1950.5	1	Male	20-24	20	5	374.110	AFG

Importing online financial data in the JSON format

In this chapter, we will also draw upon financial data from Quandl's API to create insightful visualizations. If you are not familiar with Quandl, it is a financial and economic data warehouse that stores millions of datasets from hundreds of publishers. The best thing about Quandl is that these datasets are delivered via the unified API, without worrying about the procedures to parse the data correctly. Anonymous users can get up to 50 API calls per day, and you get up to 500 free API calls if you are a registered user. Readers can sign up for a free API key at `https://www.quandl.com/?modal=register`.

At Quandl, every dataset is identified by a unique ID, as defined by the Quandl Code on each search result webpage. For example, the Quandl code GOOG/NASDAQ_SWTX defines the historical NASDAQ index data published by Google Finance. Every dataset is available in three formats--CSV, JSON, and XML.

Although an official Python client library is available from Quandl, we are not going to use that for the sake of demonstrating the general procedures of importing JSON data. According to Quandl's documentation, we can fetch JSON formatted data tables through the following API call:

```
GET https://www.quandl.com/api/v3/datasets/{Quandl code}/data.json
```

Let's try to get the Big Mac index data from Quandl.

```
from urllib.request import urlopen
import json
import time
import pandas as pd


def get_bigmac_codes():
    """Get a Pandas DataFrame of all codes in the Big Mac index dataset

    The first column contains the code, while the second header
    contains the description of the code.
    for example,
    ECONOMIST/BIGMAC_ARG,Big Mac Index - Argentina
    ECONOMIST/BIGMAC_AUS,Big Mac Index - Australia
    ECONOMIST/BIGMAC_BRA,Big Mac Index - Brazil
    Returns:
        codes: Pandas DataFrame of Quandl dataset codes"""
    codes_url = "https://www.quandl.com/api/v3/databases/ECONOMIST/codes"
    codes = pd.read_csv(codes_url, header=None, names=['Code',
'Description'],
                        compression='zip', encoding='latin_1')
    return codes

def get_quandl_dataset(api_key, code):
    """Obtain and parse a quandl dataset in Pandas DataFrame format

    Quandl returns dataset in JSON format, where data is stored as a
    list of lists in response['dataset']['data'], and column headers
    stored in response['dataset']['column_names'].
    for example, {'dataset': {...,
             'column_names': ['Date',
                              'local_price',
                              'dollar_ex',
                              'dollar_price',
                              'dollar_ppp',
                              'dollar_valuation',
                              'dollar_adj_valuation',
                              'euro_adj_valuation',
                              'sterling_adj_valuation',
                              'yen_adj_valuation',
                              'yuan_adj_valuation'],
             'data': [['2017-01-31',
                       55.0,
                       15.8575,
                       3.4683903515687,
                       10.869565217391,
```

```
                        -31.454736135007,
                        6.2671477203176,
                        8.2697553162259,
                        29.626894343348,
                        32.714616745128,
                        13.625825886047],
                       ['2016-07-31',
                        50.0,
                        14.935,
                        3.3478406427854,
                        9.9206349206349,
                        -33.574590420925,
                        2.0726096168216,
                        0.40224795003514,
                        17.56448458418,
                        19.76377270142,
                        11.643103380531]
                       ],
              'database_code': 'ECONOMIST',
              'dataset_code': 'BIGMAC_ARG',
              ... }}
    A custom column--country is added to denote the 3-letter country code.
    Args:
        api_key: Quandl API key
        code: Quandl dataset code

    Returns:
        df: Pandas DataFrame of a Quandl dataset

    """
    base_url = "https://www.quandl.com/api/v3/datasets/"
    url_suffix = ".json?api_key="

    # Fetch the JSON response
    u = urlopen(base_url + code + url_suffix + api_key)
    response = json.loads(u.read().decode('utf-8'))
    # Format the response as Pandas Dataframe
    df = pd.DataFrame(response['dataset']['data'],
columns=response['dataset']['column_names'])
    # Label the country code
    df['country'] = code[-3:]
    return df


quandl_dfs = []
codes = get_bigmac_codes()

# Replace this with your own API key
```

```
api_key = "INSERT YOUR KEY HERE"

for code in codes.Code:
    # Get the DataFrame of a Quandl dataset
    df = get_quandl_dataset(api_key, code)
    # Store in a list
    quandl_dfs.append(df)
    # Prevents exceeding the API speed limit
    time.sleep(2)
# Concatenate the list of dataframes into a single one
bigmac_df = pd.concat(quandl_dfs)
bigmac_df.head()
```

The expected output is as follows:

-	Date	local_price	dollar_ex	dollar_price	dollar_ppp	dollar_valuation	dollar_adj_valuation	euro_adj_valuation	sterling_adj_valuation	yen_adj_valuation	yuan_adj_valuation	country
0	2017-01-31	55.0	15.85750	3.468390	10.869565	-31.454736	6.26715	8.26976	29.6269	32.7146	13.6258	ARG
1	2016-07-31	50.0	14.93500	3.347841	9.920635	-33.574590	2.07261	0.402248	17.5645	19.7638	11.6431	ARG
2	2016-01-31	33.0	13.80925	2.389703	6.693712	-51.527332	-24.8619	-18.714	-18.7209	0.40859	-17.029	ARG
3	2015-07-31	28.0	9.13500	3.065134	5.845511	-36.009727	-4.7585	-0.357918	-6.01091	30.8609	5.02868	ARG
4	2015-01-31	28.0	8.61000	3.252033	5.845511	-32.107881	0.540242	-0.804495	-2.49468	34.3905	6.01183	ARG

The Big Mac index was invented by The Economist in 1986 as a lighthearted guide to check whether currencies are at their correct level. It is based on the theory of **purchasing power parity** (**PPP**) and is considered an informal measure of currency exchange rates at PPP. It measures their value against a similar basket of goods and services, in this case a Big Mac. Differing prices at market exchange rates would imply that one currency is undervalued or overvalued.

The code for parsing JSON from the Quandl API is a bit more complicated, and thus extra explanations might help you to understand it. The first function, `get_bigmac_codes()`, parses the list of all available dataset codes in the Quandl Economist database as a pandas DataFrame. Meanwhile, the second function, `get_quandl_dataset(api_key, code)`, converts the JSON response of a Quandl dataset API query to a pandas DataFrame. All datasets obtained are concatenated using `pandas.concat()`.

Visualizing the trend of data

Once we have imported the two datasets, we can set out on a further visualization journey. Let's begin by plotting the world population trends from 1950 to 2017. To select rows based on the value of a column, we can use the following syntax: `df[df.variable_name == "target"]` or `df[df['variable_name'] == "target"]`, where `df` is the dataframe object. Other conditional operators, such as larger than > or smaller than <, are also supported. Multiple conditional statements can be chained together using the "and" operator &, or the "or" operator |.

To aggregate the population across all age groups within a year, we are going to rely on `df.groupby().sum()`, as shown in the following example:

```
import matplotlib.pyplot as plt


# Select the aggregated population data from the world for both genders,
# during 1950 to 2017.
selected_data = data[(data.Location == 'WORLD') & (data.Sex == 'Both') &
(data.Time <= 2017) ]

# Calculate aggregated population data across all age groups for each year
# Set as_index=False to avoid the Time variable to be used as index
grouped_data = selected_data.groupby('Time', as_index=False).sum()

# Generate a simple line plot of population vs time
fig = plt.figure()
plt.plot(grouped_data.Time, grouped_data.Value)

# Label the axis
plt.xlabel('Year')
plt.ylabel('Population (thousands)')

plt.show()
```

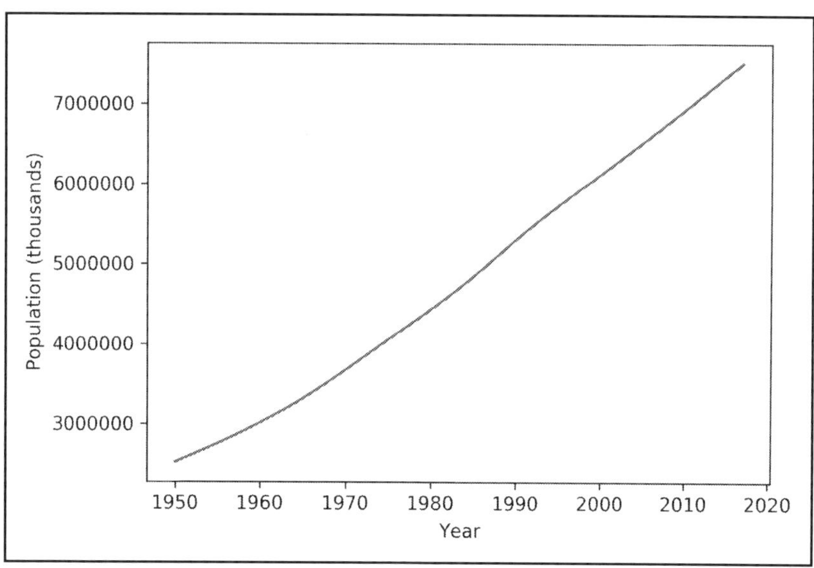

Area chart and stacked area chart

Sometimes, we may want to shade the area under the line plot with color for a greater visual impact. This can be achieved via the `fill_between` class:

```
fill_between(x, y1, y2=0, where=None, interpolate=False, step=None)
```

By default, `fill_between` shades the region between `y=0` and the line when `y2` is not specified. More complex shading behavior can be specified using the where, interpolate, and step keyword arguments. Readers can refer to the following link for more information: `https://matplotlib.org/examples/pylab_examples/fill_between_demo.html`.

Let's try to plot a more detailed chart by separating the two genders. We are going to explore the relative contribution of males and females towards the population growth. To do that, we can prepare a stacked area chart using the `stackplot` class:

```
# Select the aggregated population data from the world for each gender,
# during 1950 to 2017.
male_data = data[(data.Location == 'WORLD') & (data.Sex == 'Male') &
(data.Time <= 2017) ]
female_data = data[(data.Location == 'WORLD') & (data.Sex == 'Female') &
(data.Time <= 2017) ]

# Calculate aggregated population data across all age groups for each year
```

```
# Set as_index=False to avoid the Time variable to be used as index
grouped_male_data = male_data.groupby('Time', as_index=False).sum()
grouped_female_data = female_data.groupby('Time', as_index=False).sum()

# Create two subplots with shared y-axis (sharey=True)
fig, (ax1, ax2) = plt.subplots(nrows=1, ncols=2, figsize=(12,4),
sharey=True)

# Generate a simple line plot of population vs time,
# then shade the area under the line in sky blue.
ax1.plot(grouped_data.Time, grouped_data.Value)
ax1.fill_between(grouped_data.Time, grouped_data.Value, color='skyblue')

# Use set_xlabel() or set_ylabel() instead to set the axis label of an
# axes object
ax1.set_xlabel('Year')
ax1.set_ylabel('Population (thousands)')

# Generate a stacked area plot of population vs time
ax2.stackplot(grouped_male_data.Time, grouped_male_data.Value,
grouped_female_data.Value)

# Add a figure legend
ax2.legend(['Male', 'Female'], loc='upper left')

# Set the x-axis label only this time
ax2.set_xlabel('Year')
plt.show()
```

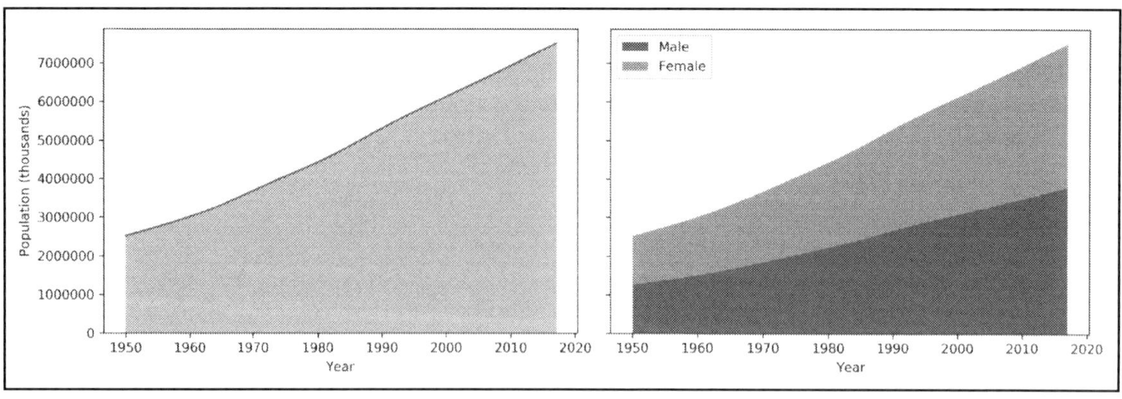

Introducing Seaborn

Seaborn by Michael Waskom is a statistical visualization library that is built on top of Matplotlib. It comes with handy functions for visualizing categorical variables, univariate distributions, and bivariate distributions. For more complex plots, various statistical methods such as linear regression models and clustering algorithms are available. Like Matplotlib, Seaborn also supports Pandas dataframes as input, plus automatically performing the necessary slicing, grouping, aggregation, and statistical model fitting to produce informative figures.

These Seaborn functions aim to bring publication-quality figures through an API with a minimal set of arguments, while maintaining the full customization capabilities of Matplotlib. In fact, many functions in Seaborn return a Matplotlib axis or grid object when invoked. Therefore, Seaborn is a great companion of Matplotlib. To install Seaborn through PyPI, you can issue the following command in the terminal:

```
pip install pandas
```

Seaborn will be imported as `sns` throughout this book. This section will not be a documentation of Seaborn. Rather our goal is to give a high-level overview of Seaborn's capabilities from the perspective of Matplotlib users. Readers can refer to the official Seaborn site (`http://seaborn.pydata.org/index.html`) for more information.

Visualizing univariate distribution

Seaborn makes the task of visualizing the distribution of a dataset much easier. Starting with the population data as discussed before, let's see how it distributes among different countries in 2017 by plotting a bar plot:

```
import seaborn as sns
import matplotlib.pyplot as plt


# Extract USA population data in 2017
current_population = population_df[(population_df.Location
                                     == 'United States of America') &
                                    (population_df.Time == 2017) &
                                    (population_df.Sex != 'Both')]

# Population Bar chart
sns.barplot(x="AgeGrp",y="Value", hue="Sex", data = current_population)

# Use Matplotlib functions to label axes rotate tick labels
```

```
ax = plt.gca()
ax.set(xlabel="Age Group", ylabel="Population (thousands)")
ax.set_xticklabels(ax.xaxis.get_majorticklabels(), rotation=45)
plt.title("Population Barchart (USA)")

# Show the figure
plt.show()
```

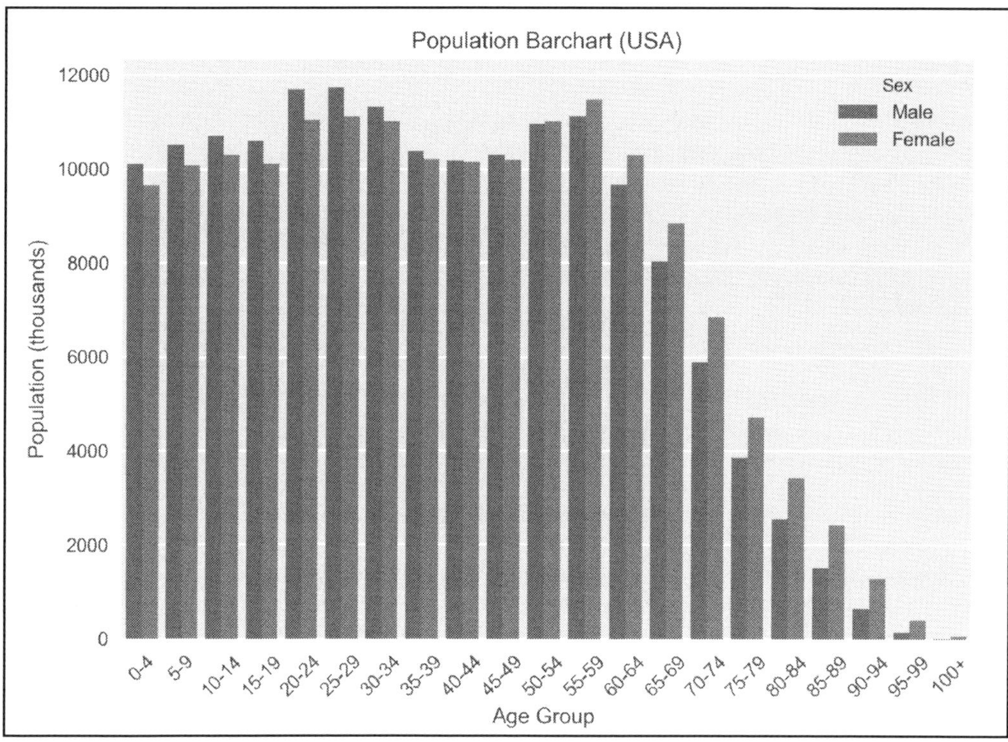

Bar chart in Seaborn

The `seaborn.barplot()` function shows a series of data points as rectangular bars. If multiple points per group are available, confidence intervals will be shown on top of the bars to indicate the uncertainty of the point estimates. Like most other Seaborn functions, various input data formats are supported, such as Python lists, Numpy arrays, pandas Series, and pandas DataFrame.

A more traditional way to show the population structure is through the use of a population pyramid.

So what is a population pyramid? As its name suggests, it is a pyramid-shaped plot that shows the age distribution of a population. It can be roughly classified into three classes, namely constrictive, stationary, and expansive for populations that are undergoing negative, stable, and rapid growth respectively. For instance, constrictive populations have a lower proportion of young people, so the pyramid base appears to be constricted. Stable populations have a more or less similar number of young and middle-aged groups. Expansive populations, on the other hand, have a large proportion of youngsters, thus resulting in pyramids with enlarged bases.

We can build a population pyramid by plotting two bar charts on two subplots with a shared *y* axis:

```
import seaborn as sns
import matplotlib.pyplot as plt

# Extract USA population data in 2017
current_population = population_df[(population_df.Location
                                     == 'United States of America') &
                                    (population_df.Time == 2017) &
                                    (population_df.Sex != 'Both')]

# Change the age group to descending order
current_population = current_population.iloc[::-1]

# Create two subplots with shared y-axis
fig, axes = plt.subplots(ncols=2, sharey=True)

# Bar chart for male
sns.barplot(x="Value",y="AgeGrp", color="darkblue", ax=axes[0],
            data = current_population[(current_population.Sex == 'Male')])
# Bar chart for female
sns.barplot(x="Value",y="AgeGrp", color="darkred", ax=axes[1],
            data = current_population[(current_population.Sex ==
'Female')])

# Use Matplotlib function to invert the first chart
axes[0].invert_xaxis()

# Use Matplotlib function to show tick labels in the middle
axes[0].yaxis.tick_right()

# Use Matplotlib functions to label the axes and titles
axes[0].set_title("Male")
axes[1].set_title("Female")
```

```
axes[0].set(xlabel="Population (thousands)", ylabel="Age Group")
axes[1].set(xlabel="Population (thousands)", ylabel="")
fig.suptitle("Population Pyramid (USA)")

# Show the figure
plt.show()
```

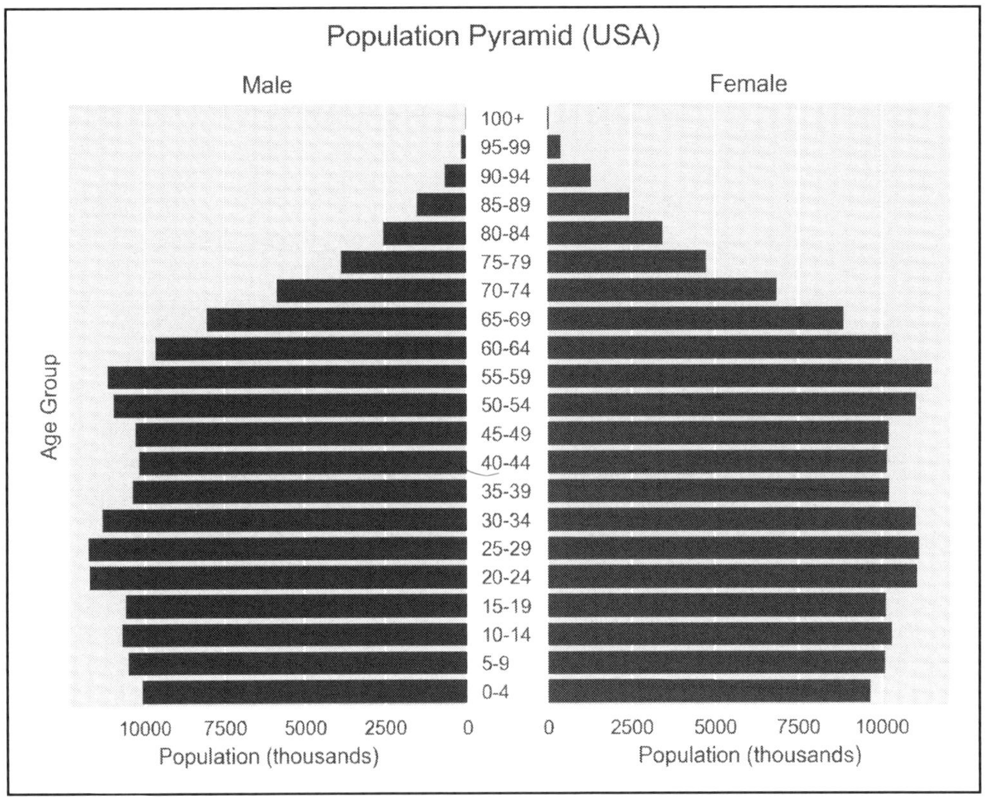

Since Seaborn is built on top of the solid foundations of Matplotlib, we can customize the plot easily using built-in functions of Matplotlib. In the preceding example, we used `matplotlib.axes.Axes.invert_xaxis()` to flip the male population plot horizontally, followed by changing the location of the tick labels to the right-hand side using `matplotlib.axis.YAxis.tick_right()`. As first introduced in `Chapter 2`, *Figure Aesthetics*, we further customized the titles and axis labels for the plot using a combination of `matplotlib.axes.Axes.set_title()`, `matplotlib.axes.Axes.set()`, and `matplotlib.figure.Figure.suptitle()`.

Let's try to plot the population pyramids for Cambodia and Japan as well by changing the line `population_df.Location == 'United States of America'` to `population_df.Location == 'Cambodia'` or `population_df.Location == 'Japan'`. Can you classify the pyramids into one of the three population pyramid classes?

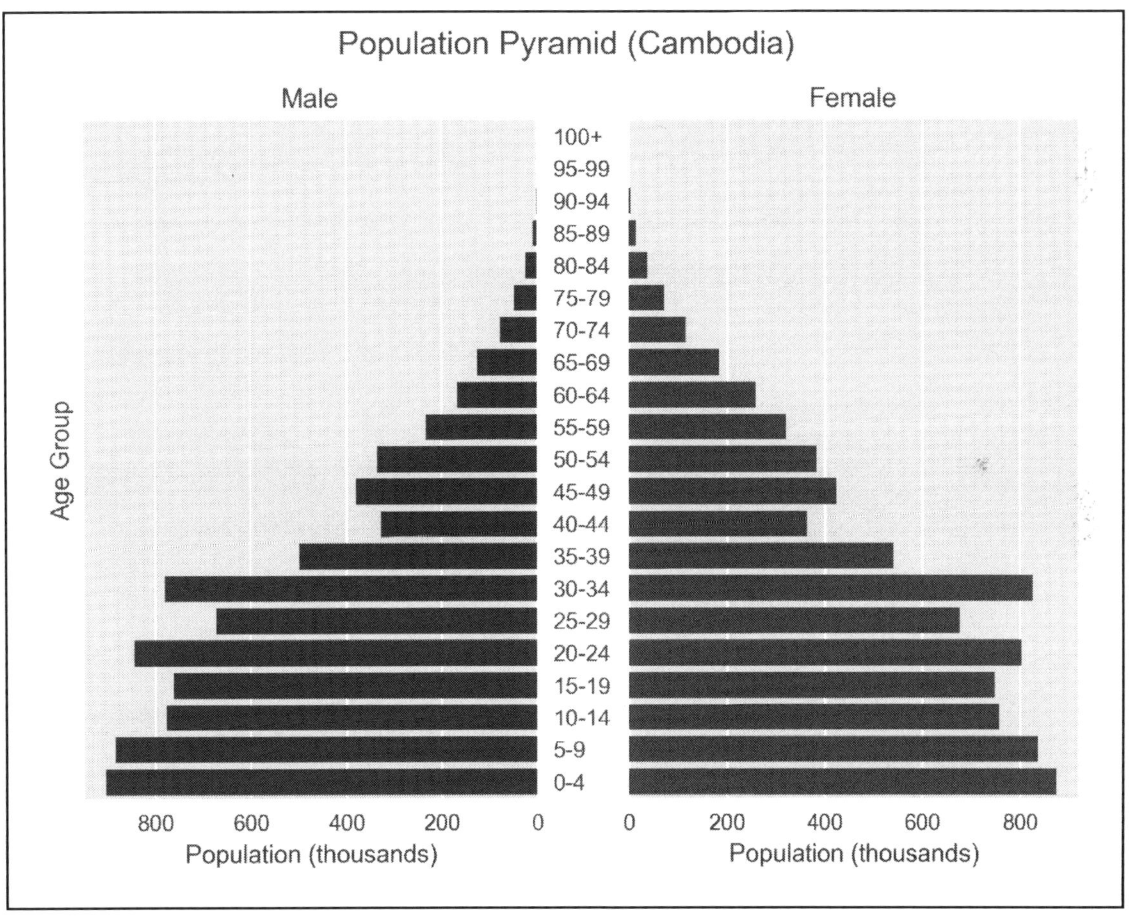

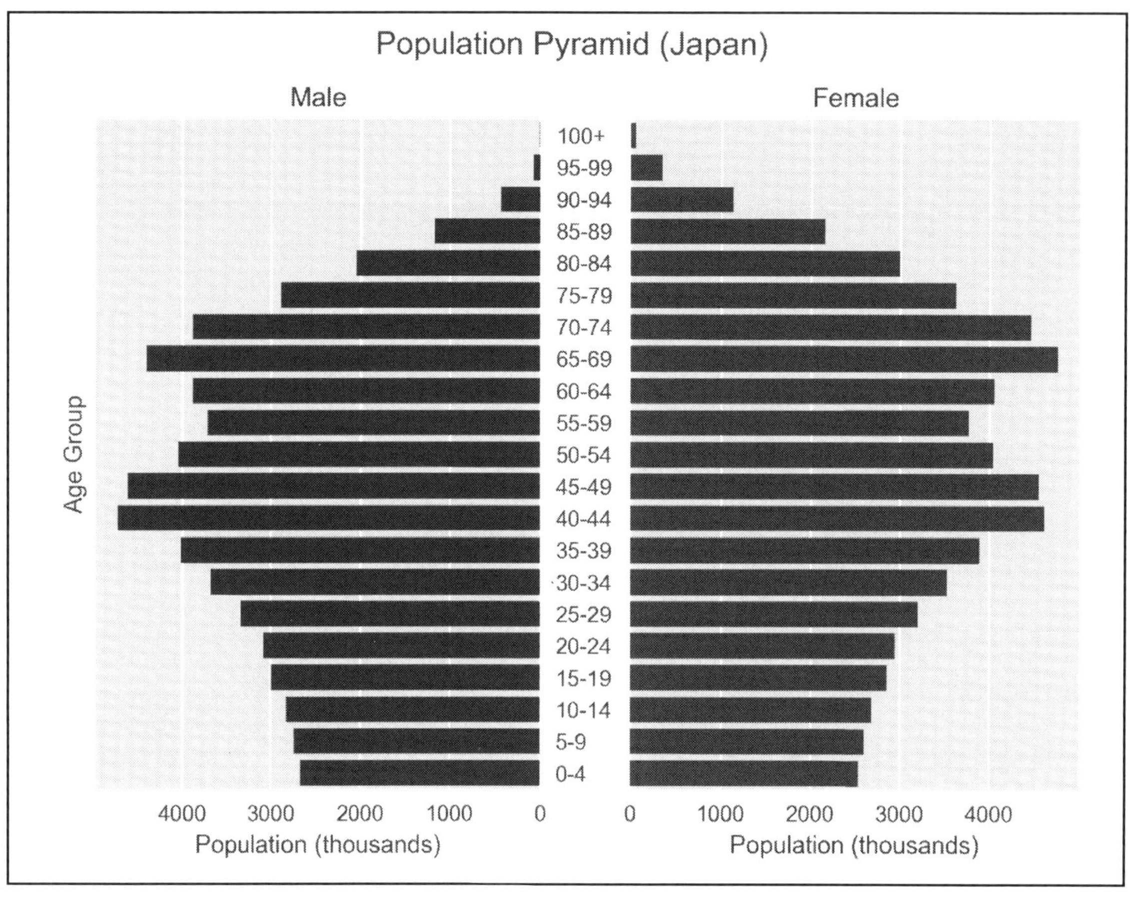

To see how Seaborn simplifies the code for relatively complex plots, let's see how a similar plot can be achieved using vanilla Matplotlib.

First, like the previous Seaborn-based example, we create two subplots with shared *y* axis:

```
fig, axes = plt.subplots(ncols=2, sharey=True)
```

Next, we plot horizontal bar charts using `matplotlib.pyplot.barh()` and set the location and labels of ticks, followed by adjusting the subplot spacing:

```
# Get a list of tick positions according to the data bins
y_pos = range(len(current_population.AgeGrp.unique()))

# Horizontal barchart for male
axes[0].barh(y_pos, current_population[(current_population.Sex ==
             'Male')].Value, color="darkblue")

# Horizontal barchart for female
axes[1].barh(y_pos, current_population[(current_population.Sex ==
             'Female')].Value, color="darkred")

# Show tick for each data point, and label with the age group
axes[0].set_yticks(y_pos)
axes[0].set_yticklabels(current_population.AgeGrp.unique())

# Increase spacing between subplots to avoid clipping of ytick labels
plt.subplots_adjust(wspace=0.3)
```

Finally, we use the same code to further customize the look and feel of the figure:

```
# Invert the first chart
axes[0].invert_xaxis()

# Show tick labels in the middle
axes[0].yaxis.tick_right()

# Label the axes and titles
axes[0].set_title("Male")
axes[1].set_title("Female")
axes[0].set(xlabel="Population (thousands)", ylabel="Age Group")
axes[1].set(xlabel="Population (thousands)", ylabel="")
fig.suptitle("Population Pyramid (USA)")

# Show the figure
plt.show()
```

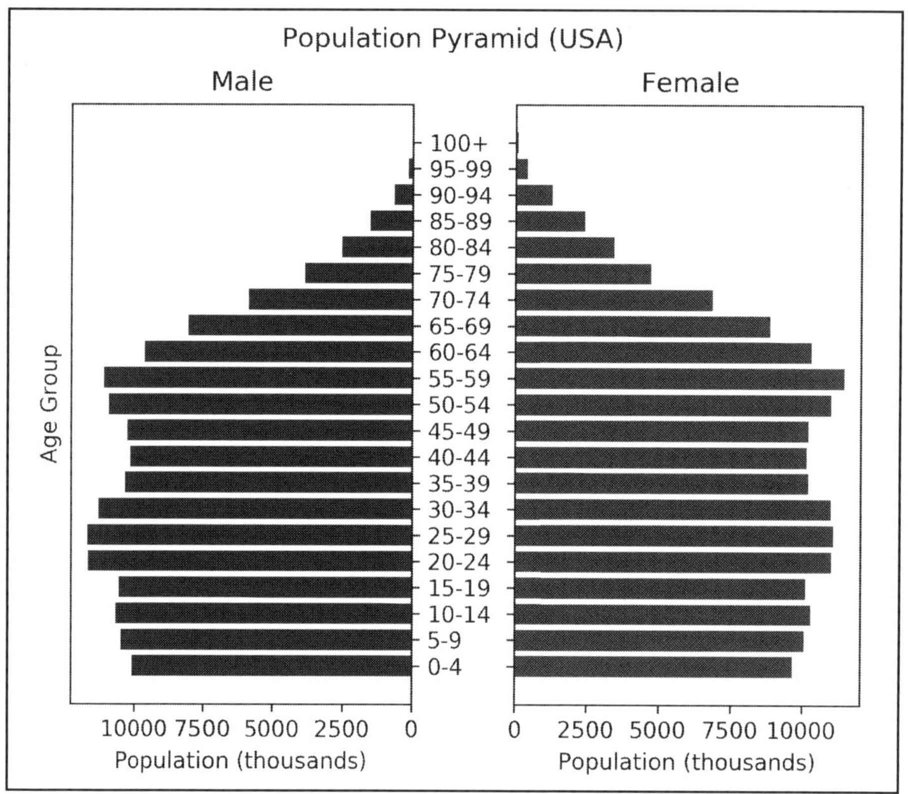

When compared to the Seaborn-based code, the pure Matplotlib implementation requires extra lines to define the tick positions, tick labels, and subplot spacing. For some other Seaborn plot types that include extra statistical calculations such as linear regression, and pearson correlation, the code reduction is even more dramatic. Therefore, Seaborn is a "batteries-included" statistical visualization package that allows users to write less verbose code.

Histogram and distribution fitting in Seaborn

In the population example, the raw data was already binned into different age groups. What if the data is not binned (for example, the BigMac Index data)? Turns out, `seaborn.distplot` can help us to process the data into bins and show us a histogram as a result. Let's look at this example:

```
import seaborn as sns
import matplotlib.pyplot as plt


# Get the BigMac index in 2017
current_bigmac = bigmac_df[(bigmac_df.Date == "2017-01-31")]

# Plot the histogram
ax = sns.distplot(current_bigmac.dollar_price)
plt.show()
```

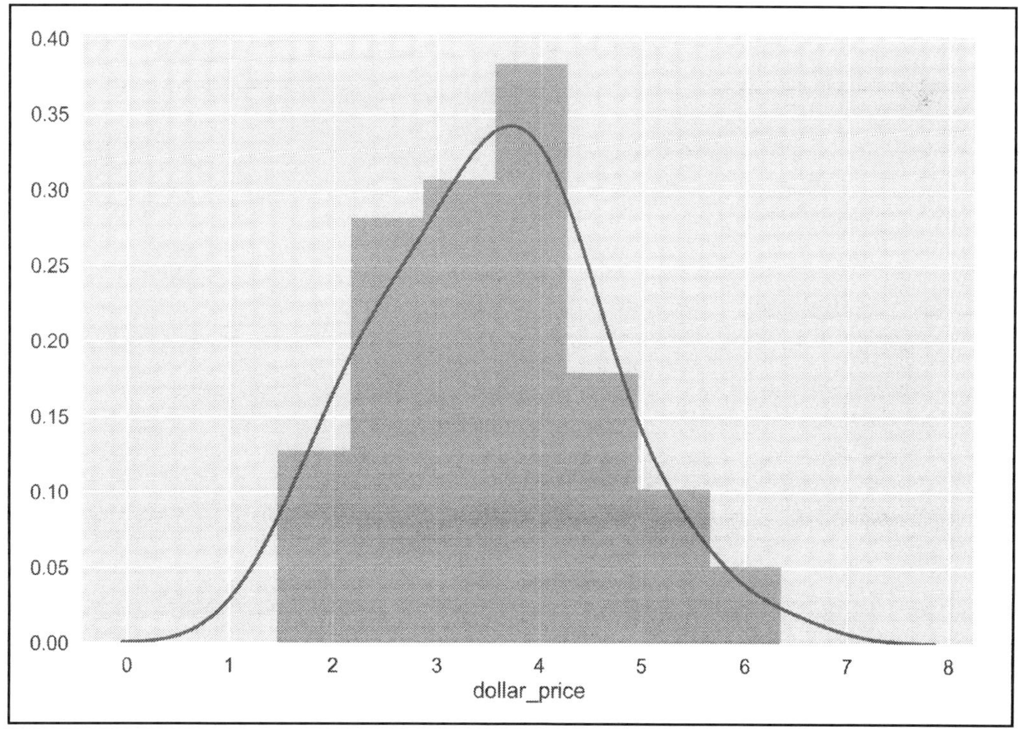

The `seaborn.distplot` function expects either pandas Series, single-dimensional numpy.array, or a Python list as input. Then, it determines the size of the bins according to the Freedman-Diaconis rule, and finally it fits a **kernel density estimate** (**KDE**) over the histogram.

KDE is a non-parametric method used to estimate the distribution of a variable. We can also supply a parametric distribution, such as beta, gamma, or normal distribution, to the `fit` argument.

In this example, we are going to fit the normal distribution from the `scipy.stats` package over the Big Mac Index dataset:

```
from scipy import stats

ax = sns.distplot(current_bigmac.dollar_price, kde=False, fit=stats.norm)
plt.show()
```

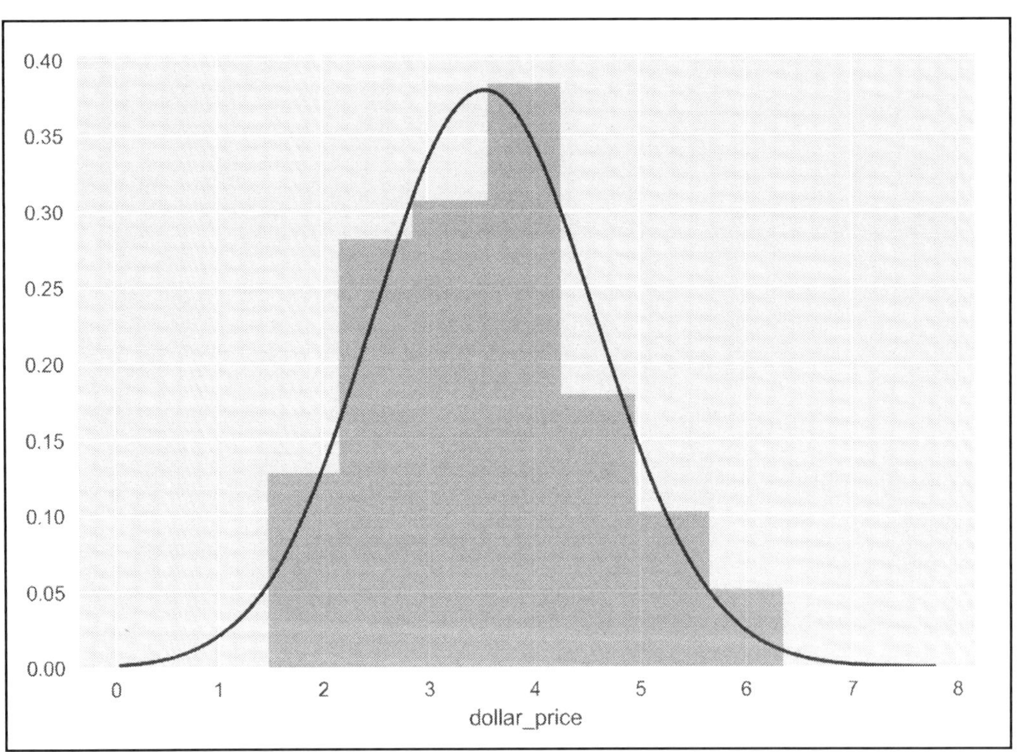

Visualizing a bivariate distribution

We should bear in mind that the Big Mac index is not directly comparable between countries. Normally, we would expect commodities in poor countries to be cheaper than those in rich ones. To represent a fairer picture of the index, it would be better to show the relationship between Big Mac pricing and **Gross Domestic Product** (**GDP**) per capita.

We are going to acquire GDP per capita from Quandl's **World Bank World Development Indicators** (**WWDI**) dataset. Based on the previous code example of acquiring JSON data from Quandl, can you try to adapt it to download the GDP per capita dataset?

For those who are impatient, here is the full code:

```
import urllib
import json
import pandas as pd
import time
from urllib.request import urlopen


def get_gdp_dataset(api_key, country_code):
    """Obtain and parse a quandl GDP dataset in Pandas DataFrame format
    Quandl returns dataset in JSON format, where data is stored as a
    list of lists in response['dataset']['data'], and column headers
    stored in response['dataset']['column_names'].

    Args:
        api_key: Quandl API key
        country_code: Three letter code to represent country

    Returns:
        df: Pandas DataFrame of a Quandl dataset
    """
    base_url = "https://www.quandl.com/api/v3/datasets/"
    url_suffix = ".json?api_key="

    # Compose the Quandl API dataset code to get GDP per capita
    # (constant 2000 US$) dataset
    gdp_code = "WWDI/" + country_code + "_NY_GDP_PCAP_KD"

    # Parse the JSON response from Quandl API
    # Some countries might be missing, so we need error handling code
    try:
        u = urlopen(base_url + gdp_code + url_suffix + api_key)
    except urllib.error.URLError as e:
        print(gdp_code,e)
        return None
```

```
    response = json.loads(u.read().decode('utf-8'))

    # Format the response as Pandas Dataframe
    df = pd.DataFrame(response['dataset']['data'],
columns=response['dataset']['column_names'])

    # Add a new country code column
    df['country'] = country_code

    return df


api_key = "INSERT YOUR KEY HERE"
quandl_dfs = []

# Loop through all unique country code values in the BigMac index DataFrame
for country_code in bigmac_df.country.unique():
    # Fetch the GDP dataset for the corresponding country
    df = get_gdp_dataset(api_key, country_code)

    # Skip if the response is empty
    if df is None:
        continue

    # Store in a list DataFrames
    quandl_dfs.append(df)

    # Prevents exceeding the API speed limit
    time.sleep(2)

# Concatenate the list of DataFrames into a single one
gdp_df = pd.concat(quandl_dfs)
gdp_df.head()
```

The expected output:

```
WWDI/EUR_NY_GDP_PCAP_KD HTTP Error 404: Not Found
WWDI/SIN_NY_GDP_PCAP_KD HTTP Error 404: Not Found
WWDI/ROC_NY_GDP_PCAP_KD HTTP Error 404: Not Found
WWDI/UAE_NY_GDP_PCAP_KD HTTP Error 404: Not Found
```

	Date	Value	country
0	2015-12-31	10501.660269	ARG
1	2014-12-31	10334.780146	ARG
2	2013-12-31	10711.229530	ARG

3	2012-12-31	10558.265365	ARG
4	2011-12-31	10780.342508	ARG

We can see that the GDP per capita dataset is not available for four geographical locations, but we can ignore that for now.

Next, we will merge the two DataFrames that contain Big Mac Index and GDP per capita respectively using `pandas.merge()`. The most recent record in WWDI's GDP per capita dataset was collected at the end of 2015, so let's pair that up with the corresponding Big Mac index dataset in the same year.

For those who are familiar with the SQL language, `pandas.merge()` supports four modes, namely left, right, inner, and outer joins. Since we are interested in rows that have matching countries in both DataFrames only, we are going to choose inner join:

```
merged_df = pd.merge(bigmac_df[(bigmac_df.Date == "2015-01-31")],
gdp_df[(gdp_df.Date == "2015-12-31")], how='inner', on='country')
merged_df.head()
```

	Date_x	local_price	dollar_ex	dollar_price	dollar_ppp	dollar_valuation	dollar_adj_valuation	euro_adj_valuation	sterling_adj_valuation	yen_adj_valuation	yuan_adj_valuation	country	Date_y	Value
0	2015-01-31	28.00	8.610000	3.252033	5.845511	-32.107881	0.540242	-0.804495	-2.49468	34.3905	6.01183	ARG	2015-12-31	10501.660269
1	2015-01-31	5.30	1.227220	4.318705	1.106472	-9.839144	-17.8995	-18.9976	-20.3778	9.74234	-13.4315	AUS	2015-12-31	54688.445933
2	2015-01-31	13.50	2.592750	5.206827	2.818372	8.702019	68.4555	66.2024	63.3705	125.172	77.6231	BRA	2015-12-31	11211.891104
3	2015-01-31	2.89	0.661594	4.368235	0.603340	-8.805115	3.11257	1.73343	0	37.8289	8.72415	GBR	2015-12-31	41182.619517
4	2015-01-31	5.70	1.228550	4.639616	1.189979	-3.139545	-2.34134	-3.64753	-5.28928	30.5387	2.97343	CAN	2015-12-31	50108.065004

Scatter plot in Seaborn

A scatter plot is one of the most common plots in the scientific and business worlds. It is particularly useful for displaying the relationship between two variables. While we can simply use `matplotlib.pyplot.scatter` to draw a scatter plot (see `Chapter 2`, *Figure Aesthetics*, for more details), we can also use Seaborn to build similar plots with more advanced features.

The two functions `seaborn.regplot()` and `seaborn.lmplot()` display a linear relationship in the form of a scatter plot, a regression line, plus the 95% confidence interval around that regression line. The main difference between the two functions is that `lmplot()` combines `regplot()` with `FacetGrid` such that we can create color-coded or faceted scatter plots to show the interaction between three or more pairs of variables. We will demonstrate the use of `lmplot()` later in this chapter and the next chapter.

The simplest form of `seaborn.regplot()` supports numpy arrays, pandas Series, or pandas DataFrames as input. The regression line and the confidence interval can be removed by specifying `fit_reg=False`.

We are going to investigate the hypothesis that Big Macs are cheaper in poorer countries, and vice versa, checking whether there is any correlation between the Big Mac index and GDP per capita:

```
import seaborn as sns
import matplotlib.pyplot as plt

# seaborn.regplot() returns matplotlib.Axes object
ax = sns.regplot(x="Value", y="dollar_price", data=merged_df,
fit_reg=False)
ax.set_xlabel("GDP per capita (constant 2000 US$)")
ax.set_ylabel("BigMac index (US$)")

plt.show()
```

The expected output:

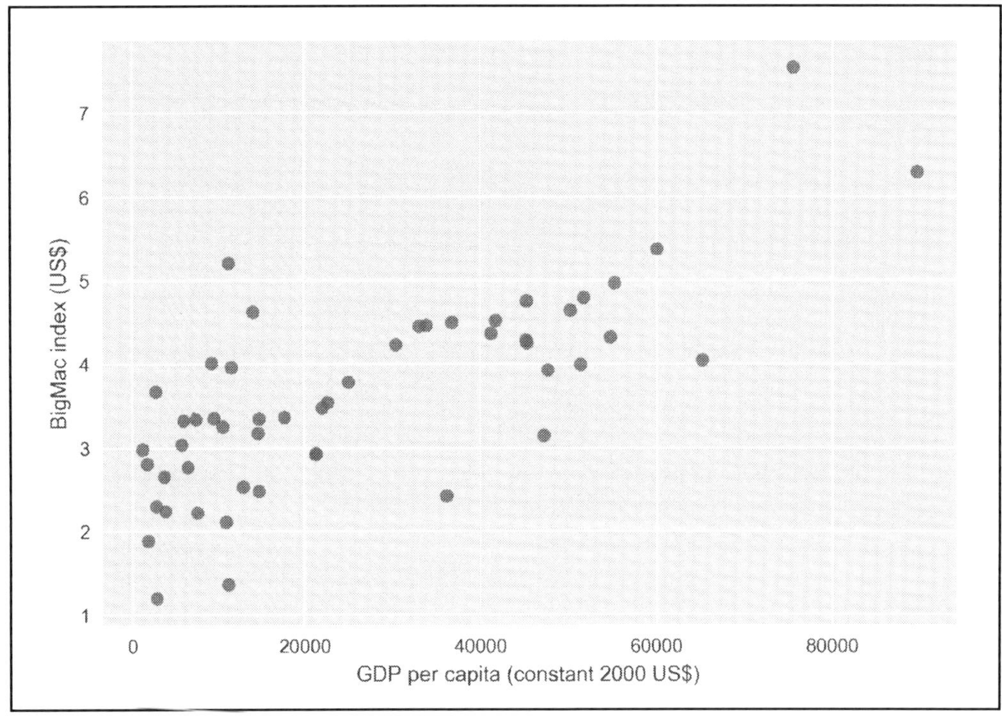

So far so good! It looks like the Big Mac index is positively correlated with GDP per capita. Let's turn the regression line back on and label a few countries that show extreme Big Mac index values:

```
ax = sns.regplot(x="Value", y="dollar_price", data=merged_df)
ax.set_xlabel("GDP per capita (constant 2000 US$)")
ax.set_ylabel("BigMac index (US$)")

# Label the country code for those who demonstrate extreme BigMac index
for row in merged_df.itertuples():
    if row.dollar_price >= 5 or row.dollar_price <= 2:
        ax.text(row.Value,row.dollar_price+0.1,row.country)

plt.show()
```

This is the expected output:

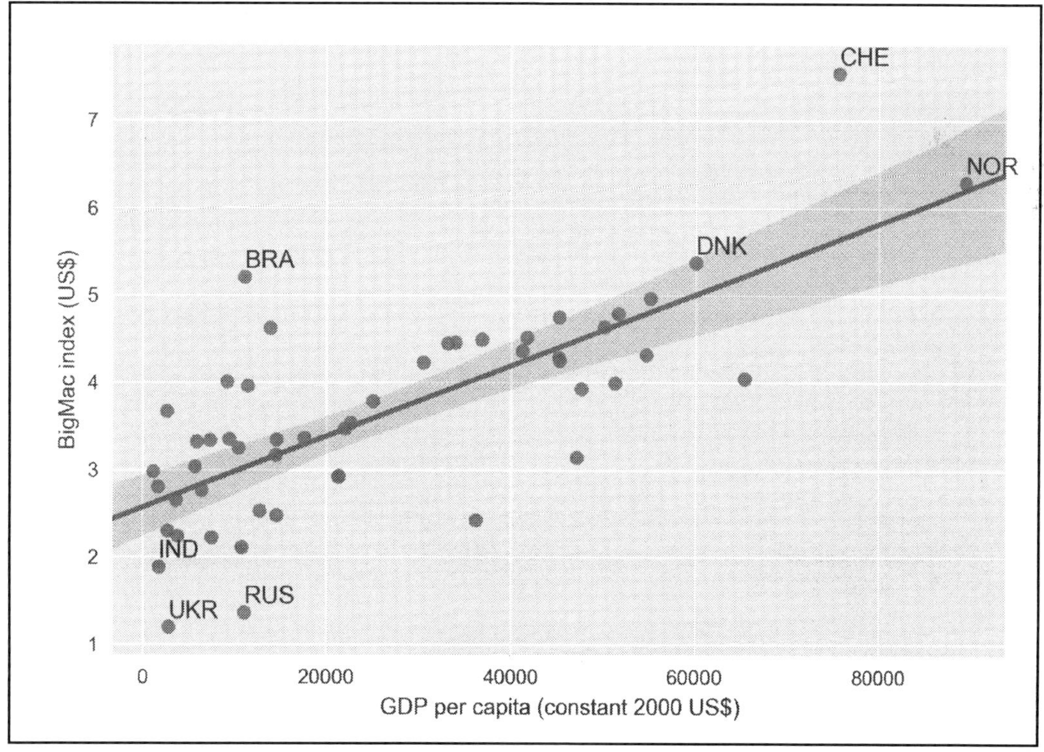

We can see that many countries fall within the confidence interval of the regression line. Given the GDP per capita level for each country, the linear regression model predicts the corresponding Big Mac index. The currency value shows signs of under- or over-valuation if the actual index deviates from the regression model.

By labeling the countries that show extremely high or low values, we can clearly see that the average price of a Big Mac in Brazil and Switzerland is overvalued, while it is undervalued in India, Russia, and Ukraine even if the differences in GDP are considered.

Since Seaborn is not a package for statistical analysis, we would need to rely on other packages, such as `scipy.stats` or `statsmodels`, to obtain the parameters of a regression model. In the next example, we are going to get the `slope` and `intercept` parameters from the regression model, and apply different colors for points that are above or below the regression line:

```
from scipy.stats import linregress


ax = sns.regplot(x="Value", y="dollar_price", data=merged_df)
ax.set_xlabel("GDP per capita (constant 2000 US$)")
ax.set_ylabel("BigMac index (US$)")

# Calculate linear regression parameters
slope, intercept, r_value, p_value, std_err = linregress(merged_df.Value,
merged_df.dollar_price)

colors = []
for row in merged_df.itertuples():
    if row.dollar_price > row.Value * slope + intercept:
        # Color markers as darkred if they are above the regression line
        color = "darkred"
    else:
        # Color markers as darkblue if they are below the regression line
        color = "darkblue"

    # Label the country code for those who demonstrate extreme BigMac index
    if row.dollar_price >= 5 or row.dollar_price <= 2:
        ax.text(row.Value,row.dollar_price+0.1,row.country)

    # Highlight the marker that corresponds to China
    if row.country == "CHN":
        t = ax.text(row.Value,row.dollar_price+0.1,row.country)
        color = "yellow"

    colors.append(color)
```

```
# Overlay another scatter plot on top with marker-specific color
ax.scatter(merged_df.Value, merged_df.dollar_price, c=colors)

# Label the r squared value and p value of the linear regression model.
# transform=ax.transAxes indicates that the coordinates are given relative
# to the axes bounding box, with 0,0 being the lower left of the axes
# and 1,1 the upper right.
ax.text(0.1, 0.9, "$r^2={0:.3f}, p={1:.3e}$".format(r_value ** 2, p_value),
transform=ax.transAxes)

plt.show()
```

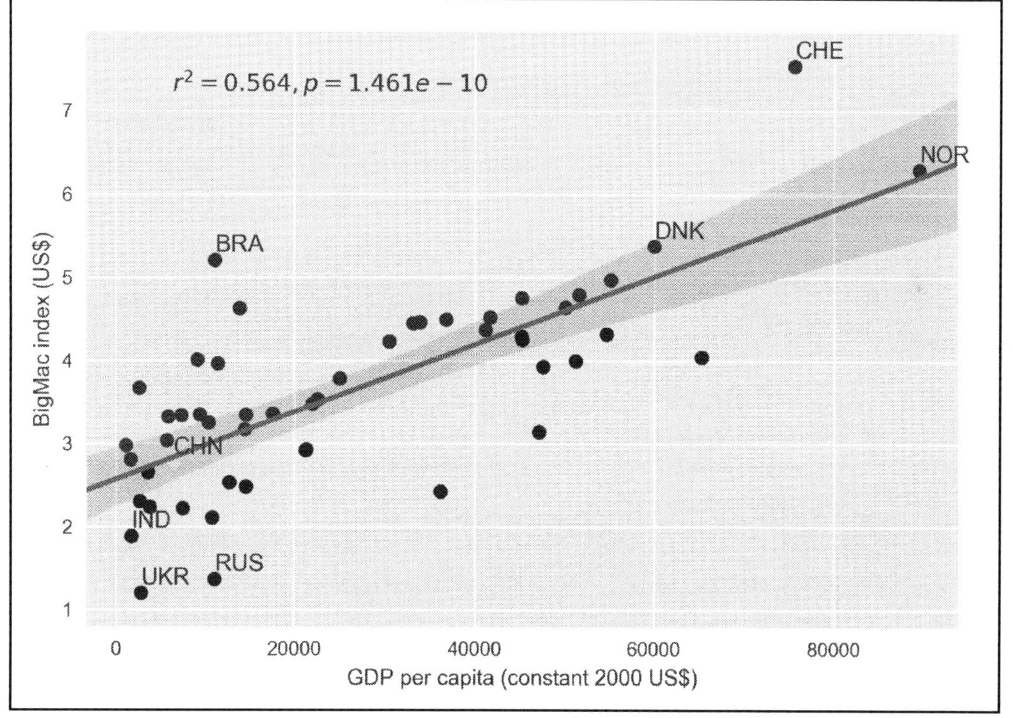

Contrary to popular belief, it looks like China's currency was not significantly under-valued in 2015, since its marker lies well within the 95% confidence interval of the regression line.

To better illustrate the distribution of values, we can combine histograms of x or y values with scatter plots using `seaborn.jointplot()`:

```
# seaborn.jointplot() returns a seaborn.JointGrid object
g = sns.jointplot(x="Value", y="dollar_price", data=merged_df)

# Provide custom axes labels through accessing the underlying axes object
# We can get matplotlib.axes.Axes of the scatter plot by calling g.ax_joint
g.ax_joint.set_xlabel("GDP per capita (constant 2000 US$)")
g.ax_joint.set_ylabel("BigMac index (US$)")

# Set the title and adjust the margin
g.fig.suptitle("Relationship between GDP per capita and BigMac Index")
g.fig.subplots_adjust(top=0.9)

plt.show()
```

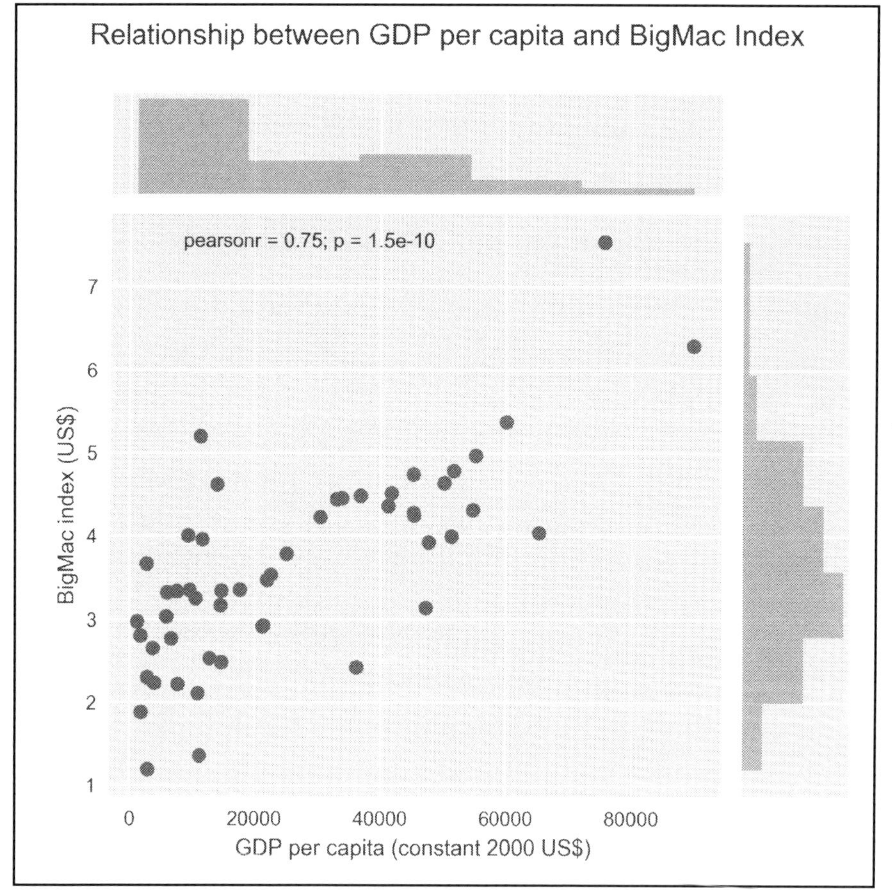

By additionally specifying the `kind` parameter in `jointplot` to `reg`, `resid`, `hex`, or `kde`, we can quickly change the plot type to regression, residual, hex bin, or KDE contour plot respectively.

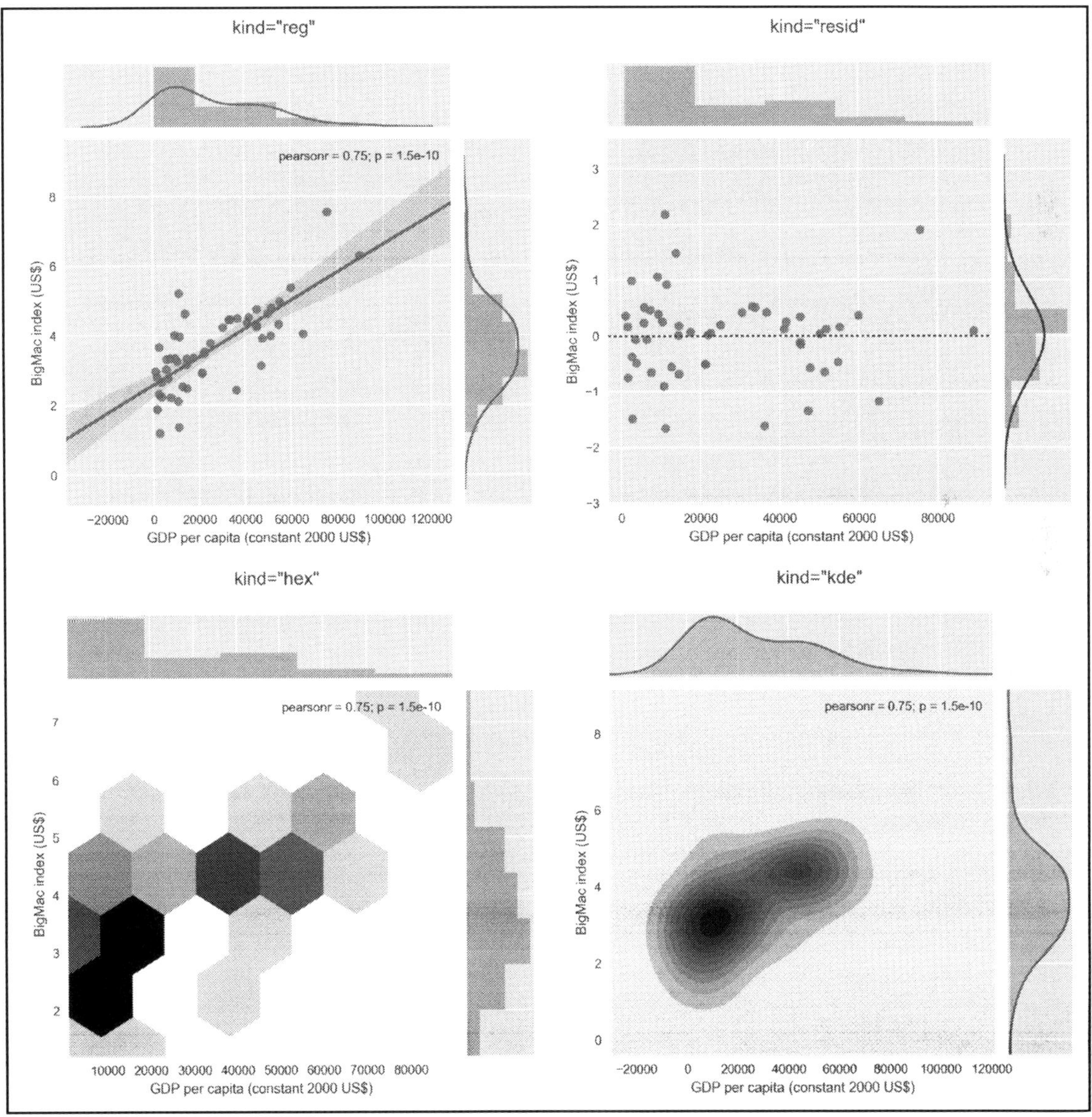

Here is a big disclaimer: with the data in our hands, it is still too early to make any conclusions about the valuation of currencies! Different business factors such as labor cost, rent, raw material costs, and taxation can all contribute to the pricing model of Big Mac, but this is beyond the scope of this book.

Visualizing categorical data

Towards the end of this chapter, let's try to integrate all datasets that we have processed so far. Remember that we briefly introduced the three categories of population structures (that is, constrictive, stable, and expansive) earlier in this chapter?

In this section, we are going to implement a naive algorithm for classifying populations into one of the three categories. After that, we will explore different techniques of visualizing categorical data.

Most references online discuss visual classification of population pyramids only (for example, `https://www.populationeducation.org/content/what-are-different-types-population-pyramids`). Clustering-based methods do exist (for example, Korenjak-Cˇ erne, Kejžar, Batagelj (2008). *Clustering of Population Pyramids*. Informatica. 32.), but to date, mathematical definitions of population categories are scarcely discussed. We will build a naive classifier based on the ratio of populations between "0-4" and "50-54" age groups in the next example:

```
import pandas as pd
import seaborn as sns
import matplotlib.pyplot as plt


# Select total population for each country in 2015
current_population = population_df[(population_df.Time == 2015) &
                                   (population_df.Sex == 'Both')]

# A list for storing the population type for each country
pop_type_list = []

# Look through each country in the BigMac index dataset
for country in merged_df.country.unique():
    # Make sure the country also exist in the GDP per capita dataset
    if not country in current_population.country.values:
       continue

    # Calculate the ratio of population between "0-4" and "50-54"
    # age groups
    young = current_population[(current_population.country == country) &
```

```
                                    (current_population.AgeGrp == "0-4")].Value

    midage = current_population[(current_population.country == country) &
                                    (current_population.AgeGrp ==
"50-54")].Value

    ratio = float(young) / float(midage)

    # Classify the populations based on arbitrary ratio thresholds
    if ratio < 0.8:
        pop_type = "constrictive"
    elif ratio < 1.2 and ratio >= 0.8:
        pop_type = "stable"
    else:
        pop_type = "expansive"

    pop_type_list.append([country, ratio, pop_type])

# Convert the list to Pandas DataFrame
pop_type_df = pd.DataFrame(pop_type_list,
columns=['country','ratio','population type'])

# Merge the BigMac index DataFrame with population type DataFrame
merged_df2 = pd.merge(merged_df, pop_type_df, how='inner', on='country')
merged_df2.head()
```

The expected output is as follows:

	Date_x	local_price	dollar_ex	dollar_price	dollar_ppp	dollar_valuation	dollar_adj_valuation	euro_adj_valuation	sterling_adj_valuation	yen_adj_valuation	yuan_adj_valuation	country	Date_y	Value	ratio	population type
0	2015-01-31	28.00	8.610000	3.252033	5.845511	-32.107881	0.540242	-0.804495	-2.49468	34.3905	6.01183	ARG	2015-12-31	10501.660269	1.695835	expansive
1	2015-01-31	5.30	1.227220	4.318705	1.106472	-9.839144	-17.8995	-18.9976	-20.3778	9.74234	-13.4315	AUS	2015-12-31	54688.445933	0.961301	stable
2	2015-01-31	13.50	2.592750	5.206827	2.818372	8.702019	68.4555	66.2024	63.3705	125.172	77.6231	BRA	2015-12-31	11211.891104	1.217728	expansive
3	2015-01-31	2.89	0.661594	4.368235	0.603340	-8.805115	3.11257	1.73343	0	37.8289	8.72415	GBR	2015-12-31	41182.619517	0.872431	stable
4	2015-01-31	5.70	1.228550	4.639616	1.189979	-3.139545	-2.34134	-3.64753	-5.28928	30.5387	2.97343	CAN	2015-12-31	50108.065004	0.690253	constrictive

Categorical scatter plot

With the data classified into categories, we can check whether different population types exhibit different Big Mac index distributions.

We can use `seaborn.lmplot` to dissect the data and create a categorical scatter plot. As a recap, `lmplot()` combines `regplot()` with `FacetGrid` for visualization of three or more pairs of variables in faceted grids or color-coded scatter plots. In the upcoming examples, we are going to assign the population type variable to the `col`, `row`, or `hue` parameters of `lmplot()`. Let's see how the results look:

```
# Horizontal faceted grids (col="population type")
g = sns.lmplot(x="Value", y="dollar_price", col="population type",
data=merged_df2)
g.set_xlabels("GDP per capita (constant 2000 US$)")
g.set_ylabels("BigMac index (US$)")

plt.show()
```

The preceding code excerpt generates:

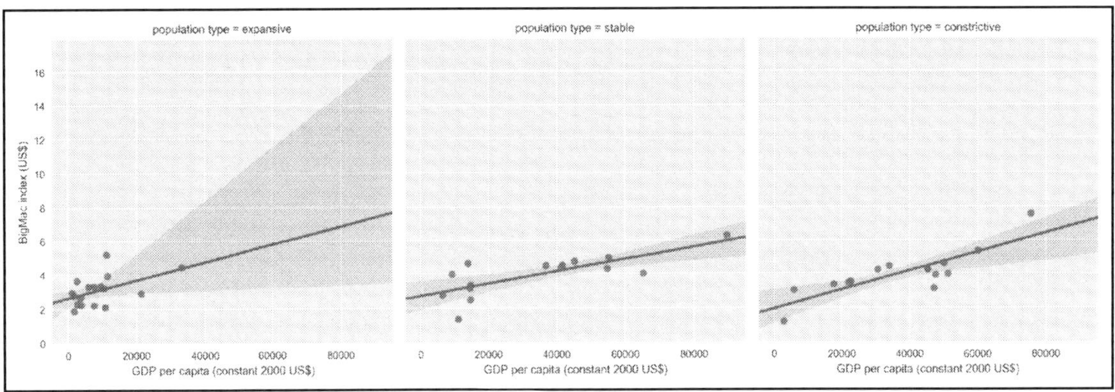

Alternatively, if we set `row="population type"` instead of `col="population type"` in the code excerpt, the following plot will be generated:

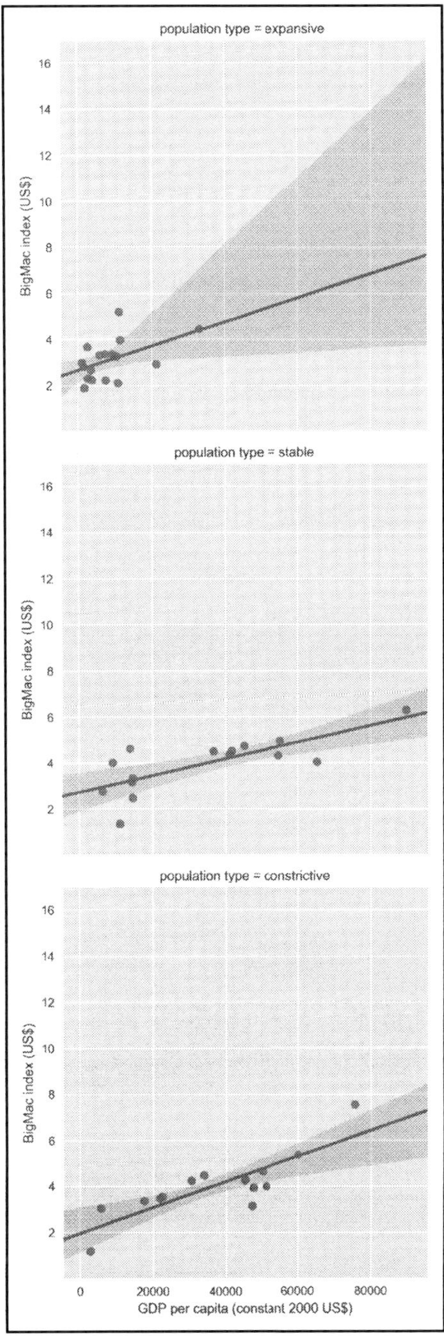
population type = expansive
population type = stable
population type = constrictive
BigMac index (US$)
GDP per capita (constant 2000 US$)
0
20000
40000
60000
80000
2
4
6
8
10
12
14
16

Finally, by changing `col="population type"` to `hue="population type"`, a color-coded categorical scatter plot will be generated:

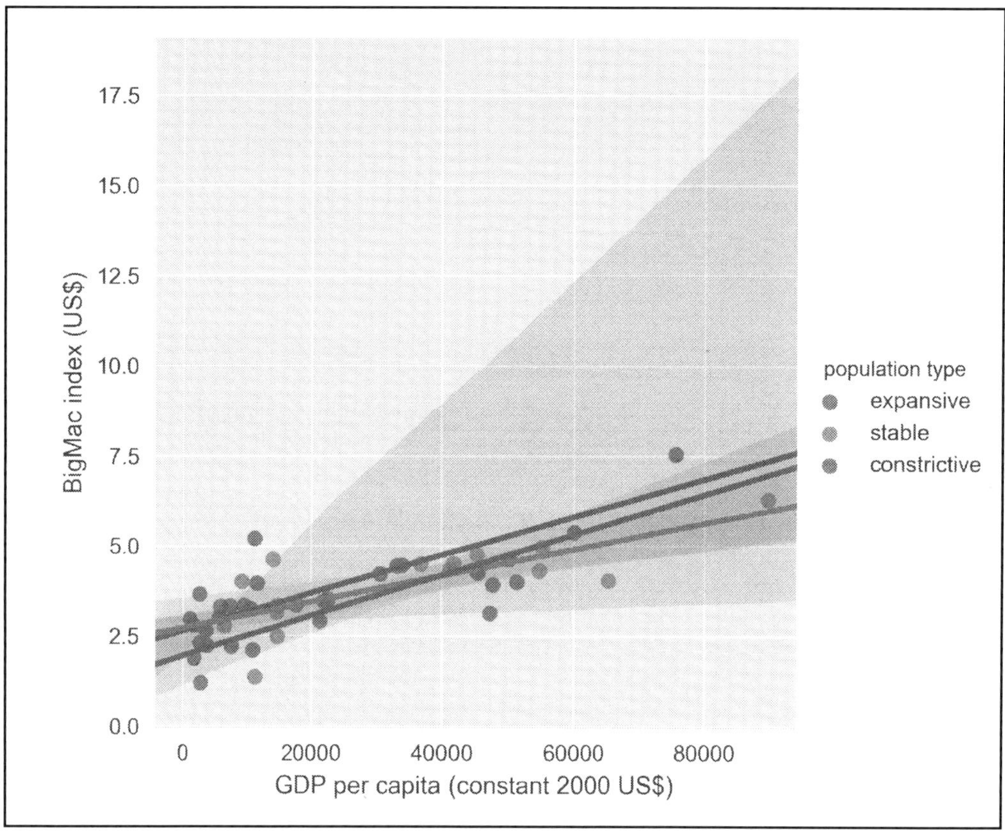

In fact, `col`, `row`, and `hue` can be mixed together to create a rich faceted grid. This is particularly useful when there are lots of dimensions in your data. Further discussion of facet grids will be available in the next chapter.

Strip plot and swarm plot

A strip is basically a scatter plot where the x axis represents a categorical variable. Typical uses of a strip plot involves applying a small random jitter value to each data point such that the separation between points becomes clearer:

```
# Strip plot with jitter value
ax = sns.stripplot(x="population type", y="dollar_price", data=merged_df2,
jitter=True)
ax.set_xlabel("Population type")
ax.set_ylabel("BigMac index (US$)")

plt.show()
```

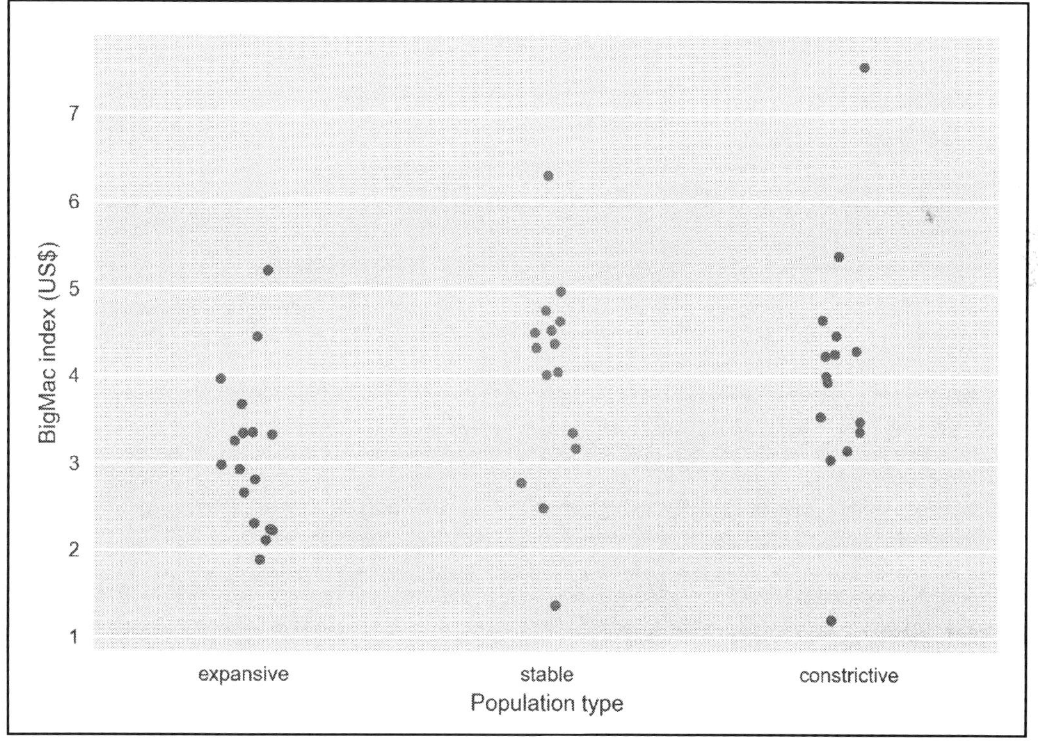

A swarm plot is very similar to a strip plot, yet the locations of points are adjusted automatically to avoid overlap even if the jitter value is not applied. These plots resemble bees swarming a position, and are likewise named.

If we change the Seaborn function call from `sns.stripplot` to `sns.swarmplot` in the preceding code excerpt, the result will be changed to this:

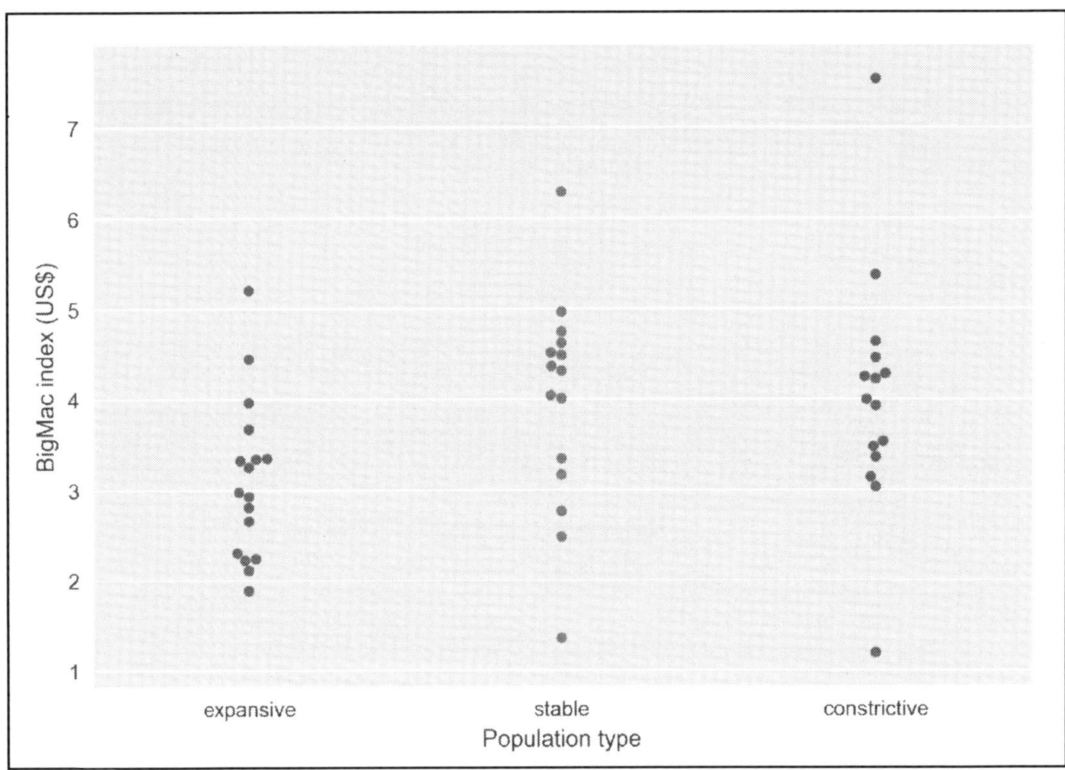

Box plot and violin plot

The way a strip plot and swarm plot represent data makes comparison difficult. Suppose you want to find out whether the stable or constrictive population type has a higher median BigMac index value. Can you do that based on the two previous example plots?

You might be tempted to think that the constrictive group has a higher median value because of the higher maximum data point, but in fact the stable group has a higher median value.

Could there be a better plot type for comparing the distribution of categorical data? Here you go! Let's try a box plot:

```
# Box plot
ax = sns.boxplot(x="population type", y="dollar_price", data=merged_df2)
ax.set_xlabel("Population type")
ax.set_ylabel("BigMac index (US$)")

plt.show()
```

The expected output:

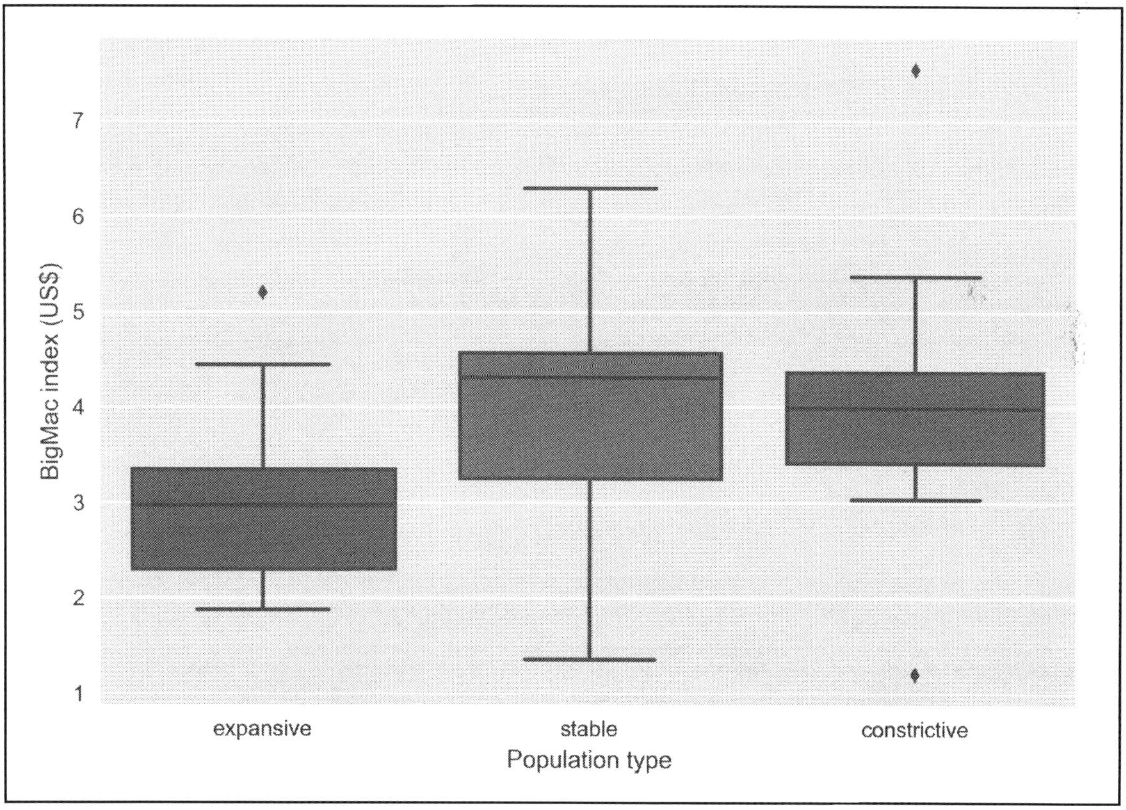

The box represents quartiles of the data, the center line denotes the median value, and the whiskers represent the full range of the data. Data points that deviate by more than 1.5 times the interquartile range from the upper or lower quartile are deemed to be outliers and show as fliers.

A violin plot combines the kernel density estimate of our data with the box plot. Both box plot and violin plot display the median and interquartile range, but a violin plot goes one step further by showing the full estimated probability distribution that is fit to the data. Therefore, we can tell whether there are peaks within the data and also compare their relative amplitude.

If we change the Seaborn function call from `sns.boxplot` to `sns.violinplot` in the code excerpt, the result would be like this:

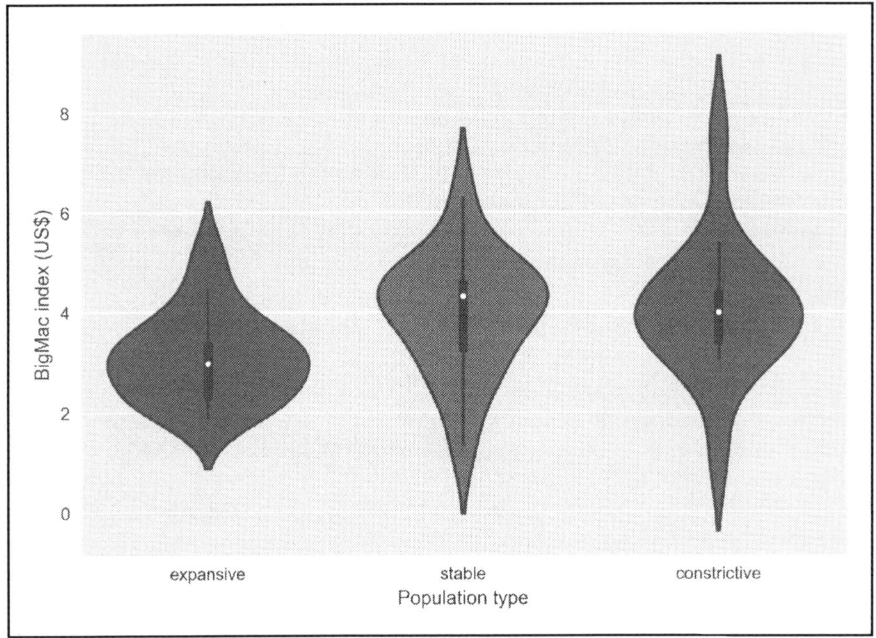

We can also overlay a strip plot or swarm plot on top of the box plot or swarm plot in order to get the best of both worlds. Here is example code:

```
# Prepare a box plot
ax = sns.boxplot(x="population type", y="dollar_price", data=merged_df2)

# Overlay a swarm plot on top of the same axes
sns.swarmplot(x="population type", y="dollar_price", data=merged_df2,
color="w", ax=ax)
ax.set_xlabel("Population type")
ax.set_ylabel("BigMac index (US$)")

plt.show()
```

The expected output:

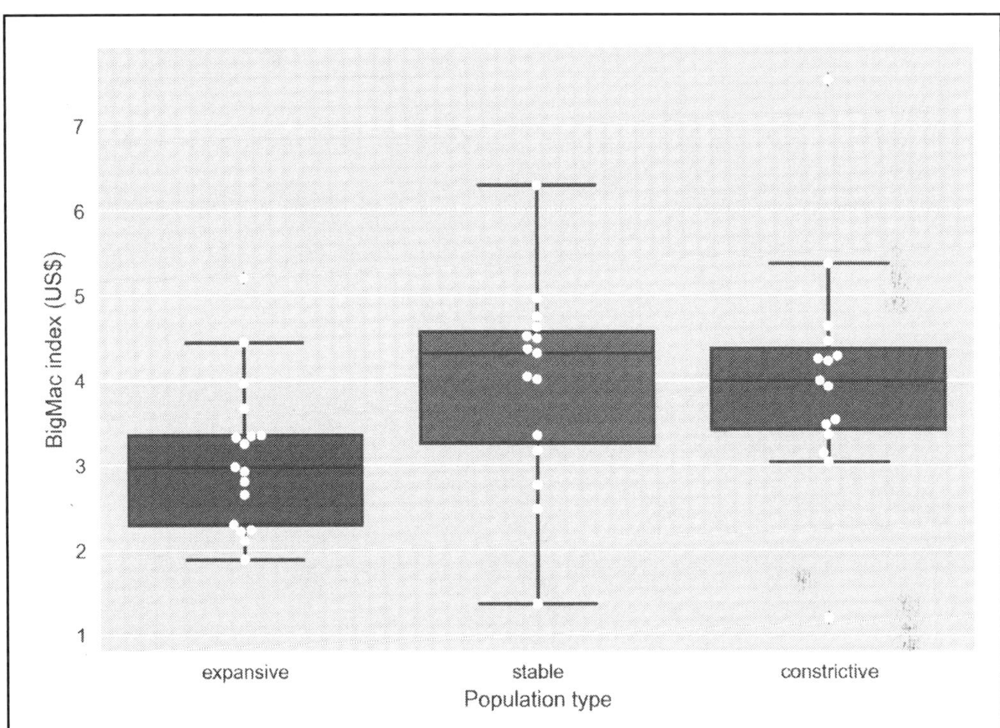

Controlling Seaborn figure aesthetics

While we can use Matplotlib to customize the figure aesthetics, Seaborn comes with several handy functions to make customization easier. If you are using Seaborn version 0.8 or later, `seaborn.set()` must be called explicitly after import if you would like to enable the beautiful Seaborn default theme. In earlier versions, `seaborn.set()` was called implicitly on import.

Preset themes

The five default themes in Seaborn, namely darkgrid, whitegrid, dark, white, and ticks, can be selected by calling the `seaborn.set_style()` function.

`seaborn.set_style()` must be called before issuing any plotting commands in order to display the theme properly.

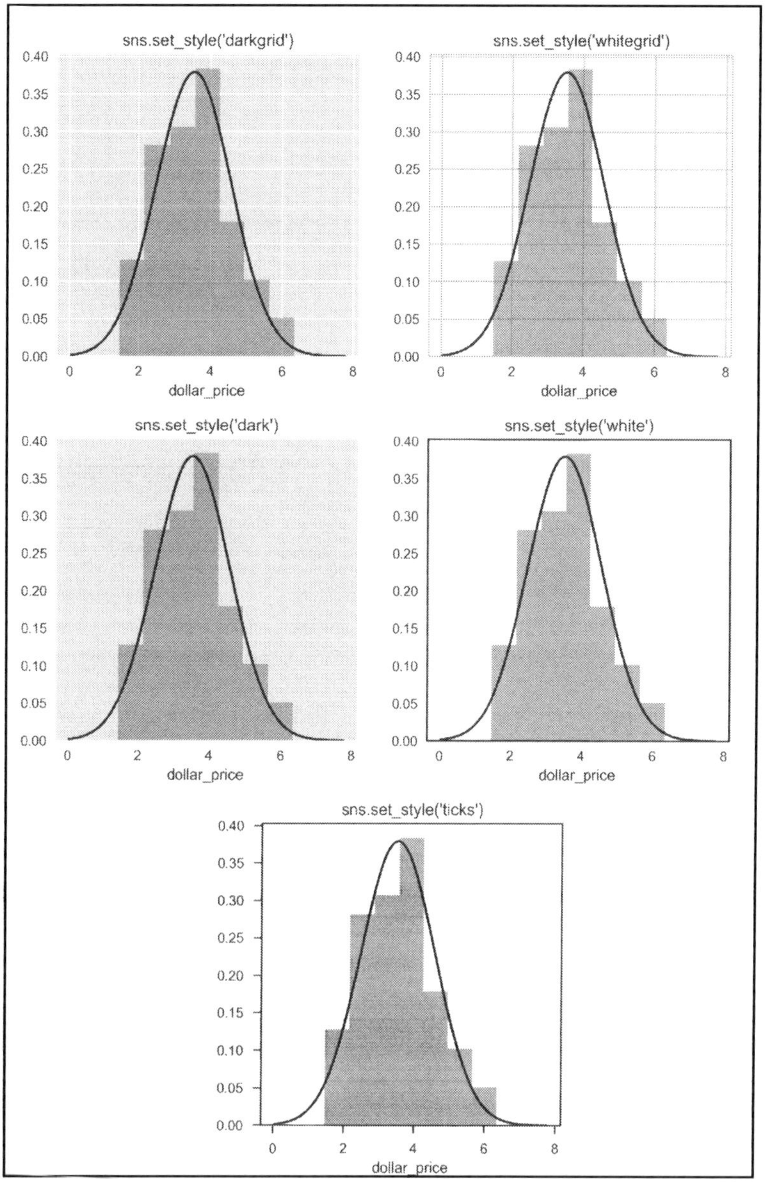

Removing spines from the figure

To remove or adjust the positions of spines, we can make use of the `seaborn.despine` function. By default, the spines on the top and right side of a figure are removed, and additional spines can be removed by setting `left=True` or `bottom=True`. Through the use of offset and trim parameters, the location of the spines can be adjusted as well.

`seaborn.despine` has to be called after calling the Seaborn plotting functions.

Here are the results of different combinations of parameters in the `seaborn.despine` function:

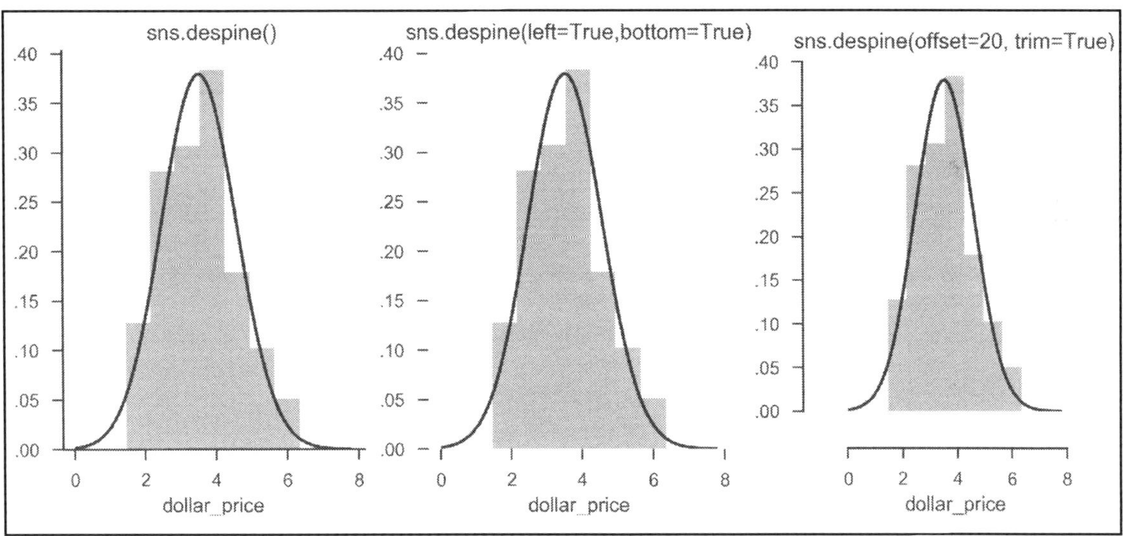

Changing the size of the figure

To control the height and width of the figure, we can of course rely on `matplotlib.pyplot.figure(figsize=(WIDTH,HEIGHT))`, which was first introduced in `Chapter 3`, *Figure Layout and Annotations*.

In this example, we are going to change the size of the previous histogram example to 8 inches wide and 4 inches tall:

```
import seaborn as sns
import matplotlib.pyplot as plt
from scipy import stats

# Note: Codes related to data preparation are skipped for brevity
# Reset all previous theme settings to defaults
sns.set()

# Change the size to 8 inches wide and 4 inches tall
fig = plt.figure(figsize=(8,4))

# We are going to reuse current_bigmac that was generated earlier
# Plot the histogram
ax = sns.distplot(current_bigmac.dollar_price)
plt.show()
```

Here is the expected output from the preceding code:

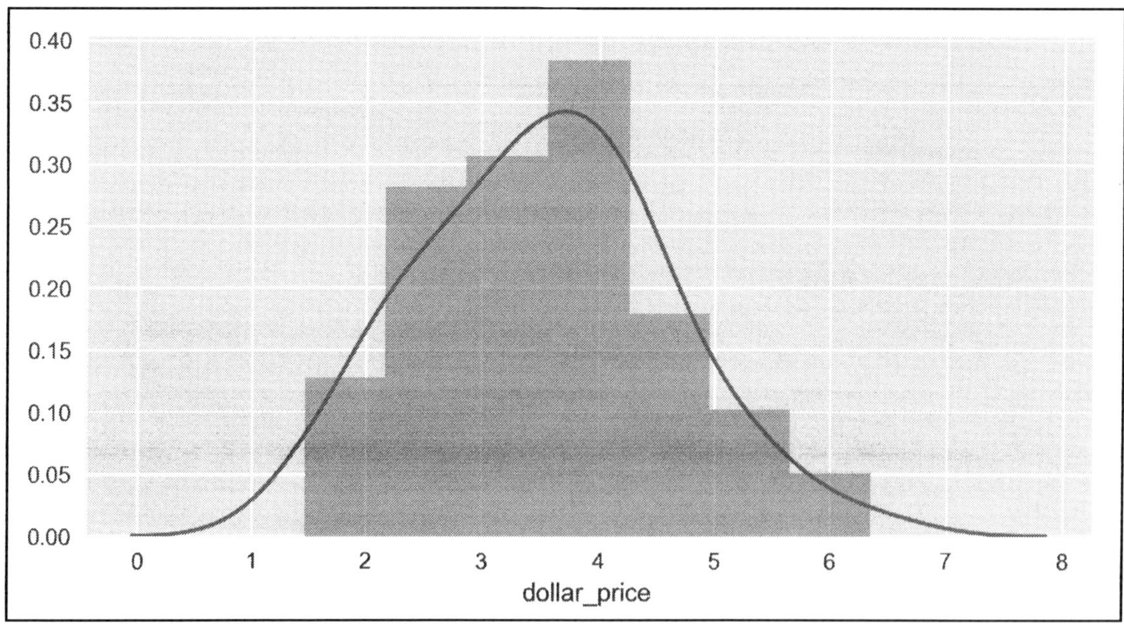

Seaborn also comes with the `seaborn.set_context()` function to control the scale of plot elements. There are four preset contexts, paper, notebook, talk, and poster, which are in ascending order of size. By default, the Notebook style is chosen. This is an example of setting the context to `poster`:

```
# Reset all previous theme settings to defaults
sns.set()

# Set Seaborn context to poster
sns.set_context("poster")

# We are going to reuse current_bigmac that was generated earlier
# Plot the histogram
ax = sns.distplot(current_bigmac.dollar_price)
plt.show()
```

Here is the expected output from the preceding code:

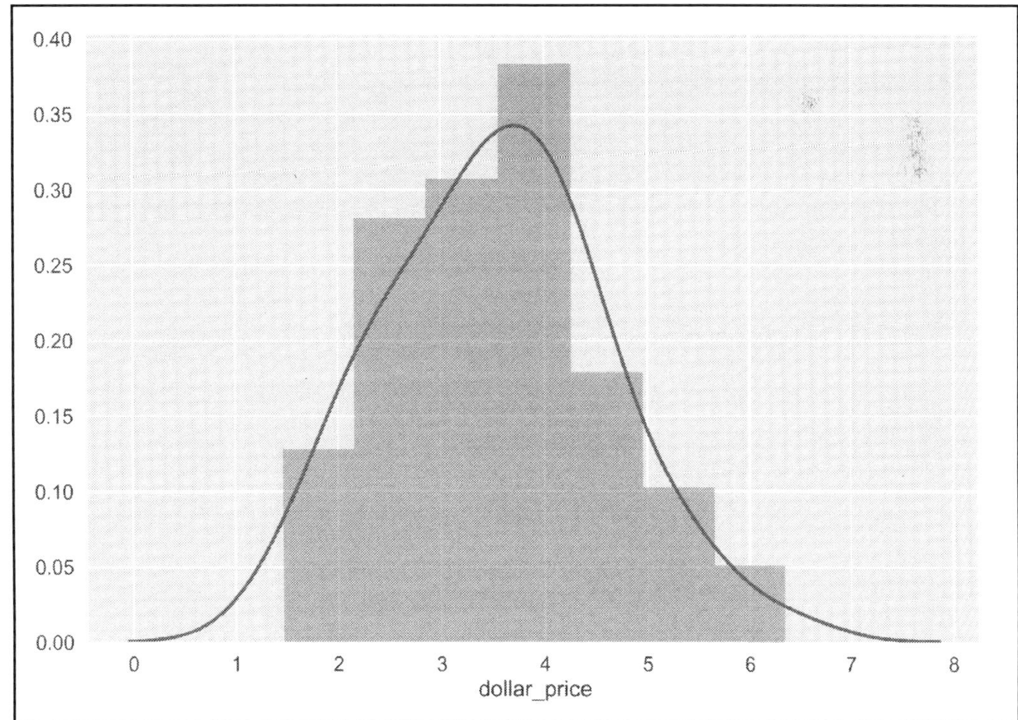

Fine-tuning the style of the figure

Almost every element in a Seaborn figure can be further customized via `seaborn.set`. Here is the list of parameters that are supported:

- `context`: One of the preset contexts--{paper, notebook, talk, poster}.
- `style`: One of the axes' styles--{darkgrid, whitegrid, dark, white, ticks}.
- `palette`: One of the color palettes as defined in `https://seaborn.pydata.org/generated/seaborn.color_palette.html#seaborn.color_palette`.
- `font`: A supported font or font family name, such as serif, sans-serif, cursive, fantasy, or monospace. For more information, visit `https://matplotlib.org/api/font_manager_api.html`.
- `font_scale`: An independent scaling factor of font elements.
- `rc`: A dictionary of extra `rc` parameters mappings. To obtain the full list of all `rc` parameters, we can run `seaborn.axes_style()`.

RC parameters that are not defined in the currently used preset context or axis style cannot be overridden. For more information on `seaborn.set()`, please visit `https://seaborn.pydata.org/generated/seaborn.set.html#seaborn.set`.

Let's try to increase the font scale, increase the line width of the KDE plot, and change the color of several plot elements:

```
# Get a dictionary of all parameters that can be changed
sns.axes_style()

"""
Returns
{'axes.axisbelow': True,
 'axes.edgecolor': '.8',
 'axes.facecolor': 'white',
 'axes.grid': True,
 'axes.labelcolor': '.15',
 'axes.linewidth': 1.0,
 'figure.facecolor': 'white',
 'font.family': [u'sans-serif'],
 'font.sans-serif': [u'Arial',
 u'DejaVu Sans',
 u'Liberation Sans',
 u'Bitstream Vera Sans',
 u'sans-serif'],
 'grid.color': '.8',
 'grid.linestyle': u'-',
```

```
 'image.cmap': u'rocket',
 'legend.frameon': False,
 'legend.numpoints': 1,
 'legend.scatterpoints': 1,
 'lines.solid_capstyle': u'round',
 'text.color': '.15',
 'xtick.color': '.15',
 'xtick.direction': u'out',
 'xtick.major.size': 0.0,
 'xtick.minor.size': 0.0,
 'ytick.color': '.15',
 'ytick.direction': u'out',
 'ytick.major.size': 0.0,
 'ytick.minor.size': 0.0}
 """

# Increase the font scale to 2, change the grid color to light grey,
# and axes label color to dark blue
sns.set(context="notebook",
 style="darkgrid",
 font_scale=2,
 rc={'grid.color': '0.6',
 'axes.labelcolor':'darkblue',
 "lines.linewidth": 2.5})

# Plot the histogram
ax = sns.distplot(current_bigmac.dollar_price)
plt.show()
```

The code generates the following histogram:

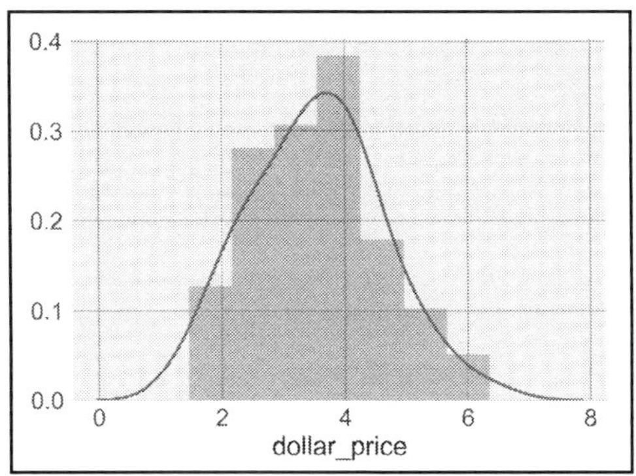

So far, only functions that control global aesthetics were introduced. What if we want to change the style of a specific plot only?

Luckily, most Seaborn plotting functions come with specific parameters for the customization of styles. This also means that there isn't a universal styling tutorial for all Seaborn plotting functions. However, we can take a closer look at this `seaborn.distplot()` code excerpt to get an idea:

```
# Note: Codes related to data preparation and imports are skipped for
# brevity
# Reset the style
sns.set(context="notebook", style="darkgrid")

# Plot the histogram with custom style
ax = sns.distplot(current_bigmac.dollar_price,
                  kde_kws={"color": "g",
                           "linewidth": 3,
                           "label": "KDE"},
                  hist_kws={"histtype": "step",
                            "alpha": 1,
                            "color": "k",
                            "label": "histogram"})

plt.show()
```

The expected result:

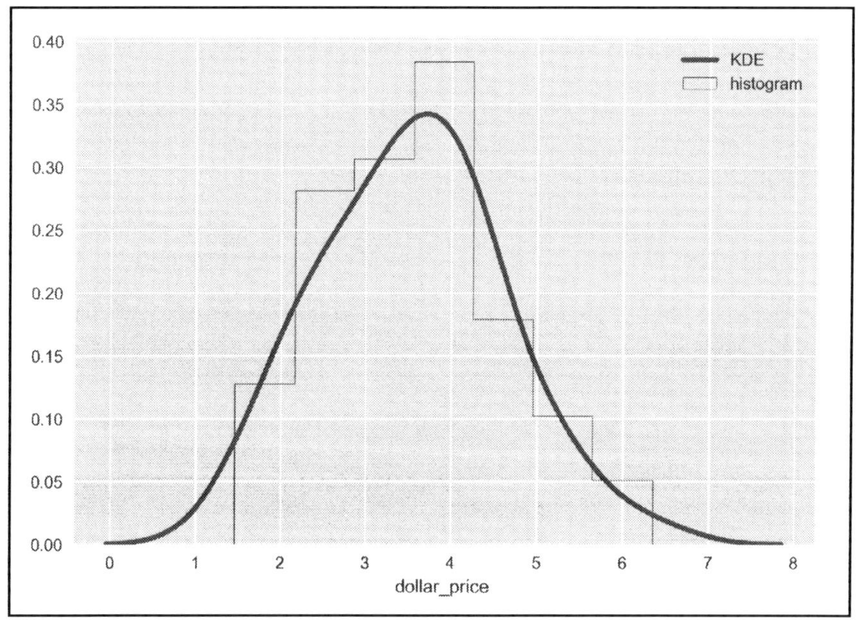

Some Seaborn functions support a more direct approach of customizing aesthetics. For example, `seaborn.barplot` can pass through keyword arguments such as `facecolor`, `edgecolor`, `ecolor`, and `linewidth` to the underlying `matplotlib.pyplot.bar` function:

```
# Note: Codes related to data preparation and imports are skipped
# for brevity
# Population Bar chart
sns.barplot(x="AgeGrp",y="Value", hue="Sex",
            linewidth=2, edgecolor="w",
            data = current_population)

# Use Matplotlib functions to label axes rotate tick labels
ax = plt.gca()
ax.set(xlabel="Age Group", ylabel="Population (thousands)")
ax.set_xticklabels(ax.xaxis.get_majorticklabels(), rotation=45)
plt.title("Population Barchart (USA)")

# Show the figure
plt.show()
```

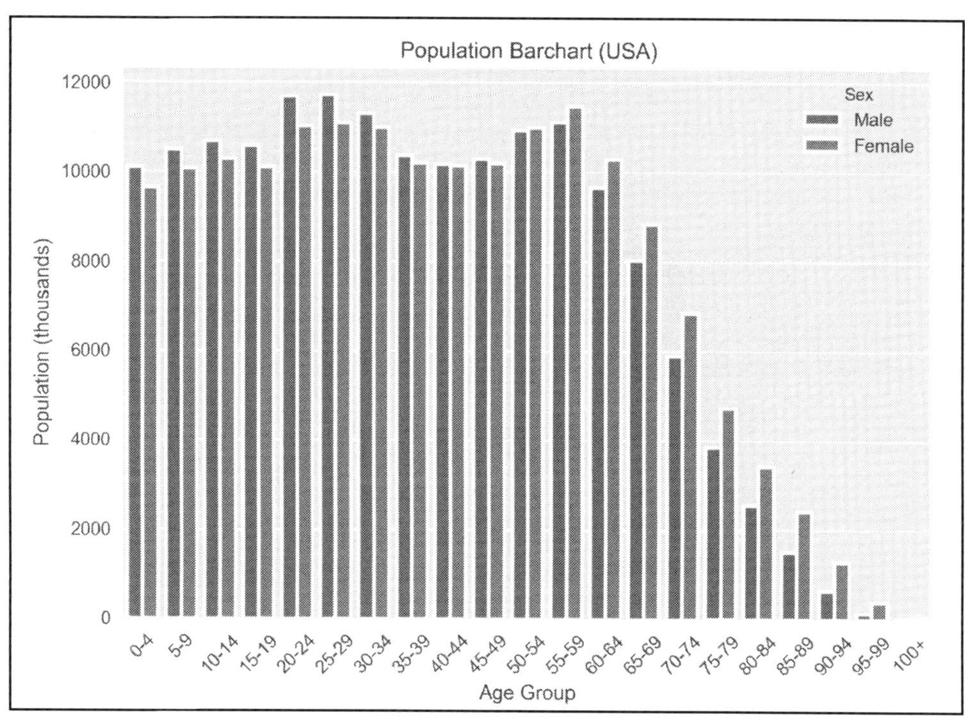

More about colors

Color is perhaps the most important aspect of figure style, and thus it deserves its own subsection. There are many great resources that discuss the principles of choosing colors in visualizations (for example, `https://betterfigures.org/2015/06/23/picking-a-colour-scale-for-scientific-graphics/` and `https://earthobservatory.nasa.gov/blogs/elegantfigures/2013/08/05/subtleties-of-color-part-1-of-6/`). The official Matplotlib documentation also contains a good overview of color maps (`http://matplotlib.org/users/colormaps.html`).

Effective use of color adds sufficient contrast to make something stand out and draw your audience's attention. Colors can also evoke emotions; for example, red is often associated with important or passionate, while green is often associated with natural or stable. If you are trying to deliver a story from your plots, do try to use an appropriate color scheme. It's estimated that 8% of men and 0.5% of women suffer from red-green color blindness, so we need to pick colors with these individuals in mind as well.

Color scheme and color palettes

There are three general kinds of color palettes available in seaborn--qualitative, diverging, and sequential:

- Qualitative palettes are best for data with discrete levels or nominal or categorical data. Custom qualitative palettes can be created by providing a list of Matplotlib colors to `seaborn.color_palette`.
- Diverging palettes are used for highlighting low and high values in a figure, with a neutrally colored midpoint. Custom diverging palettes can be created by passing two hue values plus the optional lightness and saturation values for the extremes to the `seaborn.diverging_palette` function.
- Sequential palettes are usually used for quantitative data that progresses continuously from low to high.
  Custom sequential palettes can be created by providing a single Matplotlib color to `seaborn.light_palette` or `seaborn.dark_palette`, which produces a palette that changes gradually from light or dark desaturated values to the seed color.

In the next example, we are going to plot the most commonly used qualitative, diverging, and sequential palettes, as well as a few custom palettes:

```
import numpy as np
import matplotlib.pyplot as plt
from matplotlib.colors import ListedColormap


def palplot(pal, ax):
    """Plot the values in a color palette as a horizontal array.
    Adapted from seaborn.palplot
    Args:
        p : seaborn color palette
        ax : axes to plot the color palette
    """
    n = len(pal)
    ax.imshow(np.arange(n).reshape(1, n),
              cmap=ListedColormap(list(pal)),
              interpolation="nearest", aspect="auto")
    ax.set_xticks(np.arange(n) - .5)
    ax.set_yticks([-.5, .5])
    ax.set_xticklabels([])
    ax.set_yticklabels([])
palettes = {"qualitative": ["deep", "pastel", "bright", "dark",
                            "colorblind", "Accent", "Paired",
                            "Set1", "Set2", "Set3", "Pastel1",
                            "Pastel2", "Dark2"],
            "diverging": ["BrBG", "PiYG", "PRGn", "PuOr", "RdBu",
                          "RdBu_r", "RdGy", "RdGy_r", "RdYlGn",
                          "coolwarm"],
            "sequential": ["husl", "Greys", "Blues", "BuGn_r",
                           "GnBu_d", "plasma", "viridis","cubehelix"]}

#Reset to default Seaborn style
sns.set()

# Create one subplot per palette, the x-axis is shared
fig, axarr = plt.subplots(13, 3, sharex=True, figsize=(12,11))

# Plot 9 color blocks for each palette
for i, palette_type in enumerate(palettes.keys()):
    for j, palette in enumerate(palettes[palette_type]):
        pal = sns.color_palette(palettes[palette_type][j], 9)
        palplot(pal, axarr[j,i])
        axarr[j,i].set_xlabel(palettes[palette_type][j])

# Plot a few more custom diverging palette
custom_diverging_palette = [
```

```
 sns.diverging_palette(220, 20, n=9),
 sns.diverging_palette(10, 220, sep=80, n=9),
 sns.diverging_palette(145, 280, s=85, l=25, n=9)
]

for i, palette in enumerate(custom_diverging_palette):
    palplot(palette, axarr[len(palettes["diverging"])+i,1])
    axarr[len(palettes["diverging"])+i,1].set_xlabel("custom diverging
    {}".format(i+1))

# Plot a few more custom sequential palette
other_custom_palette = [
 sns.light_palette("green", 9),
 sns.light_palette("green", 9, reverse=True),
 sns.dark_palette("navy", 9),
 sns.dark_palette("navy", 9, reverse=True),
 sns.color_palette(["#49a17a","#4aae82","#4eb98a","#55c091","#c99b5f",
 "#cbb761","#c5cc62","#accd64","#94ce65"])
]

for i, palette in enumerate(other_custom_palette):
    palplot(palette, axarr[len(palettes["sequential"])+i,2])
    axarr[len(palettes["sequential"])+i,2].set_xlabel("custom sequential
    {}".format(i+1))

# Reduce unnecessary margin space
plt.tight_layout()

# Show the plot
plt.show()
```

The expected output is as follows:

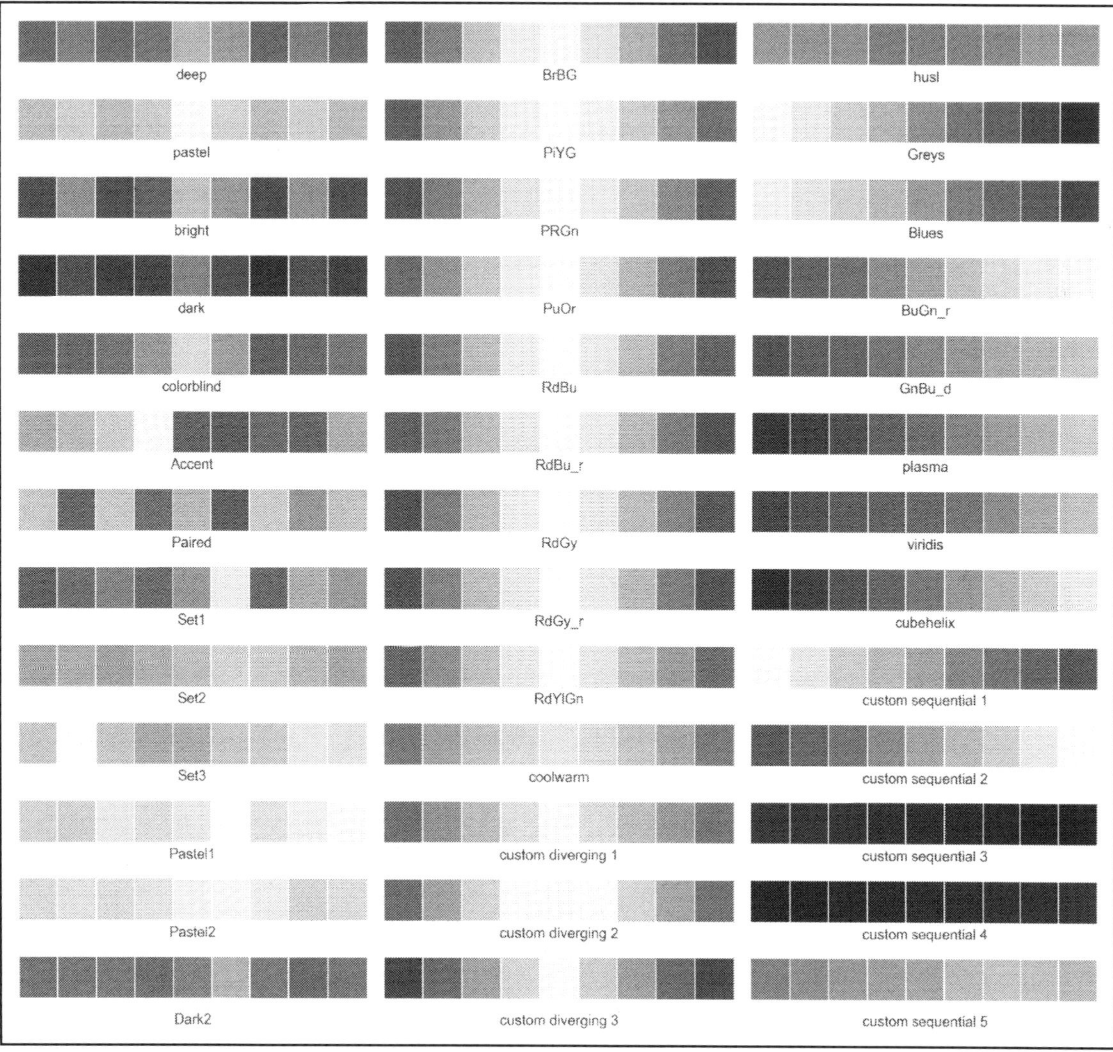

To change the color scheme of a Seaborn plot, we can use either the `color` or `palette` parameter available in most Seaborn functions. The `color` parameter supports a single color that will be applied to all of the elements. On the other hand, `palette` supports a range of colors to differentiate levels of the `hue` variable.

Some Seaborn functions support the `color` parameter only (for example, dist plot), while others can support both `color` and `palette` (for example, bar plot and box plot). Readers can refer to the official documentation to see which parameter is supported.

The following three code excerpts demonstrate the use of the `color` or `palette` parameter in a dist plot, bar plot, and box plot:

```
# Note: Codes related to data preparation and imports are skipped
# for brevity
# Change the color of histogram and KDE line to darkred
ax = sns.distplot(current_bigmac.dollar_price, color="darkred")
plt.show()
```

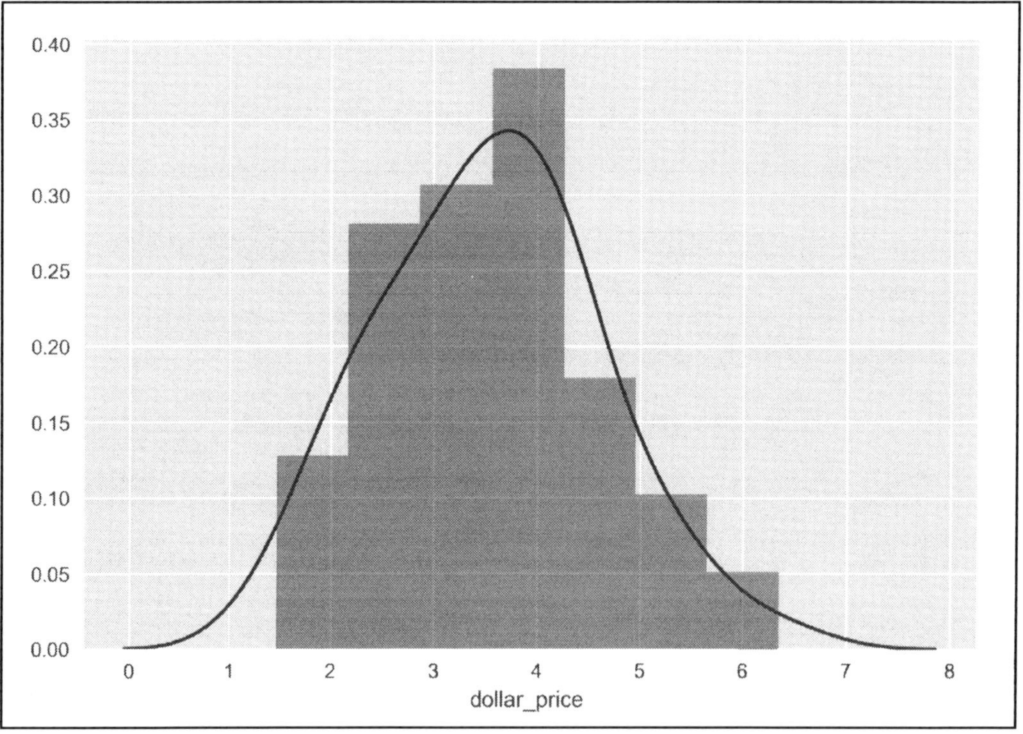

```
current_population = population_df[(population_df.Location == 'United
States of America') &
                                   (population_df.Time == 2017) &
                                   (population_df.Sex != 'Both')]
# Change the color palette of the bar chart to Paired
sns.barplot(x="AgeGrp",y="Value", hue="Sex", palette="Paired", data =
current_population)
# Rotate tick labels by 30 degree
plt.setp(plt.gca().get_xticklabels(), rotation=30,
horizontalalignment='right')
plt.show()
```

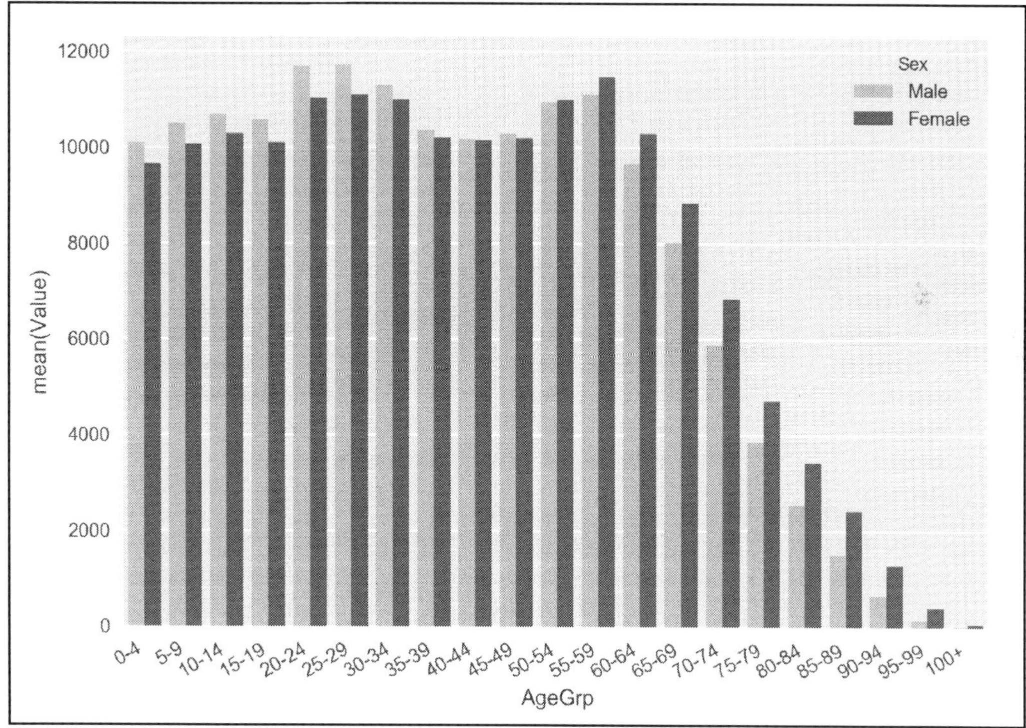

```
# Note: Codes related to data preparation and imports are skipped
# for brevity
# Change the color palette of the bar chart to Set2 from color
# brewer library
ax = sns.boxplot(x="population type", y="dollar_price", palette="Set2",
data=merged_df2)
plt.show()
```

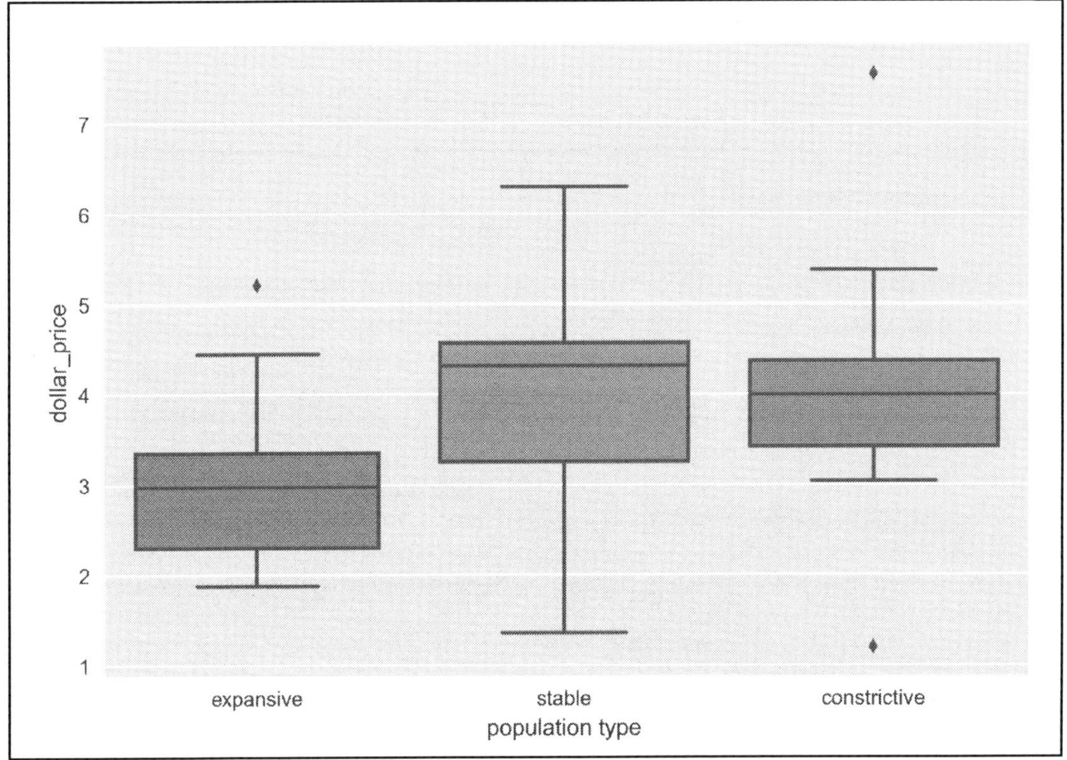

Summary

You just learned how we can parse online data in CSV or JSON formats using the versatile Pandas package. You further learned how to filter, subset, merge, and process data into insights. You have now equipped yourself with the knowledge to visualize time series, univariate, bivariate, and categorical data. The chapter concluded with a number of useful techniques to customize figure aesthetics for effective storytelling.

Phew! We have just completed a long chapter, so go grab a burger, have a break, and relax.

5
Visualizing Multivariate Data

When we have **big data** that contains many variables, the plot types in `Chapter 4`, *Visualizing Online Data* may no longer be an effective way of data visualization. We may try to cramp as many variables in a single plot as possible, but the overcrowded or cluttered details would quickly reach the boundary of a human's visual perception capabilities.

In this chapter, we aim to introduce multivariate data visualization techniques; they enable us to better understand the distribution of data and the relationships between variables. Here is the outline of this chapter:

- Getting End-of-Day (EOD) stock data from Quandl
- Two-dimensional faceted plots:
    - Factor plot in Seaborn
    - Faceted grid in Seaborn
    - Pair plot in Seaborn
- Other two-dimensional multivariate plots:
    - Heatmap in Seaborn
    - Candlestick plot in matplotlib.finance:
        - Visualizing various stock market indicators
    - Building a comprehensive stock chart
- Three-dimensional plots:
    - Scatter plot
    - Bar chart
    - Caveats of using Matplotlib 3D

First, we will discuss faceted plots, which is a divide-and-conquer approach to visualizing multivariate data. The gestalt of this approach is to slice input data into different facets such that only a handful of attributes will be represented in each visualization panel. This will reduce visual clutter by allowing inspection of variables in reduced subsets. Sometimes, finding a suitable way to represent multivariate data in a 2D graph is difficult. Therefore, we are going to introduce 3D plotting functions in Matplotlib as well. All the source codes of this chapter can be found at `https://github.com/PacktPublishing/Matplotlib-2.x-By-Example`.

The data used in this chapter was collected from Quandl's End-of-Day (EOD) stock database. Let's get the data from Quandl first.

Getting End-of-Day (EOD) stock data from Quandl

Since we are going to discuss stock data extensively, note that we do not guarantee the accuracy, completeness, or validity of the content presented; nor are we responsible for any errors or omissions that may have occurred. The data, visualizations, and analyses are provided on an "as is" basis for educational purposes only, without any representations, warranties, or conditions of any kind. Therefore, the publisher and the authors do not accept liability for your use of the content. It should be noted that past stock performance may not predict future performance. Readers should also be aware of the risks involved in stock investments and should not take any investment decisions based on the content in this chapter. In addition, readers are advised to conduct their own independent research into individual stocks before making a investment decision.

We are going to adapt the Quandl JSON API code in `Chapter 4`, *Visualizing Online Data* to get EOD stock data from Quandl. The historical stock data from January 1, 2017 to June 30, 2017 for six stock codes will be obtained: Apple Inc.(EOD/AAPL), The Procter & Gamble Company (EOD/PG), Johnson & Johnson (EOD/JNJ), Exxon Mobil Corporation (EOD/XOM), International Business Machines Corporation (EOD/IBM), and Microsoft Corporation (EOD/MSFT). Again, we will use the default `urllib` and `json` modules to handle Quandl API calls, followed by converting the data into a Pandas DataFrame:

```
from urllib.request import urlopen
import json
import pandas as pd
```

```
def get_quandl_dataset(api_key, code, start_date, end_date):
    """Obtain and parse a quandl dataset in Pandas DataFrame format

    Quandl returns dataset in JSON format, where data is stored as a
    list of lists in response['dataset']['data'], and column headers
    stored in response['dataset']['column_names'].
    Args:
        api_key: Quandl API key
        code: Quandl dataset code

    Returns:
        df: Pandas DataFrame of a Quandl dataset

    """
    base_url = "https://www.quandl.com/api/v3/datasets/"
    url_suffix = ".json?api_key="
    date = "&start_date={}&end_date={}".format(start_date, end_date)

    # Fetch the JSON response
    u = urlopen(base_url + code + url_suffix + api_key + date)
    response = json.loads(u.read().decode('utf-8'))
    # Format the response as Pandas Dataframe
    df = pd.DataFrame(response['dataset']['data'],
columns=response['dataset']
    ['column_names'])
    return df

# Input your own API key here
api_key = "INSERT YOUR KEY HERE"

# Quandl code for six US companies
codes = ["EOD/AAPL", "EOD/PG", "EOD/JNJ", "EOD/XOM", "EOD/IBM", "EOD/MSFT"]
start_date = "2017-01-01"
end_date = "2017-06-30"

dfs = []
# Get the DataFrame that contains the EOD data for each company
for code in codes:
    df = get_quandl_dataset(api_key, code, start_date, end_date)
    df["Company"] = code[4:]
    dfs.append(df)

# Concatenate all dataframes into a single one
stock_df = pd.concat(dfs)

# Sort by ascending order of Company then Date
stock_df = stock_df.sort_values(["Company","Date"])
stock_df.head()
```

-	Date	Open	High	Low	Close	Volume	Dividend	Split	Adj_Open	Adj_High	Adj_Low	Adj_Close	Adj_Volume	Company
124	2017-01-03	115.80	116.3300	114.76	116.15	28781865.0	0.0	1.0	114.833750	115.359328	113.802428	115.180830	28781865.0	AAPL
123	2017-01-04	115.85	116.5100	115.75	116.02	21118116.0	0.0	1.0	114.883333	115.537826	114.784167	115.051914	21118116.0	AAPL
122	2017-01-05	115.92	116.8642	115.81	116.61	22193587.0	0.0	1.0	114.952749	115.889070	114.843667	115.636991	22193587.0	AAPL
121	2017-01-06	116.78	118.1600	116.47	117.91	31751900.0	0.0	1.0	115.805573	117.174058	115.498159	116.926144	31751900.0	AAPL
120	2017-01-09	117.95	119.4300	117.94	118.99	33561948.0	0.0	1.0	116.965810	118.433461	116.955894	117.997132	33561948.0	AAPL

The dataframe contains **Opening, High, Low, and Closing** (**OHLC**) prices for each stock. Extra information is also available; for example, the dividend column reflects the cash dividend value on that day. The split column shows the ratio of new shares to old shares if a split occurred on that day. The adjusted prices account for price fluctuations due to distributions or corporate actions by assuming that all these actions were reinvested into the current stock. For more information about these columns, consult the documentation pages on Quandl.

Grouping the companies by industry

As you may have noticed, three of the companies (AAPL, IBM, and MSFT) are tech companies, while the remaining three companies are not. Stock analysts often group companies by industry to gain deeper insights. Let's try to label the companies by industry:

```
# Classify companies by industry
tech_companies = set(["AAPL","IBM","MSFT"])
stock_df['Industry'] = ["Tech" if c in tech_companies else "Others" for c
in stock_df['Company']]
```

Converting the date to a supported format

The `Date` column in `stock_df` is recorded as a series of Python strings. Although Seaborn can use string-formatted dates in some functions, Matplotlib cannot. To make the dates malleable to data processing and visualizations, we need to convert the values to float numbers supported by Matplotlib:

```
from matplotlib.dates import date2num


# Convert Date column from string to Python datetime object,
# then to float number that is supported by Matplotlib.
stock_df["Datetime"] = date2num(pd.to_datetime(stock_df["Date"],
format="%Y-%m-%d").tolist())
```

Getting the percentage change of the closing price

Next, we want to calculate the change of the closing price with regard to the previous day's close. The `pct_change()` function in Pandas makes this task very easy:

```
import numpy as np


# Calculate percentage change versus the previous close
stock_df["Close_change"] = stock_df["Close"].pct_change()
# Since the DataFrame contain multiple companies' stock data,
# the first record in the "Close_change" should be changed to
# NaN in order to prevent referencing the price of incorrect company.
stock_df.loc[stock_df["Date"]=="2017-01-03", "Close_change"] = np.NaN
stock_df.head()
```

Two-dimensional faceted plots

We are going to introduce three major ways to create faceted plots: `seaborn.factorplot()`, `seaborn.FacetGrid()`, and `seaborn.pairplot()`. You might have seen some faceted plots in the previous chapter, when we talked about `seaborn.lmplot()`. Actually, the `seaborn.lmplot()` function combines `seaborn.regplot()` with `seaborn.FacetGrid()`, and the definitions of data subsets can be adjusted by the `hue`, `col`, and `row` parameters.

We are going to introduce three major ways to create faceted plots: `seaborn.factorplot()`, `seaborn.FacetGrid()`, and `seaborn.pairplot()`. These functions actually work similarly to `seaborn.lmplot()` in the way of defining facets.

Factor plot in Seaborn

With the help of `seaborn.factorplot()`, we can draw categorical point plots, box plots, violin plots, bar plots, or strip plots onto a `seaborn.FacetGrid()` by tuning the `kind` parameter. The default plot type for `factorplot` is point plot. Unlike other plotting functions in Seaborn, which support a wide variety of input data formats, `factorplot` supports pandas DataFrames as input only, while variable/column names can be supplied as string to `x`, `y`, `hue`, `col`, or `row`:

```
import seaborn as sns
import matplotlib.pyplot as plt


sns.set(style="ticks")

# Plot EOD stock closing price vs Date for each company.
# Color of plot elements is determined by company name (hue="Company"),
# plot panels are also arranged in columns accordingly (col="Company").
# The col_wrap parameter determines the number of panels per row
(col_wrap=3).
g = sns.factorplot(x="Date", y="Close",
                   hue="Company", col="Company",
                   data=stock_df, col_wrap=3)

plt.show()
```

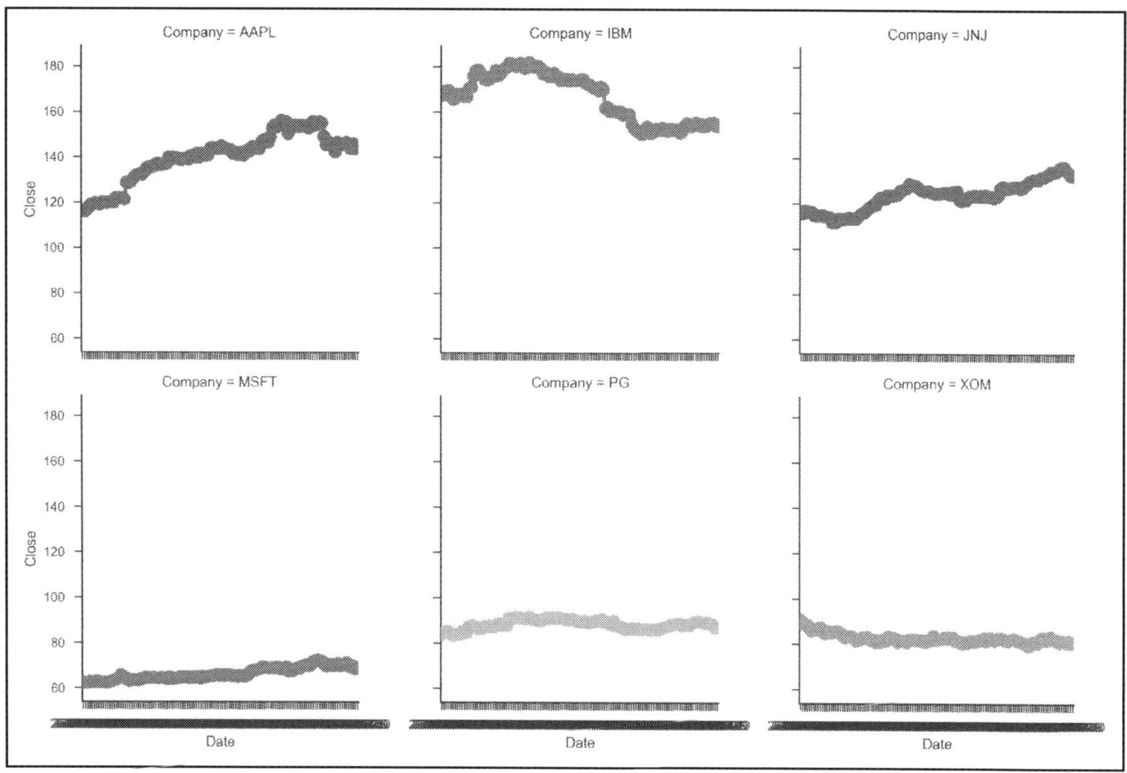

There are several issues in the preceding plot.

First, the aspect ratio (length divided by height) is slightly suboptimal for a time series chart. A wider plot would allow us to observe minute changes during the time period. We are going to adjust that using the `aspect` parameter.

Second, the lines and dots are too thick, thereby masking some details in the plot. We can reduce the size of these visual elements by tweaking the `scale` parameter.

Lastly, the ticks are too close to each other, and the tick labels are overlapping. After plotting, `sns.factorplot()` returns a FacetGrid, which was denoted as `g` in the code. We can further tweak the aesthetics of the plot, such as tick positions and labels, by calling the relevant functions in the `FacetGrid` object:

```
# Increase the aspect ratio and size of each panel
g = sns.factorplot(x="Date", y="Close",
                   hue="Company", col="Company",
                   data=stock_df,
                   col_wrap=3, size=3,
                   scale=0.5, aspect=1.5)

# Thinning of ticks (select 1 in 10)
locs, labels = plt.xticks()
g.set(xticks=locs[0::10], xticklabels=labels[0::10])

# Rotate the tick labels to prevent overlap
g.set_xticklabels(rotation=30)

# Reduce the white space between plots
g.fig.subplots_adjust(wspace=.1, hspace=.2)
plt.show()
```

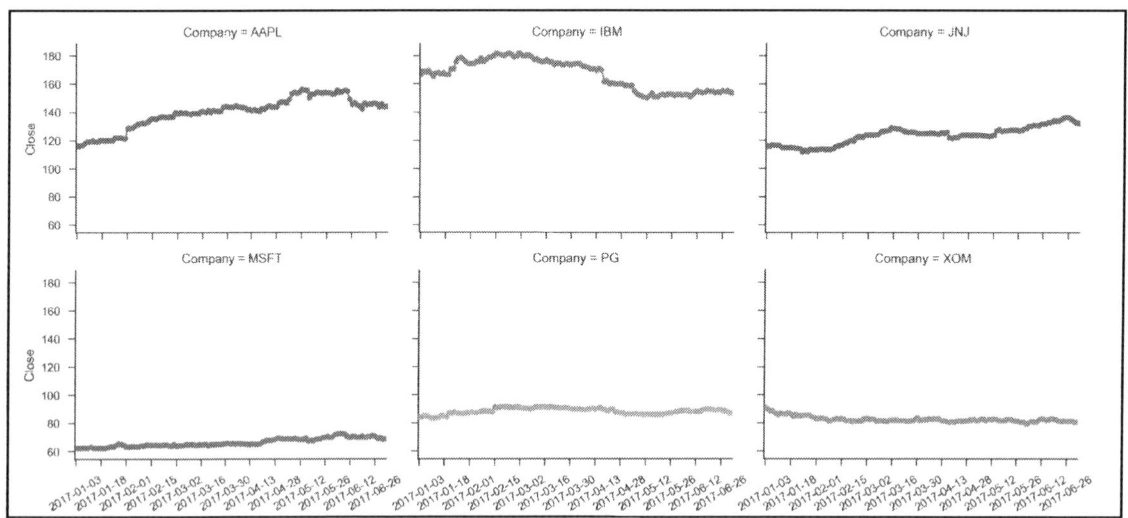

```
# Create faceted plot separated by industry
g = sns.factorplot(x="Date", y="Close",
                   hue="Company", col="Industry",
                   data=stock_df, size=4,
                   aspect=1.5, scale=0.5)

locs, labels = plt.xticks()
g.set(xticks=locs[0::10], xticklabels=labels[0::10])
g.set_xticklabels(rotation=30)
plt.show()
```

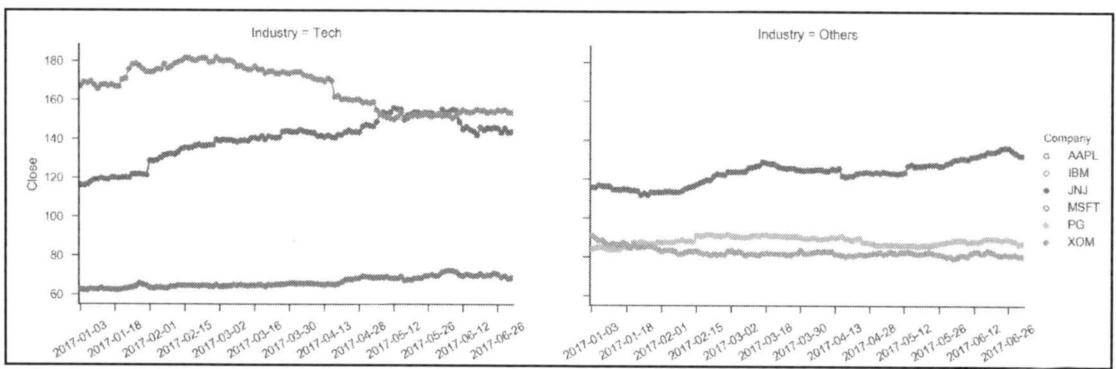

Faceted grid in Seaborn

Up until now, we have already mentioned `FacetGrid` a few times, but what exactly is it?

As you may know, `FacetGrid` is an engine for subsetting data and drawing plot panels determined by assigning variables to the rows and columns of `hue` parameters. While we can use wrapper functions such as `lmplot` and `factorplot` to scaffold plots on `FacetGrid` easily, it would be more flexible to build FacetGrid from scratch. To do that, we first supply a pandas DataFrame to the `FacetGrid` object and specify the way to lay out the grid via `col`, `row`, and `hue` parameters. Then we can assign a Seaborn or Matplotlib plotting function to each panel by calling the `map()` function of the `FacetGrid` object:

```
# Create a FacetGrid
g = sns.FacetGrid(stock_df, col="Company", hue="Company",
                  size=3, aspect=2, col_wrap=2)

# Map the seaborn.distplot function to the panels,
# which shows a histogram of closing prices.
g.map(sns.distplot, "Close")
```

```
# Label the axes
g.set_axis_labels("Closing price (US Dollars)", "Density")

plt.show()
```

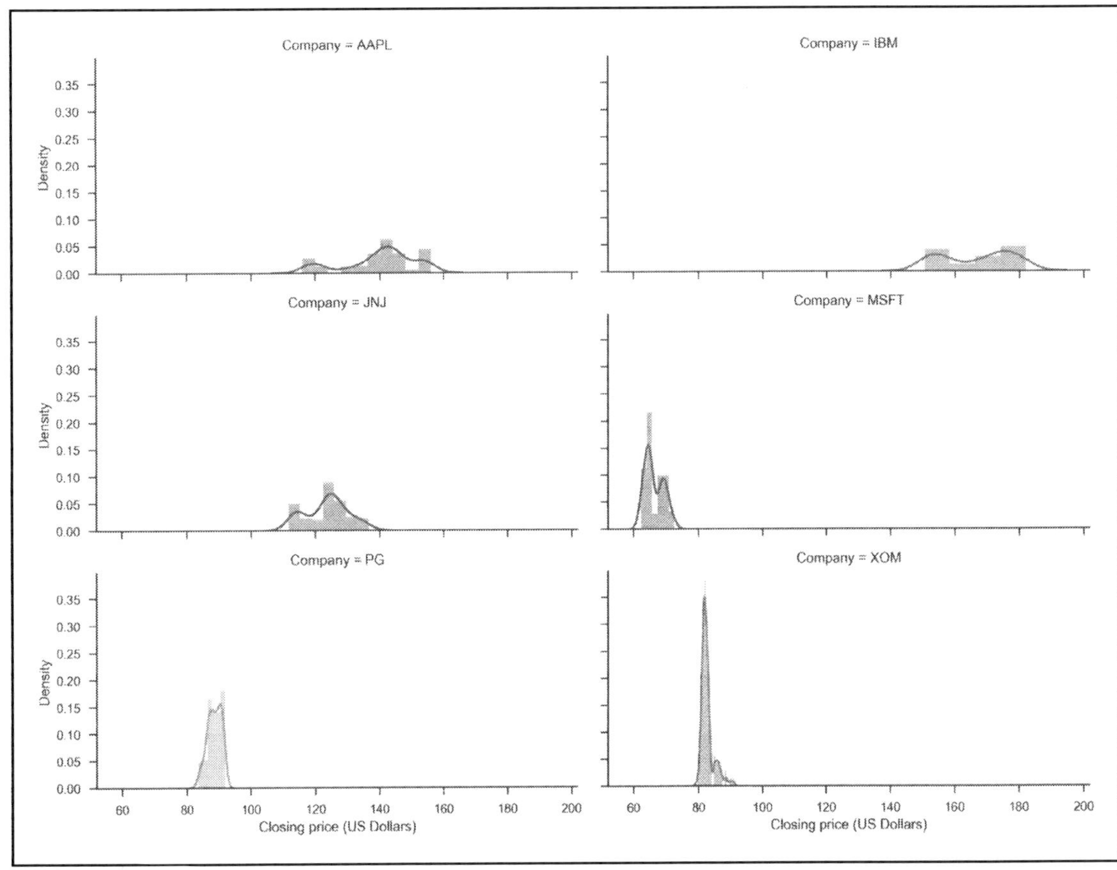

We can also supply keyword arguments to the plotting functions:

```
g = sns.FacetGrid(stock_df, col="Company", hue="Company",
                  size=3, aspect=2.2, col_wrap=2)

# We can supply extra kwargs to the plotting function.
# Let's turn off KDE line (kde=False), and plot raw
# frequency of bins only (norm_hist=False).
# By setting rug=True, tick marks that denotes the
# density of data points will be shown in the bottom.
g.map(sns.distplot, "Close", kde=False, norm_hist=False, rug=True)

g.set_axis_labels("Closing price (US Dollars)", "Density")

plt.show()
```

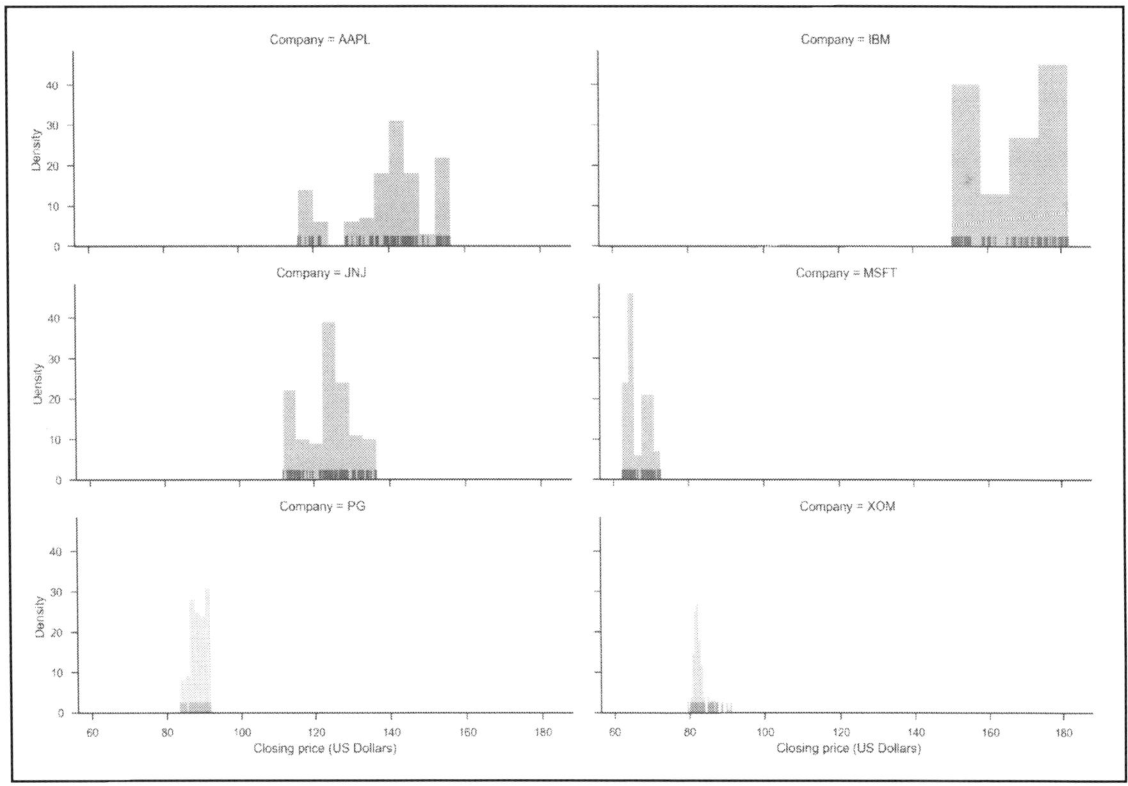

`FacetGrid` is not limited to the use of Seaborn plotting functions; let's try to map the good old `Matplotlib.pyplot.plot()` function to `FacetGrid`:

```
from matplotlib.dates import DateFormatter


g = sns.FacetGrid(stock_df, hue="Company", col="Industry",
                  size=4, aspect=1.5, col_wrap=2)

# plt.plot doesn't support string-formatted Date,
# so we need to use the Datetime column that we
# prepared earlier instead.
g.map(plt.plot, "Datetime", "Close", marker="o", markersize=3, linewidth=1)
g.add_legend()

# We can access individual axes through g.axes[column]
# or g.axes[row,column] if multiple rows are present.
# Let's adjust the tick formatter and rotate the tick labels
# in each axes.
for col in range(2):
    g.axes[col].xaxis.set_major_formatter(DateFormatter('%Y-%m-%d'))
    plt.setp(g.axes[col].get_xticklabels(), rotation=30)

g.set_axis_labels("", "Closing price (US Dollars)")
plt.show()
```

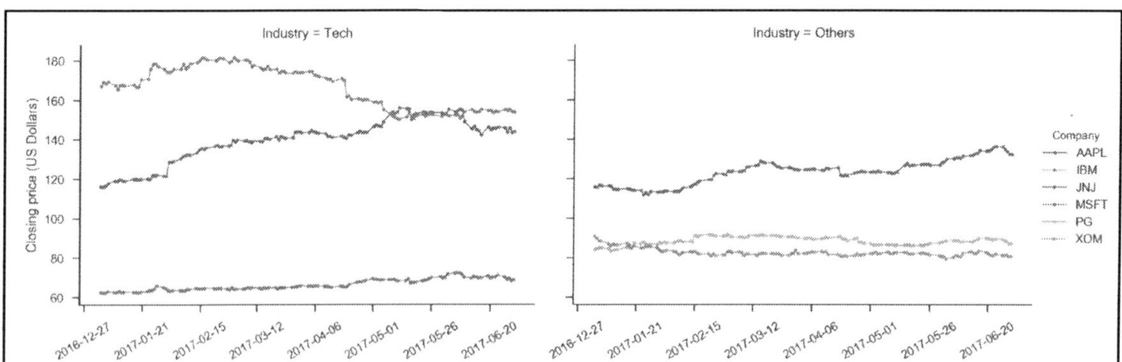

Pair plot in Seaborn

A pair plot is a special type of `FacetGrid`. Pairwise relationships between all variables in the input DataFrame will be visualized as scatter plots. In addition, a series of histograms will be displayed along the diagonal axes to show the distribution of the variable in that column:

```
# Show a pairplot of three selected variables (vars=["Open", "Volume",
"Close"])
g = sns.pairplot(stock_df, hue="Company",
                 vars=["Open", "Volume", "Close"])

plt.show()
```

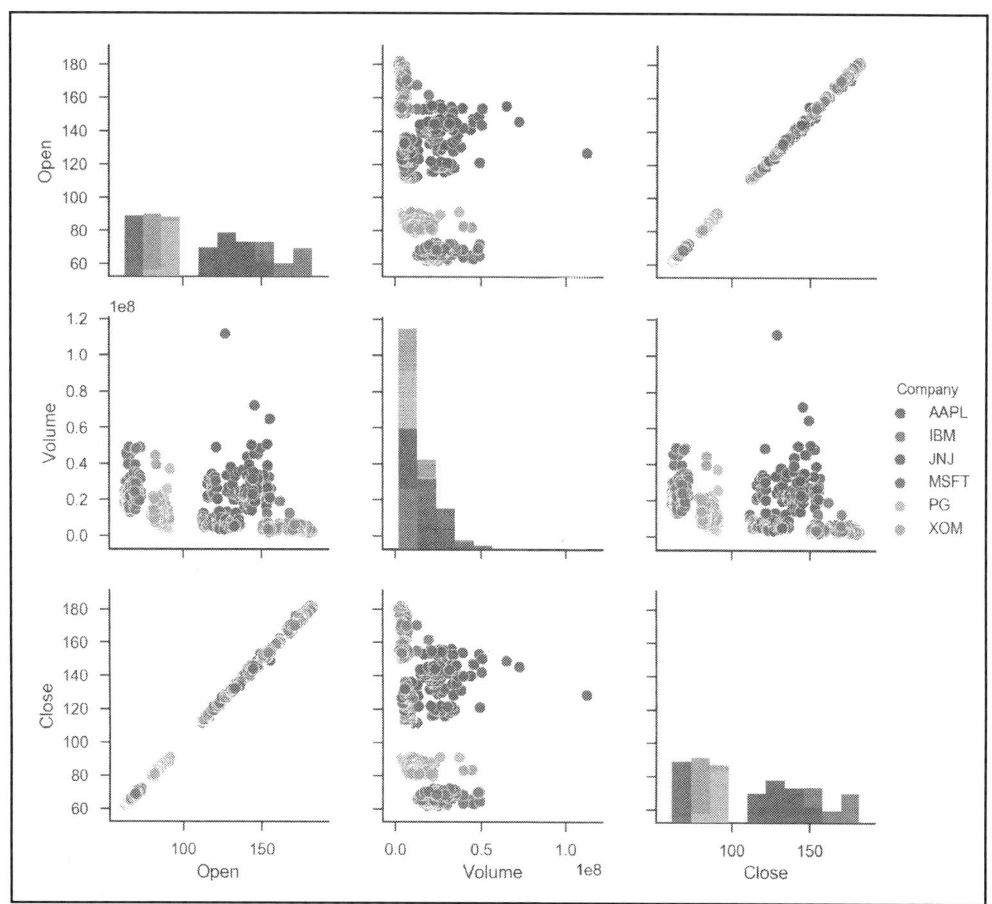

We can tweak many aspects of the plot. In the next example, we will increase the aspect ratio, change the plot type in the diagonal line to KDE plot, and adjust the aesthetics of the plots using keyword arguments:

```
# Adjust the aesthetics of the plot
g = sns.pairplot(stock_df, hue="Company",
                 aspect=1.5, diag_kind="kde",
                 diag_kws=dict(shade=True),
                 plot_kws=dict(s=15, marker="+"),
                 vars=["Open", "Volume", "Close"])

plt.show()
```

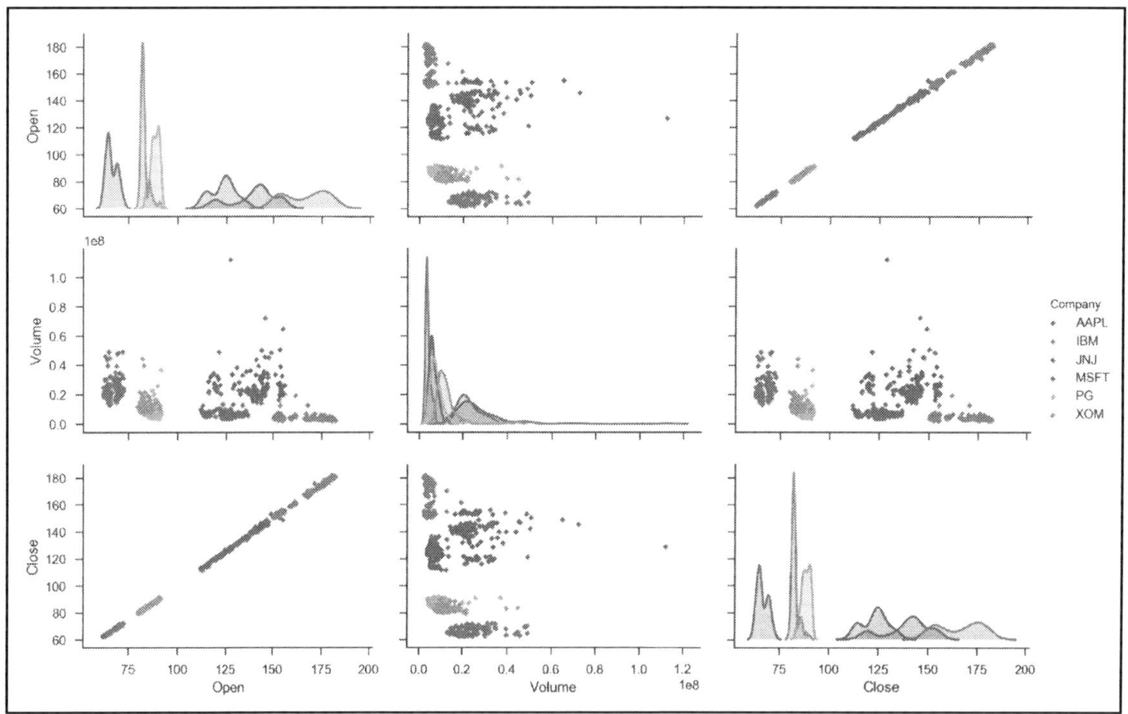

Similar to other plots based on `FacetGrid`, we can define the variables to be displayed in each panel. We can also manually define the comparisons that matter to us instead of an all-versus-all comparison by setting the `x_vars` and `y_vars` parameters. You may also use `seaborn.PairGrid()` directly if you require even higher flexibility for defining comparison groups:

```
# Manually defining the comparisons that we are interested.
g = sns.pairplot(stock_df, hue="Company", aspect=1.5,
                 x_vars=["Open", "Volume"],
                 y_vars=["Close", "Close_change"])

plt.show()
```

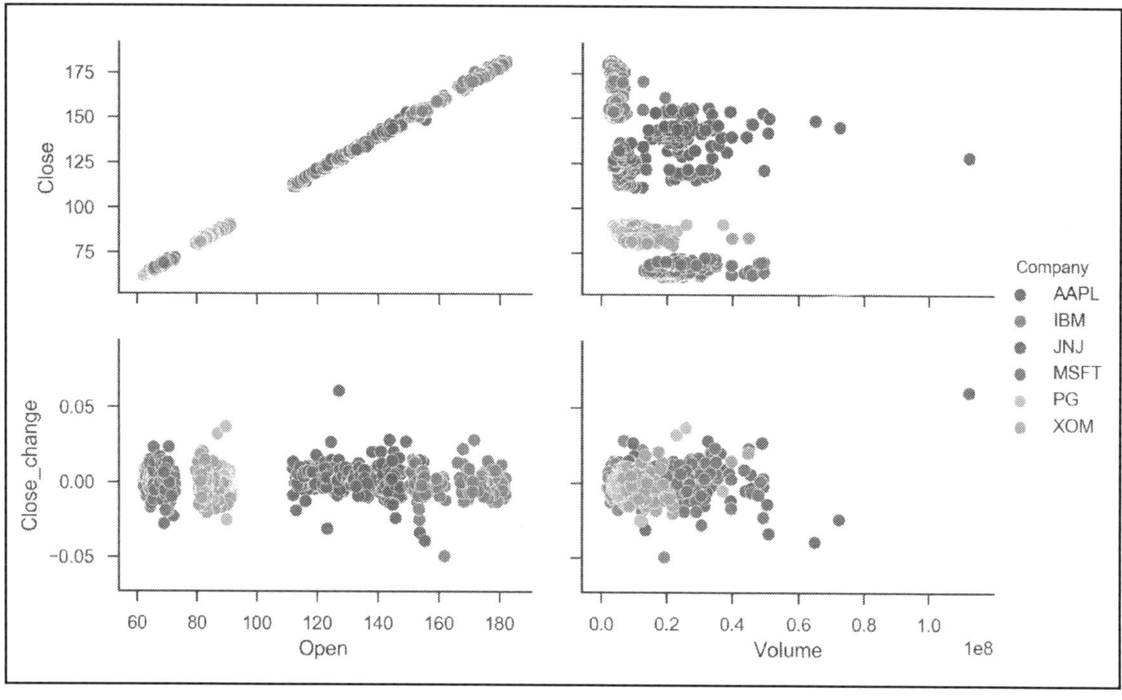

Other two-dimensional multivariate plots

FacetGrid, factor plot, and pair plot may take up a lot of space when we need to visualize more variables or samples. There are two special plot types that come in handy if you want the maximize space efficiency--Heatmaps and Candlestick plots.

Heatmap in Seaborn

A heatmap is an extremely compact way to display a large amount of data. In the finance world, color-coded blocks can give investors a quick glance at which stocks are up or down. In the scientific world, heatmaps allow researchers to visualize the expression level of thousands of genes.

The `seaborn.heatmap()` function expects a 2D list, 2D Numpy array, or pandas DataFrame as input. If a list or array is supplied, we can supply column and row labels via `xticklabels` and `yticklabels` respectively. On the other hand, if a DataFrame is supplied, the column labels and index values will be used to label the columns and rows respectively.

To get started, we will plot an overview of the performance of the six stocks using a heatmap. We define stock performance as the change of closing price when compared to the previous close. This piece of information was already calculated earlier in this chapter (that is, the `Close_change` column). Unfortunately, we can't supply the whole DataFrame to `seaborn.heatmap()` directly, since it expects company names as columns, date as index, and the change in closing price as values.

If you are familiar with Microsoft Excel, you might have experience in using pivot tables, a powerful technique to summarize the levels or values of a particular variable. pandas includes such functionality. The following code excerpt makes use of the wonderful `Pandas.DataFrame.pivot()` function to make a pivot table:

```
stock_change = stock_df.pivot(index='Date', columns='Company',
values='Close_change')
stock_change = stock_change.loc["2017-06-01":"2017-06-30"]
stock_change.head()
```

Company Date	AAPL	IBM	JNJ	MSFT	PG	XOM
2017-06-01	0.002749	0.000262	0.004133	0.003723	0.000454	0.002484
2017-06-02	0.014819	-0.004061	0.010095	0.023680	0.005220	-0.014870
2017-06-05	-0.009778	0.002368	0.002153	0.007246	0.001693	0.007799

2017-06-06	0.003378	-0.000262	0.003605	0.003320	0.000676	0.013605
2017-06-07	0.005957	-0.009123	-0.000611	-0.001793	-0.000338	-0.003694

With the pivot table ready, we can proceed to plot our first heatmap:

```
ax = sns.heatmap(stock_change)
plt.show()
```

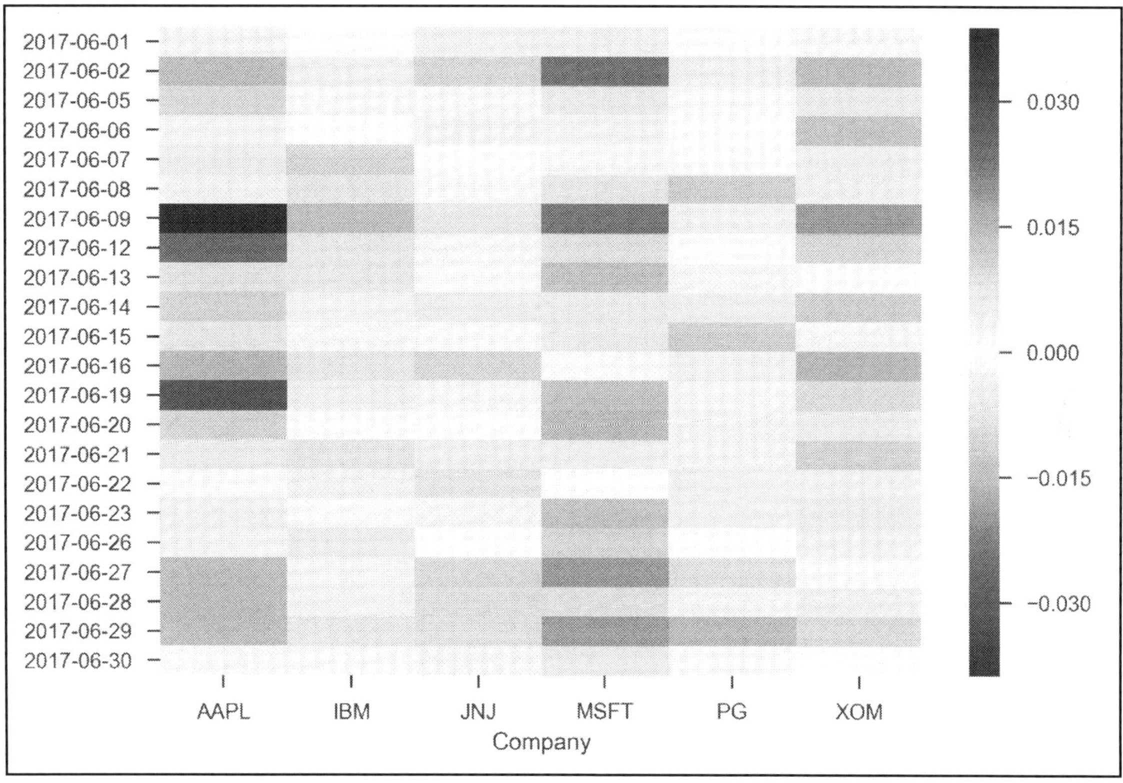

The default heatmap implementation is not really compact enough. Of course, we can resize the figure via `plt.figure(figsize=(width, height))`; we can also toggle the square parameter to create square-shaped blocks. To ease visual recognition, we can add a thin border around the blocks.

By US stock market convention, green denotes a rise and red denotes a fall in prices. Hence we can adjust the `cmap` parameter to adjust the color map. However, neither Matplotlib nor Seaborn includes a red-green color map, so we need to create our own:

At the end of `Chapter 4`, *Visualizing Online Data*, we briefly introduced functions for creating custom color maps. Here we will use `seaborn.diverging_palette()` to create the red-green color map, which requires us to specify the hues, saturation, and lightness (husl) for the negative and positive extents of the color map. You may also use this code to launch an interactive widget in Jupyter Notebook to help select the colors:

```
%matplotlib notebook
import seaborn as sns

sns.choose_diverging_palette(as_cmap=True)
```

```
# Create a new red-green color map using the husl color system
# h_neg and h_pos determines the hue of the extents of the color map.
# s determines the color saturation
# l determines the lightness
# sep determines the width of center point
# In addition, we need to set as_cmap=True as the cmap parameter of
# sns.heatmap expects matplotlib colormap object.
rdgn = sns.diverging_palette(h_neg=10, h_pos=140, s=80, l=50,
                             sep=10, as_cmap=True)

# Change to square blocks (square=True), add a thin
# border (linewidths=.5), and change the color map
# to follow US stocks market convention (cmap="RdGn").
ax = sns.heatmap(stock_change, cmap=rdgn,
                 linewidths=.5, square=True)

# Prevent x axes label from being cropped
plt.tight_layout()
plt.show()
```

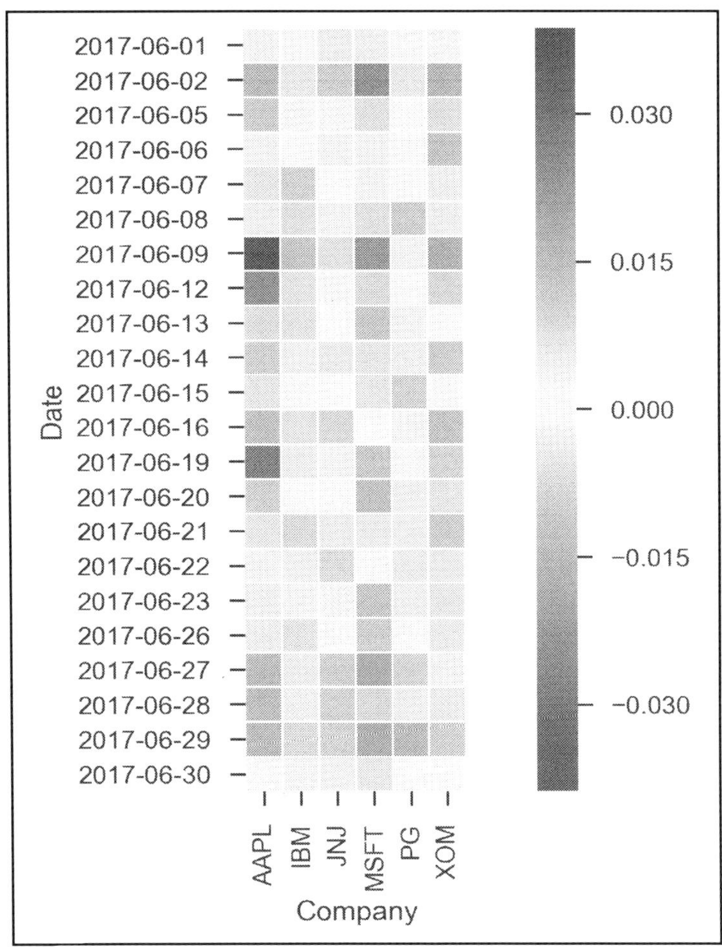

2017-06-01
2017-06-02
2017-06-05
2017-06-06
2017-06-07
2017-06-08
2017-06-09
2017-06-12
2017-06-13
2017-06-14
2017-06-15
2017-06-16
2017-06-19
2017-06-20
2017-06-21
2017-06-22
2017-06-23
2017-06-26
2017-06-27
2017-06-28
2017-06-29
2017-06-30
Date
AAPL
IBM
JNJ
MSFT
PG
XOM
Company
0.030
0.015
0.000
−0.015
−0.030

It could be hard to discern small differences in values when color is the only discriminative factor. Adding text annotations to each color block may help readers understand the magnitude of the difference:

```
fig = plt.figure(figsize=(6,8))

# Set annot=True to overlay the values.
# We can also assign python format string to fmt.
# For example ".2%" refers to percentage values with
# two decimal points.
ax = sns.heatmap(stock_change, cmap=rdgn,
                 annot=True, fmt=".2%",
                 linewidths=.5, cbar=False)
plt.show()
```

	AAPL	IBM	JNJ	MSFT	PG	XOM
17-06-01	0.27%	0.03%	0.41%	0.37%	0.05%	0.25%
17-06-02	1.48%	-0.41%	1.01%	2.37%	0.52%	-1.49%
17-06-05	-0.98%	0.24%	0.22%	0.72%	0.17%	0.78%
17-06-06	0.34%	-0.03%	0.36%	0.33%	0.07%	1.36%
17-06-07	0.60%	-0.91%	-0.06%	-0.18%	-0.03%	-0.37%
17-06-08	-0.24%	0.74%	-0.15%	-0.61%	-1.04%	-0.36%
17-06-09	-3.88%	1.31%	0.75%	-2.27%	0.35%	1.87%
17-06-12	-2.39%	0.70%	0.22%	-0.77%	0.09%	0.97%
17-06-13	0.80%	-0.60%	0.15%	1.25%	-0.20%	0.04%
17-06-14	-0.98%	-0.29%	0.57%	-0.54%	0.43%	-1.07%
17-06-15	-0.60%	0.27%	0.20%	-0.53%	1.06%	0.23%
17-06-16	-1.40%	0.75%	0.98%	0.14%	0.31%	1.50%
17-06-19	2.86%	-0.35%	-0.21%	1.24%	0.22%	-0.87%
17-06-20	-0.91%	0.07%	0.11%	-1.35%	-0.26%	-0.54%
17-06-21	0.59%	-0.75%	0.51%	0.51%	-0.26%	-1.06%
17-06-22	-0.16%	0.40%	0.85%	-0.01%	-0.41%	-0.44%
17-06-23	0.45%	-0.19%	0.28%	1.35%	0.44%	0.65%
17-06-26	-0.31%	0.73%	-0.07%	-0.95%	-0.07%	-0.45%
17-06-27	-1.43%	-0.31%	-0.98%	-1.87%	-0.84%	-0.16%
17-06-28	1.46%	0.37%	-0.88%	0.85%	-0.27%	0.52%
17-06-29	-1.47%	-0.77%	-0.88%	-1.88%	-1.56%	-1.02%
17-06-30	0.24%	-0.19%	-0.26%	0.64%	0.18%	0.04%

Company

Candlestick plot in matplotlib.finance

As you have seen in the first part of this chapter, our dataset contains the opening and closing prices as well as the highest and lowest price per trading day. None of the plots we have described thus far are able to describe the trend of all these variables in a single plot.

In the financial world, the candlestick plot is almost the default choice for describing price movements of stocks, currencies, and commodities over a time period. Each candlestick consists of the body, describing the opening and closing prices, and extended wicks illustrating the highest and lowest prices of a particular trading day. If the closing price is higher than the opening price, the candlestick is often colored black. Conversely, the candlestick is colored red if the closing price is lower. The trader can then infer the opening and closing prices based on the combination of color and the boundary of the candlestick body.

In the following example, we are going to prepare a candlestick chart of Apple Incorporation in the last 50 trading days of our DataFrame. We will also apply the tick formatter (see `Chapter 2`, *Figure Aesthetics* for more details) to label the ticks as dates:

```
import matplotlib.pyplot as plt
from matplotlib.dates import date2num, WeekdayLocator, DayLocator,
DateFormatter, MONDAY
from matplotlib.finance import candlestick_ohlc


# Extract stocks data for AAPL.
# candlestick_ohlc expects Date (in floating point number), Open, High,
Low,
# Close columns only
# So we need to select the useful columns first using DataFrame.loc[].
Extra
# columns can exist,
# but they are ignored. Next we get the data for the last 50 trading only
for
# simplicity of plots.
candlestick_data = stock_df[stock_df["Company"]=="AAPL"]\
                   .loc[:, ["Datetime", "Open", "High", "Low", "Close",
                   "Volume"]]\
                   .iloc[-50:]

# Create a new Matplotlib figure
fig, ax = plt.subplots()

# Prepare a candlestick plot
candlestick_ohlc(ax, candlestick_data.values, width=0.6)
```

```
ax.xaxis.set_major_locator(WeekdayLocator(MONDAY)) # major ticks on the
mondays
ax.xaxis.set_minor_locator(DayLocator()) # minor ticks on the days
ax.xaxis.set_major_formatter(DateFormatter('%Y-%m-%d'))
ax.xaxis_date() # treat the x data as dates
# rotate all ticks to vertical
plt.setp(ax.get_xticklabels(), rotation=90, horizontalalignment='right')

ax.set_ylabel('Price (US $)') # Set y-axis label
plt.show()
```

Starting from Matplotlib 2.0, `matplotlib.finance` is deprecated. Readers should use `mpl_finance` (`https://github.com/matplotlib/mpl_finance`) in the future instead. However, as of writing this chapter, `mpl_finance` is not yet available on PyPI, so let's stick to `matplotlib.finance` for the time being.

Visualizing various stock market indicators

The candlestick plot in the current form is a bit bland. Traders usually overlay stock indicators such as **Average True Range (ATR)**, Bollinger band, **Commodity Channel Index (CCI)**, **Exponential Moving Average (EMA)**, **Moving Average Convergence Divergence (MACD)**, **Relative Strength Index (RSI)**, and various other stats for technical analysis.

Stockstats (`https://github.com/jealous/stockstats`) is a great package for calculating these indicators/stats and many more. It wraps around pandas DataFrames and generate the stats on the fly when they are accessed. To use `stockstats`, we simply install it via PyPI: `pip install stockstats`.

Next, we can convert a pandas DataFrame to a stockstats DataFrame via `stockstats.StockDataFrame.retype()`. A plethora of stock indicators can then be accessed by following the pattern `StockDataFrame["variable_timeWindow_indicator"]`. For example, `StockDataFrame['open_2_sma']` would give us the 2-day simple moving average on the opening price. Shortcuts may be available for some indicators, so please consult the official documentation for more information:

```
from stockstats import StockDataFrame


# Convert to StockDataFrame
# Need to pass a copy of candlestick_data to StockDataFrame.retype
# Otherwise the original candlestick_data will be modified
stockstats = StockDataFrame.retype(candlestick_data.copy())

# 5-day exponential moving average on closing price
ema_5 = stockstats["close_5_ema"]
# 20-day exponential moving average on closing price
ema_20 = stockstats["close_20_ema"]
# 50-day exponential moving average on closing price
ema_50 = stockstats["close_50_ema"]
# Upper Bollinger band
boll_ub = stockstats["boll_ub"]
# Lower Bollinger band
boll_lb = stockstats["boll_lb"]
# 7-day Relative Strength Index
rsi_7 = stockstats['rsi_7']
# 14-day Relative Strength Index
rsi_14 = stockstats['rsi_14']
```

With the stock indicators ready, we can overlay them on the same candlestick chart:

```
import datetime
import matplotlib.pyplot as plt
from matplotlib.dates import date2num, WeekdayLocator, DayLocator,
DateFormatter, MONDAY
from matplotlib.finance import candlestick_ohlc


# Create a new Matplotlib figure
fig, ax = plt.subplots()

# Prepare a candlestick plot
candlestick_ohlc(ax, candlestick_data.values, width=0.6)

# Plot stock indicators in the same plot
ax.plot(candlestick_data["Datetime"], ema_5, lw=1, label='EMA (5)')
ax.plot(candlestick_data["Datetime"], ema_20, lw=1, label='EMA (20)')
ax.plot(candlestick_data["Datetime"], ema_50, lw=1, label='EMA (50)')
ax.plot(candlestick_data["Datetime"], boll_ub, lw=2, linestyle="--",
label='Bollinger upper')
ax.plot(candlestick_data["Datetime"], boll_lb, lw=2, linestyle="--",
label='Bollinger lower')

ax.xaxis.set_major_locator(WeekdayLocator(MONDAY)) # major ticks on
# the mondays
ax.xaxis.set_minor_locator(DayLocator()) # minor ticks on the days
ax.xaxis.set_major_formatter(DateFormatter('%Y-%m-%d'))
ax.xaxis_date() # treat the x data as dates
# rotate all ticks to vertical
plt.setp(ax.get_xticklabels(), rotation=90, horizontalalignment='right')

ax.set_ylabel('Price (US $)') # Set y-axis label

# Limit the x-axis range from 2017-4-23 to 2017-7-1
datemin = datetime.date(2017, 4, 23)
datemax = datetime.date(2017, 7, 1)
ax.set_xlim(datemin, datemax)

plt.legend() # Show figure legend
plt.tight_layout()
plt.show()
```

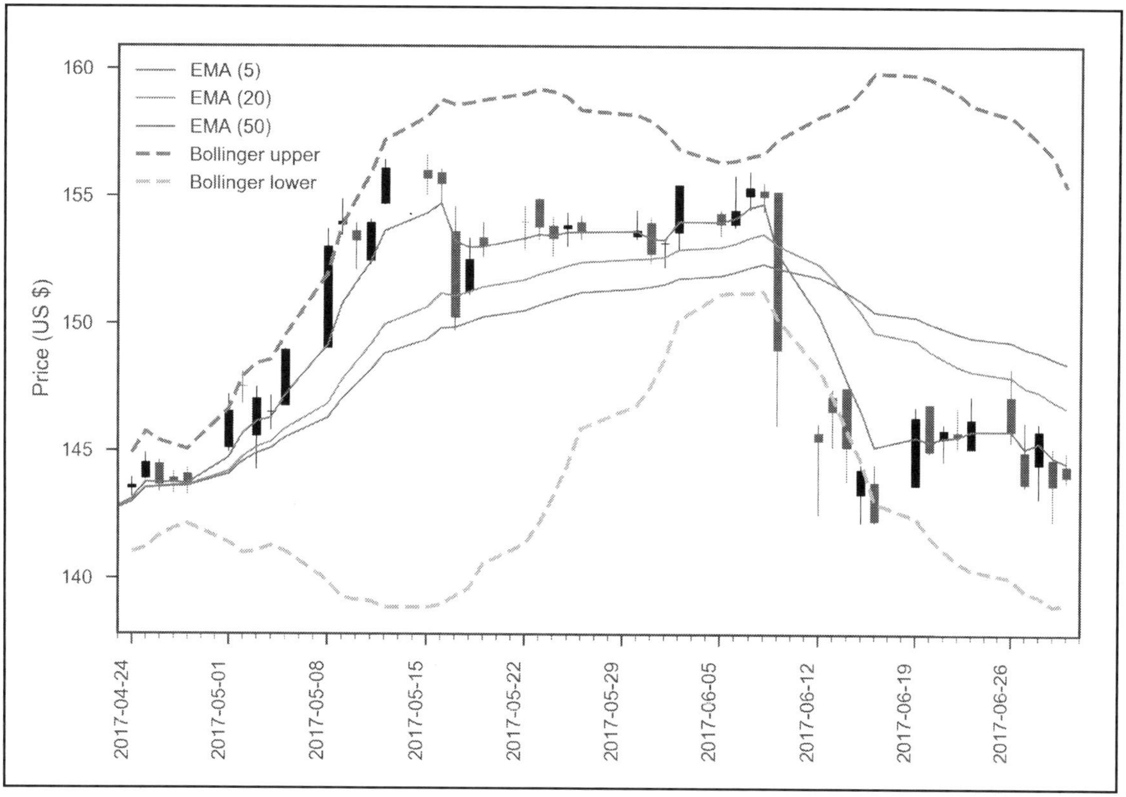

Building a comprehensive stock chart

In the following elaborate example, we are going to apply the many techniques that we have covered thus far to create a more comprehensive stock chart. In addition to the preceding plot, we will add a line chart to display the **Relative Strength Index** (**RSI**) and a bar chart to show trade volume. A special market event (`http://markets.businessinsider.com/news/stocks/apple-stock-price-falling-new-iphone-speed-2017-6-1002082799`) is going to be annotated on the chart as well:

If you look closely at the charts, you might notice some missing dates. These days are usually non-trading days or public holidays that were not present in our DataFrame.

```
import datetime
import matplotlib.pyplot as plt
from matplotlib.dates import date2num, WeekdayLocator, DayLocator,
```

```
DateFormatter, MONDAY
from matplotlib.finance import candlestick_ohlc
from matplotlib.ticker import FuncFormatter


# FuncFormatter to convert tick values to Millions
def millions(x, pos):
    return '%dM' % (x/1e6)

# Create 3 subplots spread acrosee three rows, with shared x-axis.
# The height ratio is specified via gridspec_kw
fig, axarr = plt.subplots(nrows=3, ncols=1, sharex=True, figsize=(8,8),
                          gridspec_kw={'height_ratios':[3,1,1]})

# Prepare a candlestick plot in the first axes
candlestick_ohlc(axarr[0], candlestick_data.values, width=0.6)

# Overlay stock indicators in the first axes
axarr[0].plot(candlestick_data["Datetime"], ema_5, lw=1, label='EMA (5)')
axarr[0].plot(candlestick_data["Datetime"], ema_20, lw=1, label='EMA (20)')
axarr[0].plot(candlestick_data["Datetime"], ema_50, lw=1, label='EMA (50)')
axarr[0].plot(candlestick_data["Datetime"], boll_ub, lw=2, linestyle="--",
label='Bollinger upper')
axarr[0].plot(candlestick_data["Datetime"], boll_lb, lw=2, linestyle="--",
label='Bollinger lower')

# Display RSI in the second axes
axarr[1].axhline(y=30, lw=2, color = '0.7') # Line for oversold threshold
axarr[1].axhline(y=50, lw=2, linestyle="--", color = '0.8') # Neutral RSI
axarr[1].axhline(y=70, lw=2, color = '0.7') # Line for overbought threshold
axarr[1].plot(candlestick_data["Datetime"], rsi_7, lw=2, label='RSI (7)')
axarr[1].plot(candlestick_data["Datetime"], rsi_14, lw=2, label='RSI (14)')

# Display trade volume in the third axes
axarr[2].bar(candlestick_data["Datetime"], candlestick_data['Volume'])

# Mark the market reaction to the Bloomberg news
# https://www.bloomberg.com/news/articles/2017-06-09/apple-s-new
# -iphones-said-to-miss-out-on-higher-speed-data-links
# http://markets.businessinsider.com/news/stocks/apple-stock-price
# -falling-new-iphone-speed-2017-6-1002082799
axarr[0].annotate("Bloomberg News",
                  xy=(datetime.date(2017, 6, 9), 155), xycoords='data',
                  xytext=(25, 10), textcoords='offset points', size=12,
                  arrowprops=dict(arrowstyle="simple",
                  fc="green", ec="none"))

# Label the axes
```

```
axarr[0].set_ylabel('Price (US $)')
axarr[1].set_ylabel('RSI')
axarr[2].set_ylabel('Volume (US $)')

axarr[2].xaxis.set_major_locator(WeekdayLocator(MONDAY)) # major ticks on
the mondays
axarr[2].xaxis.set_minor_locator(DayLocator()) # minor ticks on the days
axarr[2].xaxis.set_major_formatter(DateFormatter('%Y-%m-%d'))
axarr[2].xaxis_date() # treat the x data as dates
axarr[2].yaxis.set_major_formatter(FuncFormatter(millions)) # Change the y-
axis ticks to millions
plt.setp(axarr[2].get_xticklabels(), rotation=90,
horizontalalignment='right') # Rotate x-tick labels by 90 degree

# Limit the x-axis range from 2017-4-23 to 2017-7-1
datemin = datetime.date(2017, 4, 23)
datemax = datetime.date(2017, 7, 1)
axarr[2].set_xlim(datemin, datemax)

# Show figure legend
axarr[0].legend()
axarr[1].legend()

# Show figure title
axarr[0].set_title("AAPL (Apple Inc.) NASDAQ", loc='left')

# Reduce unneccesary white space
plt.tight_layout()
plt.show()
```

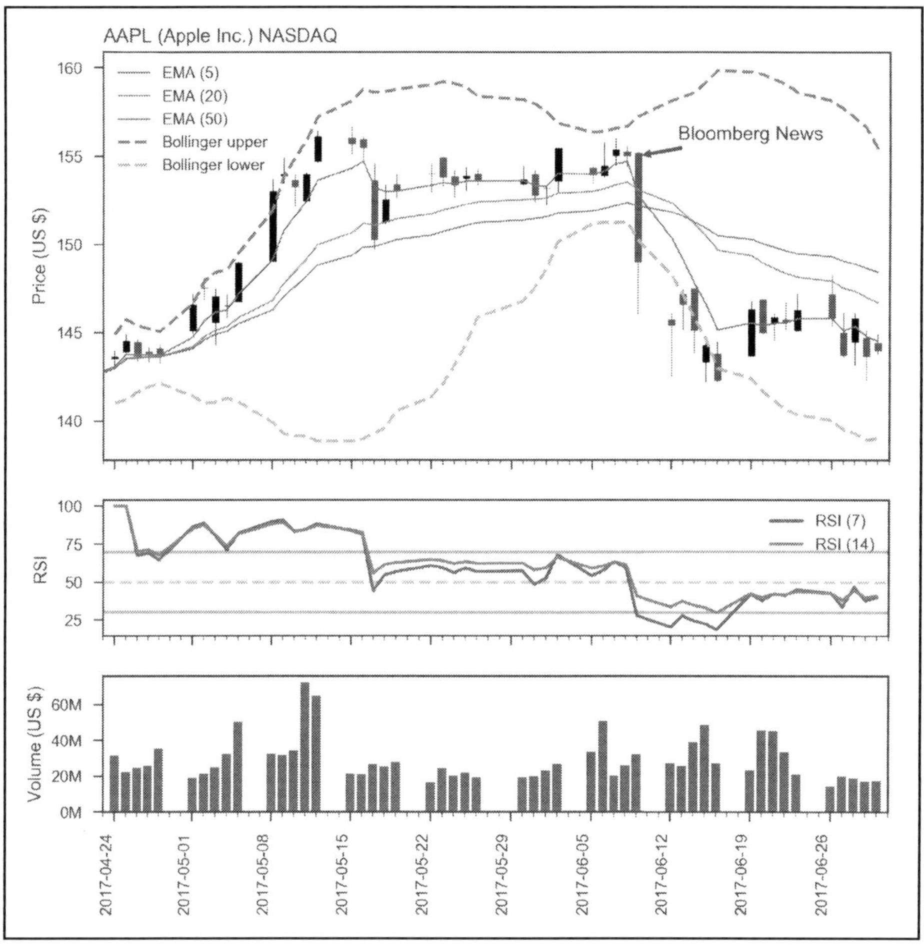

Three-dimensional (3D) plots

By transitioning to the three-dimensional space, you may enjoy greater creative freedom when creating visualizations. The extra dimension can also accommodate more information in a single plot. However, some may argue that 3D is nothing more than a visual gimmick when projected to a 2D surface (such as paper) as it would obfuscate the interpretation of data points.

In Matplotlib version 2, despite significant developments in the 3D API, annoying bugs or glitches still exist. We will discuss some workarounds toward the end of this chapter. More powerful Python 3D visualization packages do exist (such as MayaVi2, Plotly, and VisPy), but it's good to use Matplotlib's 3D plotting functions if you want to use the same package for both 2D and 3D plots, or you would like to maintain the aesthetics of its 2D plots.

For the most part, 3D plots in Matplotlib have similar structures to 2D plots. As such, we will not go through every 3D plot type in this section. We will put our focus on 3D scatter plots and bar charts.

3D scatter plot

In `Chapter 1`, *Hello Plotting World!*, we have already explored scatter plots in two dimensions. In this section, let's try to create a 3D scatter plot. Before doing that, we need some data points in three dimensions (x, y, z):

```
import pandas as pd

source =
"https://raw.githubusercontent.com/PointCloudLibrary/data/master/tutorials/
ism_train_cat.pcd"
cat_df = pd.read_csv(source, skiprows=11, delimiter=" ",
names=["x","y","z"], encoding='latin_1')
cat_df.head()
```

Point	x	y	z
0	-17.034178	18.972282	40.482403
1	-16.881481	21.815451	44.156799
2	-16.749582	18.154911	34.131474
3	-16.876919	20.598286	36.271809
4	-16.849340	17.403711	42.993984

To declare a 3D plot, we first need to import the `Axes3D` object from the `mplot3d` extension in `mpl_toolkits`, which is responsible for rendering 3D plots in a 2D plane. After that, we need to specify `projection='3d'` when we create subplots:

```
from mpl_toolkits.mplot3d import Axes3D
import matplotlib.pyplot as plt

fig = plt.figure()
ax = fig.add_subplot(111, projection='3d')
ax.scatter(cat_df.x, cat_df.y, cat_df.z)

plt.show()
```

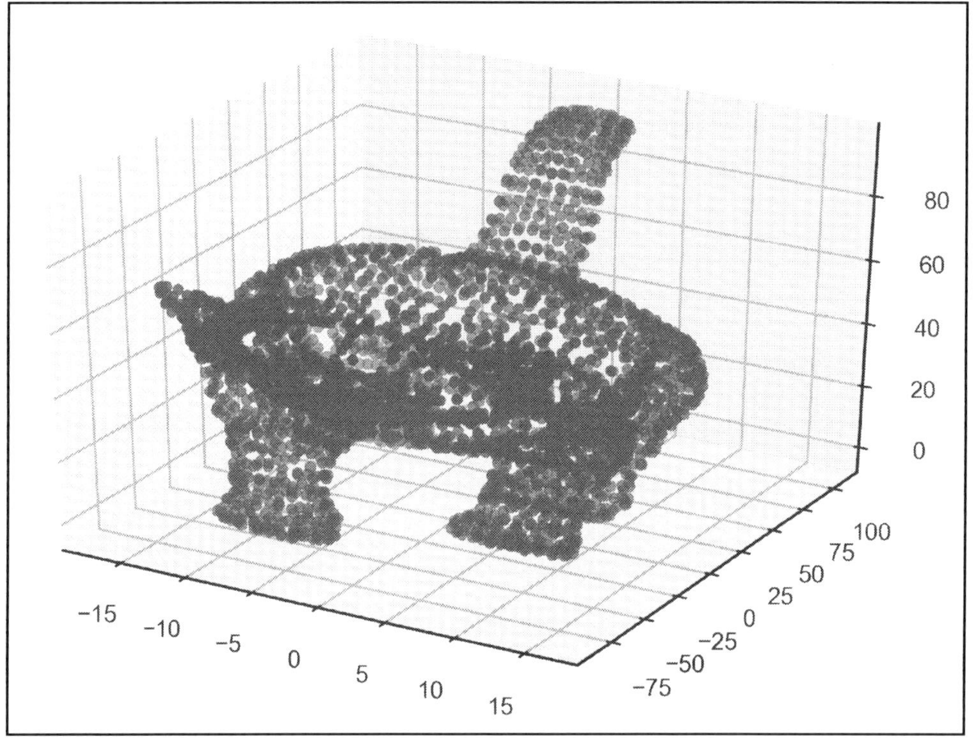

Behold, the mighty sCATter plot in 3D. Cats are currently taking over the internet. According to the New York Times, cats are "the essential building block of the Internet" (`https://www.nytimes.com/2014/07/23/upshot/what-the-internet-can-see-from-your-cat-pictures.html`). Undoubtedly, they deserve a place in this chapter as well.

Contrary to the 2D version of `scatter()`, we need to provide X, Y, and Z coordinates when we are creating a 3D scatter plot. Yet the parameters that are supported in 2D `scatter()` can be applied to 3D `scatter()` as well:

```
fig = plt.figure()
ax = fig.add_subplot(111, projection='3d')

# Change the size, shape and color of markers
ax.scatter(cat_df.x, cat_df.y, cat_df.z, s=4, c="g", marker="o")

plt.show()
```

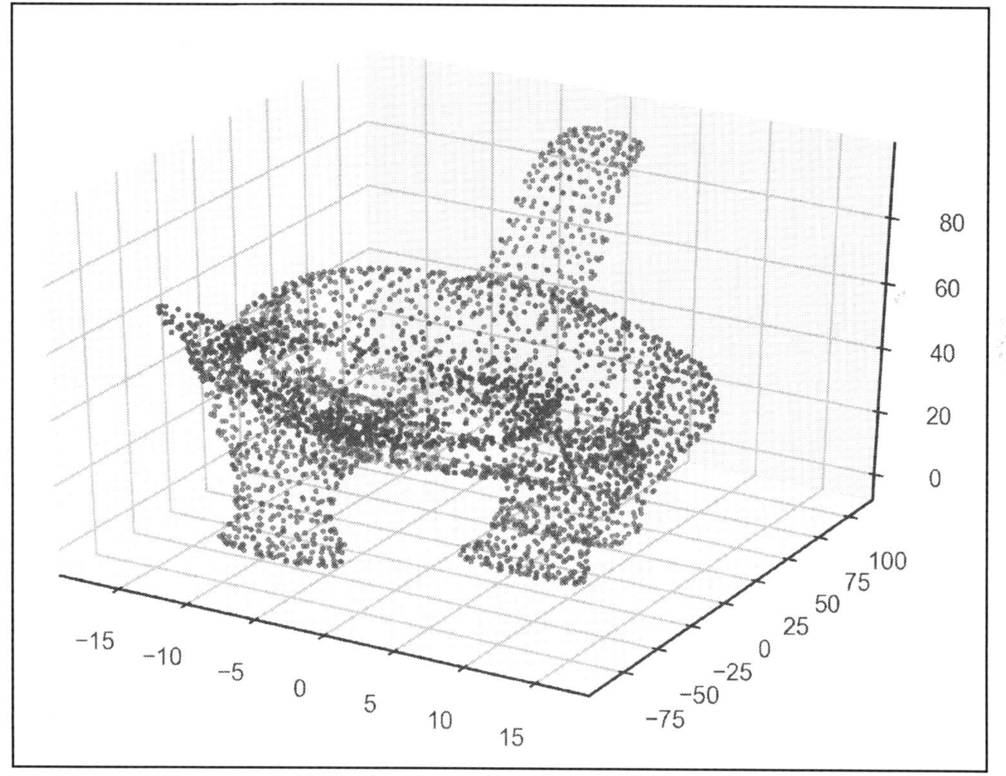

To change the viewing angle and elevation of the 3D plot, we can make use of `view_init()`. The `azim` parameter specifies the azimuth angle in the X-Y plane, while `elev` specifies the elevation angle. When the azimuth angle is 0, the X-Y plane would appear to the north from you. Meanwhile, an azimuth angle of 180 would show you the south side of the X-Y plane:

```
fig = plt.figure()
ax = fig.add_subplot(111, projection='3d')
ax.scatter(cat_df.x, cat_df.y, cat_df.z,s=4, c="g", marker="o")

# elev stores the elevation angle in the z plane azim stores the
# azimuth angle in the x,y plane
ax.view_init(azim=180, elev=10)

plt.show()
```

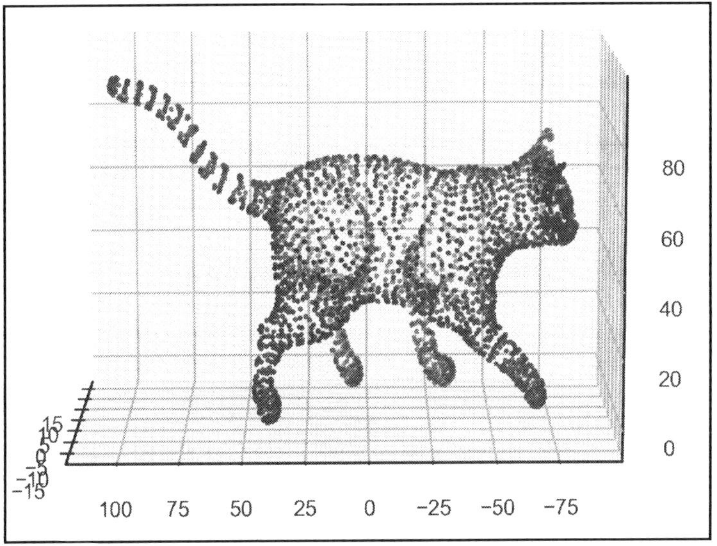

3D bar chart

We introduced candlestick plots for showing **Open-High-Low-Close** (**OHLC**) financial data. In addition, a 3D bar chart can be employed to show OHLC across time. The next figure shows a typical example of plotting a 5-day OHLC bar chart:

```
import matplotlib.pyplot as plt
import numpy as np
from mpl_toolkits.mplot3d import Axes3D
```

```
# Get 1 and every fifth row for the 5-day AAPL OHLC data
ohlc_5d = stock_df[stock_df["Company"]=="AAPL"].iloc[1::5, :]

fig = plt.figure()
ax = fig.add_subplot(111, projection='3d')

# Create one color-coded bar chart for Open, High, Low and Close prices.
for color, col, z in zip(['r', 'g', 'b', 'y'], ["Open", "High", "Low",
                         "Close"], [30, 20, 10, 0]):
    xs = np.arange(ohlc_5d.shape[0])
    ys = ohlc_5d[col]
    # Assign color to the bars
    colors = [color] * len(xs)
    ax.bar(xs, ys, zs=z, zdir='y', color=colors, alpha=0.8, width=5)

plt.show()
```

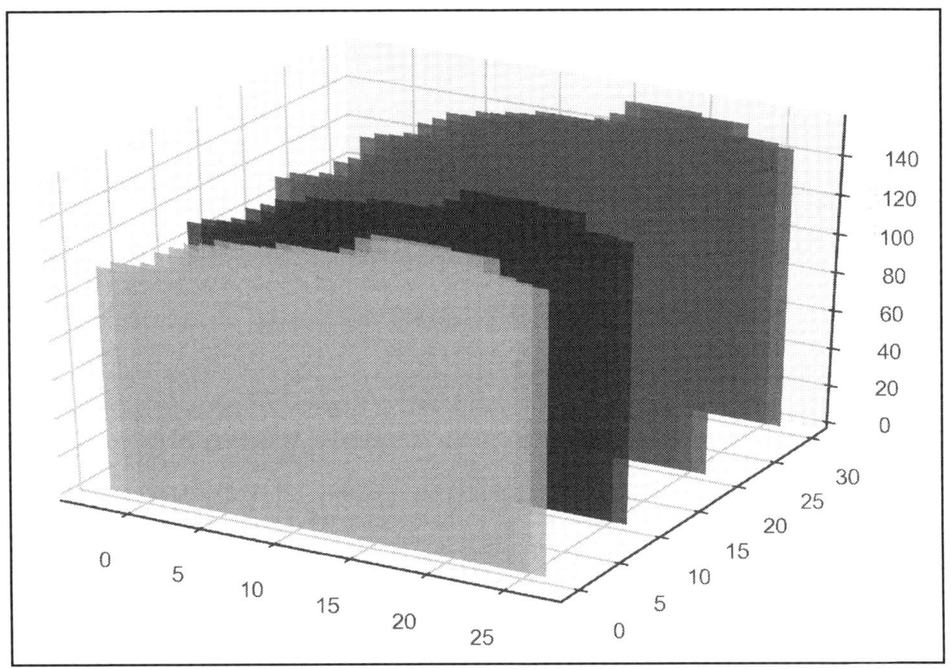

The method for setting ticks and labels is similar to other Matplotlib plotting functions:

```
fig = plt.figure(figsize=(9,7))
ax = fig.add_subplot(111, projection='3d')

# Create one color-coded bar chart for Open, High, Low and Close prices.
for color, col, z in zip(['r', 'g', 'b', 'y'], ["Open", "High", "Low",
                          "Close"], [30, 20, 10, 0]):
    xs = np.arange(ohlc_5d.shape[0])
    ys = ohlc_5d[col]
    # Assign color to the bars
    colors = [color] * len(xs)
    ax.bar(xs, ys, zs=z, zdir='y', color=colors, alpha=0.8)

# Manually assign the ticks and tick labels
ax.set_xticks(np.arange(ohlc_5d.shape[0]))
ax.set_xticklabels(ohlc_5d["Date"], rotation=20,
                   verticalalignment='baseline',
                   horizontalalignment='right',
                   fontsize='8')
ax.set_yticks([30, 20, 10, 0])
ax.set_yticklabels(["Open", "High", "Low", "Close"])

# Set the z-axis label
ax.set_zlabel('Price (US $)')

# Rotate the viewport
ax.view_init(azim=-42, elev=31)
plt.tight_layout()
plt.show()
```

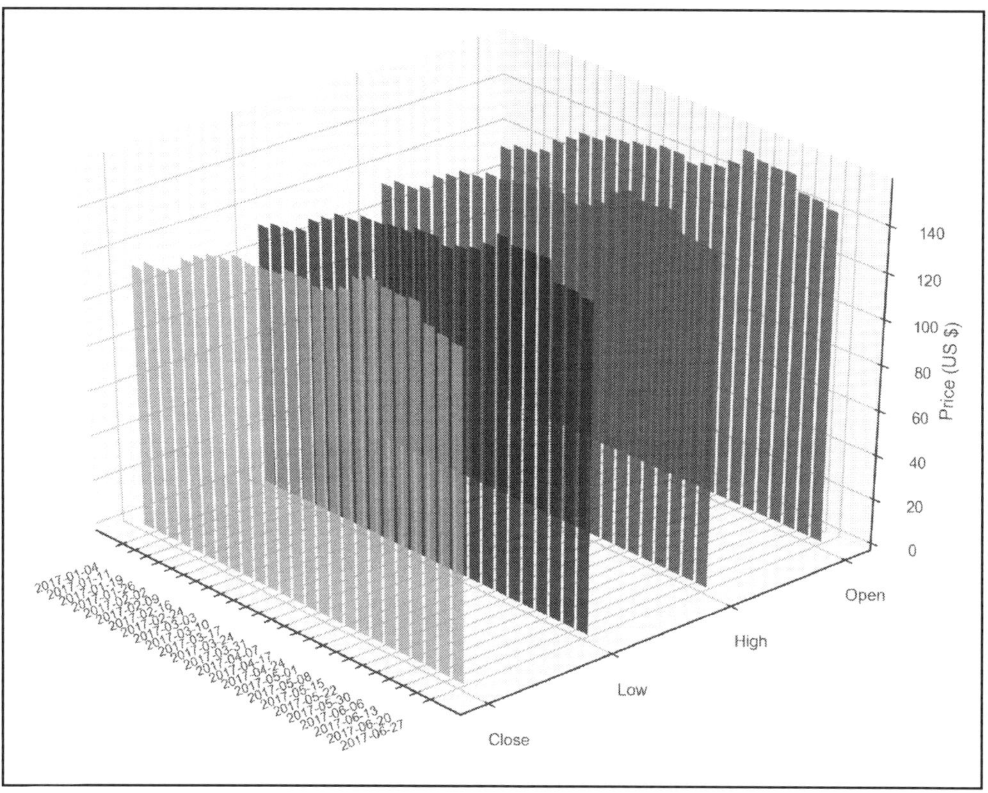

Caveats of Matplotlib 3D

Due to the lack of a true 3D graphical rendering backend (such as OpenGL) and proper algorithm for detecting 3D objects' intersections, the 3D plotting capabilities of Matplotlib are not great but just adequate for typical applications. In the official Matplotlib FAQ (`https://matplotlib.org/mpl_toolkits/mplot3d/faq.html`), the author noted that 3D plots may not look right at certain angles. Besides, we also reported that `mplot3d` would failed to clip bar charts if zlim is set (`https://github.com/matplotlib/matplotlib/issues/8902`; see also `https://github.com/matplotlib/matplotlib/issues/209`). Without improvements in the 3D rendering backend, these issues are hard to fix.

To better illustrate the latter issue, let's try to add `ax.set_zlim3d(bottom=110, top=150)` right above `plt.tight_layout()` in the previous 3D bar chart:

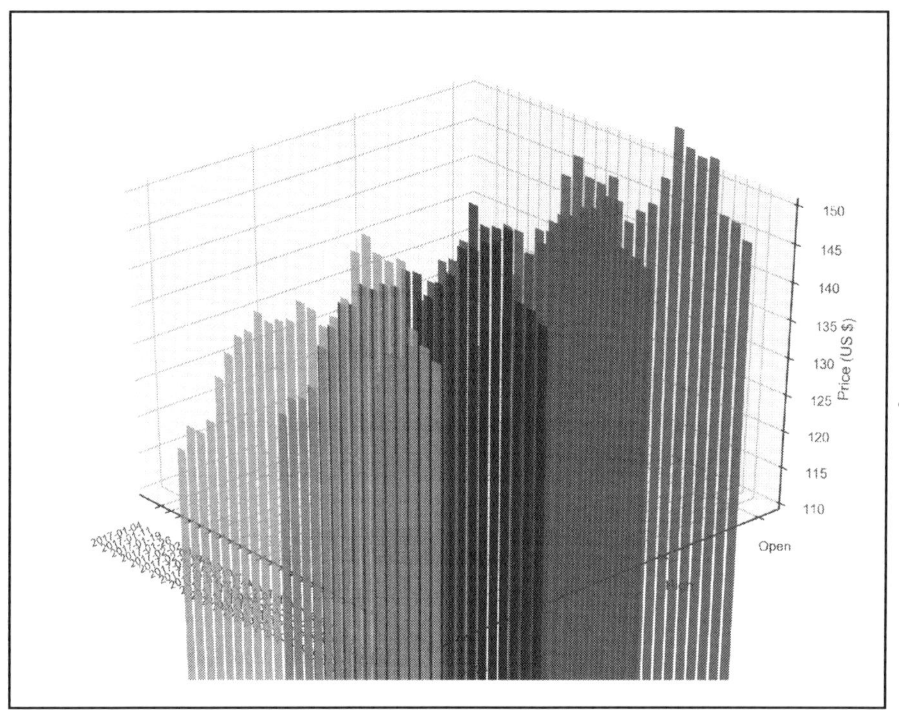

Clearly, something is going wrong, as the bars overshoot the lower boundary of the axes. We will try to address the latter issue through the following workaround:

```
# FuncFormatter to add 110 to the tick labels
def major_formatter(x, pos):
    return "{}".format(x+110)

fig = plt.figure(figsize=(9,7))
ax = fig.add_subplot(111, projection='3d')

# Create one color-coded bar chart for Open, High, Low and Close prices.
for color, col, z in zip(['r', 'g', 'b', 'y'], ["Open", "High", "Low",
                          "Close"], [30, 20, 10, 0]):
    xs = np.arange(ohlc_5d.shape[0])
    ys = ohlc_5d[col]

    # Assign color to the bars
    colors = [color] * len(xs)
```

```
    # Truncate the y-values by 110
    ax.bar(xs, ys-110, zs=z, zdir='y', color=colors, alpha=0.8)

# Manually assign the ticks and tick labels
ax.set_xticks(np.arange(ohlc_5d.shape[0]))
ax.set_xticklabels(ohlc_5d["Date"], rotation=20,
                   verticalalignment='baseline',
                   horizontalalignment='right',
                   fontsize='8')

# Set the z-axis label
ax.set_yticks([30, 20, 10, 0])
ax.set_yticklabels(["Open", "High", "Low", "Close"])
ax.zaxis.set_major_formatter(FuncFormatter(major_formatter))
ax.set_zlabel('Price (US $)')

# Rotate the viewport
ax.view_init(azim=-42, elev=31)

plt.tight_layout()
plt.show()
```

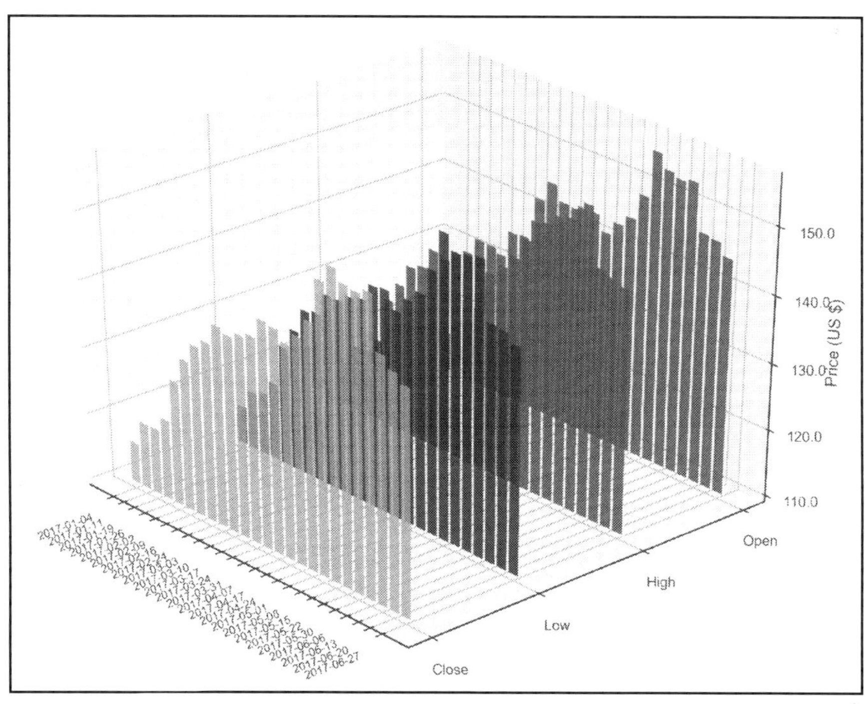

Basically, we truncated the y values by 110, and then we used a tick formatter (`major_formatter`) to shift the tick value back to the original. For 3D scatter plots, we can simply remove the data points that exceed the boundary of `set_zlim3d()` in order to generate a proper figure. However, these workarounds may not work for every 3D plot type.

Summary

You have successfully learned the techniques for visualizing multivariate data in 2D and 3D forms. Although most examples in this chapter revolved around the topic of stock trading, the data processing and visualization methods can be applied readily to other fields as well. In particular, the divide-and-conquer approach used to visualize multivariate data in facets is extremely useful in the scientific field.

We didn't go into too much detail of the 3D plotting capability of Matplotlib, as it is yet to be polished. For simple 3D plots, Matplotlib already suffices. The learning curve can be reduced if we use the same package for both 2D and 3D plots. You are advised to take a look at MayaVi2, Plotly, and VisPy if you require more powerful 3D plotting functions.

6

Adding Interactivity and Animating Plots

As a book focusing on the use of Matplotlib through elaborate examples, we opted to defer or simplify our discussion of the internals. For those of you who want to understand the nuts and bolts that make Matplotlib tick, you are advised to read *Mastering matplotlib* by Duncan M. McGreggor. At some point during our Matplotlib journey, it becomes inevitable for us to discuss more about backends, which turn plotting commands to graphics. These backends can be broadly classified as non-interactive or interactive. We will give examples that are pertinent to each backend class.

Matplotlib was not designed as an animation package from the get-go, thus it will appear sluggish in some advanced usages. For animation-centric applications, PyGame is a very good alternative (`https://www.pygame.org`); it supports OpenGL- and Direct3D-accelerated graphics for the ultimate speed in animating objects. Nevertheless, Matplotlib has acceptable performance most of the time, and we will guide you through the steps to create animations that are more engaging than static plots.

The examples in this chapter will be based on unemployment rates and earnings by educational attainment (2016), available from `data.gov` and curated by the Bureau of Labor Statistics, U.S. Department of Labor. Here is the outline of this chapter:

- Scraping information from websites
- Non-interactive backends
- Interactive backends
    - Tkinter, Jupyter, and Plot.ly
- Creating an animated plot
- Exporting an animation as a video

Scraping information from websites

Governments or jurisdictions around the world are increasingly embracing the importance of open data, which aims to increase citizen involvement and informs about decision making, making policies more open to public scrutiny. Some examples of open data initiatives around the world include `data.gov` (United States of America), `data.gov.uk` (United Kingdom), and `data.gov.hk` (Hong Kong).

These data portals often provide Application Programming Interfaces (APIs; see `Chapter 4`, *Visualizing Online Data,* for more details) for programmatic access to data. However, APIs are not available for some datasets; hence, we resort to good old web scraping techniques to extract information from websites.

BeautifulSoup (`https://www.crummy.com/software/BeautifulSoup/`) is an incredibly useful package used to scrape information from websites. Basically, everything marked with an HTML tag can be scraped with this wonderful package, from text, links, tables, and styles, to images. Scrapy is also a good package for web scraping, but it is more like a framework for writing powerful web crawlers. So, if you just need to fetch a table from a page, BeautifulSoup offers simpler procedures.

We are going to use BeautifulSoup version 4.6 throughout this chapter. To install BeautifulSoup 4, we can once again rely on PyPI:

```
pip install beautifulsoup4
```

The data of USA unemployment rates and earnings by educational attainment (2016) is available at `https://www.bls.gov/emp/ep_table_001.htm`. Currently, BeautifulSoup does not handle HTML requests. So we need to use the `urllib.request` or `requests` package to fetch a web page for us. Of the two options, the `requests` package is probably easier to use, due to its higher-level HTTP client interface. If `requests` is not available on your system, you can install it through PyPI:

```
pip install requests
```

Let's take a look at the web page before we write the web scraping code. If we use the Google Chrome browser to visit the Bureau of Labor Statistics website, we can inspect the HTML code corresponding to the table we need by right-clicking:

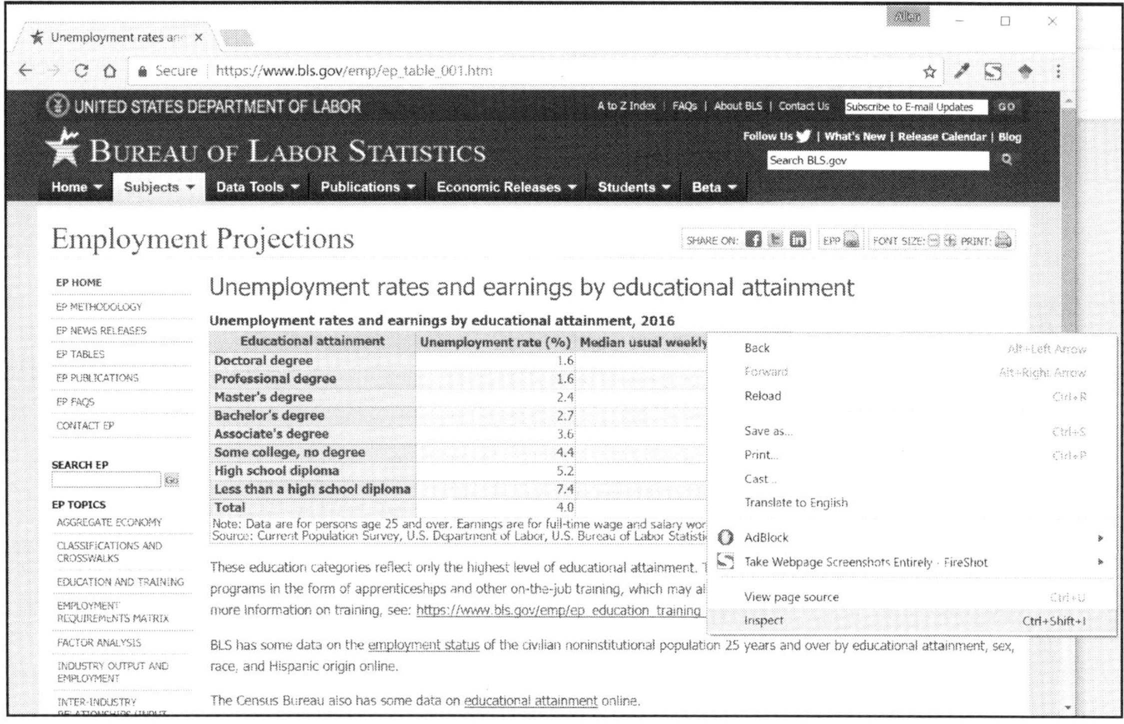

A pop-up window for code inspection will be shown, which allows us to read the code for each of the elements on the page.

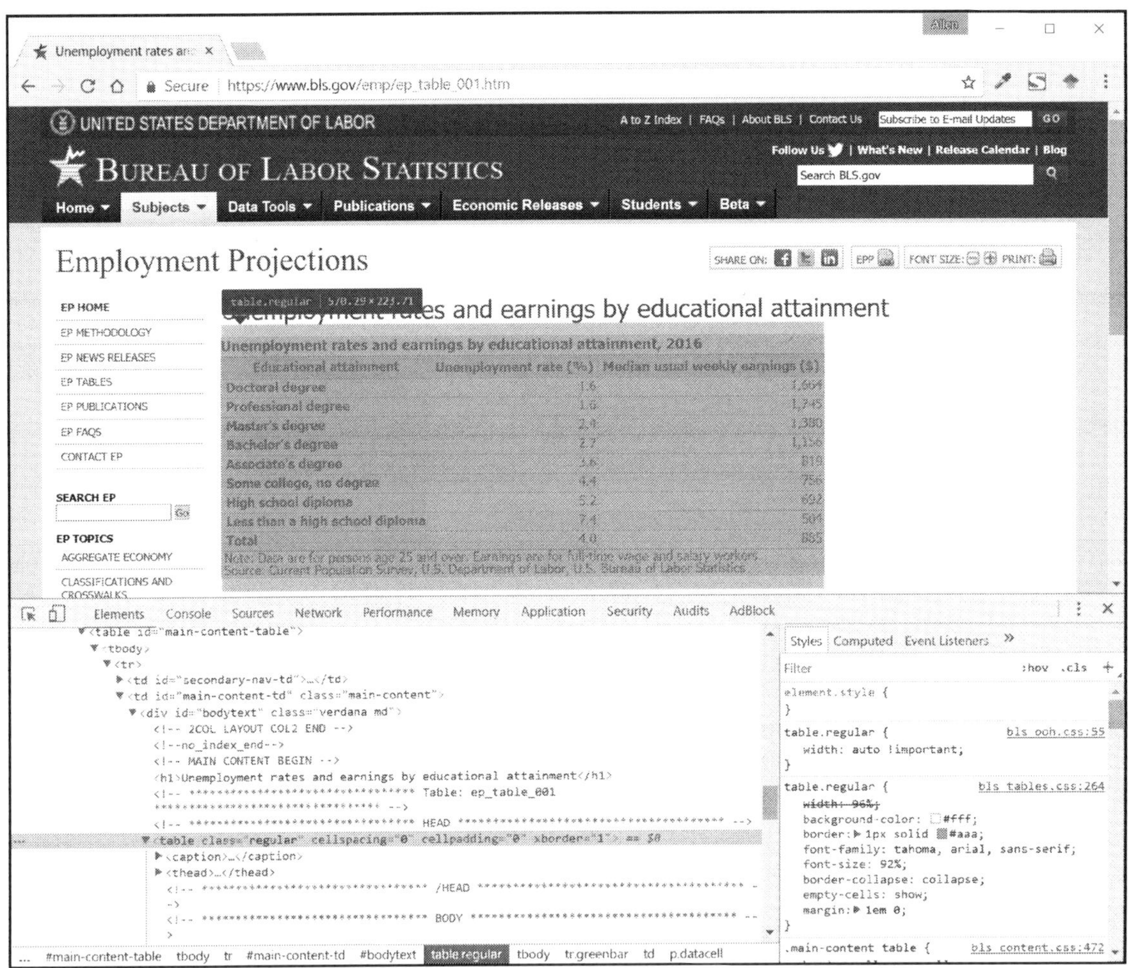

More specifically, we can see that the column names are defined in the `<thead>...</thead>` section, while the table content is defined in the `<tbody>...</tbody>` section.

In order to instruct BeautifulSoup to scrape the information we need, we need to give clear directions to it. We can right-click on the relevant section in the code inspection window and copy the unique identifier in the format of the CSS selector.

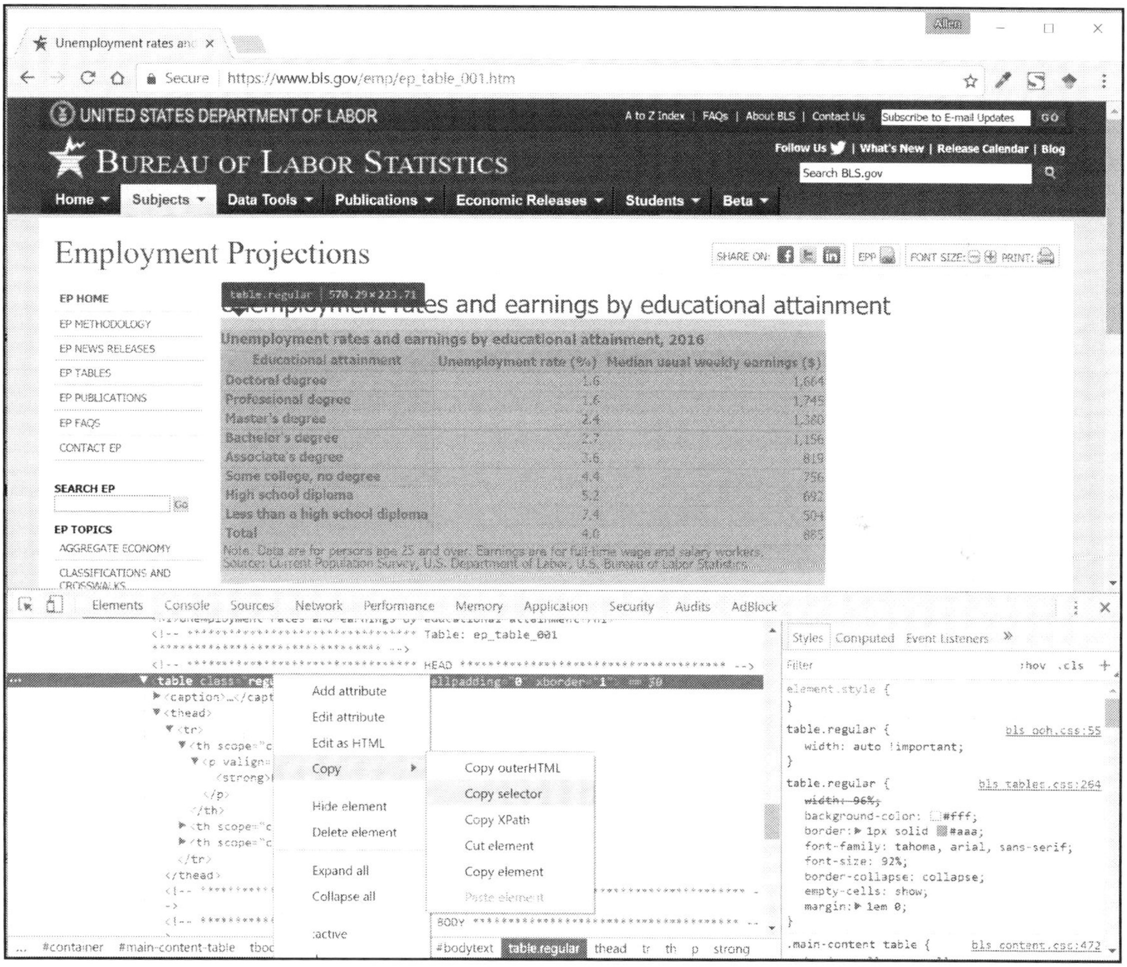

Cascading Style Sheets (**CSS**) selectors were originally designed for applying element-specific styles to a website. For more information, visit the following page: `https://www.w3schools.com/cssref/css_selectors.asp`.

Let's try to get the CSS selectors for `thead` and `tbody`, and use the `BeautifulSoup.select()` method to scrape the respective HTML code:

```
import requests
from bs4 import BeautifulSoup


# Specify the url
url = "https://www.bls.gov/emp/ep_table_001.htm"

# Query the website and get the html response
response = requests.get(url)

# Parse the returned html using BeautifulSoup
bs = BeautifulSoup(response.text)

# Select the table header by CSS selector
thead = bs.select("#bodytext > table > thead")[0]

# Select the table body by CSS selector
tbody = bs.select("#bodytext > table > tbody")[0]

# Make sure the code works
print(thead)
```

We see the following output from the previous code:

```
<thead> <tr> <th scope="col"><p align="center"
valign="top"><strong>Educational attainment</strong></p></th> <th
scope="col"><p align="center" valign="top">Unemployment rate (%)</p></th>
<th scope="col"><p align="center" valign="top">Median usual weekly earnings
($)</p></th> </tr> </thead>
```

Next, we are going to find all instances of `<th>...</th>` in `<thead>...</thead>`, which contains the name of each column. We will build a dictionary of lists with headers as keys to hold the data:

```
# Get the column names
headers = []

# Find all header columns in <thead> as specified by <th> html tags
for col in thead.find_all('th'):
    headers.append(col.text.strip())

# Dictionary of lists for storing parsed data
data = {header:[] for header in headers}
```

Finally, we parse the remaining rows (`<tr>...</tr>`) from the body (`<tbody>...</tbody>`) of the table and convert the data into a pandas DataFrame:

```
import pandas as pd


# Parse the rows in table body
for row in tbody.find_all('tr'):
    # Find all columns in a row as specified by <th> or <td> html tags
    cols = row.find_all(['th','td'])

    # enumerate() allows us to loop over an iterable,
    # and return each item preceded by a counter
    for i, col in enumerate(cols):
        # Strip white space around the text
        value = col.text.strip()

        # Try to convert the columns to float, except the first column
        if i > 0:
            value = float(value.replace(',','')) # Remove all commas in
            # string

        # Append the float number to the dict of lists
        data[headers[i]].append(value)

# Create a dataframe from the parsed dictionary
df = pd.DataFrame(data)

# Show an excerpt of parsed data
df.head()
```

	Educational attainment	Median usual weekly earnings ($)	Unemployment rate (%)
0	Doctoral degree	1664.0	1.6
1	Professional degree	1745.0	1.6
2	Master's degree	1380.0	2.4
3	Bachelor's degree	1156.0	2.7
4	Associate's degree	819.0	3.6

We have now fetched the HTML table and formatted it as a structured pandas DataFrame.

Non-interactive backends

The code for plotting graphs is considered the frontend in Matplotlib terminology. We first mentioned backends in `Chapter 1`, *Hello Plotting World!*, when we were talking about output formats. In reality, Matplotlib backends differ much more than just in the support of graphical formats. Backends handle so many things behind the scenes! And that determines the support for plotting capabilities. For example, LaTeX text layout is only supported by AGG, PDF, PGF, and PS backends.

We have been using non-interactive backends so far, which include AGG, Cairo, GDK, PDF, PGF, PS, and SVG. Most of these backends work without extra dependencies, yet Cairo and GDK would require the Cairo graphics library or GIMP Drawing Kit, respectively, to work.

Non-interactive backends can be further classified into two groups--vector and raster. Vector graphics describe images in terms of points, paths, and shapes that are calculated using mathematical formulas. A vector graphic will always appear smooth, irrespective of scale, and its size is usually much smaller than its raster counterpart. PDF, PGF, PS, and SVG backends belong to the "vector" group.

Raster graphics describe images in terms of a finite number of tiny color blocks (pixels). So, if we zoom in enough, we start to see a blurry image, or in other words, pixelation. By increasing the resolution or **Dots Per Inch** (**DPI**) of the image, we are less likely to observe pixelation. AGG, Cairo, and GDK belong to this group of backends. This table summarizes the key functionalities and differences among the non-interactive backends:

Backend	**Vector/Raster**	**Output formats**
Agg	Raster	PNG
Cairo	Vector/Raster	PDF, PNG, PS, or SVG
PDF	Vector	PDF
PGF	Vector	PDF or PGF
PS	Vector	PS
SVG	Vector	SVG
GDK (Deprecated in Matplotlib 2.0)	Raster	PNG, JPEG, or TIFF

Normally, we don't need to manually select a backend, as the default choice would work great for most tasks. On the other hand, we can specify a backend through the `matplotlib.use()` method before importing `matplotlib.pyplot`:

```
import matplotlib
matplotlib.use('SVG') # Change to SVG backend
import matplotlib.pyplot as plt
import textwrap # Standard library for text wraping


# Create a figure
fig, ax = plt.subplots(figsize=(6,7))

# Create a list of x ticks positions
ind = range(df.shape[0])

# Plot a bar chart of median usual weekly earnings by educational
# attainments
rects = ax.barh(ind, df["Median usual weekly earnings ($)"], height=0.5)

# Set the x-axis label
ax.set_xlabel('Median weekly earnings (USD)')

# Label the x ticks
# The tick labels are a bit too long, let's wrap them in 15-char lines
ylabels=[textwrap.fill(label,15) for label in df["Educational attainment"]]
ax.set_yticks(ind)
ax.set_yticklabels(ylabels)

# Give extra margin at the bottom to display the tick labels
fig.subplots_adjust(left=0.3)

# Save the figure in SVG format
plt.savefig("test.svg")
```

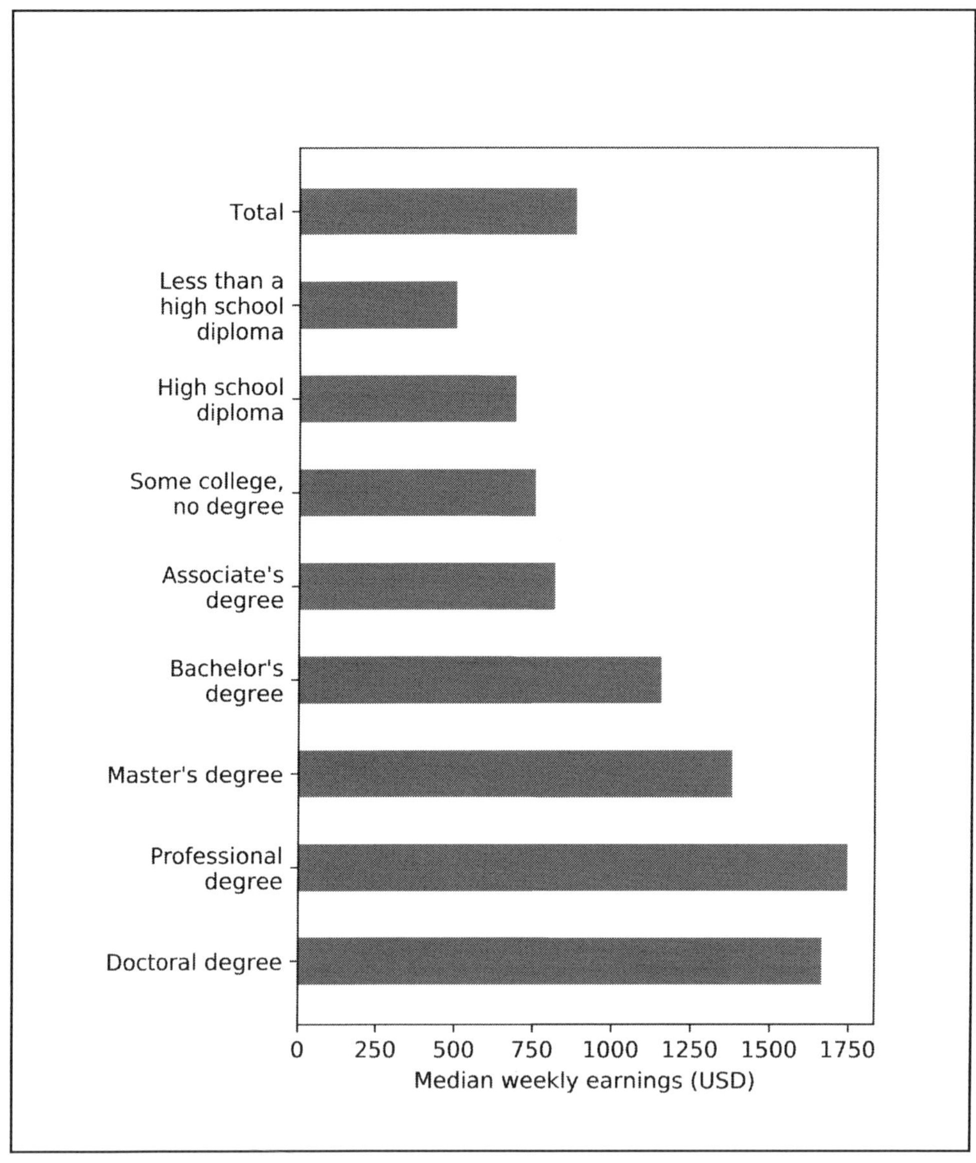
Total
Less than a high school diploma
High school diploma
Some college, no degree
Associate's degree
Bachelor's degree
Master's degree
Professional degree
Doctoral degree
0
250
500
750
1000
1250
1500
1750
Median weekly earnings (USD)

Interactive backends

Matplotlib can build interactive figures that are far more engaging for readers. Sometimes, a plot might be overwhelmed with graphical elements, making it hard to discern individual data points. On other occasions, some data points may appear so similar that it becomes hard to spot the differences with the naked eye. An interactive plot can address these two scenarios by allowing us to zoom in, zoom out, pan, and explore the plot in the way we want.

Through the use of interactive backends, plots in Matplotlib can be embedded in Graphical User Interface (GUI) applications. By default, Matplotlib supports the pairing of the Agg raster graphics renderer with a wide variety of GUI toolkits, including wxWidgets (Wx), GIMP Toolkit (GTK+), Qt, and Tkinter (Tk). As Tkinter is the de facto standard GUI for Python, which is built on top of Tcl/Tk, we can create an interactive plot just by calling `plt.show()` in a standalone Python script.

Tkinter-based backend

Let's try to copy the following code to a separate text file and name it `chapter6_gui.py`. After that, type `python chapter6_gui.py` in your terminal (Mac/Linux) or Command Prompt (Windows). If you are unsure about how to open a terminal or Command Prompt, refer to `Chapter 1`, *Hello Plotting World!*, for more details:

```
import matplotlib
import matplotlib.pyplot as plt
import textwrap # Standard library for text wraping
import requests
import pandas as pd
from bs4 import BeautifulSoup


# Specify the url
url = "https://www.bls.gov/emp/ep_table_001.htm"

# Query the website and get the html response
response = requests.get(url)

# Parse the returned html using BeautifulSoup
bs = BeautifulSoup(response.text)

# Select the table header by CSS selector
thead = bs.select("#bodytext > table > thead")[0]
```

```
# Select the table body by CSS selector
tbody = bs.select("#bodytext > table > tbody")[0]

# Get the column names
headers = []

# Find all header columns in <thead> as specified by <th> html tags
for col in thead.find_all('th'):
    headers.append(col.text.strip())

# Dictionary of lists for storing parsed data
data = {header:[] for header in headers}

# Parse the rows in table body
for row in tbody.find_all('tr'):
    # Find all columns in a row as specified by <th> or <td> html tags
    cols = row.find_all(['th','td'])

    # enumerate() allows us to loop over an iterable,
    # and return each item preceded by a counter
    for i, col in enumerate(cols):
        # Strip white space around the text
        value = col.text.strip()

        # Try to convert the columns to float, except the first column
        if i > 0:
            value = float(value.replace(',','')) # Remove all commas in
            # string

        # Append the float number to the dict of lists
        data[headers[i]].append(value)

# Create a dataframe from the parsed dictionary
df = pd.DataFrame(data)

# Create a figure
fig, ax = plt.subplots(figsize=(6,7))

# Create a list of x ticks positions
ind = range(df.shape[0])

# Plot a bar chart of median usual weekly earnings by educational
# attainments
rects = ax.barh(ind, df["Median usual weekly earnings ($)"], height=0.5)

# Set the x-axis label
ax.set_xlabel('Median weekly earnings (USD)')
```

```
# Label the x ticks
# The tick labels are a bit too long, let's wrap them in 15-char lines
ylabels=[textwrap.fill(label,15) for label in df["Educational attainment"]]
ax.set_yticks(ind)
ax.set_yticklabels(ylabels)

# Give extra margin at the bottom to display the tick labels
fig.subplots_adjust(left=0.3)

# Show the figure in a GUI
plt.show()
```

We see a pop-up window similar to the following. We can pan, zoom to selection, configure subplot margins, save, and go back and forth between different views by clicking on the buttons on the bottom toolbar. If we put our mouse over the plot, we can also observe the exact coordinates in the bottom-right corner. This feature is extremely useful for dissecting data points that are close to each other.

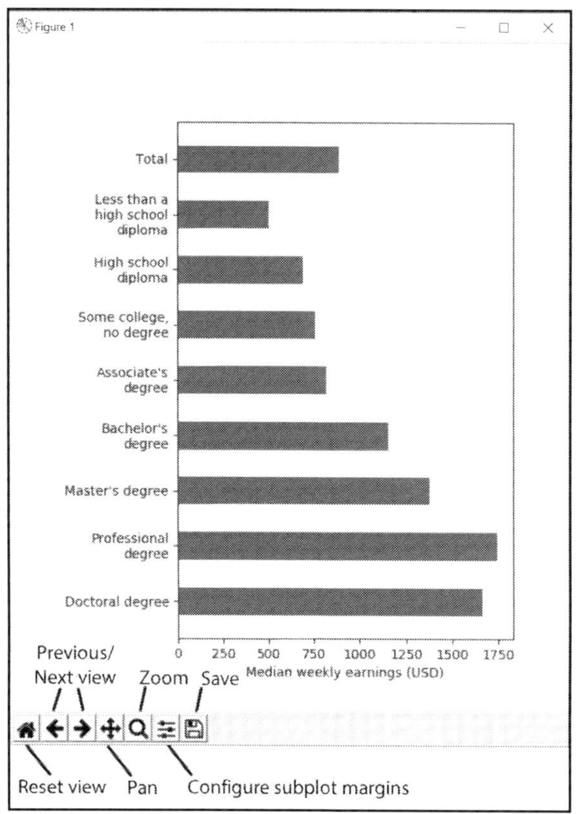

Next, we are going to extend the application by adding a radio button widget on top of the figure, such that we can switch between the display of weekly earnings or unemployment rates. The radio button can be found in `matplotlib.widgets`, and we are going to attach a data updating function to the `.on_clicked()` event of the button. You can paste the following code right before the `plt.show()` line in the previous code example (`chapter6_gui.py`). Let's see how it works:

```
# Import Matplotlib radio button widget
from matplotlib.widgets import RadioButtons

# Create axes for holding the radio selectors.
# supply [left, bottom, width, height] in normalized (0, 1) units
bax = plt.axes([0.3, 0.9, 0.4, 0.1])
radio = RadioButtons(bax, ('Weekly earnings', 'Unemployment rate'))

# Define the function for updating the displayed values
# when the radio button is clicked
def radiofunc(label):
    # Select columns from dataframe, and change axis label depending on
    # selection
    if label == 'Weekly earnings':
        data = df["Median usual weekly earnings ($)"]
        ax.set_xlabel('Median weekly earnings (USD)')
    elif label == 'Unemployment rate':
        data = df["Unemployment rate (%)"]
        ax.set_xlabel('Unemployment rate (%)')

    # Update the bar heights
    for i, rect in enumerate(rects):
        rect.set_width(data[i])

    # Rescale the x-axis range
    ax.set_xlim(xmin=0, xmax=data.max()*1.1)

    # Redraw the figure
    plt.draw()

# Attach radiofunc to the on_clicked event of the radio button
radio.on_clicked(radiofunc)
```

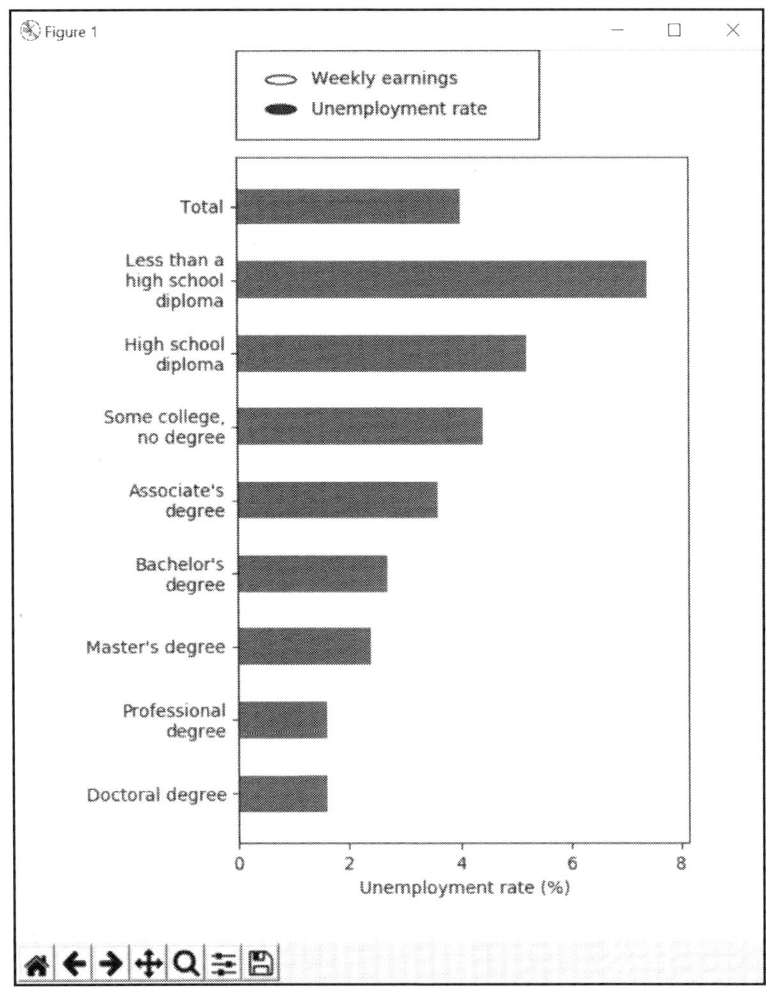

You will be welcomed by a new radio selector box at the top of the figure. Try switching between the two states and see if the figure is updated accordingly. The complete code is also available as `chapter6_tkinter.py` in our code repository.

Interactive backend for Jupyter Notebook

Before we conclude this section, we are going to introduce two more interactive backends that are rarely covered by books. Starting with Matplotlib 1.4, there is an interactive backend specifically designed for Jupyter Notebook. To invoke that, we simply need to paste `%matplotlib notebook` at the start of our notebook. We are going to adapt one of the earlier examples in this chapter to use this backend:

```
# Import the interactive backend for Jupyter notebook
%matplotlib notebook
import matplotlib
import matplotlib.pyplot as plt
import textwrap


fig, ax = plt.subplots(figsize=(6,7))
ind = range(df.shape[0])
rects = ax.barh(ind, df["Median usual weekly earnings ($)"], height=0.5)
ax.set_xlabel('Median weekly earnings (USD)')
ylabels=[textwrap.fill(label,15) for label in df["Educational attainment"]]
ax.set_yticks(ind)
ax.set_yticklabels(ylabels)
fig.subplots_adjust(left=0.3)

# Show the figure using interactive notebook backend
plt.show()
```

You will see an interactive interface coming up, with buttons similar to a Tkinter-based application:

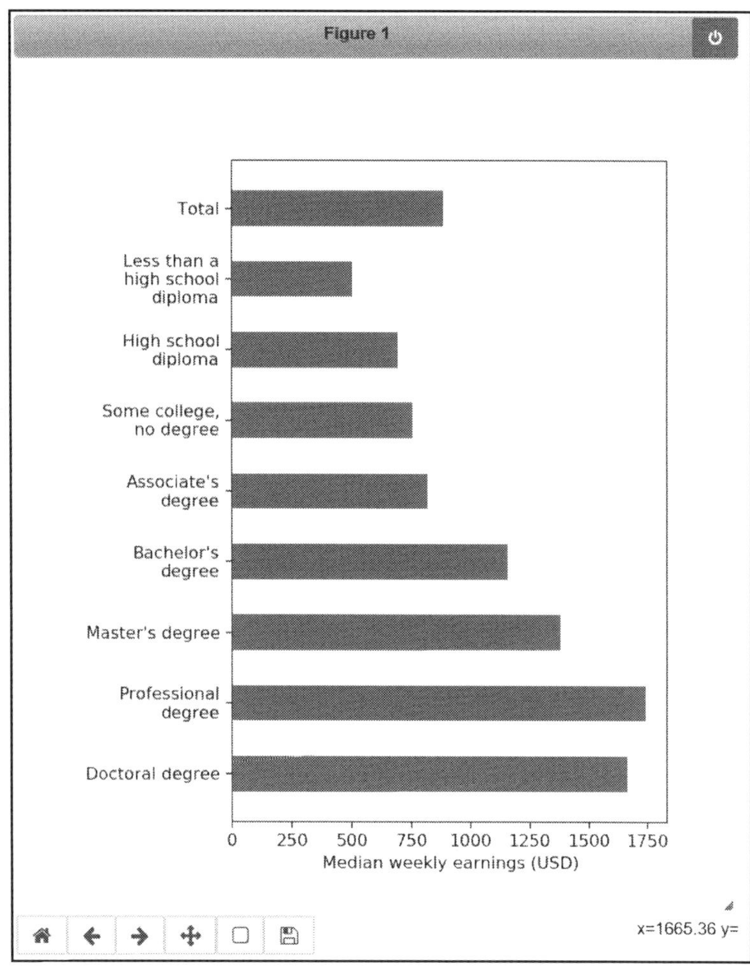

Plot.ly-based backend

Lastly, we will talk about Plot.ly, which is a D3.js-based interactive graphing library with many programming language bindings, including Python. Plot.ly has quickly gained traction in the area of online data analytics due to its powerful data dashboard, high performance, and detailed documentation. For more information, please visit Plot.ly's website (`https://plot.ly`).

Plot.ly offers easy transformation of Matplotlib figures into online interactive charts through its Python bindings. To install Plotly.py, we can use PyPI:

```
pip install plotly
```

Let us show you a quick example of integrating Matplotlib with Plot.ly:

```
import matplotlib.pyplot as plt
import numpy as np
import plotly.plotly as py
from plotly.offline import init_notebook_mode, enable_mpl_offline,
iplot_mpl


# Plot offline in Jupyter Notebooks, not required for standalone script
# Note: Must be called before any plotting actions
init_notebook_mode()

# Convert mpl plots to locally hosted HTML documents, not required if you
# are a registered plot.ly user and have a API key
enable_mpl_offline()

# Create two subplots with shared x-axis
fig, axarr = plt.subplots(2, sharex=True)

# The code for generating "df" is skipped for brevity, please refer to the
# "Tkinter-based backend" section for details of generating "df"
ind = np.arange(df.shape[0]) # the x locations for the groups
width = 0.35

# Plot a bar chart of the weekly earnings in the first axes
axarr[0].bar(ind, df["Median usual weekly earnings ($)"], width)

# Plot a bar chart of the unemployment rate in the second axes
axarr[1].bar(ind, df["Unemployment rate (%)"], width)

# Set the ticks and labels
axarr[1].set_xticks(ind)
# Reduce verbosity of labels by removing " degree"
axarr[1].set_xticklabels([value.replace(" degree","") for value in
df["Educational attainment"]])

# Offline Interactive plot using plot.ly
# Note: import and use plotly.offline.plot_mpl instead for standalone
# Python scripts
iplot_mpl(fig)
```

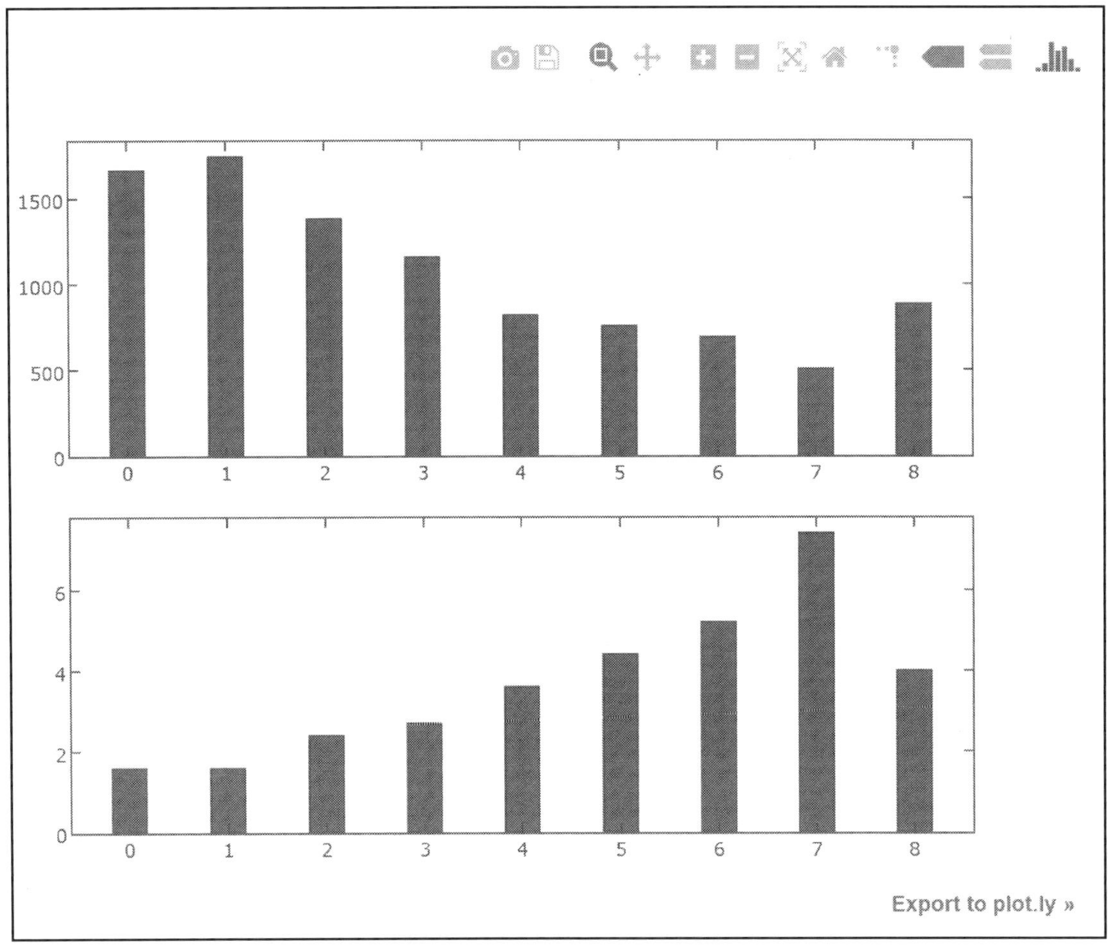

You may be greeted by the following error message when you run the preceding Plot.ly example:

```
IOPub data rate exceeded. The notebook server will temporarily stop sending
output to the client in order to avoid crashing it.
To change this limit, set the config variable
--NotebookApp.iopub_data_rate_limit.
```

To circumvent this error, you can relaunch Jupyter Notebook by setting a higher `iopub_data_rate_limit`:

```
jupyter notebook --NotebookApp.iopub_data_rate_limit=1.0e10
```

You may also notice that the tick labels cannot be displayed properly, despite clear specifications in the code. This issue is also reported on the official GitHub page (`https://github.com/plotly/plotly.py/issues/735`). Unfortunately, there is no fix for this issue to date.

We admit that there are numerous materials online that describe the integration of Matplotlib plots in different GUI applications. Due to page limits, we are not going to go through each of these backends here. For readers who want to read more about these interactive backends, Alexandre Devert has written an excellent chapter (*Chapter 8, User Interface*) in *matplotlib Plotting Cookbook*. In *Chapter 8, User Interface* of that book, Alexandre has provided recipes for creating GUI applications using wxWidgets, GTK, and Pyglet as well.

Creating animated plots

As explained at the start of this chapter, Matplotlib was not originally designed for making animations, and there are GPU-accelerated Python animation packages that may be more suitable for such a task (such as PyGame). However, since we are already familiar with Matplotlib, it is quite easy to adapt existing plots to animations.

Installation of FFmpeg

Before we start making animations, we need to install either FFmpeg, avconv, MEncoder, or ImageMagick on our system. These additional dependencies are not bundled with Matplotlib, and so we need to install them separately. We are going to walk you through the steps of installing FFmpeg.

For Debian-based Linux users, FFmpeg can be installed by issuing the following command in the terminal:

```
sudo apt-get install ffmpeg
```

FFmpeg may not be available on Ubuntu 14.04 or earlier. To install FFmpeg on Ubuntu 14.04, please follow the steps below:

```
sudo add-apt-repository ppa:mc3man/trusty-media
```

Press *Enter* to confirm the addition of the repository.

```
Also note that with apt-get a sudo apt-get dist-upgrade
is needed for initial setup & with some package upgrades
More info:
https://launchpad.net/~mc3man/+archive/ubuntu/trusty-medi
a
Press [ENTER] to continue or ctrl-c to cancel adding it
```

Update and upgrade a few packages before installing FFmpeg.

```
sudo apt-get update
sudo apt-get dist-upgrade
```

Finally, proceed with the normal procedure of installing FFmpeg via `apt-get`:

```
sudo apt-get install ffmpeg
```

For Mac users, Homebrew (`https://brew.sh/`) is the simplest way to search and install the FFmpeg package. For those who don't have Homebrew, you can paste the following code in your terminal to install it:

```
/usr/bin/ruby -e "$(curl -fsSL
https://raw.githubusercontent.com/Homebrew/install/master/install)"
```

After that, we can install FFmpeg by issuing the following command in the terminal app:

```
brew install ffmpeg
```

Alternatively, you may install FFmpeg by copying the binaries (`https://evermeet.cx/ffmpeg/`) to the system path (for example, `/usr/local/bin`). Readers may visit the following page for more details: `http://www.renevolution.com/ffmpeg/2013/03/16/how-to-install-ffmpeg-on-mac-os-x.html`

The installation steps for Windows users are quite a bit more involved, as we need to download the executable ourselves, followed by adding the executable to the system path. Therefore, we have prepared a series of screen captures to guide you through the process.

First, we need to obtain a prebuilt binary from `http://ffmpeg.zeranoe.com/builds/`. Choose the CPU architecture that matches with your system, and select the latest release and static linked libraries.

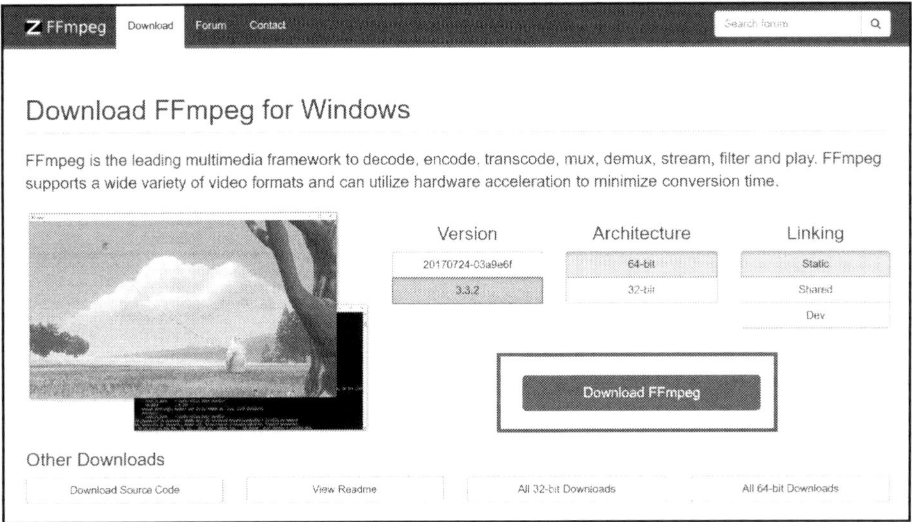

Next, we need to extract the downloaded ZIP file to the `C` drive as `c:\ffmpeg`, and add the folder `c:\ffmpeg\bin` to the `Path` variable. To do this, go to **Control Panel** and click on the **System and Security** link, followed by clicking on **System**. In the **System** window, click on the **Advanced system settings** link to the left:

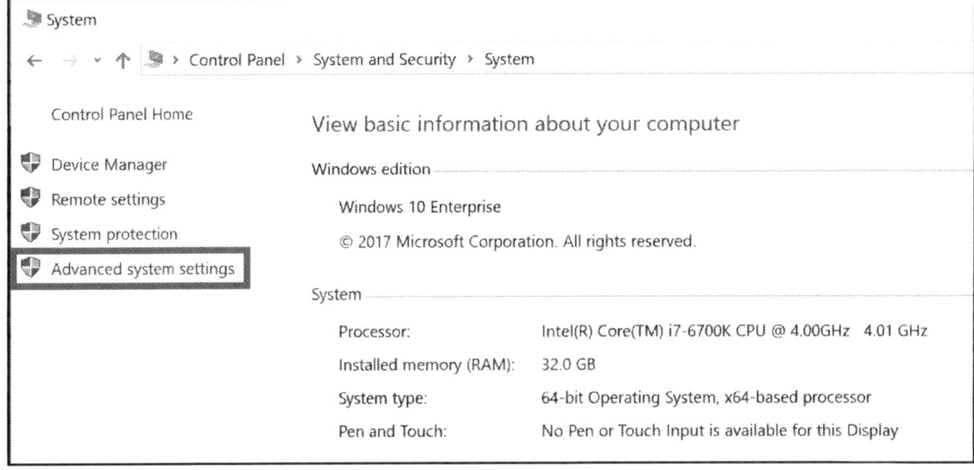

In the pop-up **System Properties** window, click on the **Environmental Variables...** button:

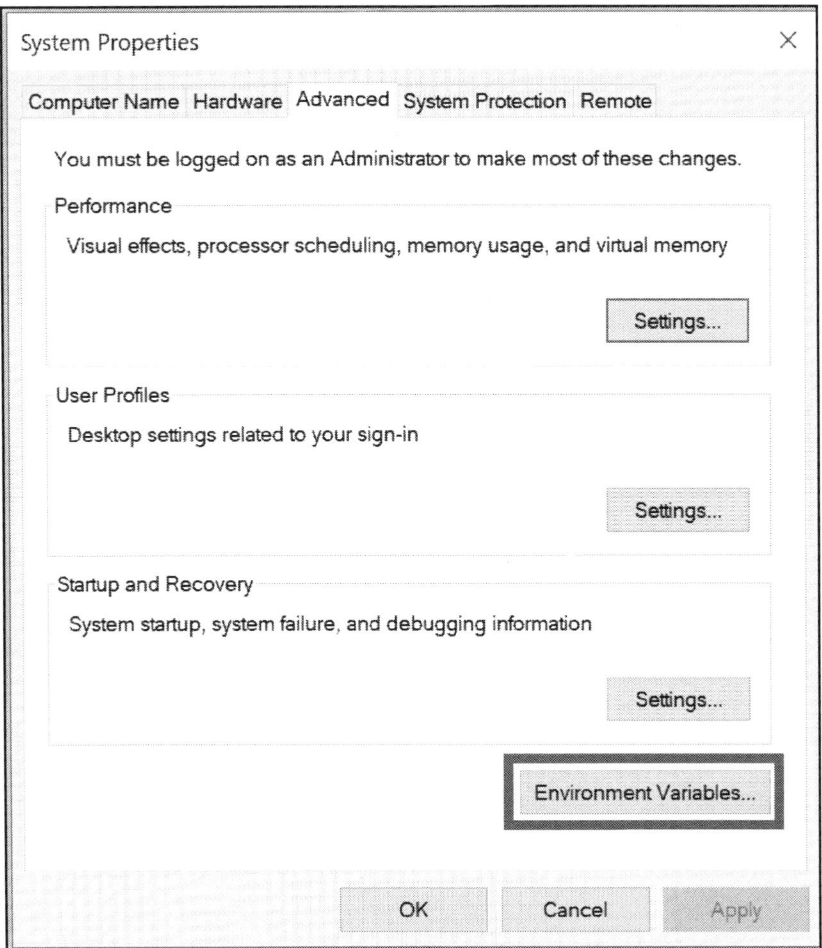

Select the **Path** entry, and click on the **Edit...** button:

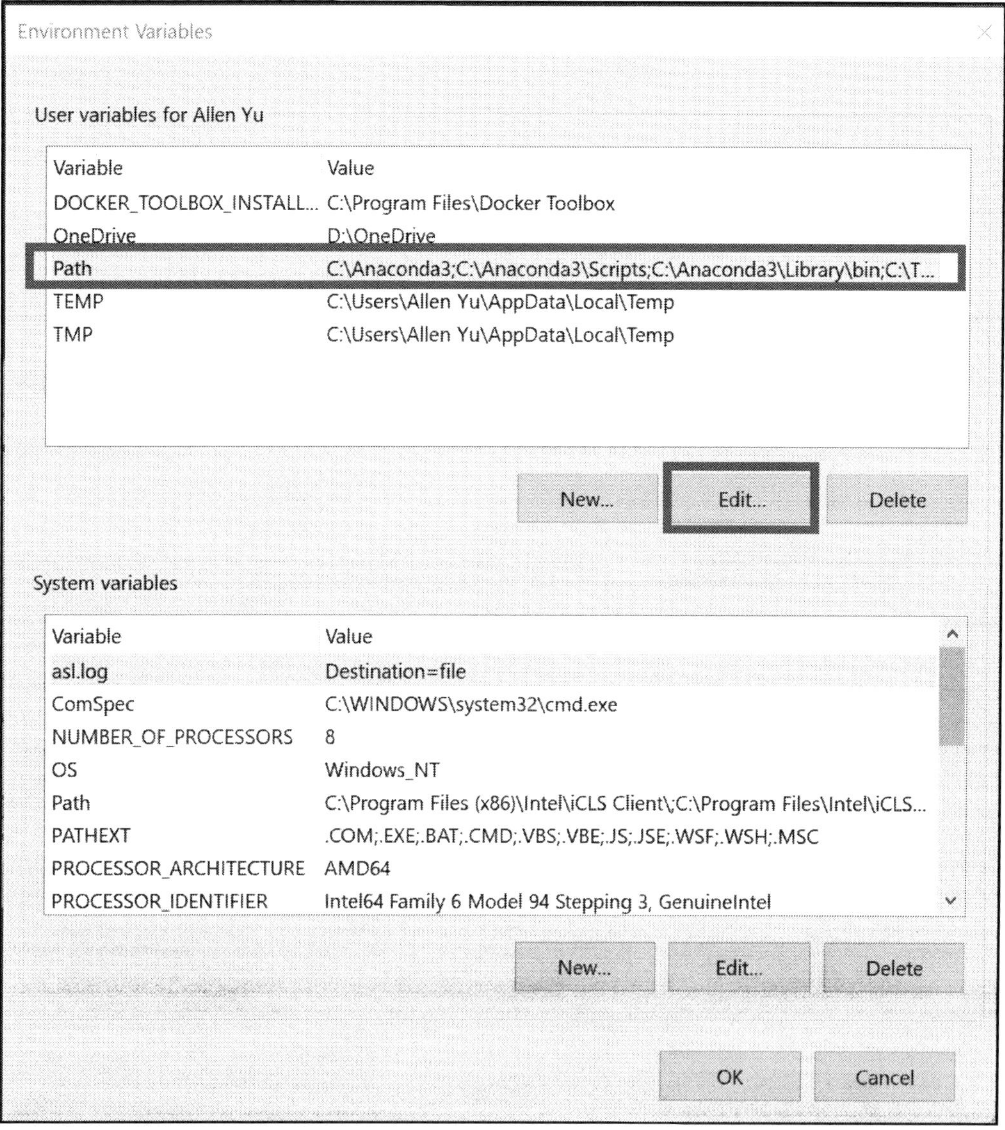

In the **Edit environmental variable** window, create a new entry that shows `c:\ffmpeg\bin`. Click on **OK** in all pop-up windows to save your changes. Restart Command Prompt and Jupyter Notebook and you are good to go.

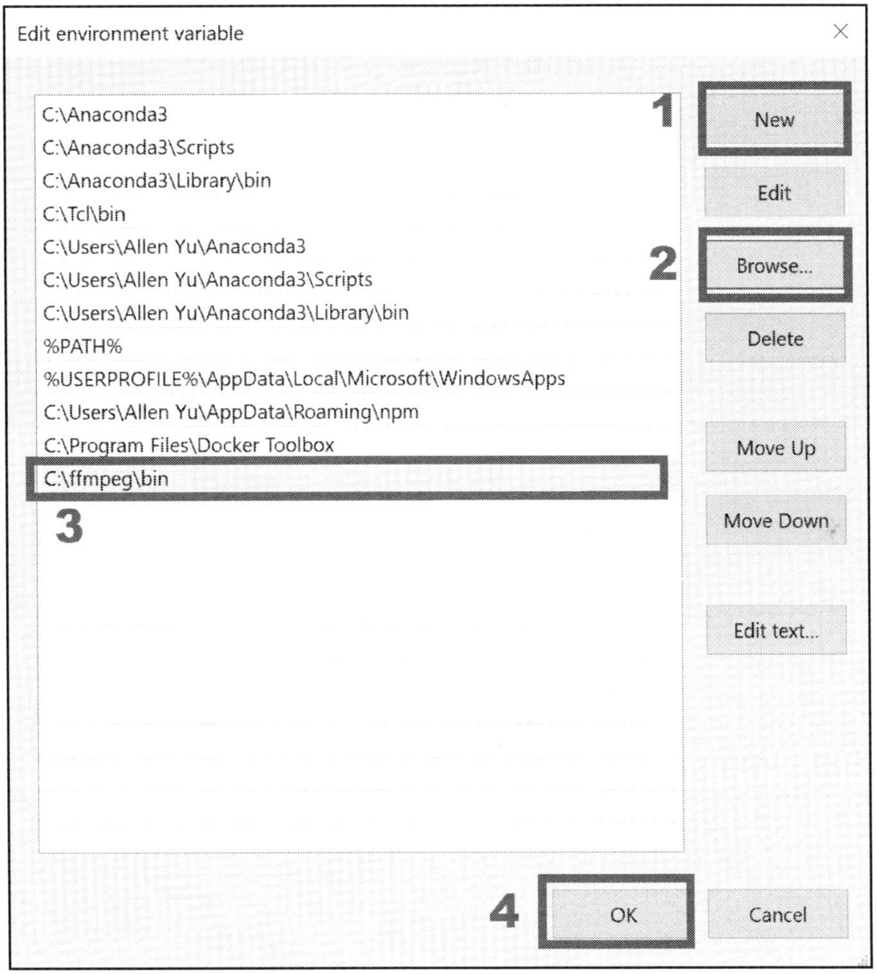

Visit Wikihow (`http://www.wikihow.com/Install-FFmpeg-on-Windows`) for instructions on installing FFmpeg on Windows 7.

Creating animations

Matplotlib provides two main interfaces for creating animations: `TimedAnimation` and `FuncAnimation`. `TimedAnimation` is useful for creating time-based animations, while `FuncAnimation` can be used to create animations according to a custom-defined function. Given the much higher level of flexibility offered by `FuncAnimation`, we will only explore the use of `FuncAnimation` in this section. Readers can refer to the official documentation (`https://matplotlib.org/api/animation_api.html`) for more information about `TimedAnimation`.

`FuncAnimation` works by repeatedly calling a function that changes the properties of Matplotlib objects in each frame. In the following example, we've simulated the change in median weekly earnings by assuming a 5% annual increase. We are going to create a custom function--animate--which returns Matplotlib Artist objects that are changed in each frame. This function will be supplied to `animation.FuncAnimation()` together with a few more extra parameters:

```
import textwrap
import matplotlib.pyplot as plt
import random
# Matplotlib animation module
from matplotlib import animation
# Used for generating HTML video embed code
from IPython.display import HTML


# Adapted from previous example, codes that are modified are commented
fig, ax = plt.subplots(figsize=(6,7))
ind = range(df.shape[0])
rects = ax.barh(ind, df["Median usual weekly earnings ($)"], height=0.5)
ax.set_xlabel('Median weekly earnings (USD)')
ylabels=[textwrap.fill(label,15) for label in df["Educational attainment"]]
ax.set_yticks(ind)
ax.set_yticklabels(ylabels)
fig.subplots_adjust(left=0.3)

# Change the x-axis range
ax.set_xlim(0,7600)

# Add a text annotation to show the current year
title = ax.text(0.5,1.05, "Median weekly earnings (USD) in 2016",
                bbox={'facecolor':'w', 'alpha':0.5, 'pad':5},
                transform=ax.transAxes, ha="center")

# Animation related stuff
```

```
n=30 #Number of frames

# Function for animating Matplotlib objects
def animate(frame):
    # Simulate 5% annual pay rise
    data = df["Median usual weekly earnings ($)"] * (1.05 ** frame)

    # Update the bar heights
    for i, rect in enumerate(rects):
        rect.set_width(data[i])

    # Update the title
    title.set_text("Median weekly earnings (USD) in {}".format(2016+frame))

    return rects, title

# Call the animator. Re-draw only the changed parts when blit=True.
# Redraw all elements when blit=False
anim=animation.FuncAnimation(fig, animate, blit=False, frames=n)

# Save the animation in MPEG-4 format
anim.save('test.mp4')

# OR--Embed the video in Jupyter notebook
HTML(anim.to_html5_video())
```

Here is the screen capture of one of the video frames:

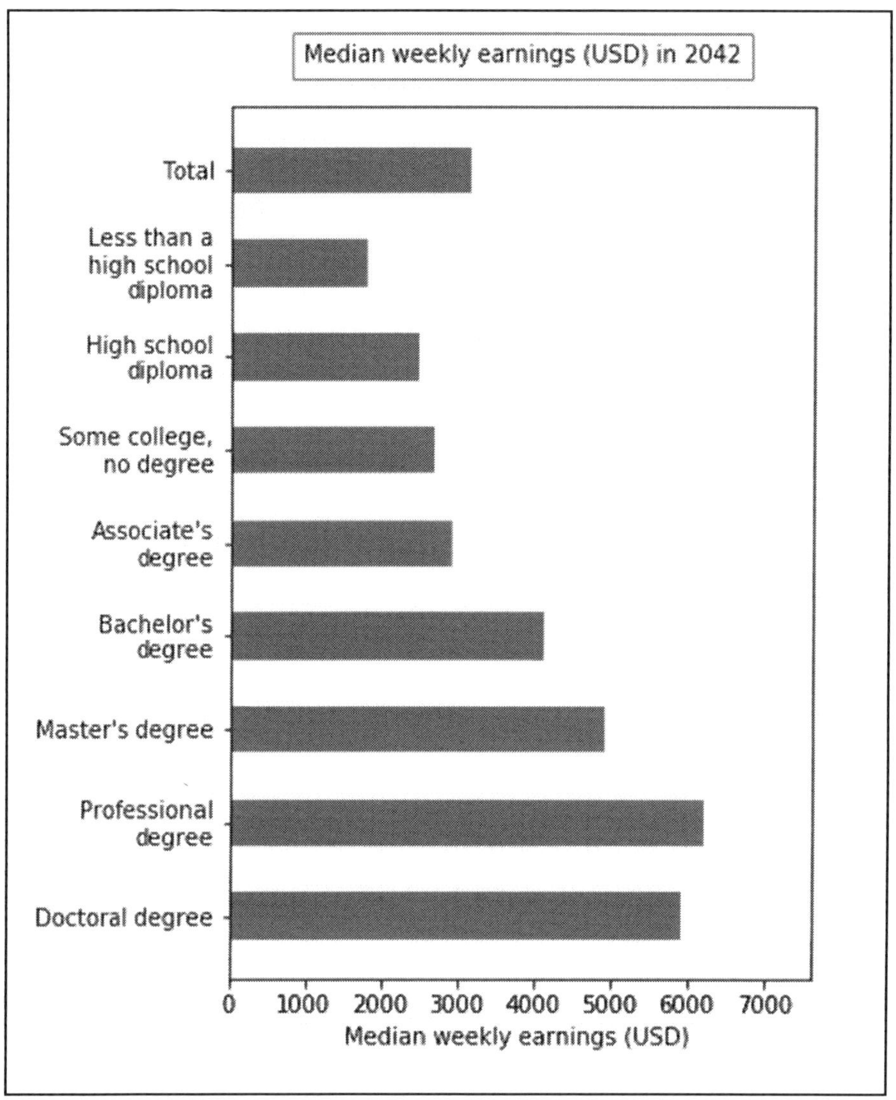

In this example, we output the animation in the form of MPEG-4-encoded videos. The video can also be embedded in Jupyter Notebook in the form of an H.264-encoded video. All you need to do is call the `Animation.to_html5_video()` method and supply the returned object to `IPython.display.HTML`. Video encoding and HTML5 code generation will happen automagically behind the scenes.

Summary

In this chapter, you further enriched your techniques for obtaining online data through the use of the BeautifulSoup web scraping library. You successfully learned the different ways of creating interactive figures and animations. These techniques will pave the way for you to create intuitive and engaging visualizations in more advanced applications.

In the next chapter, we will explore the use of Matplotlib in the context of scientific visualizations.

7
A Practical Guide to Scientific Plotting

Creating scientific figures is where art meets science. Any scientific data visualization should be "of substance, statistics and design" (pg. 51, Tufte, Edward R. *The Visual Display of Quantitative Information*, Graphics Press: Cheshire, CT, 1983; pp 1-197). We say a picture is worth a thousand words, but not all graphics are created equal. A well-drawn visual attracts audience and soundly delivers messages. On the contrary, poorly made plots can impede understanding, or even be misleading. We now have a myriad of tools for data plotting; virtually anyone can convert numbers to graphics before grasping the purpose or nature of these graphs. Such convenience makes good planning and careful crafting your actual survival skills in data visualization.

Undoubtedly, accuracy and clarity are the basic criteria to communicate scientific facts. It is more than labeling each axis properly with International System of Units (SI). The level of statistical significance is important in determining the validity of scientific discoveries. Statistical testing results are therefore often necessary to be marked on plots for quick referral. There are also other common practices in scientific plotting, some to comply with conventions and some for ethics that we should adhere to.

Finally, it is always an advantage to think from a designer's perspective. Unlike business marketing and pure art, scientists should not aim at attracting eyeballs in a fancy or extravagant manner. Nevertheless, it does not diminish the need to create appealing visuals to convey messages well. It is a well-recognized fact in psychology and cognitive science that certain properties such as colors and space influence our perception. These are termed preattentive attributes, which can aid comprehension if used effectively. There is a subtle balance between smart emphasis and misrepresentation, being informative and cluttering. Communication at various occasions warrants attention at different points as well.

We have come a long way to learn about diversified plot types and ways to fine-tune each component. In this chapter, we'll take our skills to the next level by getting the gist of professional scientific plotting. Let's have a look at the topics covered:

- General rules of effective visualization
    - Planning your figure
        - Choosing the right plot type
        - Targeting your audience
    - Crafting your graph
        - The science of visual perception
        - Giving emphasis and avoiding clutter
        - Styling plots for slideshows, posters, and journal articles
- Scientific practice
    - Bar chart: stacked versus layered
    - Replacing bar charts with mean-and-error plots
    - Indicating statistical significance:
        - Adding "stars" to indicate significance
    - Methods of dimension reduction:
        - Principal Component Analysis (PCA)
        - t-distributed Stochastic Neighbour Embedding (t-SNE)

After this chapter, you will master quality figure-making for scientific communication through different media.

General rules of effective visualization

In `Chapter 2`, *Figure Aesthetics*, we briefly introduced ways to fine-tune figure aesthetics, focusing more on the coding techniques. Before a deeper discussion of science-specific plotting skills, we would like to introduce some general guidelines for making effective visuals.

Planning your figure

I have my numbers. I have my plot recipes. Now what? Plo... Wait a minute. To plot or not to plot? That is the question. We are not switching to philosophy or literature. Scientific figures are not simply decorations to add colors to your manuscript or presentation, but should each bring out a unique message.

To achieve this, it is essential for us to consider the context when planning our figures. Just like writing essays, we can do so by thinking about the 6Ws--"Why", "What", "Who", "When", "Where", and "How".

Do we need the plot?

We set out plotting a graph by knowing its purpose: "why". In preparing manuscripts to submit to journals, slideshows, or poster presentations, we always have a coherent main theme throughout, or at least within a section. Figures inserted are the evidence that guides us step by step to drawing the conclusion consistent with the theme.

Knowing the purpose of figures, "when" the dataset is worth a plot, depends on determining how it shapes a sound argument toward the conclusion. Note that this does not mean we should hide away contradictory results. Instead, given the limited space and time (and more importantly, the effective attention that our audience can give), we can save on redundant information. Necessary but unimportant information can be summarized in supplementary sections sometimes.

Choosing the right plot

Having introduced so many plot types in previous chapters, it would be great for us to have a quick summary here. The choice of plot types should be primarily based on data type, followed by the target usage of the plots:

- Are we trying to compare and contrast different groups of data?
- Are we trying to show the relationship between groups?
- Are we trying to show the distribution of data?
- Are we trying to show the ratio or composition of groups?

Finally, we need to understand the advantages and limitations of different plot types in order to make the right decision. We have summarized the major considerations of choosing plot types in this table:

Data type	**Plot type**	**Suitable for showing**	**Notes**
Trend / time series	Line chart (`Chapter 1`, *Hello Plotting World!*, `Chapter 2`, *Figure Aesthetics*, and `Chapter 4`, *Visualizing Online Data*)	Comparison, relationship	Simple yet versatile.
-	Area chart (`Chapter 4`, *Visualizing Online Data*)	Distribution	More verbose than line chart.
-	Stacked area chart (`Chapter 4`, *Visualizing Online Data*)	Composition	It may be difficult to compare the relative sizes due to different baselines.
Univariate distribution	Bar chart (`Chapter 3`, *Figure Layout and Annotations* and `Chapter 4`, *Visualizing Online Data*)	Comparison	Good for comparing against zero. Not suitable if zero is not a meaningful value.
-	Histogram (`Chapter 4`, *Visualizing Online Data*)	Distribution	-
-	Kernel density estimation (`Chapter 4`, *Visualizing Online Data*)	Distribution	More informative than histograms, as the full distribution of data can be shown, and the data points are not grouped into discrete bins.
-	Line chart (`Chapter 1`, *Hello Plotting World!*, `Chapter 2`, *Figure Aesthetics*, and `Chapter 4`, *Visualizing Online Data*)	Comparison, relationship	-
-	Point plot (`Chapter 5`, *Visualizing Multivariate Data* and `Chapter 7`, *A Practical Guide to Scientific Plotting*)	Comparison, relationship	Similar to line chart. Yet it can display confidence intervals or standard deviation.

Bivariate distribution	Scatter plot (`Chapter 3`, *Figure Layout and Annotations* and `Chapter 4`, *Visualizing Online Data*)	Relationship	-
-	Hexbin chart (`Chapter 4`, *Visualizing Online Data*)	Distribution	-
-	Kernel density estimation (`Chapter 4`, *Visualizing Online Data*)	Distribution	More informative than a hexbin chart, as the full distribution of data can be shown, and the data points are not grouped into discrete bins.
-	Line chart (`Chapter 1`, *Hello Plotting World!*, `Chapter 2`, *Figure Aesthetics*, and `Chapter 4`, *Visualizing Online Data*)	Relationship	-
Categorical data	Box plot (`Chapter 4`, *Visualizing Online Data*)	Distribution	-
-	Categorical scatter plot (`Chapter 4`, *Visualizing Online Data*)	Distribution	-
-	Pie chart (`Chapter 3`, *Figure Layout and Annotations*)	Composition	It is hard to make comparison between similar groups based on the size of slices alone, as the curved surfaces obscure the perception of size.
-	Swarm plot (`Chapter 4`, *Visualizing Online Data*)	Distribution	-
-	Violin plot (`Chapter 4`, *Visualizing Online Data*)	Distribution	More informative than boxplots, as the full distribution of data can be shown. Meanwhile, boxplots can only show the quartiles of data.

Multivariate distribution	Candlestick plot (`Chapter 5`, *Visualizing Multivariate Data*)	Comparison	-
-	Faceted plot (`Chapter 5`, *Visualizing Multivariate Data*)	Comparison	Not scalable to a large number of variables.
-	Heatmap (`Chapter 5`, *Visualizing Multivariate Data*)	Comparison	An extremely compact form of visualization.
-	Multiaxes chart (`Chapter 5`, *Visualizing Multivariate Data*)	Comparison, composition, distribution, relationship	-
-	Pair plot (`Chapter 5`, *Visualizing Multivariate Data*)	Comparison, relationship	Not scalable to large number of variables.
-	3D scatter plot (`Chapter 5`, *Visualizing Multivariate Data*)	Relationship	3D plots should be avoided, as the proportions would be skewed when projected to 2D space.
-	3D bar chart (`Chapter 5`, *Visualizing Multivariate Data*)	Comparison	3D plots should be avoided, as the proportions would be skewed when projected to 2D space.

Targeting your audience

"Who" and "where" are your audience? Are they readers of your manuscript, field experts in a scientific conference, or the general public in a science promotion seminar? This sets the context of the graphics and will influence how you present your data.

We need to consider the knowledge scope of the audience in choosing between some more specific and complex field-standard plots and ones easier to understand but losing details. Figures in slideshows, posters, and journal articles also need different adaptations, which we will list in the next section.

Crafting your graph

Now you should be clear about the purpose and overall plan for every plot to make. It is time to make it *good*.

We made a nice start by choosing the right plot for the right results. Still, careful crafting of details defines how easily your figures can be comprehended. In this section, we will introduce some basic concepts of human visual perception, which is the science behind design principles. We will then learn to adapt our figures to make them more digestible for the brain.

The science of visual perception

Data visualization is not rocket science, but there are reasons why some figures can be made easier to understand just with different styling. Researchers have identified visual properties that human can quickly process with high accuracy by the low-level visual system, including color, size, similarity, and space. These properties are termed preattentive attributes. Making good use of these attributes can help us organize our visuals and highlight important messages.

The Gestalt principles of visual perception

Gestalt is a German word that stands for *form* or *shape*. The Gestalt principles are a series of theories developed in the 1920s by German researches, which discuss how we perceive visual elements. These principles are well known to graphic designers. More and more scientists are recognizing their importance in data visualization.

Here is a selected array of examples demonstrating these principles:

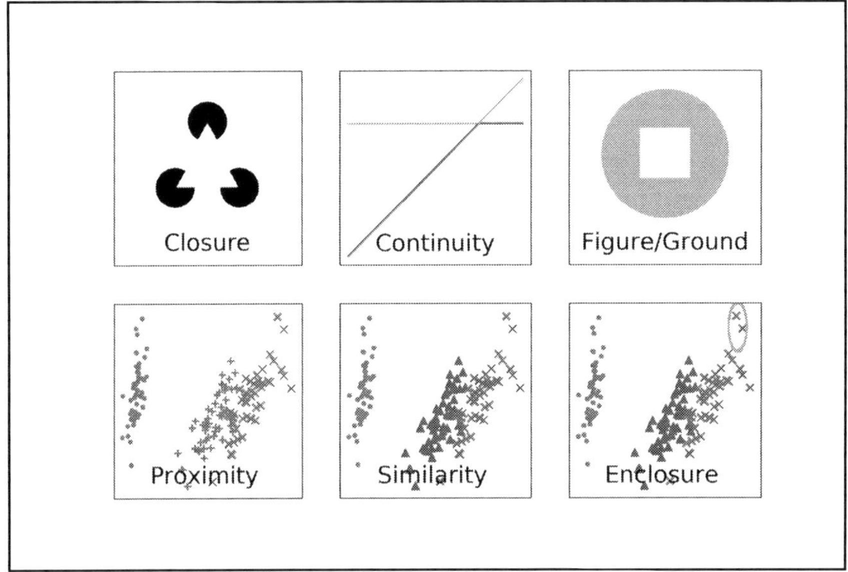

On the top row, we can see the Kanizsa triangle, which is a famous demonstration of an illusory contour. We also have a tendency to follow and extend lines that flow smoothly. In the top middle box, it may be more intuitive to think there are two straight lines instead of kinked lines, if the lines had similar colors. For figure and ground, we generally take the form with the larger area as the ground.

The bottom row shows the techniques that are most relevant to data visualization, especially for scatter plots. By nature, the distance between groups of dots represents the amount of difference between these groups of samples. When other visual cues are not obvious, as in the bottom-left case with the same color and two similar markers, it is difficult to differentiate between the two groups on the right. Higher contrast is added in the next subplot so that the three groups now become distinct by similarity of in-group marker colors and shapes. The final box shows how we can insert an extra enclosure to point out interesting features, such as outliers in a group here.

These examples were drawn in Matplotlib. As we are discussing from the designer's perspective, making them is left as a challenge for you. You can check out the code from our GitHub repository for this book.

Getting organized

Layout and organization guide the flow of readers' attention. Getting organized is a simple way to keep your audience attentive. As each figure is an argument step towards your final conclusion, presenting them in a logical order lets the audience follow your ideas closely.

Ordering plots and data series logically

When grouping multiple subplots, it is more intuitive to start from left to right, and top to bottom. As our eyes are on the same level, we have a wider horizontal field of view of 200° than the vertical 135°. It is much easier to draw a mental straight line within the same view to compare the levels, than to remember the position on an upper graph and look down for comparison. The horizontal-then-vertical arrangement reduces eye saccades which are known to cause "change blindness". Hence, it is more intuitive to place plots to be compared horizontally where possible, and let the readers scroll down row by row.

Within one graph, data series should also be ordered logically. For example, when we are preparing a visualization of drug efficacy, it would make more sense to order as control, intermediate conditions, and disease instead of having the intermediate conditions on either side.

Grouping

Here are some visualization techniques that might facilitate the display of groups:

- Use contrasting features such as marker types, as previously shown
- Have more space between groups of bars than between bars within a group
- Use enclosure methods such as adding circles or background colors to selected regions

Giving emphasis and avoiding clutter

Preattentive attributes can highlight important messages in visuals, while nonstrategic use can be distracting. To let readers focus on the plot information instead of struggling to find a point to focus on, legibility and minimalism are the two main application principles.

Color and hue

- Use plain colors without gradient or shadow
- Use the same color at least within each data series
- Use distinctive colors to mark categories
- Use warm colors to highlight features among cold or greyscale colors

Size and weight

- Make sure all sizes and lines are large and heavy enough to be legible
- Apply selective bolding to give emphasis

Spacing

- Try not to cramp in too many words and annotations within small figures
- Set the scales and limits of axes to center your object of interest within enough space

Typography

- Use a large enough font size
- Use a sans-serif font such as Arial
- Keep the same font family unless necessary, for example, symbols
- Use hierarchical font size and weight, up to three types in general
- Give emphasis with selective bolding

Use minimal marker shapes

- Use pairs of open and filled shapes such as ●○▲△ to reduce the number of shapes used
- Use solid lines with different colors instead if there are too many datasets

Styling plots for slideshows, posters, and journal articles

Scientific plots mostly reside in any of the three media: slideshows, posters, and journal articles. Because of the different environmental settings and amount of time our audience can spend on reading a figure, we need to adapt our graphics accordingly.

We now list the common considerations and corresponding adaptations.

Display time

Figures in slideshows have a very limited display time, usually less than 1 minute per slide. Poster and journal article readers may spend more time on a figure at their own pace. As a result, the complexity of visuals should be adjusted accordingly.

Space allowed

The slide dimension limits the figure dimension and layout in slideshows. We may set our own layout to assign different amounts of space to each figure in our poster, whereas the overall poster size and shape are usually fixed by the conference organizer. Sometimes a team poster template will be followed. More figures are packed in a journal article to include supporting data comprehensively, with figure dimensions specified by the journal.

Distance from the audience

An oral presentation can happen anywhere from small conference room to a huge lecture theater. Poster readers typically stand within a meter. Simpler graphs with larger element sizes and higher color contrast are needed in slideshows and posters, as compared to journal articles. There are built-in style sheets such as `'seaborn-talk'`, `'seaborn-poster'`, and `'seaborn-paper'` to use or modify from.

Adaptations

A graph can be simplified by reducing the number of subplots, showing representative examples instead of all datasets, using heavier font and line weights, and highlighting points of interest. Elements such as vertical text at the y axis label can be used in journals to save space, but they should be avoided on slideshows as they are too counter-intuitive to catch within a short time.

Summary of styling plots for slideshows, posters, and journal articles

-	Slideshow	Poster	Journal article
Time to study	Very limited; usually <1 min	Variable; usually within several minutes	Variable; readers can spend extended time and revisit the figures
Distance from audience	Far	Within a meter	Close; readers can enlarge the image
Dimensions and space allowed	Total space limited by screen; it is 4:3 or 16:9	Can customize the poster layout to assign space and dimensions. The overall poster size usually set by the conference organizer.	Per journal specification; figure dimensions and maximum number of main text figures may be fixed
Medium	Screen projector	Paper or fabric	Computer screen via online access or on printed paper.
Number of figures to show in one view	One main figure, with up to a few supporting or parallel figures	One to a few put together. All figures may be in sight.	Multiple subplots and relevant figures are usually grouped and viewed together as one main figure according to the flow of content in the main text. More supporting evidence for the same message can be added.
Complexity	Simplest	Preferably simple.	Can afford higher complexity for more details. Note the trade-off with clarity.
Size and weight	Bold	Clearly legible at one meter distance; hierarchy is important	Clearly legible, but often more space is allowed for the plot body.
Color	RGB; higher contrast preferred	CMYK; higher contrast preferred	Per journal requirement; adhere to the clarity principle.
Resolution	>72 dpi	>300 dpi	Per journal requirement; usually >300 dpi

Stylistic coherency	Preferred	Stringent	Preferred. Sometimes taken care of by the journal. Still preferable but less stringent for supplementary figures.

It's great to summarize the general visualization guidelines through bad and good examples. The leftmost plot below is a bad example where there are illegibly small fonts, inconsistent font sizes and weights, counter-intuitive highlighting colors, and unnecessary annotations. All these are fixed in the middle plot, which is good enough to be viewed online or on printed articles. For slideshows and poster presentation, we can improve further by removing clutters and increasing the font weight to enhance readability.

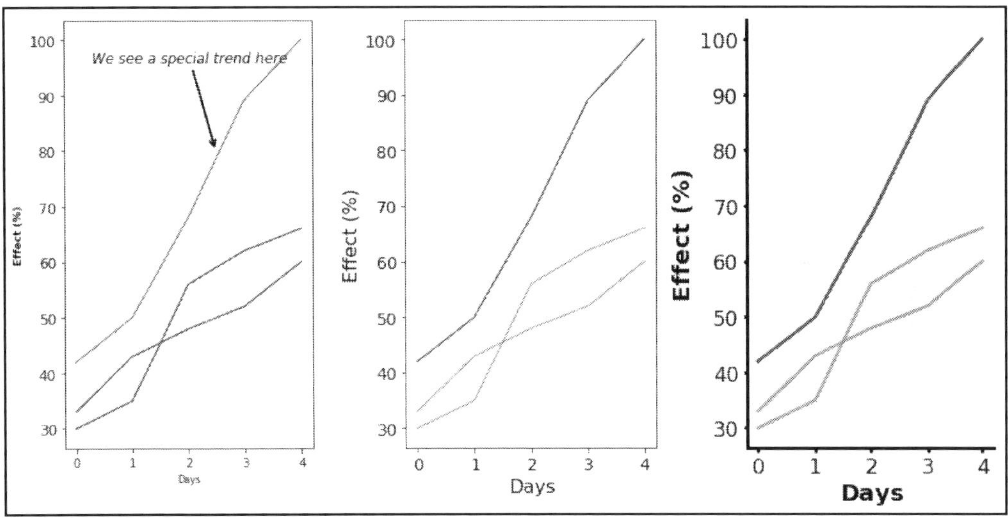

If you are interested in more design concepts for scientific presentations, here is a nice collection of articles published on the blog of Nature Methods: `http://blogs.nature.com/methagora/2013/07/data-visualization-points-of-view.html`.

In the next section, we are going to discuss the statistical aspects of scientific plotting.

Visualizing statistical data more intuitively

Science is based on statistics. We propose hypotheses from observations. We test and reject the null hypothesis when its probability, the p value, is lower than a threshold, so that observed phenomena are not likely arisen from mere chance; that is, our proposed hypothesis is supported.

There are some specific plot types that can ease the visualization of descriptive and inferential statistics. We will first revisit more variants of bar charts–stacked bar chart and layered histograms, which are commonly used in scientific publications to summarize and describe data.

Stacked bar chart and layered histogram

In `Chapter 4`, *Visualizing Online Data*, we showed the procedures to create bar charts using Matplotlib and Seaborn. It is little known that the pandas package can be used for visualization, as most people only concentrate on its data analysis capabilities. Since the pandas visualization module was built on top of Matplotlib, we can exploit the powerful APIs in the Matplotlib ecosystem to customize our figures. For more information about the pandas plotting API, please visit `https://pandas.pydata.org/pandas-docs/stable/generated/pandas.DataFrame.plot.html`.

In some cases, Pandas can create decent-looking figures that are relatively hard to make with Matplotlib or Seaborn. Stacked bar charts and layered histograms are two such examples. For instance, this blogger (`http://randyzwitch.com/creating-stacked-bar-chart-seaborn/`) took 4 hours to figure out the way to a create stacked bar chart using Seaborn.

A stacked bar chart enables us to compare the relative contribution of variables towards the total. Meanwhile, a layered histogram makes cross-comparison between conditions much easier. Therefore, they are commonly used in scientific publications. We will first show you how we can make a stacked bar chart with only a few lines of code:

```
import numpy as np
import pandas as pd
import matplotlib.pyplot as plt


# Generate 20 random variables in three groups
df = pd.DataFrame({'Condition 1': np.random.rand(20),
                   'Condition 2': np.random.rand(20)*0.9,
                   'Condition 3': np.random.rand(20)*1.1})
```

```
# Create a figure with one axes
fig, ax = plt.subplots()

# Plot a stacked bar chart
df.plot.bar(ax=ax, stacked=True)

# Add axes labels using Matplotlib's API
ax.set_xlabel("Variable")
ax.set_ylabel("Total")

plt.show()
```

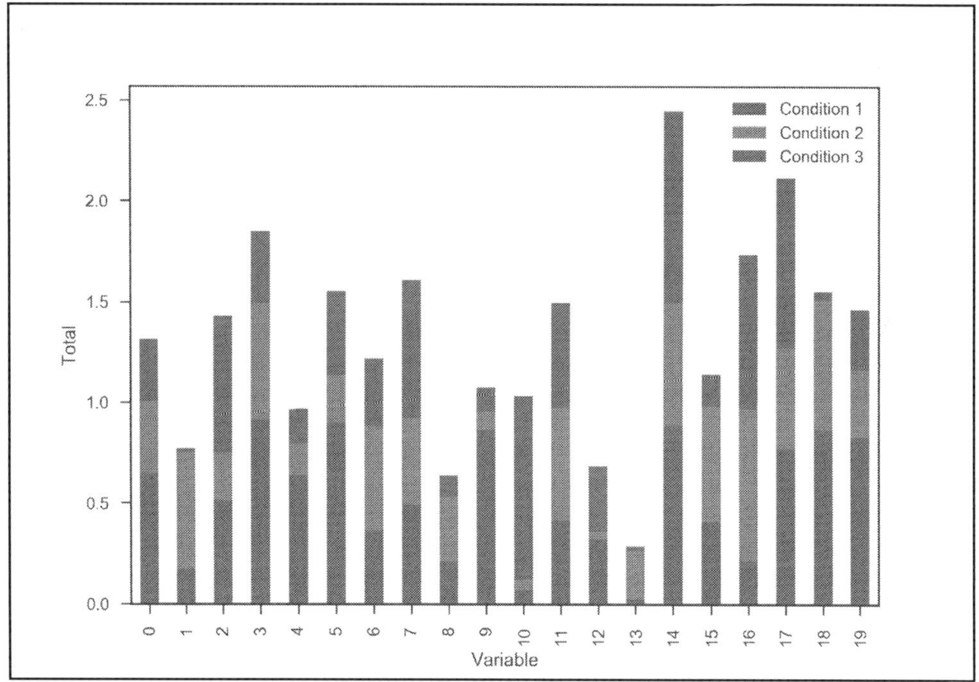

As we can see in the preceding example, a stacked bar plot can be created by simply specifying `stacked=True` in `pandas.DataFrame.plot.bar()`. With slight modifications, we can convert this plot into a stacked percentage bar plot:

```
from matplotlib.ticker import FuncFormatter


# Get the ratio of each condition by dividing each data point by
# its column sum
df_ratio = df.div(df.sum(axis=1), axis=0)
```

```
# Create a figure with one axes
fig, ax = plt.subplots()

# Plot a stacked bar chart
df_ratio.plot.bar(ax=ax, stacked=True)

# Add axes labels using Matplotlib's API
ax.set_xlabel("Variable")
ax.set_ylabel("Percentage")

# Apply a FuncFormatter to convert y-tick labels to percentage
ax.yaxis.set_major_formatter(FuncFormatter(lambda y, _:
'{:.0%}'.format(y)))

# Put legend outside the plotting area
ax.legend(bbox_to_anchor=(0., 1.02, 1., .102), loc=3,
          ncol=3, mode="expand", borderaxespad=0.)

plt.show()
```

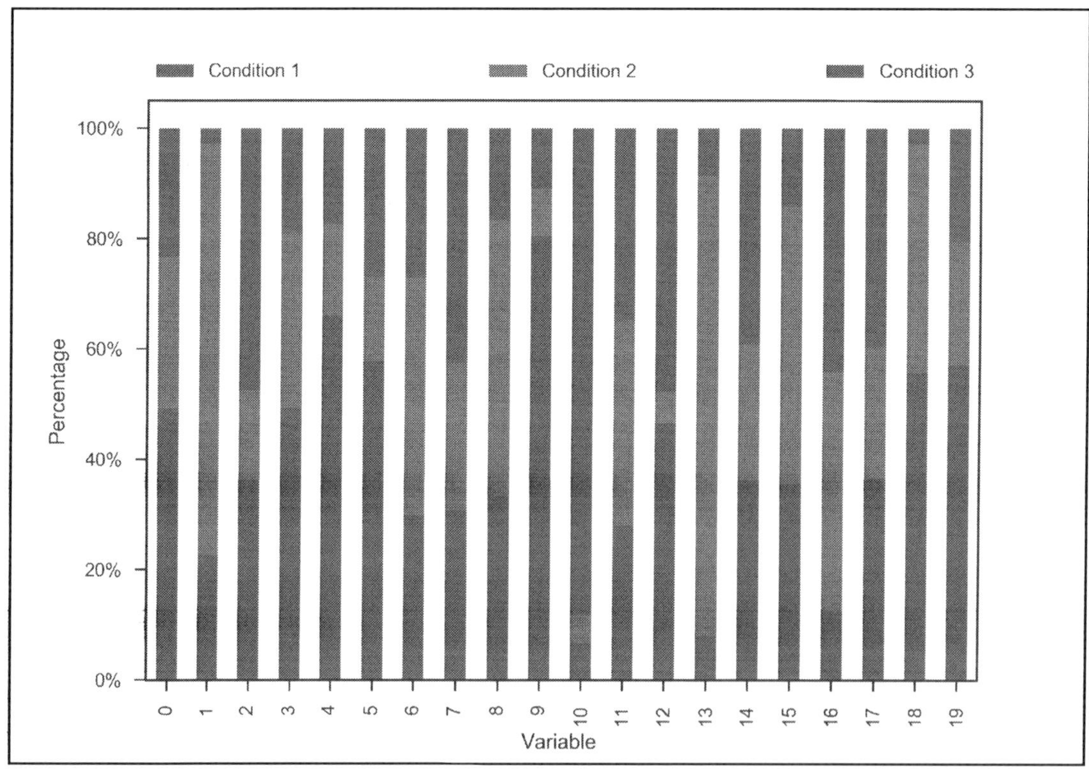

Likewise, the creation of layered histograms is also much simplified by pandas:

```
# Let's generate another random dataset with 200 random variables
df2 = pd.DataFrame({'Condition 1': np.random.randn(200),
                    'Condition 2': np.random.randn(200)*0.5+0.5,
                    'Condition 3': np.random.randn(200)-0.5})

# Create a figure with one axes
fig, ax = plt.subplots()

# Plot a layered histogram, alpha controls the transparency level
df2.plot.hist(ax=ax, alpha=0.5)

# Add axes labels using Matplotlib's API
ax.set_xlabel("Variable")
ax.set_ylabel("Total")

plt.show()
```

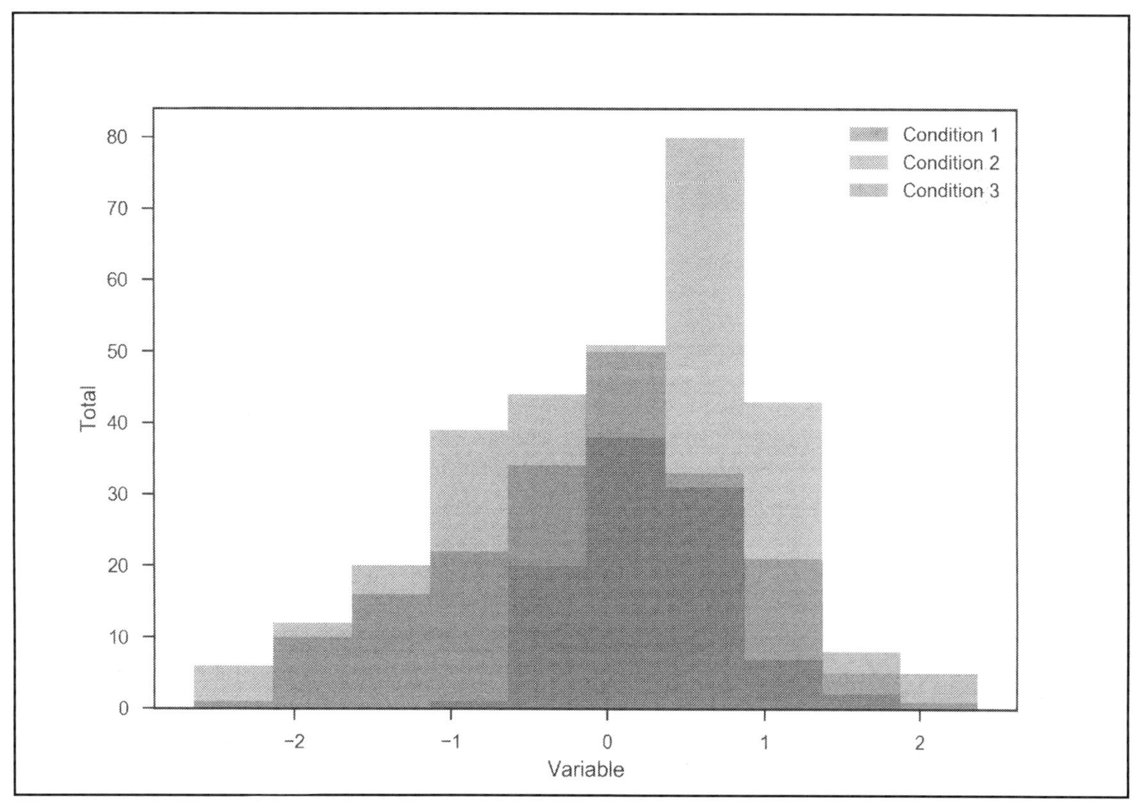

By fiddling with the `stacked` and `bins` parameters, we can instead create a stacked histogram with a customized number of bins:

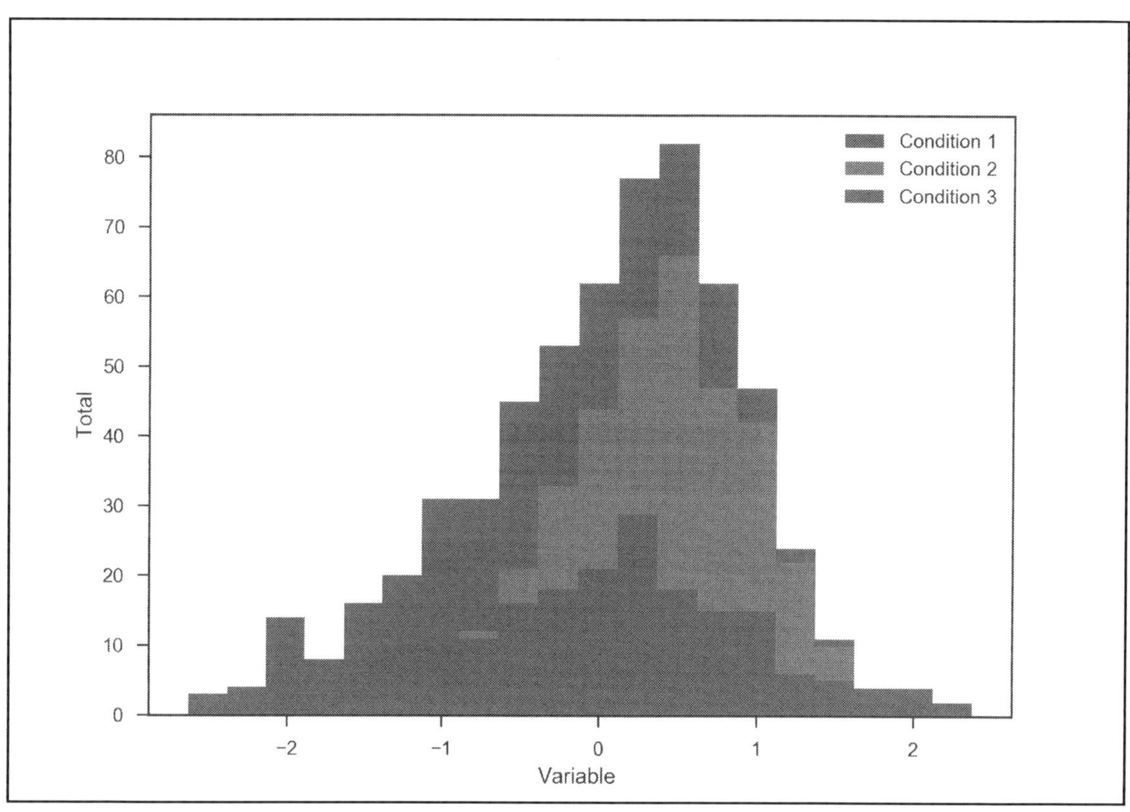

Replacing bar charts with mean-and-error plots

One of the main goals of scientific visualization is to allow intuitive comparison between cases and controls. Stacked bar charts or layered histograms do look aesthetically pleasing, but they could be confusing to readers, such as the first stacked bar chart example in this chapter. Can you tell whether variable 16 or 17 is larger in condition 3? This comparison is difficult because of the floating baseline. Similarly, layered histograms are harder to interpret, because the meanings of mixed colors have to be inferred and are not defined in the legend.

We can use `seaborn.pointplot()` to create a less verbose mean-and-error plot for comparisons between groups. To change the confidence intervals depicted by the error bars, we can change the value of the `ci` parameter. Setting `ci="sd"` would change the error bars to display standard deviation instead. Let's see how pointplot works from this example:

```
import numpy as np
import pandas as pd
import matplotlib.pyplot as plt
import seaborn as sns


# Generate 30 individuals with random disease states, gender and response
df = pd.DataFrame({'Condition': np.random.choice(["Disease",
"Intermediate", "Control"], 30),
                   'Gender': np.random.choice(["Male", "Female"], 30),
                   'Response': np.random.randint(10, high=100, size=30)})

# Create a figure
fig= plt.figure()

# Plot a pointplot
ax = sns.pointplot(x="Condition", y="Response", hue="Gender", ci="sd",
data=df)

plt.show()
```

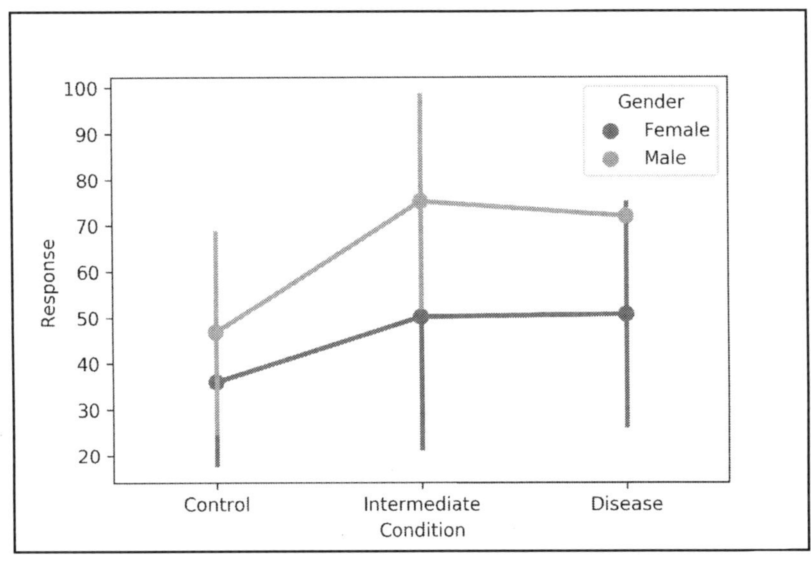

The error bars are currently overlapping, which may obscure interpretation. We can add a slight horizontal spacing between the data series using the `dodge` parameter to separate the lines. Some scientific journals are black and white only, so we can change the style of lines and markers to further separate the two data series. Besides, as per the conventions of many scientific journals, error bars are usually capped. We can create capped error bars using the `capsize` parameter:

```
# Create a figure
fig= plt.figure()

# Plot a pointplot, with horizontal spacing and different styles
# between series
ax = sns.pointplot(x="Condition", y="Response",
                   hue="Gender", ci="sd",
                   dodge=True,
                   markers=["o", "x"],
                   linestyles=["-", "--"],
                   capsize=.1,
                   data=df)
plt.show()
```

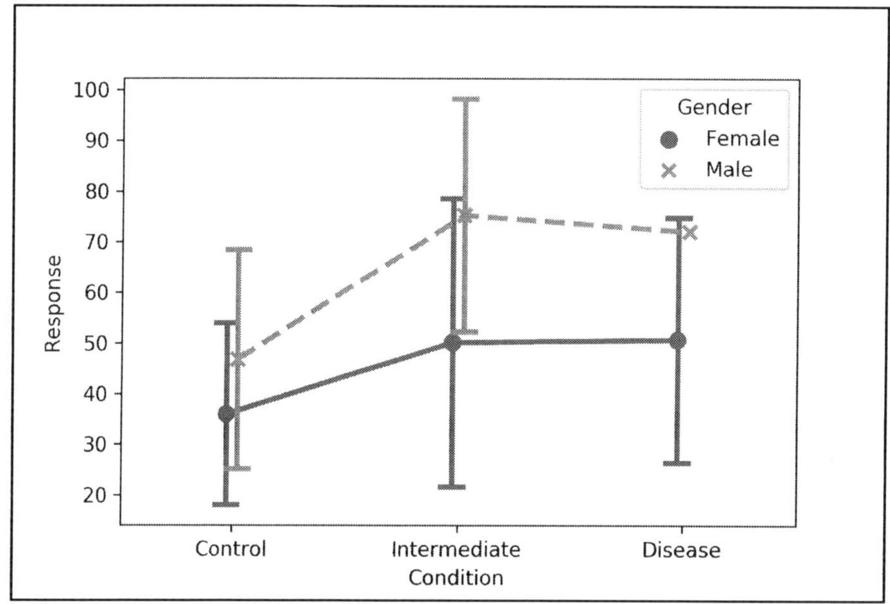

Some may argue that adding lines between groups falsely implies a relationship or dependence of data points. If the measurement groups are independent, we may consider the use of a box plot instead, which shows the distribution of data points without any connecting lines:

```
# Create a figure
fig= plt.figure()

# Plot a boxplot
ax = sns.boxplot(x="Condition", y="Response",
                 hue="Gender", data=df)

plt.show()
```

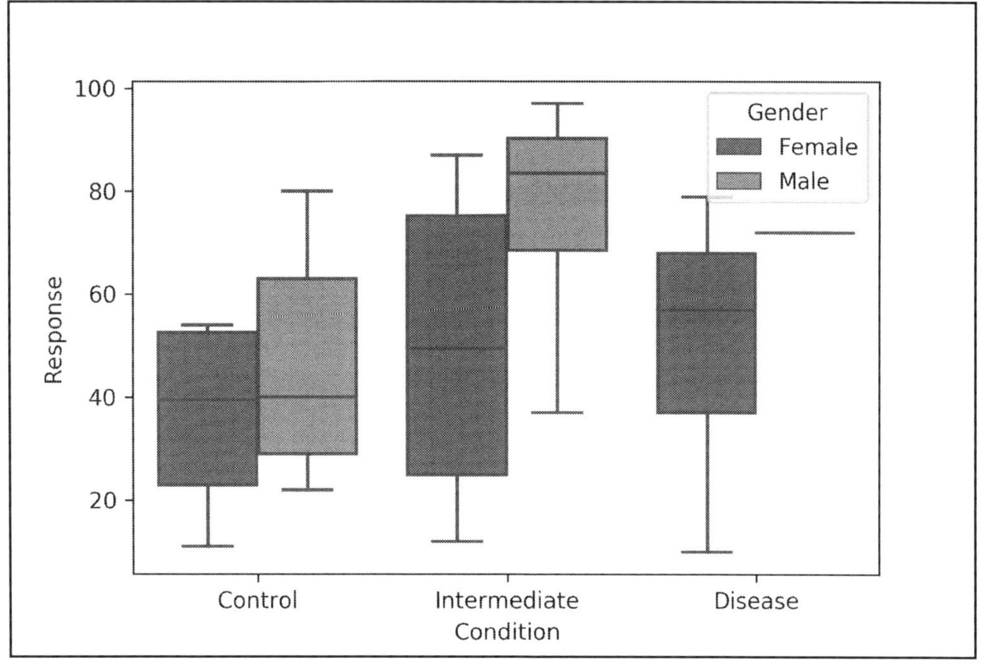

Indicating statistical significance

For journals that are following the formatting guidelines from the **American Psychological Association** (**APA**) or the **New England Journal of Medicine** (**NEJM**), we can use asterisks to indicate statistical significance in plots. Here is a table that summarizes the notation at different levels of P value, and in general, no more than four asterisks are allowed:

Symbol	**P value**
ns	>0.05
*	≤ 0.05
**	≤ 0.01
***	≤ 0.001

Neither Matplotlib nor Seaborn provides a way to annotate statistical significance easily, so we need to do that on our own. First, we need to construct brackets using `Matplotlib.Axes.plot`, followed by the addition of text annotations using `Matplotlib.Axes.text`. Please take a look at the following code excerpt to get an idea of how this works:

```
# Create a figure
fig= plt.figure()

# Plot a pointplot
ax = sns.pointplot(x="Condition", y="Response",
                   dodge=True, capsize=.1,
                   data=df)

# Top margin for asterisk position
h = 2
# Bracket location
y = df["Response"].max()

# Tick positions for each group
group1 = 0
group2 = 1
group3 = 2

# Plot a bracket across the first two groups
ax.plot([group1+0.1, group1+0.1, group2-0.1, group2-0.1], [y, y+h, y+h, y],
lw=1.5, c="k")
# Plot a bracket across the last two groups
ax.plot([group2+0.1, group2+0.1, group3-0.1, group3-0.1], [y, y+h, y+h, y],
lw=1.5, c="k")
```

```
# Indicate the statistical significance between the first two groups
ax.text((group1+group2)/2, y+h, "**", ha='center', va='bottom')
# Indicate the statistical significance between the last two groups
ax.text((group2+group3)/2, y+h, "*", ha='center', va='bottom')

# Increase the y-axis limit to show the new elements in full
ax.set_ylim(0,110)

plt.show()
```

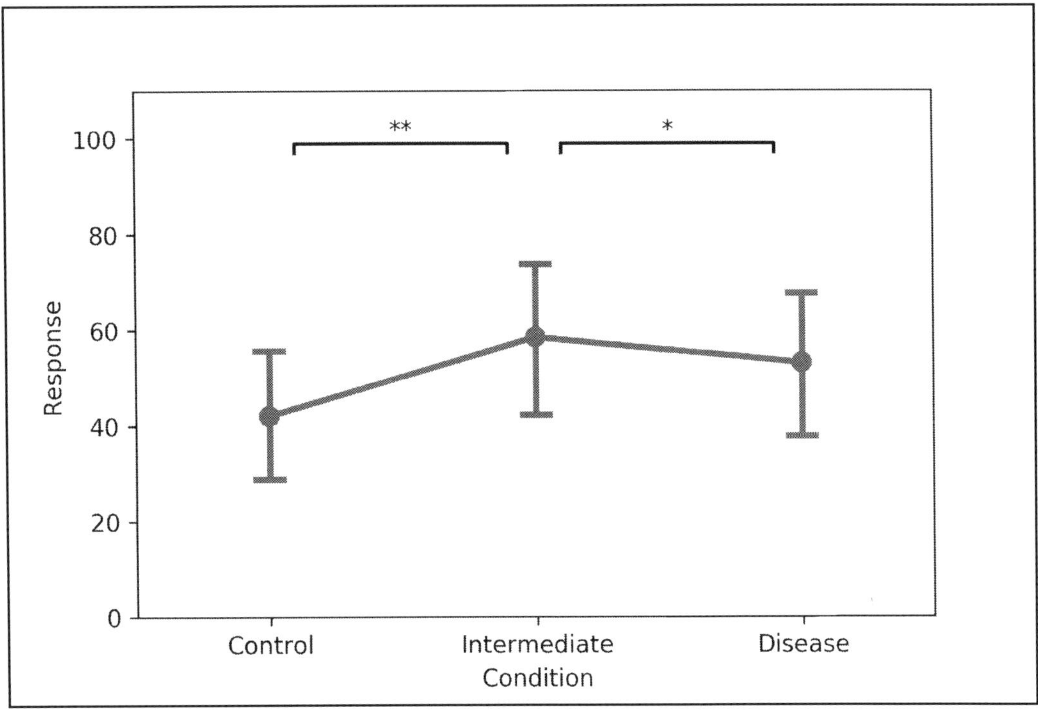

Methods for dimensions reduction

In the era of big data analysis, it is common to deal with datasets with a large number of features or dimensions. Visualization of data with high dimensionality is extremely challenging, as we will show later in this chapter, because we need to project all these dimensions to two-dimensional space (for example, a screen or paper).

In general, there are two types of dimensionality reduction approaches: linear and non-linear. Here are a few examples of each category for your information:

Method	**Type**
Principal component analysis (PCA)	Linear
Linear discriminant analysis (LDA)	Linear
Generalized discriminant analysis (GDA)	Linear
t-distributed stochastic neighbor embedding (t-SNE)	Non-linear
Isomap	Non-linear
Sammon's mapping	Non-linear
Curvilinear component analysis (CCA)	Non-linear
Multidimensional scaling (MDS)	Non-linear
Laplacian eigenmaps	Non-linear

In this chapter, we are going to focus on PCA and t-SNE only, which are commonly used approaches in their respective category.

To better illustrate the techniques for dealing with data with high dimensionality, we are going to use the recently published cervical cancer dataset from the machine learning repository at the University of Califonia, Irvine (`https://archive.ics.uci.edu/ml/datasets/Cervical+cancer+%28Risk+Factors%29`). There are 36 features in this dataset, consisting of demographic information, daily habits, sexual habits, risk factors, medical records, and cancer diagnosis, which are obtained from 858 patients. For more details about this dataset, please refer to the following publication:

Kelwin Fernandes, Jaime S. Cardoso, and Jessica Fernandes. *Transfer Learning with Partial Observability Applied to Cervical Cancer Screening*. Iberian Conference on Pattern Recognition and Image Analysis. Springer International Publishing, 2017.

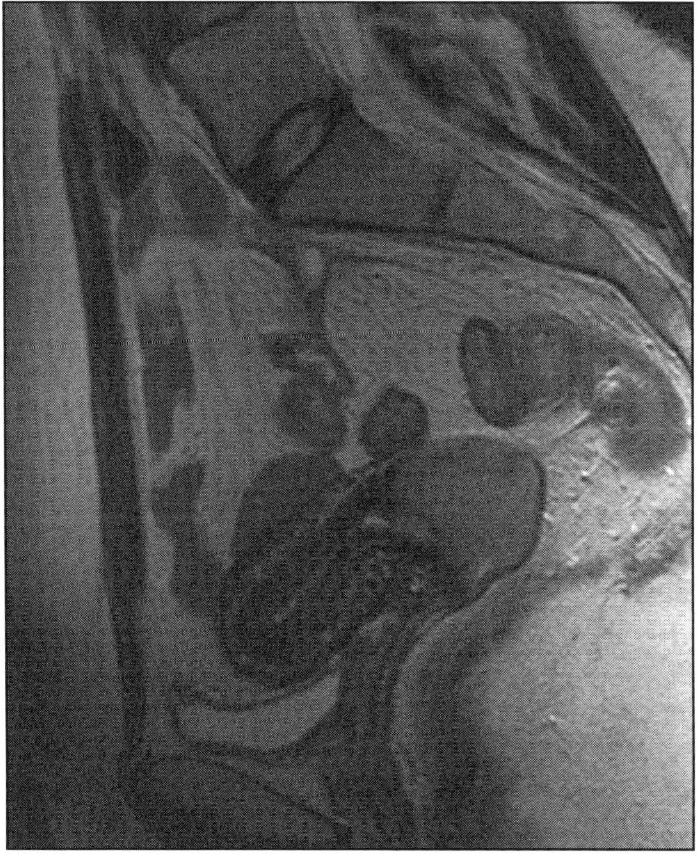

MR image of cervical cancer (source: Rádiológ-wikipedia.org)

This dataset was recorded in CSV format. As discussed in `Chapter 4`, *Visualizing Online Data,* we can use pandas to parse a CSV file into a DataFrame. Let's try to import the dataset first:

```
import pandas as pd


url =
'https://archive.ics.uci.edu/ml/machine-learning-databases/00383/risk_facto
rs_cervical_cancer.csv'
df = pd.read_csv(url, na_values="?") # NaN values are given as ? in
# the dataset
df.head() # Show the first 5 rows
```

-	Age	Number of sexual partners	First sexual intercourse	Num of pregnancies	Smokes	Smokes (years)	Smokes (packs/year)	Hormonal Contraceptives	Hormonal Contraceptives (years)	IUD	...	STDs: Time since first diagnosis	STDs: Time since last diagnosis	Dx:Cancer	Dx:CIN	Dx:HPV	Dx	Hinselmann	Schiller	Citology	Biopsy
0	18	4.0	15.0	1.0	0.0	0.0	0.0	0.0	0.0	0.0	...	NaN	NaN	0	0	0	0	0	0	0	0
1	15	1.0	14.0	1.0	0.0	0.0	0.0	0.0	0.0	0.0	...	NaN	NaN	0	0	0	0	0	0	0	0
2	34	1.0	NaN	1.0	0.0	0.0	0.0	0.0	0.0	0.0	...	NaN	NaN	0	0	0	0	0	0	0	0
3	52	5.0	16.0	4.0	1.0	37.0	37.0	1.0	3.0	0.0	...	NaN	NaN	1	0	1	0	0	0	0	0
4	46	3.0	21.0	4.0	0.0	0.0	0.0	1.0	15.0	0.0	...	NaN	NaN	0	0	0	0	0	0	0	0

As you can imagine, some of these questions are quite personal, and thus some patients are reluctant to answer them due to privacy concerns. These missing values are represented by NaN in the DataFrame, and they will affect our downstream analysis. The simplest workaround would be to drop all rows that contain missing values, but this may cause a huge reduction in the data size. To get rid of them while minimizing the extent of skewing the data, we can make use of a technique called **imputation**.

The `scikit-learn` package includes many simple and efficient tools for data mining, data analysis, and machine learning. Imputation is one of these, which is available via `sklearn.preprocessing.Imputer`. We can simply install `scikit-learn` via PyPI:

```
pip install scikit-learn
```

By default, `sklearn.preprocessing.Imputer` replaces missing values using the mean along the feature column. Please refer to the following code excerpt for the implementation of imputation:

```
from sklearn.preprocessing import Imputer


# Impute missing values, and transform the data
impute = pd.DataFrame(Imputer().fit_transform(df))
impute.columns = df.columns
impute.index = df.index

impute.head()
```

-	Age	Number of sexual partners	First sexual intercourse	Num of pregnancies	Smokes	Smokes (years)	Smokes (packs/year)	Hormonal Contraceptives	Hormonal Contraceptives (years)	IUD	...	STDs: Time since first diagnosis	STDs: Time since last diagnosis	Dx:Cancer	Dx:CIN	Dx:HPV	Dx	Hinselmann	Schiller	Citology	Biopsy
0	18.0	4.0	15.0000	1.0	0.0	0.0	0.0	0.0	0.0	0.0	...	6.140845	5.816901	0.0	0.0	0.0	0.0	0.0	0.0	0.0	0.0
1	15.0	1.0	14.0000	1.0	0.0	0.0	0.0	0.0	0.0	0.0	...	6.140845	5.816901	0.0	0.0	0.0	0.0	0.0	0.0	0.0	0.0
2	34.0	1.0	16.9953	1.0	0.0	0.0	0.0	0.0	0.0	0.0	...	6.140845	5.816901	0.0	0.0	0.0	0.0	0.0	0.0	0.0	0.0
3	52.0	5.0	16.0000	4.0	1.0	37.0	37.0	1.0	3.0	0.0	...	6.140845	5.816901	1.0	0.0	1.0	0.0	0.0	0.0	0.0	0.0
4	46.0	3.0	21.0000	4.0	0.0	0.0	0.0	1.0	15.0	0.0	...	6.140845	5.816901	0.0	0.0	0.0	0.0	0.0	0.0	0.0	0.0

We can now proceed to plot the pairwise relationship of features. As you can see, an inter-comparison of eight features would already generate a colossal pair plot. Therefore, a full 36 x 36 featured pair plot would be beyond human vision acuity, unless we print it on a large poster:

```
import seaborn as sns
import matplotlib.pyplot as plt


# 8 selected features, ranked by importance
cols = ['Dx:HPV', 'Dx',
        'Dx:CIN', 'First sexual intercourse',
        'Age', 'Num of pregnancies',
        'Hormonal Contraceptives (years)', 'Smokes (packs/year)']

# Prepare a Seaborn pairplot based on the features above
sns.pairplot(impute,
             x_vars = cols,
             y_vars = cols,
             hue = 'Dx:Cancer')

plt.show()
```

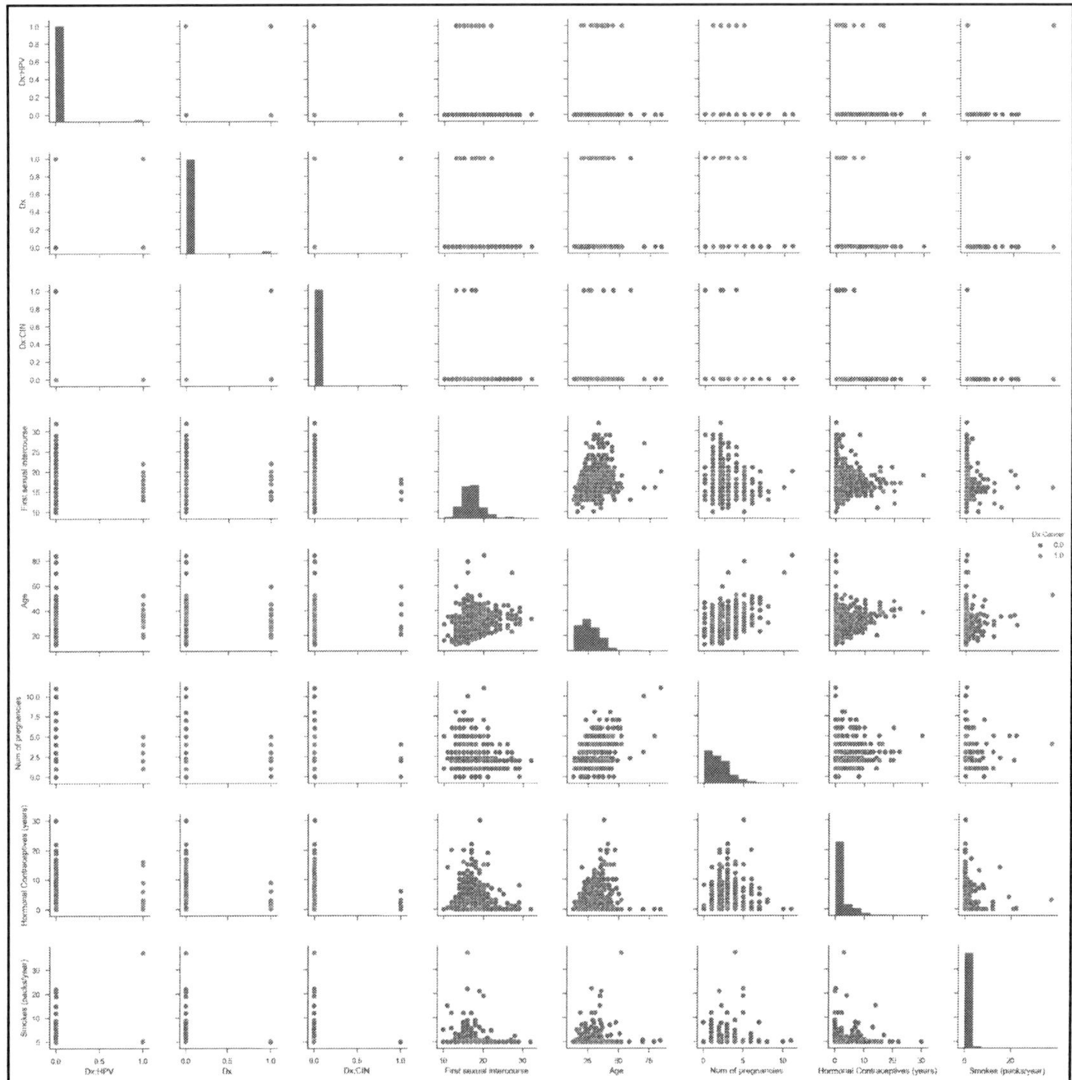
Dx:HPV
Dx
Dx:CIN
First sexual intercourse
Age
Num of pregnancies
Hormonal Contraceptives (years)
Smokes (packs/year)
Dx:Cancer
0.0
1.0

You may also wonder why I selected these eight particular features; in fact, they are the most informative features according to the **EXTremely RAndomized Trees** (**Extra Trees**) classifier. Details about Extra Trees is beyond the scope of this book, but you can see that we can get an importance score for each feature after we run this code excerpt:

```
import matplotlib.pyplot as plt
from sklearn.ensemble import ExtraTreesClassifier


# Extra tree classifier
model = ExtraTreesClassifier()
model.fit(features, df["Dx:Cancer"])

# Rank features by relative importance
importance = list(zip(model.feature_importances_, features.columns))
importance.sort(reverse=True)

# Print the feature importance
for value, name in importance:
    print("{}: {}".format(name, value))
```

The expected output is as follows:

```
Dx:HPV: 0.45595117263686297
Dx: 0.2148147929827533
Dx:CIN: 0.06677116402116405
IUD (years): 0.04313436199597205
Age: 0.028542184633573626
IUD: 0.025259632501241247
Num of pregnancies: 0.02299566539908205
Hormonal Contraceptives (years): 0.022270781247661107
STDs:HPV: 0.022142548465740583
Number of sexual partners: 0.015488778178822679
Biopsy: 0.011746015888621408
Hinselmann: 0.011286648947097027
Smokes (years): 0.00899440033143179
Citology: 0.008207518923794696
Smokes (packs/year): 0.007761904215165942
First sexual intercourse: 0.007637652091270976
STDs: 0.0053215601646868695
Schiller: 0.004763074266517777
Hormonal Contraceptives: 0.004198519571256589
Smokes: 0.003778148067827674
STDs:HIV: 0.0025237050960735205
STDs:condylomatosis: 0.0022492598675526386
STDs:vulvo-perineal condylomatosis: 0.002097078892237549
STDs: Number of diagnosis: 0.0010254107490949638
STDs (number): 0.00048315523182110114
```

```
STDs:Hepatitis B: 0.00017171648494756104
STDs:genital herpes: 0.00014973441431358995
STDs:molluscum contagiosum: 0.00013590906448047885
STDs: Time since last diagnosis: 5.158730158730069e-05
STDs:syphilis: 4.591836734690656e-05
STDs:vaginal condylomatosis: 0.0
STDs:pelvic inflammatory disease: 0.0
STDs:cervical condylomatosis: 0.0
STDs:AIDS: 0.0
STDs: Time since first diagnosis: 0.0
```

Five features received a zero importance score: `STDs:vaginal condylomatosis`, `STDs:pelvic inflammatory disease`, `STDs:cervical condylomatosis`, `STDs:AIDS`, and `STDs:Time since first diagnosis`. We may consider removing these features as they wouldn't add much information towards the classification of cervical cancer.

Principal Component Analysis (PCA)

Going by the preceding example, I hope you are convinced that it is difficult to visualize datasets with a large number of dimensions using scatter plots, histograms, or other simple 2D plots. Even if you are able to pack as many plots as possible in a limited space, it is very difficult for anyone to scale the charts to hundreds if not thousands of features. Besides better visualization, reducing the dimensions of data would also benefit other applications such as regression, classification, or machine learning in general.

To better make sense of the data, we can employ dimensionality reduction techniques. In this section, we are going to showcase **Principal Component Analysis** (**PCA**), which belongs to the group of linear dimensionality reduction techniques.

PCA works by projecting all dimensions to a lower-dimensional space that is defined by the eigenvectors of the co-variance matrix of the input data. It is common to sort the eigenvectors in descending order of their corresponding eigenvalues, or the percentage of explained variance. These eigenvectors would thus capture the directions where the maximum amount of variation occurs in the dataset, in other words, the directions where the dataset appears to be the most spread out.

We will not cover the mathematical theory behind PCA in this book. For those who are interested in the background information of PCA, please refer to the official Scikit-learn documentation (`http://scikit-learn.org/stable/modules/generated/sklearn.decomposition.PCA.html`), or a book written by Jolliffe, I. T. in 2002: Principal component analysis (Springer).

Let's learn how we can use the PCA implementation in scikit-learn to reduce the multi-dimensional dataset to just three principal components. Next, we will apply what we learned in `Chapter 5`, *Visualizing Multivariate Data* to visualize the three principal components using a 3D scatter plot:

```
%matplotlib notebook
import numpy as np
import matplotlib.pyplot as plt
from sklearn.decomposition import PCA
from mpl_toolkits.mplot3d import Axes3D


sns.set(style='ticks')

# We would like to separate features from class labels.
# In this dataset, the Dx:Cancer column defines if the individual
# has cervical cancer.
# The rest of the columns can be treated as features for the prediction
# of cervical cancer.
features = impute.drop('Dx:Cancer', axis=1)
y = impute["Dx:Cancer"]

# Perform PCA
pca = PCA(n_components=3)
X_r = pca.fit_transform(features)

# Percentage of variance explained for each components
print("Explained variance:\nPC1 {:.2%}\nPC2 {:.2%}\nPC3 {:.2%}"
      .format(pca.explained_variance_ratio_[0],
              pca.explained_variance_ratio_[1],
              pca.explained_variance_ratio_[2]))

# Show as 3D scatter plot
fig = plt.figure()
ax = Axes3D(fig)

ax.scatter(X_r[:, 0], X_r[:, 1], X_r[:, 2], c=y, cmap=plt.cm.coolwarm)

# Label the axes
ax.set_xlabel('PC1')
```

```
ax.set_ylabel('PC2')
ax.set_zlabel('PC3')

plt.show()
```

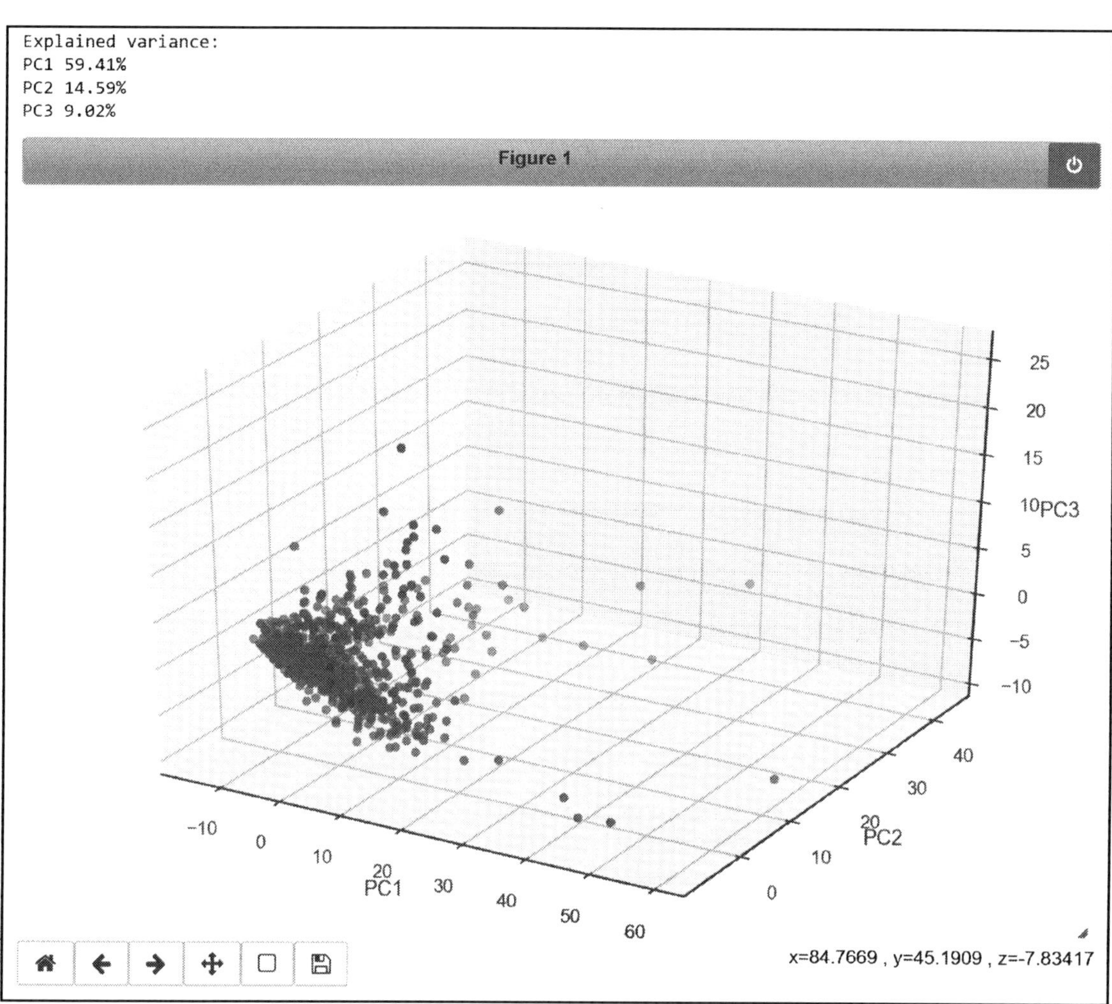

In this example, we used PCA to reduce 35 features to 3 principal components. The first principal component captured the highest level of variance at 59.41%, while the second one captured 14.59%, and the third one captured 9.02%. In this dimensionality reduction exercise, we can explain 83.02% of the total variance of the input dataset using just three dimensions. It is important to note that when the multi-dimensional data is mapped to a lower-dimensional space, we may no longer infer the input features from the results. In fact, this applies to other dimensionality reduction techniques as well, such as t-SNE, which will be discussed in the next section.

t-distributed Stochastic Neighbor Embedding (t-SNE)

Since PCA is designed for datasets with a linear relationship between the features, it might not work well if a more complex, non-linear relationship exists between them. Besides, although PCA works well in separating dissimilar data points, it is not particularly competent in placing similar data points close to each other.

We are going to explore the realm of non-linear dimension reduction techniques through the use of t-SNE, which stands for t-distributed stochastic neighbor embedding. Unlike PCA, t-SNE is a probabilistic approach to dimension reduction, rather than a mathematical function that generates an exact solution. It works by building a pair-wise data similarity matrix of input features based on Student-t distributions (one degree of freedom). Next, a similar probability distribution is constructed over the low-dimensional map, and it seeks to minimize the divergence between the two distributions such that the input can be best represented using fewer dimensions.

Based on the work of Stochastic Neighbor Embedding in 2002, Laurens van der Maaten and Geoffrey Hinton developed t-SNE in 2008. Readers can refer to their original paper for more information about the mathematical background (`http://jmlr.csail.mit.edu/papers/volume9/vandermaaten08a/vandermaaten08a.pdf`).

Now that you have a brief idea of how t-SNE works, let's see how we can use `scikit-learn` to implement t-SNE for reducing dimensions:

```
%matplotlib notebook
import numpy as np
import matplotlib.pyplot as plt
from sklearn.manifold import TSNE
from mpl_toolkits.mplot3d import Axes3D
```

```
sns.set(style='ticks')

# Perform t-SNE
tsne = TSNE(n_components=3, init='pca', random_state=0)
X_tsne = tsne.fit_transform(features)
y = impute["Dx:Cancer"]

# Show as 3D scatter plot
fig = plt.figure()
ax = Axes3D(fig)

ax.scatter(X_tsne[:, 0], X_tsne[:, 1], X_tsne[:, 2], c=y,
cmap=plt.cm.coolwarm)

# Label the axes
ax.set_xlabel('Component 1')
ax.set_ylabel('Component 2')
ax.set_zlabel('Component 3')

plt.show()
```

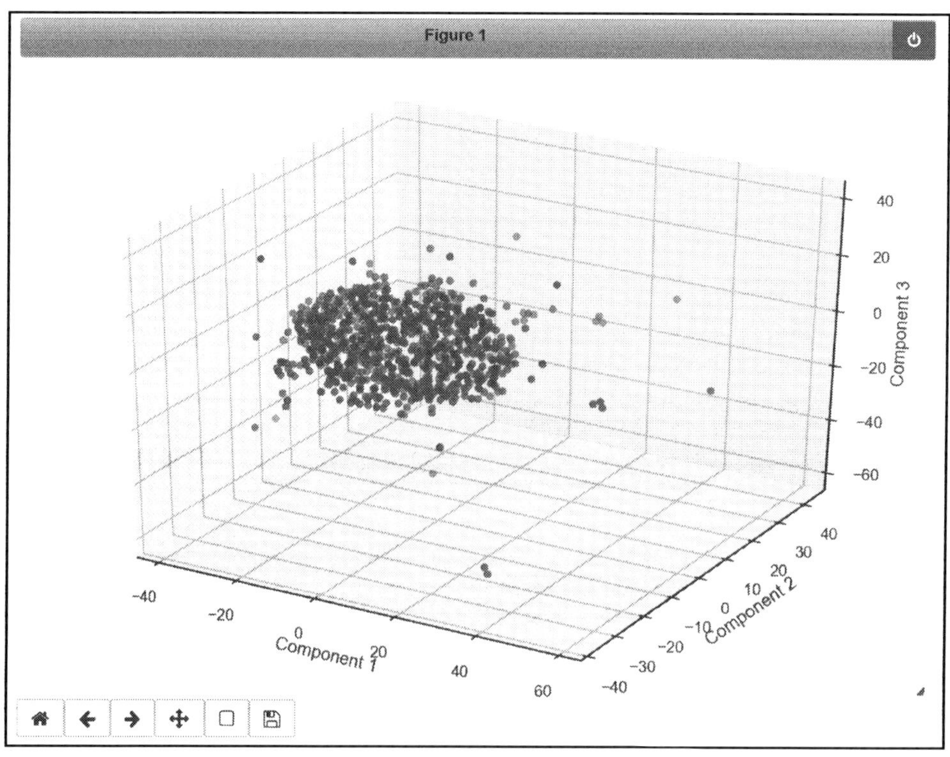

From the results, it looks like t-SNE is less capable of separating cancer patients (red) from controls (blue). In general, t-SNE performs better than PCA if a non-linear relationship exists. Perhaps the relationship between features in this cervical cancer dataset is mostly linear.

Summary

Scientific data visualization embodies topics in art, programming, and science. While we have mastered the techniques of creating various plot types in previous chapters, we hope that you have gained more understanding of creating effective plots from the art and science perspectives.

You learned how to think like a designer so that key points can be emphasized properly without causing too much clutter. You also learned how to think like a scientist so that you will be aware of some plotting conventions, such as the methods of reducing dimensions and the way to show statistical significance.

In the next and last chapter, we will explore the process of creating geographical infographics, which is entirely different from what we've learned so far. Please stay tuned for more details!

8
Exploratory Data Analytics and Infographics

Let the data speak for themselves.

This is a well-known quote to many data scientists in the field. However, it is often not trivial to capture the hidden characteristics or features in big data, and some exploratory data analysis must be done before we fully understand the dataset.

In this chapter, we aim to perform some exploratory data analysis on two datasets, using the techniques that we have discussed in previous chapters. Here is a brief outline of this chapter:

- Visualizing categorical data
- Visualizing geographical data
- GeoPandas library
- Working with images using the PIL library
- Importing/transforming images
- Multiple subplots
- Heatmap
- Survival graph

We assume that the readers are now comfortable with the use of pandas DataFrame as it will be heavily used in this chapter.

Readers should also be noted that most exploratory data analyses actually involve a significant amount of statistics, including dimension reduction approaches such as PCA or tSNE as mentioned in `Chapter 7`, *A Practical Guide to Scientific Plotting*. Yet the goal of this book is to demonstrate ways for data visualization through Python; therefore, we are only performing some basic statistics analysis such as linear regression, clustering, and non-parametric methods on survival analysis. Readers who are interested in becoming a data scientist should also have a good understanding of statistics and mathematics.

Visualizing population health information

The following section will be dedicated to combining both geographical and population health information of the US. Since this is a tutorial on Python, we focus more on ways to visualize the data, rather than to draw solid conclusions from it. However, many of the findings below actually concur with the population health research and news reports that one may find online.

To begin, let us first download the following information:

- Top 10 leading causes of death in the United States from 1999 to 2013 from Healthdata.gov
- 2016 TIGER GeoDatabase from US Census Bureau
- Survival data of various type of cancers from The Cancer Genome Atlas (TCGA) project (`https://cancergenome.nih.gov/`)

Since some of the information does not allow direct download through links, we have included the raw data in our code repository:

- Top 10 leading causes of death in the United States from 1999-2013: `https://www.healthdata.gov/dataset/nchs-age-adjusted-death-rates-top-10-leading-causes-death-united-states-2013`
- TIGER GeoDatabase: `https://www.census.gov/geo/maps-data/data/tiger-geodatabases.html`
- Cartographic boundary shapefiles (states): `https://www.census.gov/geo/maps-data/data/cbf/cbf_state.html`

First of all, we load the top 10 leading causes of death in the United States from 1999 to 2013 and then what the table looks like:

```
import numpy as np
import pandas as pd
import matplotlib.pyplot as plt
plt.rcParams.update({'figure.max_open_warning': 0})

# Read the file and format it as Pandas Dataframe
census_info =
pd.read_csv('https://github.com/PacktPublishing/Matplotlib-2.x-By-Example/b
lob/master/NCHS_-_Age-
adjusted_Death_Rates_for_the_Top_10_Leading_Causes_of_Death__United_States_
_2013.csv')

# .head() shows the header and the first 5 lines of the file
census_info.head()
```

-	YEAR	113_CAUSE_NAME	CAUSE_NAME	STATE	DEATHS	AADR
0	1999	All Causes	All Causes	Alabama	44806	1009.3
1	1999	All Causes	All Causes	Alaska	2708	838.9
2	1999	All Causes	All Causes	Arizona	40050	818.4
3	1999	All Causes	All Causes	Arkansas	27925	975.3
4	1999	All Causes	All Causes	California	229380	802.3

This dataframe contains `YEAR`, `CAUSE_NAME`, `STATE`, `DEATHS`, and `AADR`; almost all the information is self-explanatory except AADR. **AADR** stands for **Age-Adjusted Death Rate**, which is a normalized number on the original death counts based on the population size and age distribution of that corresponding state. Also, since this dataset contains the top 10 causes of different states in US from 1999 to 2013, it is obvious that there will be more than 10 causes of death in the entire dataset. Therefore, we have to know what the total number of causes is and what they are individually.

To quickly show what the leading causes of death in the United States from 1999 to 2013 are:

```
# .unique() allows the dataframe to return the unique value of the given
# column name
all_death_cause = census_info['CAUSE_NAME'].unique()

# The following code shows number of causes of death, as well as their
# identities
print(len(all_death_cause), 'Unique causes of death: ')
for death_cause in all_death_cause:
    print('-',death_cause)
```

The expected output from the preceding code:

```
17 Unique causes of death:
- All Causes
- Alzheimer's disease
- Cancer
- Chronic liver disease and cirrhosis
- CLRD
- Diabetes
- Diseases of Heart
- Essential hypertension and hypertensive renal disease
- Homicide
- Influenza and pneumonia
- Kidney Disease
- Parkinson's disease
- Pneumonitis due to solids and liquids
- Septicemia
- Stroke
- Suicide
- Unintentional Injuries
```

As expected, there are more than 10 causes of death in the dataset. The titles of the causes of death are easily understandable, except for **CLRD**, which stands for **Chronic Lower Respiratory Diseases**. By simply looking at the causes of death, one may assume that death causes by disease will have a different distribution than death causes by human action, such as suicide and unintentional injuries. To extract data from just one specific year, say 1999, we can use the following approach:

```
# Extracting data that belongs to YEAR 1999 only
year1999_df = census_info.loc[census_info['YEAR']==1999]
year1999_df.head()
```

-	YEAR	113_CAUSE_NAME	CAUSE_NAME	STATE	DEATHS	AADR
0	1999	All Causes	All Causes	Alabama	44806	1009.3
1	1999	All Causes	All Causes	Alaska	2708	838.9
2	1999	All Causes	All Causes	Arizona	40050	818.4
3	1999	All Causes	All Causes	Arkansas	27925	975.3
4	1999	All Causes	All Causes	California	229380	802.3

With the code provided above, we are now able to do some quick exploratory analysis on the current dataset. Let us first try to visualize the 10 major causes of death in the United States when compared to a specific state--`California`:

```
# We use seaborn here to quickly construct a barplot
import seaborn as sns

# setting the style of seaborn as whitegrid
sns.set(style="whitegrid")

# Constructing two dataframes for California data and the United States
# data California 1999 dataframe constructed
cali_year1999_df = year1999_df.loc[census_info['STATE']=='California',:]

# the United States 1999 dataframe constructed
us_year1999_df = year1999_df.loc[census_info['STATE']=='the United
States',:]

# Cast the value of the DEATHS and AADR to numeric for downstream plotting
# It is possible to do it at the beginning, but we want to cast the value
# here to remind the readers that it is important to check the value type
# before doing visualization!
cali_year1999_df[['DEATHS','AADR']]=cali_year1999_df[['DEATHS','AADR']].app
ly(pd.to_numeric)

us_year1999_df[['DEATHS','AADR']]=us_year1999_df[['DEATHS','AADR']].apply(p
d.to_numeric)

# Here is the 10 major causes of death that we are interested in showing
ranking_death = ['All Causes','Diseases of Heart',
                 'Cancer','Stroke','CLRD',\
                 'Unintentional Injuries','Diabetes',
                 'Influenza and pneumonia',\
                 'Alzheimer\'s disease','Kidney Disease']

# Plot Boxplot, initialize plt and set figure size
```

```
f, ax = plt.subplots()

# To draw a set of horizontal bars, we put the CAUSE_NAME as y-axis
# and DEATHS as x-axis
sns.set_color_codes("muted")
sns.barplot(x="DEATHS",y="CAUSE_NAME", data=us_year1999_df, label='Total
death in the United States',order=ranking_death,color='b')
sns.barplot(x="DEATHS", y="CAUSE_NAME", data=cali_year1999_df, label="Death
in California",order=ranking_death,color="g")

# Put figure legend, with frame around it
ax.legend(ncol=2, loc="lower right", frameon=True)
ax.set(xlim=(0, 2400000), ylabel="", xlabel="Leading causes of death in
California, comparing to the total in U.S. (1999)")

# .despine() is useful in removing the spines from plot(s)
sns.despine(left=True, bottom=True)

# Remove unnecessary whitespace
plt.tight_layout()

plt.show()
```

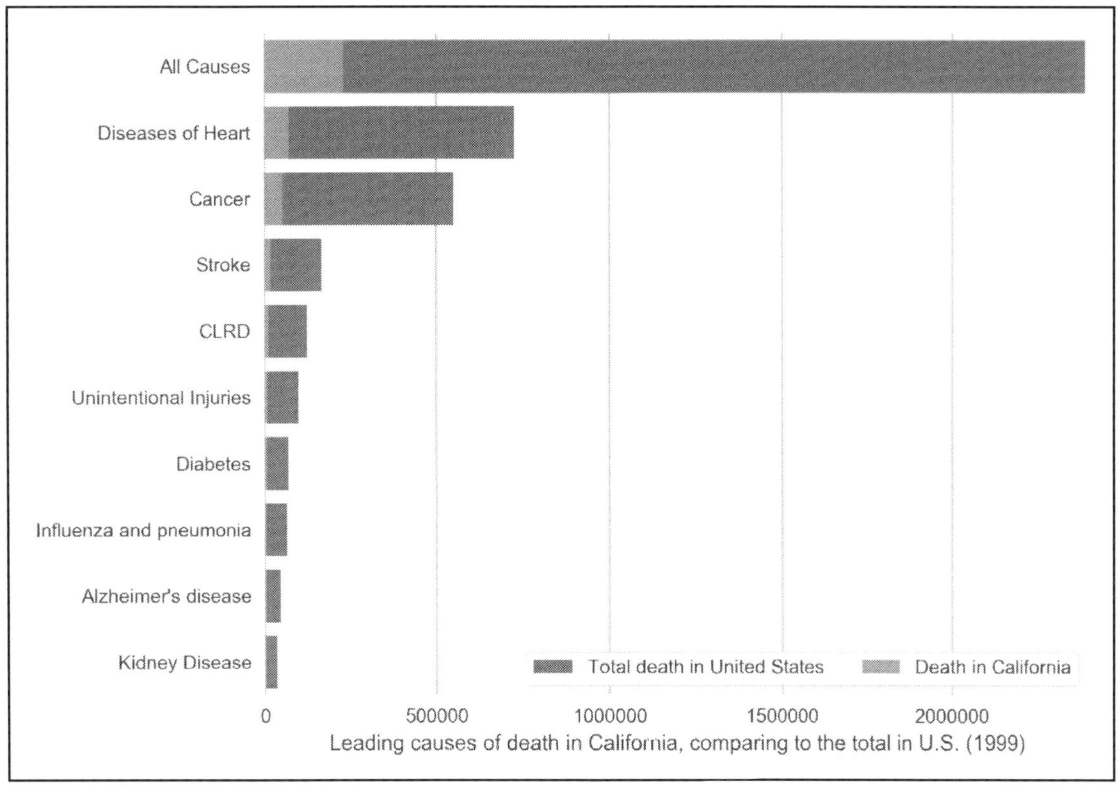

The 10 causes of death are in descending order based on the death toll from the US dataframe `us_year1999_df`. As one can tell, California is contributing close to 10% of the number of deaths for all causes in the United States.

We are sure that the readers will immediately toss the book into the trash if we are using 50 bar charts showing the number of deaths across the 50 states, even if the bar charts are nicely organized as multiplots in one figure. And in fact, classical statistical graphs are not the best way to show geographical information. Why don't we just pull out a map and start coloring?

Map-based visualization for geographical data

The following code will incorporate a map-based visualization, which is powered by the GeoPandas library. GeoPandas is very powerful in map-based visualization, especially as it incorporates Shapely for geometry visualization, Fiona for quick map-shape file access, and Descartes and Matplotlib for plotting. GeoPandas can be easily installed by simply using `pip`:

```
pip install geopandas
```

There are some dependencies for GeoPandas, such as numpy, pandas, shapely, fiona, six, and pyrpoj. Readers may refer to the installation page of GeoPandas for more information (`http://geopandas.org/install.html`).

Getting GeoPandas to work on Windows is not an easy feat, due to strict version requirements for some dependencies. The easiest way to resolve such dependencies is to use the `conda` package manager from Anaconda Python (`https://docs.continuum.io/anaconda/`):
`conda install -c conda-forge geopandas`
Readers can also refer to `https://stackoverflow.com/questions/34427788/how-to-successfully-install-pyproj-and-geopandas` for alternative methods that are applicable to standard Python distributions.

```
# To begin, we import the geopandas library as gpd
import geopandas as gpd

# One easy map that you can used is 'naturalearth_lowres'
# Use .read_file() to load in the data as pandas dataframe
world = gpd.read_file(gpd.datasets.get_path('naturalearth_lowres'))

# What is in the pandas dataframe? .head() to show the first 5 lines
world.head()
```

-	continent	gdp_md_est	geometry	iso_a3	name	pop_est
0	Asia	22270.0	POLYGON ((61.21081709172574 35.65007233330923,...	AFG	Afghanistan	28400000.0
1	Africa	110300.0	(POLYGON ((16.32652835456705 -5.87747039146621...	AGO	Angola	12799293.0
2	Europe	21810.0	POLYGON ((20.59024743010491 41.85540416113361,...	ALB	Albania	3639453.0
3	Asia	184300.0	POLYGON ((51.57951867046327 24.24549713795111,...	ARE	United Arab Emirates	4798491.0
4	South America	573900.0	(POLYGON ((-65.50000000000003 -55.199999999999...	ARG	Argentina	40913584.0

At first glance, readers can tell that `iso_a3` is actually the country code. The `name` is the country name, and each country is defined by a POLYGON and stored under the header `geometry`. Their respective continents are shown in the column `continent` and there is even a population size estimation for each country under the column `pop_est`.

To visualize the map, it is as simple as this:

```
import matplotlib.pyplot as plt


# Construct your first world map!
f, ax = plt.subplots()
world.plot(ax=ax)
plt.show()
```

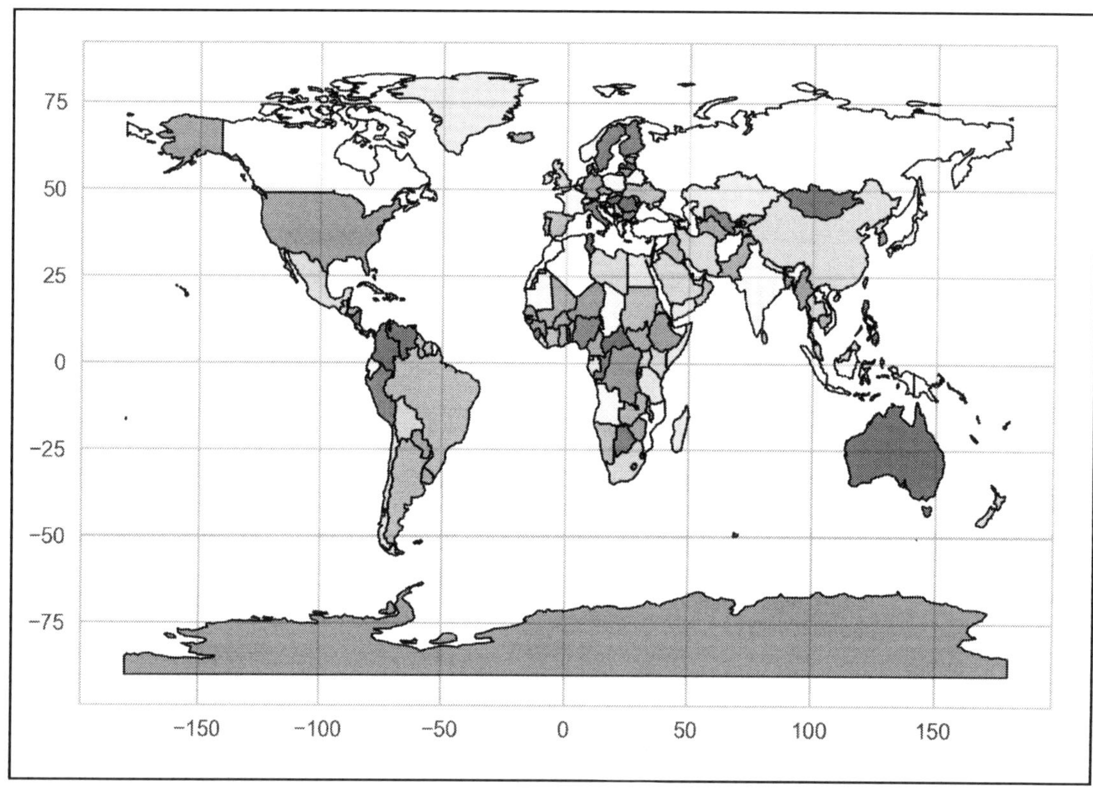

You have just constructed your first world map in Python! It is very straightforward to do so. Let us modify the map a bit. Although we love penguins and seals, there is not a lot of information on human population and diseases regarding Antarctica. How about first removing Antarctica from the map?

```
f, ax = plt.subplots()

# Removing Antarctica from the map
# The way to do so is just normal Pandas dataframe operation
world_without_antarctica = world[world['name']!='Antarctica']
world_without_antarctica.plot(ax=ax)

plt.show()
```

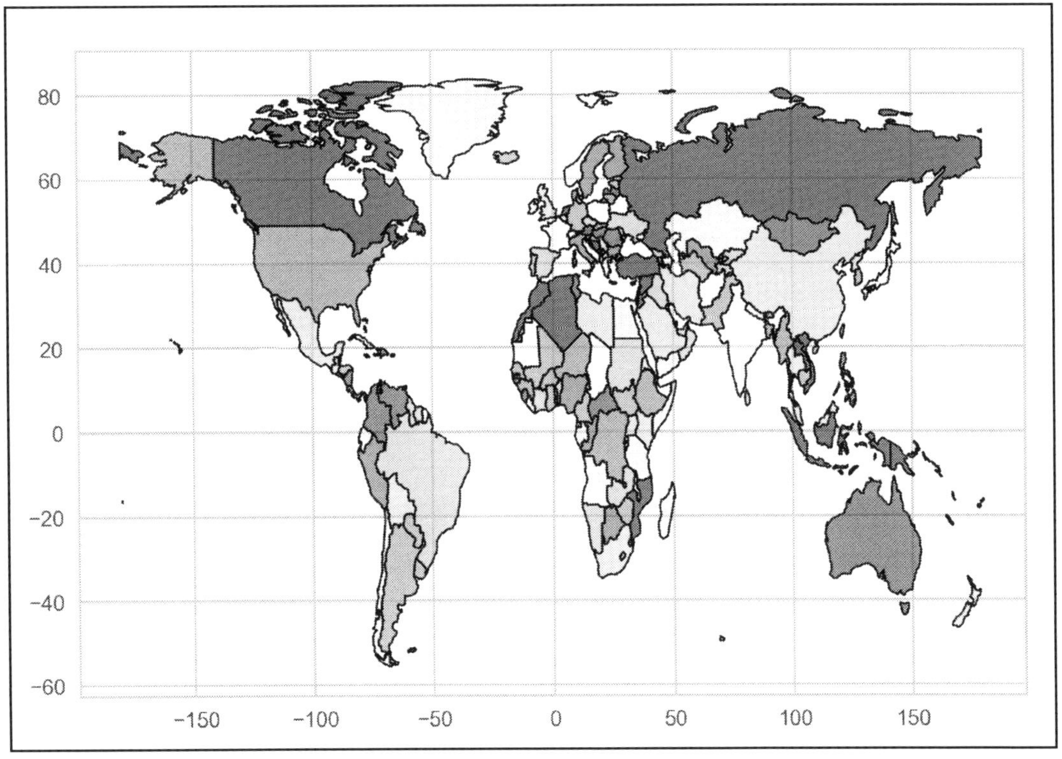

So far so good. Now remember that our data is from the US; let's focus on the United States for the time being. We would like to highlight the US in a specific color--red--as shown in the code:

```
f, ax = plt.subplots()

# Using the map without antarctica here
# High-light the United States in red and plot the figure
# This is simply pandas dataframe operation
world_without_antarctica[world_without_antarctica['name']=='the United
States'].plot(ax=ax, edgecolor='grey', facecolor='red', linewidth=1,
alpha=1)

# Also include other countries but we are coloring them in light grey
world_without_antarctica[world_without_antarctica['name']!='the United
States'].plot(ax=ax, edgecolor='grey', facecolor='lightgrey', linewidth=1,
alpha=1)

plt.show()
```

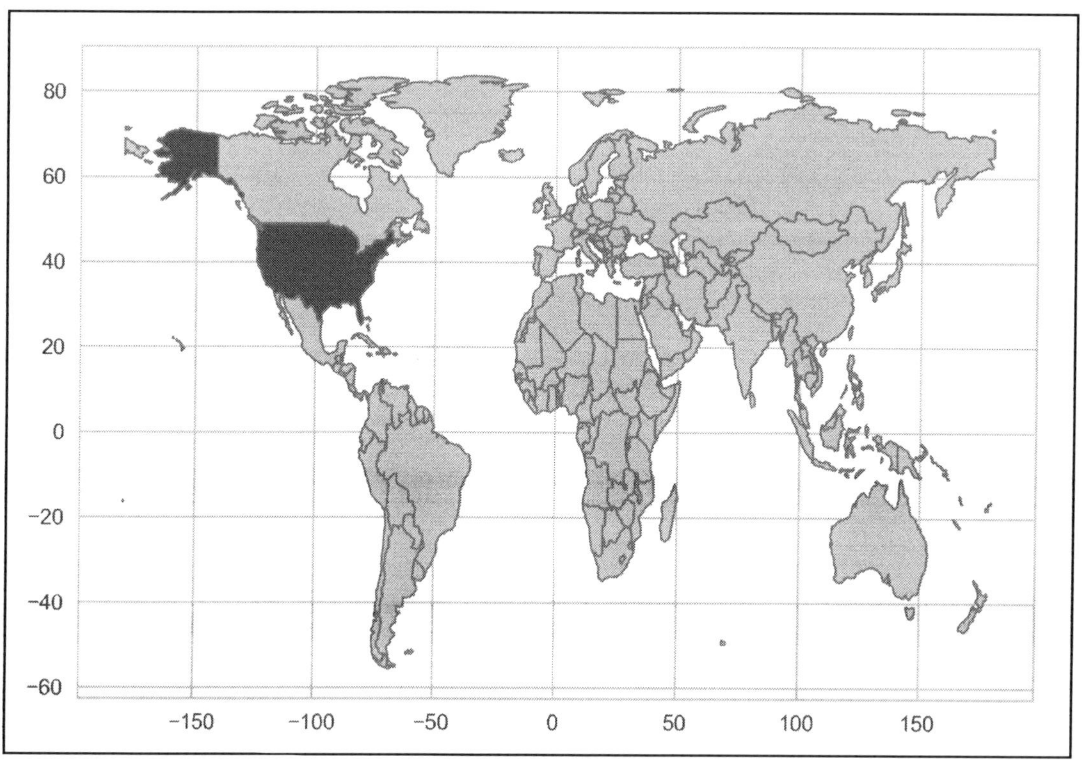

As shown here, the United States is now highlighted in red (dark gray as shown in grayscale).

However, readers may realize that this current map does not show any state information in the United States. Thus it is impossible for us to overlay our current population health information into it as there is no state information in the pandas DataFrame. We need a GeoPandas dataframe that contains a POLYGON of states. Fortunately, this can be obtained from census.gov as cartographic boundary shapefiles, which can be easily read by Fiona (a dependency of GeoPandas). The cartographic boundary shapefiles used in this chapter were obtained from `http://www2.census.gov/geo/tiger/GENZ2016/shp/cb_2016_us_state_500k.zip`.

From the link, we can obtain the `cb_2016_us_state_500k.shp` file and import it into GeoPandas.

One thing to notice is that, for ease of visualization, we have removed the state of Hawaii and islands such as Guam and Puerto Rico. The places that are removed are explicitly stated in the code:

```
# From here, we import the cartographic boundary shapefile obtained
# from census.gov
# Download and extract all the data files (e.g. to D: drive) manually
first:
# https://github.com/PacktPublishing/Matplotlib-2.x-By-
# Example/blob/master/cb_2016_us_state_500k.zip
states = gpd.read_file('D:/cb_2016_us_state_500k.shp')
states.head()
```

-	AFFGEOID	ALAND	AWATER	GEOID	LSAD	NAME	STATEFP	STATENS	STUSPS	geometry
0	0400000US01	131173688951	4593686489	01	00	Alabama	01	01779775	AL	(POLYGON ((-88.053375 30.506987, -88.051087999...
1	0400000US02	1477946266785	245390495931	02	00	Alaska	02	01785533	AK	(POLYGON ((-134.737262 58.261354, -134.73441 5...
2	0400000US04	294198560125	1027346486	04	00	Arizona	04	01779777	AZ	POLYGON ((-114.816294 32.508038, -114.814321 3...
3	0400000US05	134771517596	2960191698	05	00	Arkansas	05	00068085	AR	POLYGON ((-94.6178329666013 36.4994141203285, ...

4	0400000US06	403501101370	20466718403	06	00	California	06	01779778	CA	(POLYGON ((-118.604415 33.478552, -118.598783 ...

As one can tell, the headers between the two dataframes `state` and `world` are different. But what matters the most is the `geometry` column, which contains the POLYGON data for each state. The state names are explicitly recorded in the column `name`, with their abbreviations recorded in `STUSPS`. There is also some other information in the dataframe but we will not be using it in this chapter. Let us first visualize the states on the map to see how it goes!

```
# Importing the PIL library for image processing
from PIL import Image, ImageChops


# Image.MAX_IMAGE_PIXELS is set to be a large number to avoid warning
# from Python
Image.MAX_IMAGE_PIXELS = 1000000000

# This function identifies the border of the image and perform a trimming
# The crop() function further crop the image and zoom to US in here
def trim(image):
    img = Image.open(image)
    border = Image.new(img.mode, img.size, img.getpixel((0, 0)))
    diff = ImageChops.difference(img, border)
    diff = ImageChops.add(diff, diff, 2.0, -100)
    bbox = diff.getbbox()
    if bbox:
        img = img.crop(bbox)
    img_crop = img.crop((1000,2500,8000,6000))
    return img_crop

# Initializing a new subplot
f, ax = plt.subplots()

# Using standard Pandas operation, we remove the following places from
# the states geopandas dataframe
refined_states =
states[(states['STUSPS']!='GU')&(states['STUSPS']!='PR')&(states['STUSPS']!
='MP')&(states['STUSPS']!='VI')&(states['STUSPS']!='HI')&(states['STUSPS']!
='AS')]

# We plot the refined states as shown below, with a figsize of (100,40)
# The coloring can be specified using column='STUSPS'
refined_states.plot(figsize=(100,40), column='STUSPS')
plt.axis('equal')
```

```
# Since we are cropping the image at later steps, we put the title
# right above the map
plt.annotate('Map of the United States',xy=(-135,75),color='black',size=25)
plt.savefig('states_map.png', dpi=300)
visualizing_states_img = trim('states_map.png')
visualizing_states_img.save('states_map_crop.png')
visualizing_states_img
```

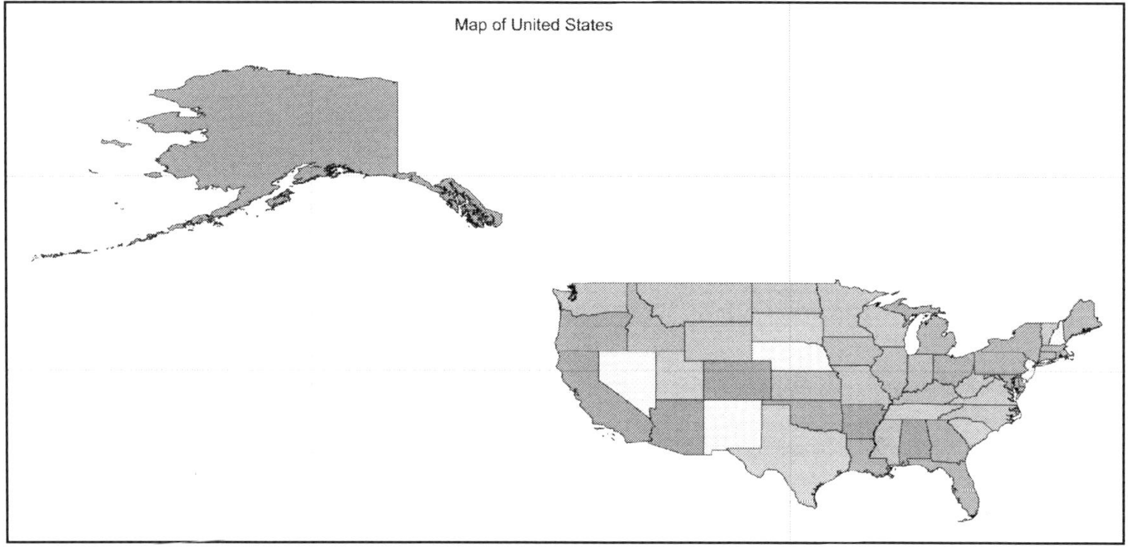

Readers may find out that there is a function called `trim()` in the code. This function uses the PIL library, which allows numerous image processing operations. The preceding code shows how to crop a given image.

Combining geographical and population health data

Remember that from the preceding bar graph, the highest number of deaths were caused by cancer in California in 1999. Let's overlay the cancer information on the graphs now. This can be done by merging two pandas DataFrames--the state boundaries dataframe and cancer death in 1999 dataframe--into one dataframe, followed by the GeoPandas plot function with `column` and `cmap` specified.

However, one minor issue is that the `states` in the `refined_states` dataframe are named under the column `NAME` instead of `STATE`. We will have to rename that particular column in `refined_states dataframe` before we perform the merger. Here is the code:

```
# Extracting all the cancer data in year 1999
cancer_year1999_df = year1999_df.loc[census_info['CAUSE_NAME']=='Cancer']

# Renaming the column name in refined_states dataframe
refined_states = refined_states.rename(columns = {'NAME':'STATE'})

# Perform merging of two dataframes, the merge depends on the column
"STATE"
merged_cancer_1999_df = pd.merge(refined_states,cancer_year1999_df,
on='STATE')

# Again, we want to stress the importance of casting data before doing any
# visualization
merged_cancer_1999_df[['DEATHS','AADR']]=merged_cancer_1999_df[['DEATHS','A
ADR']].apply(pd.to_numeric)
merged_cancer_1999_df.head()
```

-	AFFGEOID	ALAND	AWATER	GEOID	LSAD	STATE	STATEFP	STATENS	STUSPS	geometry	YEAR	113_CAUSE_NAME	CAUSE_NAME	DEATHS	AADR
0	0400000US01	131173688951	4593686489	01	00	Alabama	01	01779775	AL	(POLYGON ((-88.053375 30.506987, -88.051087999...	1999	Malignant neoplasms (C00-C97)	Cancer	9506	210.90
1	0400000US02	1477946266785	245390495931	02	00	Alaska	02	01785533	AK	(POLYGON ((-134.737262 58.261354, -134.73441 5...	1999	Malignant neoplasms (C00-C97)	Cancer	633	190.54
2	0400000US04	294198560125	1027346486	04	00	Arizona	04	01779777	AZ	POLYGON ((-114.816294 32.508038, -114.814321 3...	1999	Malignant neoplasms (C00-C97)	Cancer	9006	179.90
3	0400000US05	134771517596	2960191698	05	00	Arkansas	05	00068085	AR	POLYGON ((-94.6178329666013 36.4994141203285, ...	1999	Malignant neoplasms (C00-C97)	Cancer	6137	214.07
4	0400000US06	403501101370	20466718403	06	00	California	06	01779778	CA	(POLYGON ((-118.604415 33.478552, -118.598783 ...	1999	Malignant neoplasms (C00-C97)	Cancer	53067	184.86

We've now got the merged dataframe and it is called `merged_cancer_1999_df`; let us now visualize the number of deaths caused by cancer across the states in 1999:

```
# Initializing a new subplot
f, ax = plt.subplots()
# Plotting the map using the merged dataframe
merged_cancer_1999_df.plot(column='DEATHS',cmap='Reds',figsize=(100,40))
plt.axis('equal')

# Annotating the plot
plt.annotate('Death caused by cancer in US,
1999',xy=(-140,75),color='black',size=25)
plt.savefig('US_cancer_death_num_1999.png',dpi=300)

# Trimming the plot to give a larger image using PIL library and
# Image processing
cancer_death_visualization_img = trim('US_cancer_death_num_1999.png')
cancer_death_visualization_img.save('US_cancer_death_num_1999_crop.png')
cancer_death_visualization_img
```

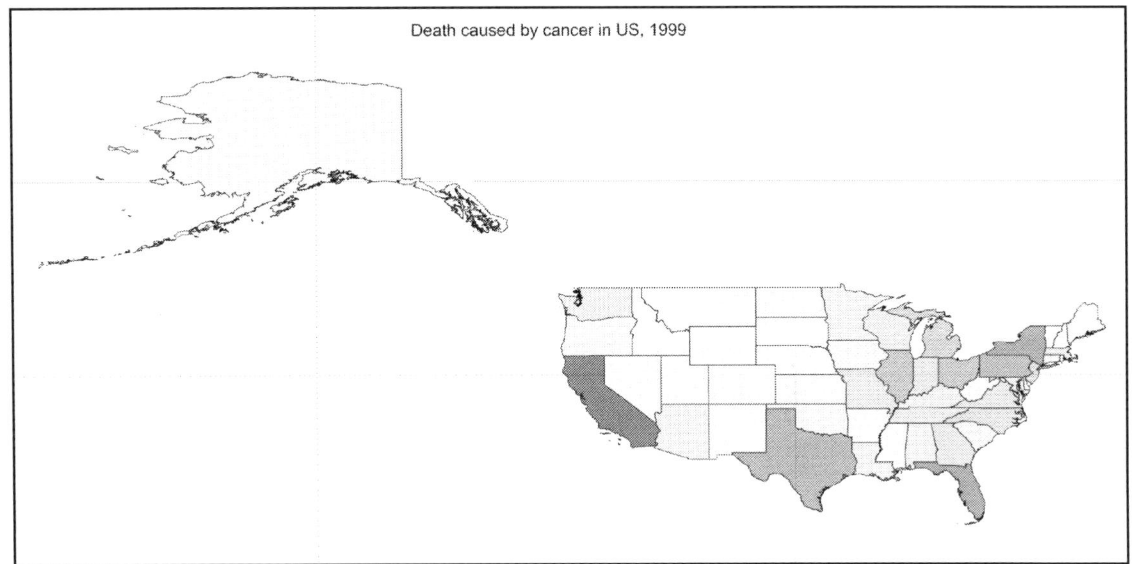

Readers may find that the legend is missing in this figure. The reason is that currently the GeoPandas library does not support legends with non-categorical data. Yet this can be done by adding annotations to the `ax` object and we left the code implementation as a challenge for you.

From the preceding figure, it is obvious that California is having the highest number of deaths caused by cancer in 1999. However, this number is definitely biased to the population size of the respective states, as well as the age group distribution. Therefore, a normalization can be done, and that is the **age-adjusted death rate** (**AADR**) value in the dataset. Let's try to visualize the AADR of cancer in 1999 across the USA and see how different the result is:

```
# Initializing a new subplot
f, ax = plt.subplots()

# Plotting the map again, this time the value is extracted from column
# 'AADR' instead of 'DEATHS'
merged_cancer_1999_df.plot(column='AADR',cmap='Reds',figsize=(100,40))
ax.grid(False)
plt.axis('equal')

# Annotating the plot
plt.annotate('Age-adjusted death rate of cancer in US,
1999',xy=(-141,75),color='black',size=25)
plt.savefig('US_cancer_AADR_1999.png',dpi=300)

# Trimming the plot to give a larger image using PIL library and
# Image processing
cancer_visualization_img = trim('US_cancer_AADR_1999.png')
cancer_visualization_img.save('US_cancer_AADR_1999_crop.png')
cancer_visualization_img
```

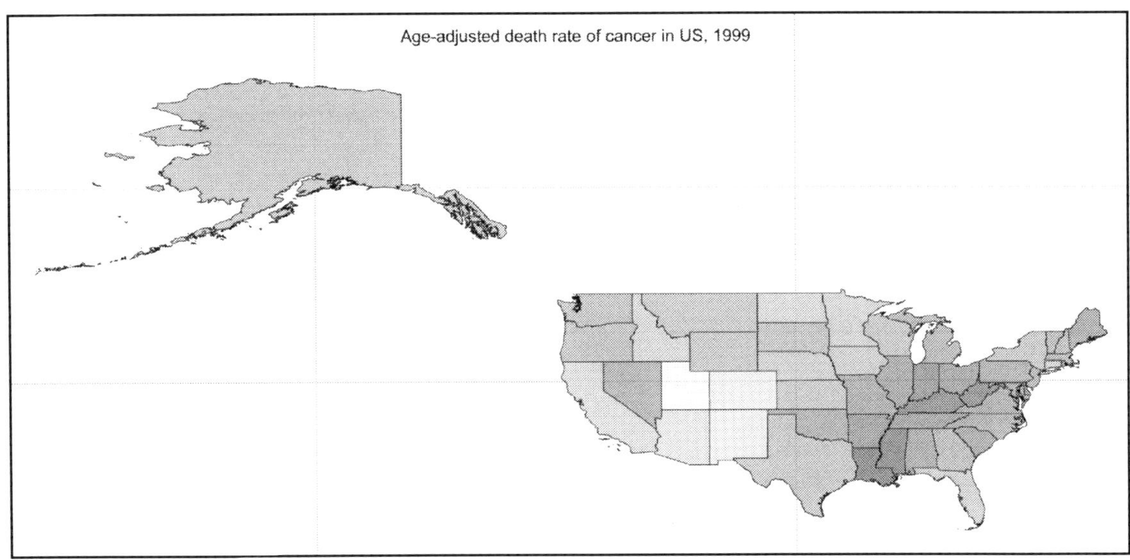

Interestingly, upon adjustment of the population size and age group effects, California is no longer the state with the highest death rate due to cancer. Therefore, it is noteworthy that normalizing data is an essential step in understanding it without bias. Depending on the nature of the data, there are different normalization methods in the field that readers may choose from.

Another cause of deaths that is also intriguing to look at is unintentional injury; this should correspond to deaths caused by accidents in different states. It is reasonable to assume that it has a very different AADR when compared to diseases such as cancer and heart disease:

```
#Initializing a new subplot
f, ax = plt.subplots()

# Similar to what we have done previously
# we are extracting the data correspond to unintentional injuries from
# year 1999
unintent_death_1999_df = year1999_df.loc[census_info['CAUSE_NAME'] ==
'Unintentional Injuries']
merged_unintent_death_1999_df = pd.merge(refined_states,
unintent_death_1999_df, on='STATE')
merged_unintent_death_1999_df[['DEATHS','AADR']]=merged_unintent_death_1999
_df[['DEATHS','AADR']].apply(pd.to_numeric)

# Plotting the map showing AADR of unintentional injuries in US, 1999
merged_unintent_death_1999_df.plot(column='AADR',cmap='Reds',figsize=(100,4
0))
ax.grid(False)
```

```
plt.axis('equal')
plt.annotate('Age-Adjusted Death Rate of unintentional injuries in US,
1999',xy=(-148,75),color='black',size=25)
plt.savefig('US_unintent_AADR_1999.png',dpi=300)

# Trimming the plot to give a larger image using PIL library and
# Image processing
unintent_death_visualization_img = trim('US_unintent_AADR_1999.png')
unintent_death_visualization_img.save('US_unintent_AADR_1999_crop.png')
unintent_death_visualization_img
```

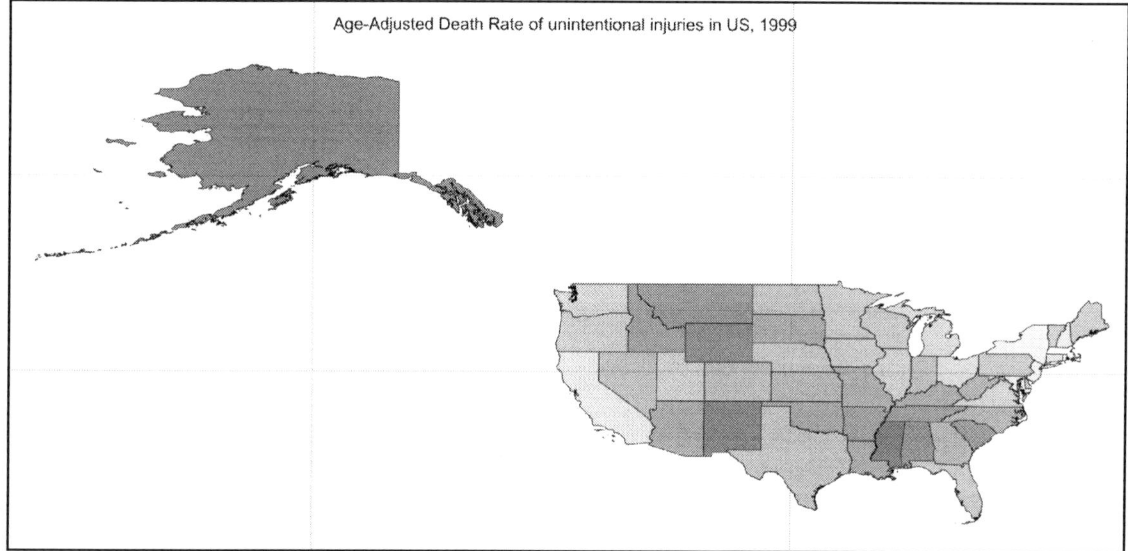

By simply contrasting the color distribution of the two maps *AADR of cancer in US 1999* and *AADR of unintentional injuries in US 1999*, readers can tell that the two causes of death have vastly different distributions. Yet we also want to know the trend of the causes of death from 1999 to 2013, as this is very important for the prediction of causes of death in the future.

With this in mind, let us go back to the cancer data and see the changes in AADR across the 25 states (for ease of visualization, we are picking 25 states only as they can be easily fitted into a 5 x 5 multiplot):

```
# Instead of extracting only information from 1999
# this time we are extracting all the data with the 'CAUSE_NAME' as cancer
complete_cancer_state_df = census_info.loc[census_info['CAUSE_NAME']
=='Cancer']
complete_cancer_state_df[['DEATHS','AADR']]=complete_cancer_state_df[['DEAT
```

```
HS','AADR']].apply(pd.to_numeric)

# Picking the top 25 states with the highest cancer AADR
selected_25_states = ['California','Florida','New York','Texas',
                      'Pennsylvania',\'Ohio','Illinois','Michigan',
                      'New Jersey','North Carolina',\
                      'Massachusetts','Virginia','Georgia','Indiana',
                      'Missouri',\
                      'Tennessee','Wisconsin','Washington','Maryland',
                      'Alabama',\
                      'Louisiana','Arizona','Kentucky','Minnesota','South
                       Carolina'][::-1]

# Here defines the maximum and minimum value of the y-axis for the plot
# to visualize cancer AADR data across these 25 states
cancer_aadr_list = complete_cancer_state_df['AADR']
ylim_max = max(cancer_aadr_list)
ylim_min = min(cancer_aadr_list)

# Initializing plots, explicitly stating that we are going to construct
# a 5x5 multiplots
fig, axs = plt.subplots(ncols=5,nrows=5,figsize=(30,30))

# Main title of the plot
sns.plt.suptitle('Age-adjusted death rate of cancer in 25 states from
1999-2013',fontsize=25)

# Construct the 25 plot individually through these 2 for loops
for i in range(0,5):
    for j in range(0,5):
        # Pop the state name from the list - "selected_25_states"
        current_state = selected_25_states.pop()
        # Create a dataframe to store the disease information for the
current state,
        # prepare for seaborn plot
        curr_state_cancer_df = complete_cancer_state_df.loc
        [complete_cancer_state_df['STATE']==current_state]
        # Construct seaborn plot with regplot(),
        # ax = axs[i,j] indicates where the plot will be placed in the
        # figure
        sns.regplot(x="YEAR", y="AADR", data=curr_state_cancer_df,
ax=axs[i,j])

        #input information for each subplots
        axs[i,j].set_title(current_state)
        axs[i,j].set_xlabel('')
        axs[i,j].set_ylabel('AADR')
        axs[i,j].set_ylim(ylim_min,ylim_max)
```

```
        axs[i,j].set_xlim(1998,2014)
plt.show()
```

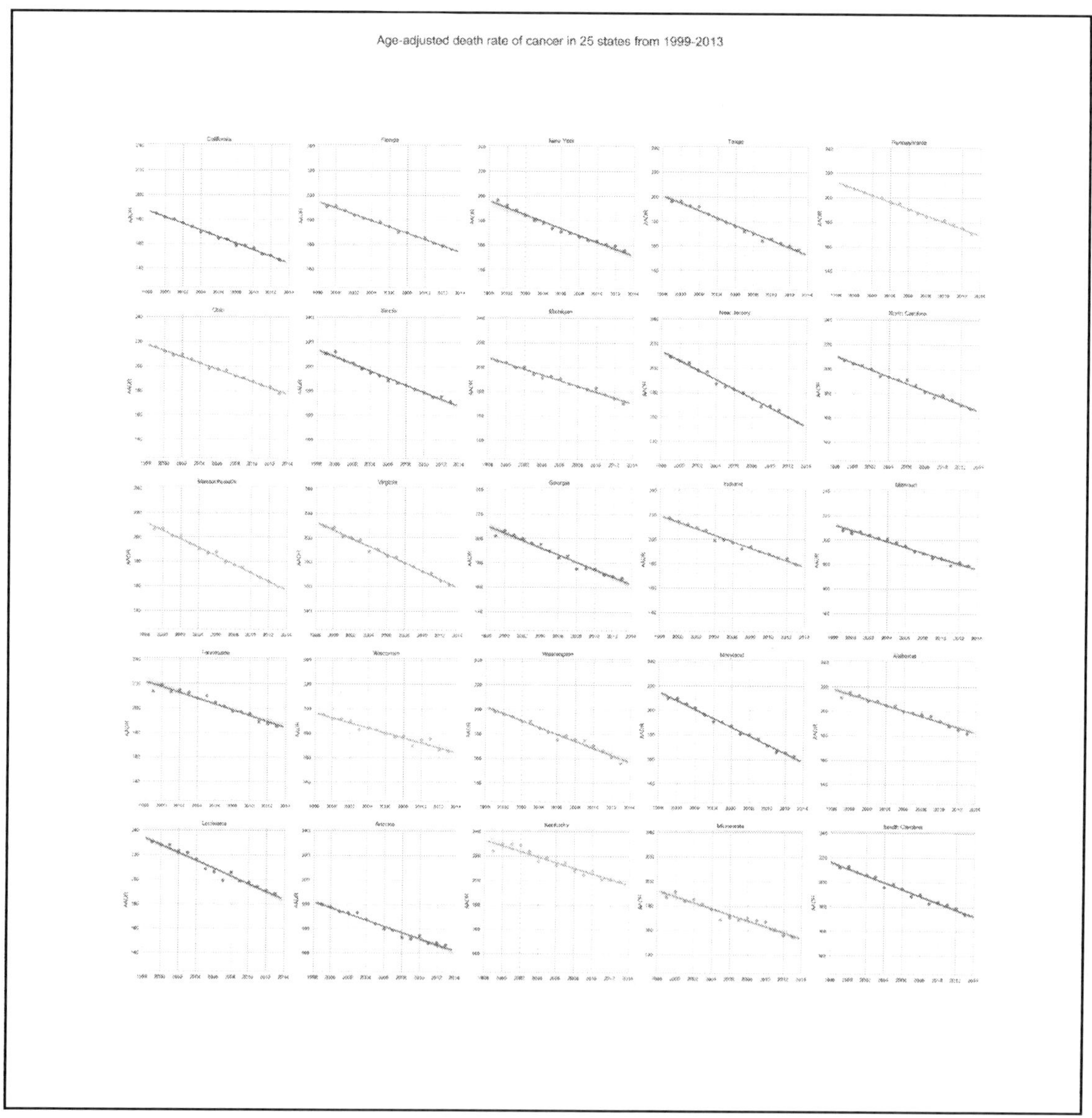

From the preceding figure, readers can tell that the 25 states are showing a decreasing trend in AADR of cancer from 1999-2013 in the USA. More analyses show that other diseases such as heart disease and neurological disorders are in general following the same trend (readers can explore on their own). However, the AADR of suicide is increasing in general, which is quite alarming. Let us explore which state has the highest AADR of suicide in the US from 1999-2013:

```
plt.clf() # Clear figure
# Constructing new dataframe that contains all the information from
# 'Suicide'
complete_suicide_state_df = census_info.loc[census_info
['CAUSE_NAME']=='Suicide']
complete_suicide_state_df[['DEATHS','AADR']]=complete_suicide_state_df[['DE
ATHS','AADR']].apply(pd.to_numeric)

# Initialize dictionary that could store the total AADR of suicide for
# individual states
# Initial value assigned as ZERO
all_states = set(complete_suicide_state_df['STATE'])
all_states_total_suicidal_dict = dict(zip(all_states,[0]*len(all_states)))

# Initialize dictionary that could store every AADR of suicide for
# individual states
# Data structure : Dictionary of List
# This will be useful for the next section
all_states_independent_suicidal_dict = {}
for each_state in all_states:
    all_states_independent_suicidal_dict[each_state]=[]

# Assigning AADR to the two dictionaries that we have initialized just now
for each_state in all_states:
    for year in range(1999,2014):
        # Construct new dataframe that contains suicide information for
        # independent state
        temp_state_suicide_df = complete_suicide_state_df.loc
        [complete_suicide_state_df['STATE']==each_state]
        # Obtain dataframe that contains suicide information for
        # independent state for a particular year
        temp_year_df = temp_state_suicide_df.loc
        [temp_state_suicide_df['YEAR']==year]
        #Assign the AADR value to the two dictionaries initialized above
all_states_total_suicidal_dict[each_state]=all_states_total_suicidal_dict[e
ach_state]+float(temp_year_df['AADR'])
all_states_independent_suicidal_dict[each_state].append(float(temp_year_df[
'AADR']))

# Determine the mean AADR of suicide for each state
```

```
for state, total_suicidal_aadr in all_states_total_suicidal_dict.items():
    all_states_total_suicidal_dict[state]=
    total_suicidal_aadr/len(range(1999,2014))

# Identify the top 25 states that has the highest mean AADR of suicide
top_25_ranked_states = sorted(all_states_total_suicidal_dict,
key=all_states_total_suicidal_dict.get,reverse=True)[0:25][::-1]

# Determining the maximum and minimum value of y-axis for visualization
# across these 25 states
suicide_aadr_list = complete_suicide_state_df['AADR']
ylim_max = max(suicide_aadr_list)
ylim_min = min(suicide_aadr_list)

# Initialize plots, explicitly stating its a 5x5 multiplot
fig, axs = plt.subplots(ncols=5,nrows=5,figsize=(30,30))
# Main title of the plot
sns.plt.suptitle('Age-adjusted death rate of suicide in 25 states from
1999-2013',fontsize=25)
# Similar to the plot shown above, here are the 2 for-loops that assign
# different subplots to their respective position
for i in range(0,5):
    for j in range(0,5):
        # Extract the state by popping them from the list
        current_state = top_25_ranked_states.pop()
        # Construct new dataframe for that particular state
        curr_state_suicide_df = complete_suicide_state_df.loc
        [complete_suicide_state_df['STATE']==current_state]
        # Construct subgraph using sns.regplot
        sns.regplot(x="YEAR", y="AADR", data=curr_state_suicide_df,
ax=axs[i,j])
        # input information for each subplots
        axs[i,j].set_title(current_state)
        axs[i,j].set_xlabel('')
        axs[i,j].set_ylabel('AADR')
        axs[i,j].set_ylim(ylim_min,ylim_max)
        axs[i,j].set_xlim(1998,2014)
plt.show()
```

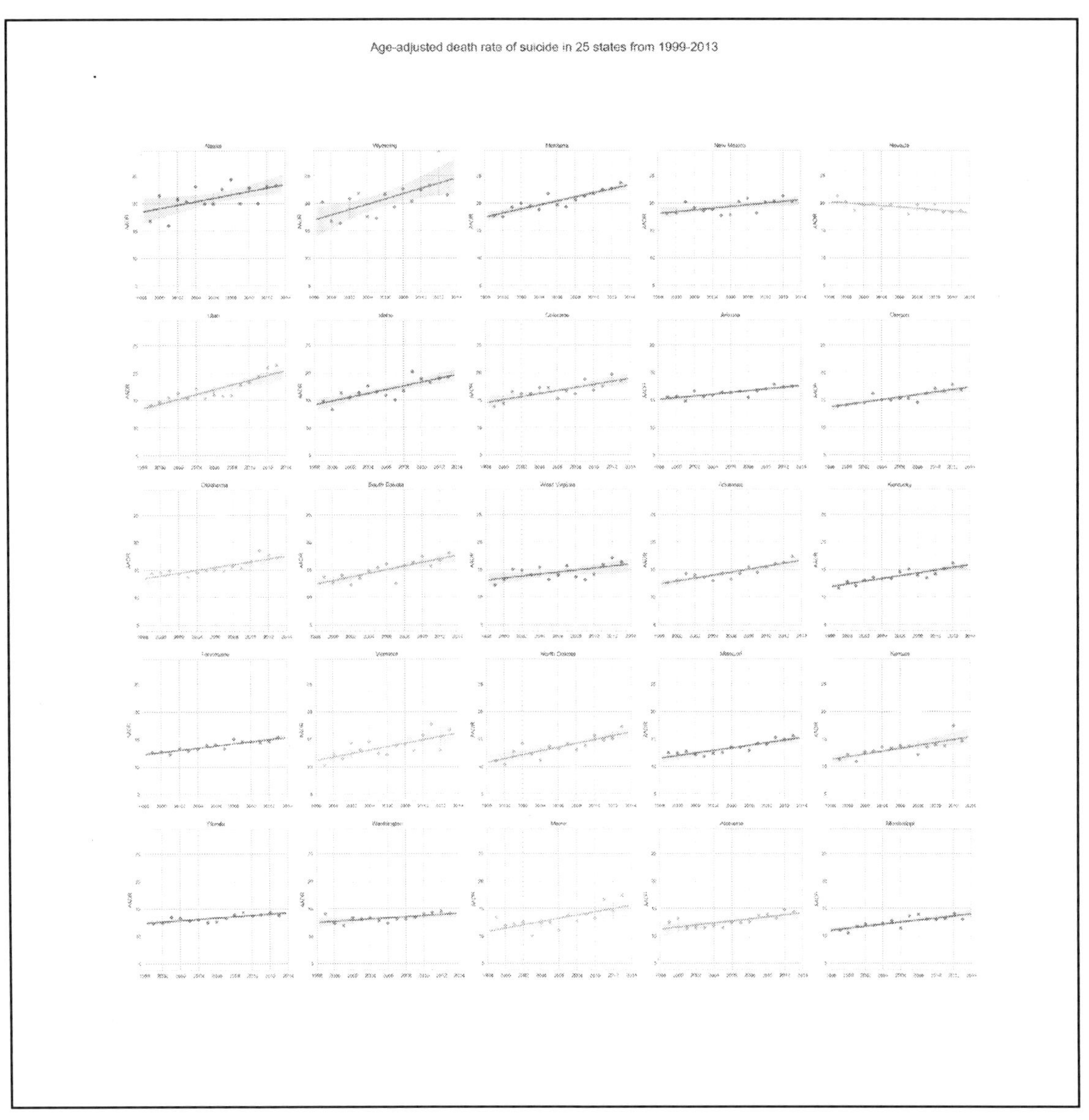
Age-adjusted death rate of suicide in 25 states from 1999-2013

The ranks of the states are assigned from left to right, top to bottom, in descending order. Therefore, Alaska was having the highest average AADR of suicide across the US from 1999 to 2013. Readers may be confused by a few things in here. First of all, the figure is ranked based on the average AADR of each states, but a higher average AADR value does not indicate an increasing trend of suicide of that particular state. To assess whether there is an increasing or decreasing trend of AADR of suicide for a particular state, we can assume that the data has a linear relationship, and fit a line to the dataset to determine the changing rate of AADR of all states from 1999 to 2013:

```
plt.clf()

f,ax=plt.subplots()
# Initialize dictionary to store the fitted rate of AADR from 1999-2013
all_states_fitted_AADR_trend = {}
x_line = range(0,15)

# In this for-loop, we are trying to fit a line to all the data point
# and estimate the slope of that
for each_state, suicidal_list in
    all_states_independent_suicidal_dict.items():
    # Line fitting
    poly_fit = np.polyfit(x_line,suicidal_list,1)
    # Extracting slope information for each state - the respective trend
    all_states_fitted_AADR_trend[each_state]=poly_fit[0]
    # Showcasing the process with the state Wyoming
    if each_state=='Wyoming':
        plt.suptitle('Age-adjusted death rate of suicide in Wyoming
        from 1999-2013')
        plt.plot(x_line,suicidal_list,'.')
        plt.plot(x_line,poly_fit[0]*x_line+poly_fit[1],'-')
        plt.xticks(x_line,range(1999,2014))
        plt.ylabel('AADR')
        plt.annotate('y = '+str(poly_fit[0])+'x +
        '+str(poly_fit[1]),(10,24),ha='center',color='b')

plt.show()
```

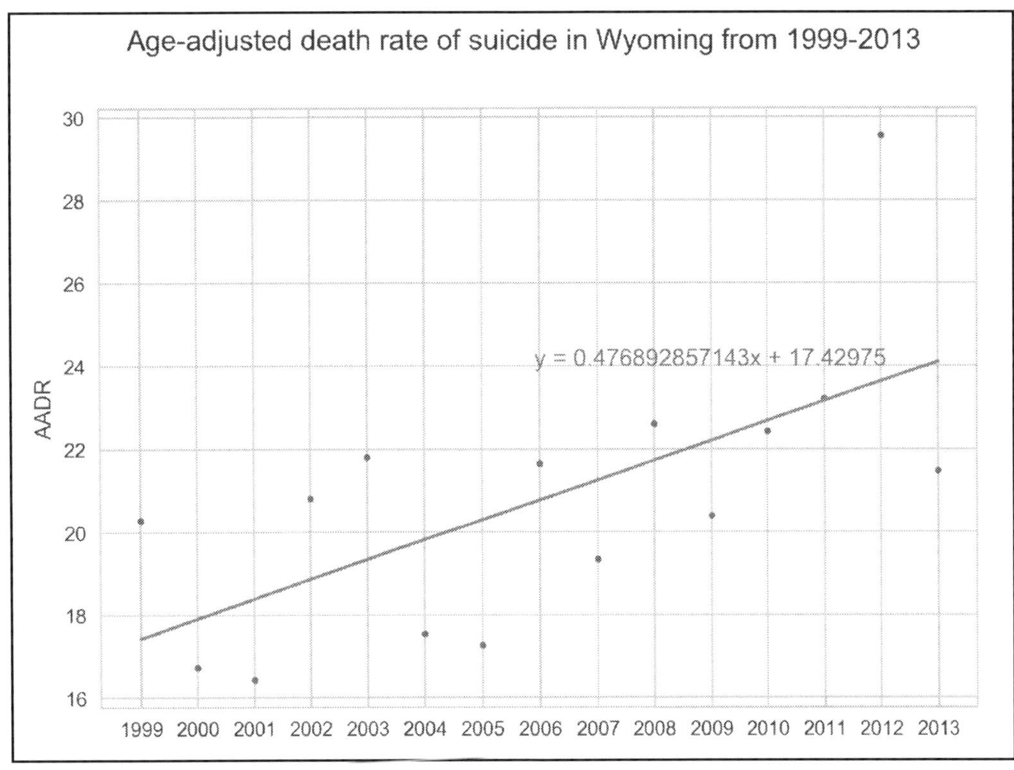

From the preceding figure, we can tell that for Wyoming, the trend is positive (slope with a value of 0.48). We can therefore calculate the slope for every state with the same method. Let's try to visualize all of the trend information from the map:

```
# Converting dictionary to dataframe, prepare for merging with
# refined_states GeoPandas dataframe
suicidal_rates_df = pd.DataFrame(list(all_states_fitted_AADR_trend.
                    items()),columns=['STATE','INCREMENT RATE'])

# Merging with GeoPandas dataframe and prepare for map plotting
merged_suicide_increment_df = pd.merge(refined_states,suicidal_rates_df,
on='STATE')

# More tricks on labeling the map
# Let's modify the dataframe and introduce a new column called
# 'stusps_coords'
# This column will store the coordinate information for each state
# abbreviation
merged_suicide_increment_df['stusps_coords'] =
merged_suicide_increment_df['geometry'].apply(lambda x:
```

```
x.representative_point().coords[:])
merged_suicide_increment_df['stusps_coords'] = [coords[0] for coords in
merged_suicide_increment_df['stusps_coords']]

# Plotting map, with color indicating the increment rate
merged_suicide_increment_df.plot(column='INCREMENT
RATE',cmap='bwr',figsize=(100,40))
# Putting state abbreviation onto the map
for idx, row in merged_suicide_increment_df.iterrows():
    plt.annotate(s=row['STUSPS'],xy=row['stusps_coords'],
    horizontalalignment='center')

plt.axis('equal')
plt.annotate('Trend of Age-Adjusted Death Rate of suicide in US,
1999-2013',xy=(-148,75),color='black',size=25)
plt.savefig('Trend_of_AADR_of_suicide_in_US.png',dpi=300)

# Trimming the plot to give a larger image using PIL library and
# Image processing
suicide_increment_visualization_img =
trim('Trend_of_AADR_of_suicide_in_US.png')
suicide_increment_visualization_img.save('Trend_of_AADR_of_suicide_in_US_cr
op.png')
suicide_increment_visualization_img
```

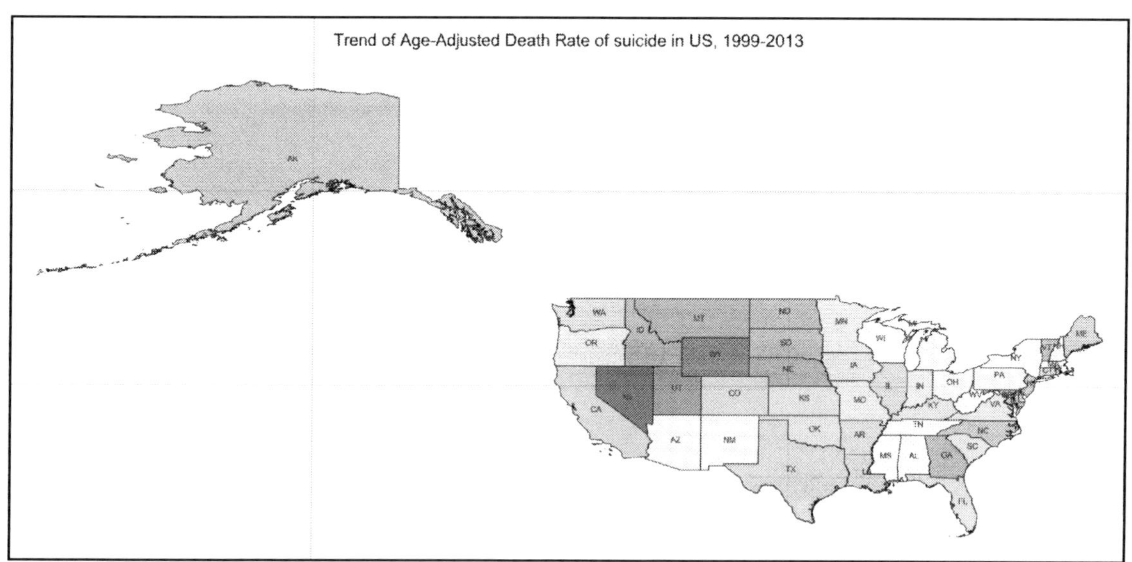

We have added two things here:

- Modified color spectrum from `reds` to `bwr` enables us to plot the increasing trend in suicide rate in red and the decreasing trend in blue. Wyoming is the state with the highest increasing trend.
- By using the shapely method `representative_point()`, we are able to calculate a point that must be within the geometric object, and we further assign the states' abbreviations to that particular point.

With this, we are now able to put together an even more informative map to visualize the trend of AADR of suicide in the US from 1999 to 2013. Interestingly, despite the fact that Nevada is having a relatively high AADR of suicide in US, it has the strongest decreasing trend in AADR of suicide as well.

Rather than using a map, we are also able to visualize geographical information, time, and AADR in one figure by using a heatmap:

```
plt.clf() # Clear figure

# By using the .pivot() method in Pandas library, readers can create
# a pivot table and simply parse it to seaborn for visualization
heatmap_df = complete_suicide_state_df.pivot('YEAR','STATE','AADR')

sns.set()
f,ax = plt.subplots(figsize=(15,15))
# plotting heatmap with the seaborn library
sns.heatmap(heatmap_df, linewidths=0.3, ax=ax)

plt.show()
```

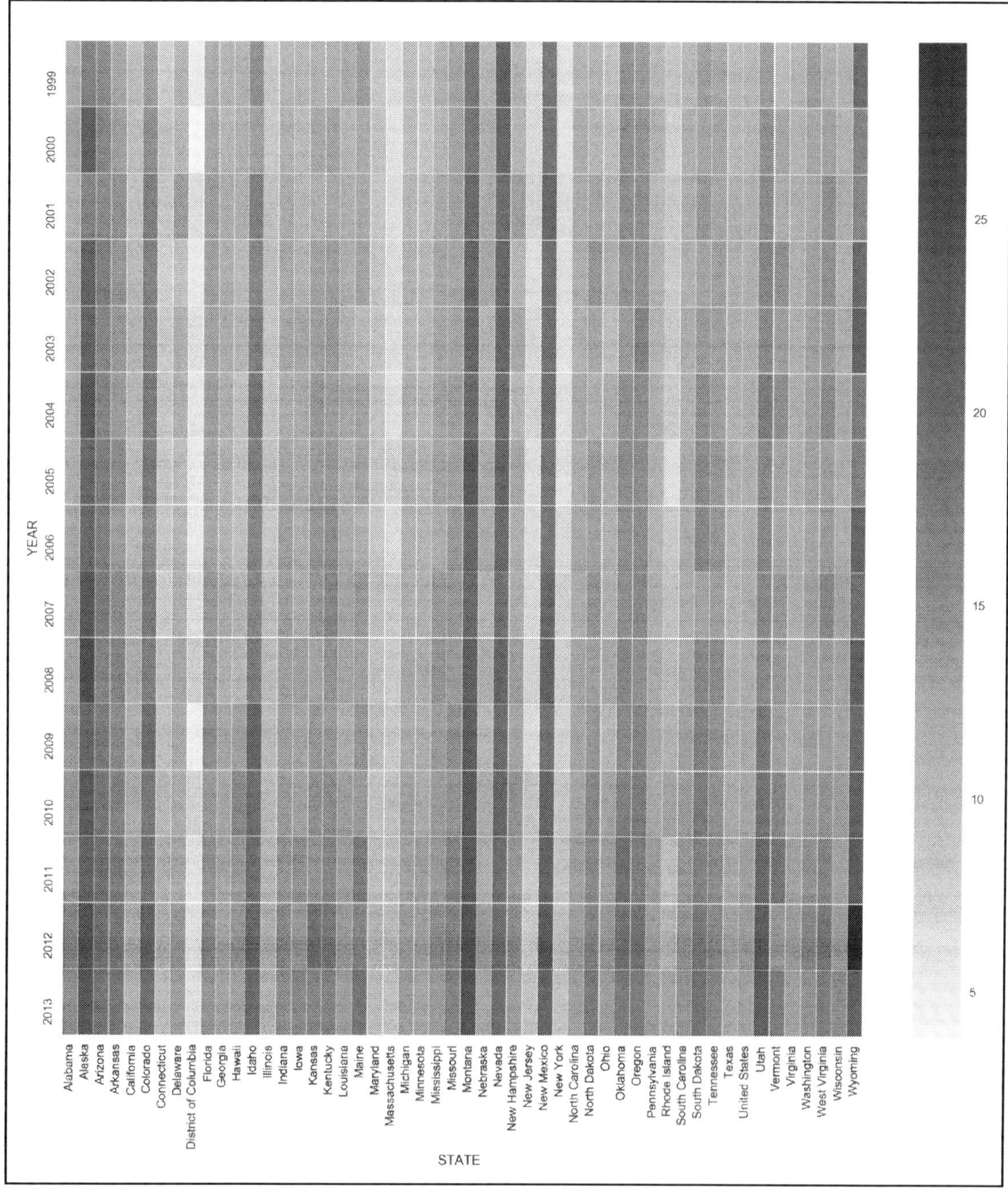
YEAR
1999
2000
2001
2002
2003
2004
2005
2006
2007
2008
2009
2010
2011
2012
2013
STATE
Alabama
Alaska
Arizona
Arkansas
California
Colorado
Connecticut
Delaware
District of Columbia
Florida
Georgia
Hawaii
Idaho
Illinois
Indiana
Iowa
Kansas
Kentucky
Louisiana
Maine
Maryland
Massachusetts
Michigan
Minnesota
Mississippi
Missouri
Montana
Nebraska
Nevada
New Hampshire
New Jersey
New Mexico
New York
North Carolina
North Dakota
Ohio
Oklahoma
Oregon
Pennsylvania
Rhode Island
South Carolina
South Dakota
Tennessee
Texas
United States
Utah
Vermont
Virginia
Washington
West Virginia
Wisconsin
Wyoming
25
20
15
10
5

This heatmap shows the AADR of suicide for every state in the USA from 1999 to 2013. To observe the correlation between the states, we can use the `.corr()` function from the pandas library:

```
# Calculate correlation among states
corr_df = heatmap_df.corr()
# Show the first 5 lines from the correlation dataframe
corr_df.head()
```

STATE	Alabama	Alaska	Arizona	Arkansas	California	Colorado	Connecticut	Delaware	District of Columbia	Florida	...	Tennessee	Texas	the United States	Utah	Vermont	Virginia	Washington	West Virginia	Wisconsin	Wyoming
STATE	-	-	-	-	-			-	-	-	-	-	-	-	-	-	-	-	-	-	-
Alabama	1.000000	0.441934	0.667451	0.667113	0.606576	0.507087	0.768300	0.443227	-0.080866	0.589588	...	0.683404	0.593106	0.796376	0.765944	0.387141	0.801539	0.637074	0.338000	0.630335	0.619940
Alaska	0.441934	1.000000	0.405809	0.456981	0.615688	0.386017	0.272008	-0.003831	0.238349	0.375888	...	0.618279	0.299035	0.526681	0.470049	0.572059	0.355524	0.350219	0.405381	0.551696	0.386371
Arizona	0.667451	0.405809	1.000000	0.686619	0.646841	0.624618	0.556479	-0.052349	-0.098132	0.529121	...	0.694571	0.674694	0.824260	0.809134	0.722823	0.755421	0.705047	0.537982	0.624330	0.575614
Arkansas	0.667113	0.456981	0.686619	1.000000	0.576276	0.727726	0.630535	0.498206	0.414993	0.762468	...	0.787560	0.805496	0.921564	0.845354	0.682375	0.885685	0.553653	0.626923	0.840058	0.581870
California	0.606576	0.615688	0.646841	0.576276	1.000000	0.431089	0.424057	0.122522	0.254083	0.610889	...	0.711576	0.571418	0.743295	0.597420	0.678870	0.665242	0.767222	0.269360	0.684559	0.640033

With the correlation dataframe, we can now plot the heatmap again and see whether the states follow the same trend in general:

```
sns.set()
f,ax = plt.subplots(figsize=(20,15))
# plotting heatmap with the seaborn library
sns.heatmap(corr_df, linewidths=0.5, ax=ax)

plt.show()
```

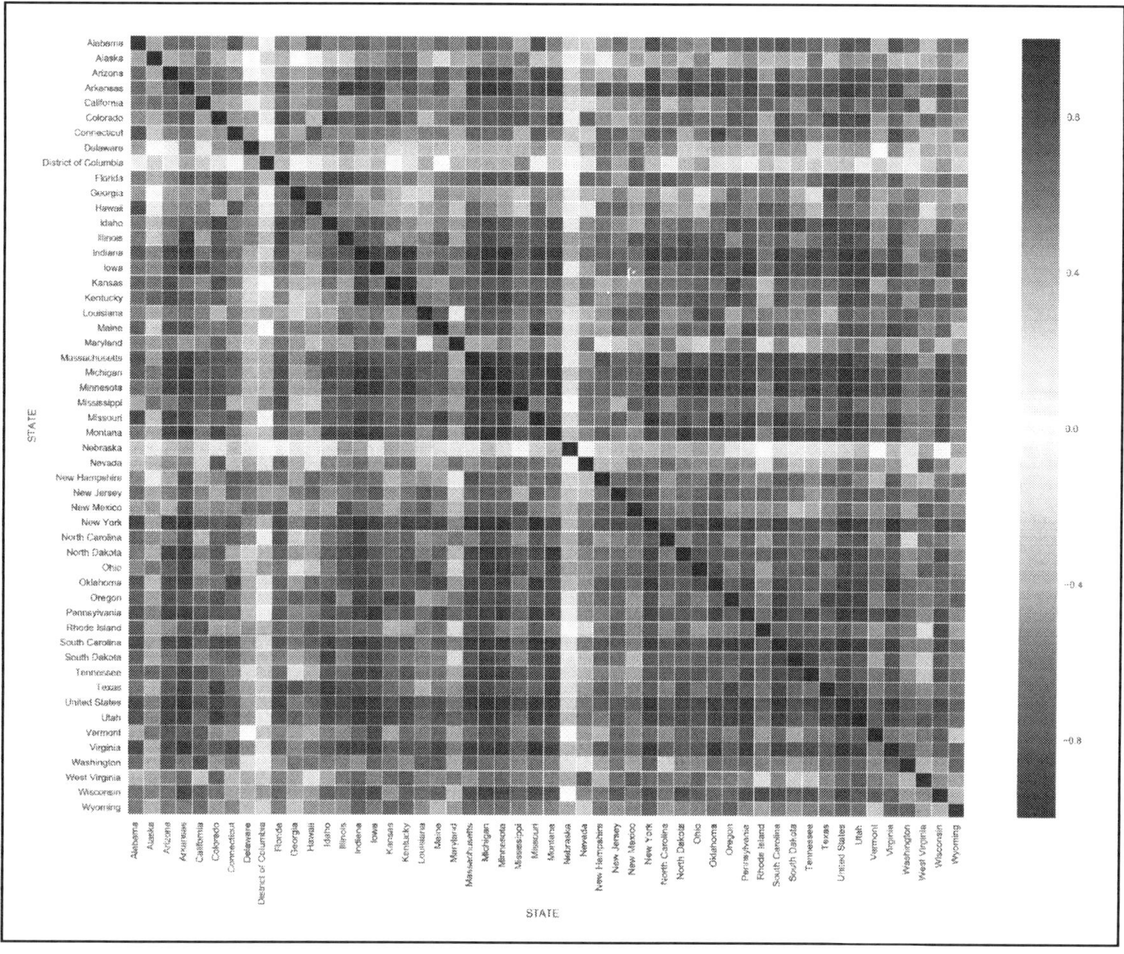

The preceding heatmap shows the correlation of AADR between all the states. The diagonal is always at a correlation coefficient of 1, as a state is always perfectly correlated with itself. Surprisingly, Nevada is showing a distinctly opposite trend when compared to all other states. Let us extract the suicide data of Nevada and see how it behaves on a line plot:

```
plt.clf()
f,ax=plt.subplots(nrows=1,ncols=1)

# Similar to script above, but this time we are showing the graph
# fitting results from Nevada
for each_state, suicidal_list in all_states_independent_suicidal
    _dict.items():
    poly_fit = np.polyfit(x_line,suicidal_list,1)
    if each_state=='Nevada':
```

```
        plt.plot(x_line,suicidal_list,'.')
        plt.plot(x_line,poly_fit[0]*x_line+poly_fit[1],'-')
        plt.xticks(x_line,range(1999,2014))
        plt.annotate('y = '+str(poly_fit[0])+'x +
'+str(poly_fit[1]),(6,20),ha='center',color='b')
        plt.ylabel('AADR')
        plt.suptitle('Age-adjusted death rate of suicide in Nevada from
1999-2013')

plt.show()
```

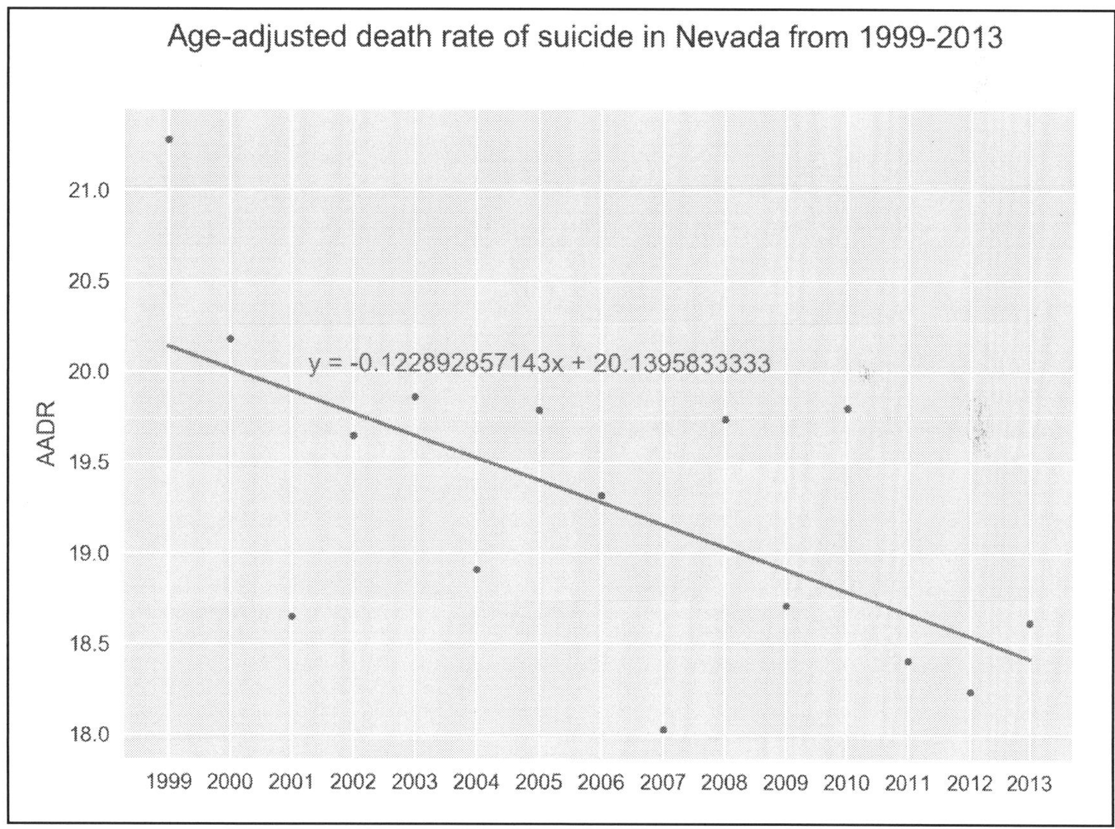

Although Nevada seems to have a higher AADR due to suicide, the trend is decreasing. This concurs with the map showing the trend of AADR of suicide in the US as aforementioned.

Survival data analysis on cancer

Since we've spent a significant amount of time discussing death rate, let us conclude this chapter with one final analysis of two cancer datasets. We have obtained the de-identified clinical dataset of breast cancer and brain tumor from `http://www.cbioportal.org/`; our goal is to see what the overall survival outcome looks like, and whether the two cancers are having statistically different survival outcomes. The datasets are being explored only for research purposes:

```
# The clinical dataset are in tsv format
# We can use the .read_csv() method and add an argument sep='\t'
# to construct the dataframe
gbm_df = pd.read_csv('https://github.com/PacktPublishing/Matplotlib-2.x-
By-Example/blob/master/gbm_tcga_clinical_data.tsv',sep='\t')
gbm_primary_df = gbm_df[gbm_df['Sample Type']=='Primary Tumor']
.dropna(subset=['Overall Survival (Months)'])

brca_df = pd.read_csv('https://github.com/PacktPublishing/Matplotlib-2.x-
By-Example/blob/master/brca_metabric_clinical_data.tsv',sep='\t')
brca_primary_df = brca_df[brca_df['Sample
Type']=='Primary'].dropna(subset=['Overall Survival (Months)'])

brca_primary_df.head()
```

-	Patient ID	Sample ID	Nottingham prognostic index	Cancer Type	Cancer Type Detailed	Cellularity	Chemotherapy	Cohort	ER Status	ER status measured by IHC	...	3-Gene classifier subtype	Patient's Vital Status	Primary Tumor Laterality	Radio Therapy	Cancer Studies	Sample Type	Tumor Other Histologic Subtype	Tumor Size	Tumor Stage	Type of Breast Surgery
0	MB-0002	MB-0002	4.020	Breast Cancer	Breast Invasive Ductal Carcinoma	high	NO	1.0	+	pos	...	ER+/HER2- High Prolif	Living	r	YES	brca_metabric	Primary	IDC	10.0	1.0	BREAST CONSERVING
1	MB-0005	MB-0005	4.030	Breast Cancer	Breast Invasive Ductal Carcinoma	high	YES	1.0	+	pos	...	NaN	Died of Disease	r	NO	brca_metabric	Primary	IDC	15.0	2.0	MASTECTOMY
2	MB-0006	MB-0006	4.050	Breast Cancer	Breast Invasive Ductal Carcinoma	moderate	YES	1.0	+	pos	...	NaN	Living	r	YES	brca_metabric	Primary	IDC	25.0	2.0	MASTECTOMY
3	MB-0010	MB-0010	4.062	Breast Cancer	Breast Invasive Ductal Carcinoma	moderate	NO	1.0	+	pos	...	ER+/HER2- High Prolif	Died of Disease	l	YES	brca_metabric	Primary	IDC	31.0	4.0	MASTECTOMY
4	MB-0014	MB-0014	4.020	Breast Cancer	Breast Invasive Ductal Carcinoma	moderate	YES	1.0	+	pos	...	NaN	Living	r	YES	brca_metabric	Primary	IDC	10.0	2.0	BREAST CONSERVING

As one can tell, there is a tremendous amount of information from this clinical data, but what we need now is just the *Overall Survival (months)* and the *Overall Survival Status* from the dataframe. With these, we are able to perform **Kaplan-Meier** (**KM**) survival analysis. KM survival analysis is a non-parametric method in estimating the probability of survival given a set of time points and census record (whether the patient is alive or deceased). This can be done simply by using the Lifelines library in Python. Lifelines also makes use of Matplotlib for graphical illustration. Before we start, let's install Lifelines via PyPI:

```
pip install lifelines
```

In the following analysis, GBM stands for glioblastoma, a type of brain cancer, and **BRCA** stands for **breast cancer** in broad terms:

```
# We need to use the lifelines library for this analysis
from lifelines.statistics import logrank_test
from lifelines import KaplanMeierFitter

# Initialize a new subplot
fig, ax = plt.subplots()

# Shaping the brain cancer data, extracting the Overall Survival (Months)
# information to a list
gbm_overall_survival_original = gbm_primary_df['Overall Survival (Months)']
# Type casting, make sure all values in the list are in type 'float'
gbm_overall_survival_input = [float(x) for x in
gbm_overall_survival_original]
# Extracting the Overall Survival Status
gbm_censored_original = gbm_primary_df['Overall Survival Status']
# Convert the Overall Survival Status to the lifelines format, it accepts 1
# as deceased and 0 as alive for input
gbm_censored_input = []
for record in gbm_censored_original:
    if record == 'DECEASED':
        gbm_censored_input.append(1)
    else:
        gbm_censored_input.append(0)

# Doing the same for breast cancer data, extracting the Overall Survival
# (Months) information to a list
brca_overall_survival_original = brca_primary_df['Overall Survival
(Months)']
# Type casting, make sure all values in the list are in type 'float'
brca_overall_survival_input = [float(x) for x in
brca_overall_survival_original]
# Extracting the Overall Survival Status
brca_censored_original = brca_primary_df['Overall Survival Status']
# Convert the Overall Survival Status to the lifelines format, it accepts 1
```

```
as deceased and 0 as alive for input
brca_censored_input = []
for record in brca_censored_original:
    if record == 'DECEASED':
        brca_censored_input.append(1)
    else:
        brca_censored_input.append(0)

# Initialize KaplanMeierFitter for Kaplan-Meier (KM) survival analysis
# and visualization
kmf = KaplanMeierFitter()
# Fitting brain cancer survival data to the graph
kmf.fit(gbm_overall_survival_input,event_observed=gbm_censored_input,label=
'Brain cancer survival')
kmf.plot(ax=ax,show_censors=False,ci_show=True)
# Fitting breast cancer survival data to the graph
kmf.fit(brca_overall_survival_input,event_observed=brca_censored_input,labe
l='Breast cancer survival')
kmf.plot(ax=ax,show_censors=False,ci_show=True)
# Labeling the graphs
plt.ylabel('Survival')
plt.xlabel('Months')

plt.show()
```

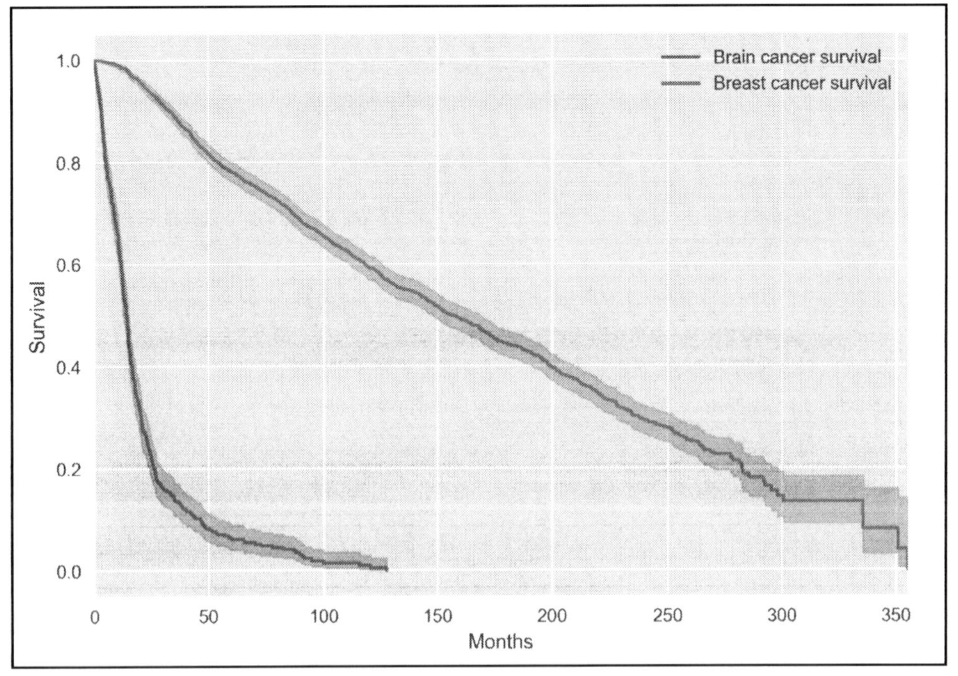

From this figure, one can tell that the survival outcomes from the two cancer types are drastically different. While 50% of the patients with breast cancer can survive up to 150 months, 50% of the patients with brain cancer (GBM) cannot live more than a year. To further test the significance between the two cancer types, we can use the log-rank test. The log-rank test is a non-parametric test done to compare the survival distributions of two samples; the code is straightforward and is shown here:

```
# Performing log rank test
gbm_brca_lgr_result =
logrank_test(gbm_overall_survival_input,brca_overall_survival_input,\
event_observed_A=gbm_censored_input,event_observed_B=brca_censored_input)
gbm_brca_lgr_result

<lifelines.StatisticalResult:
Results
   t 0: -1
   test: logrank
   alpha: 0.95
   null distribution: chi squared
   df: 1

   __ p-value ___|__ test statistic __|____ test result ____|__ is
significant __
         0.00000 |             2211.578 |      Reject Null     |         True
>
```

As stated from the results, the `p-value` is very significant (`p-value = 0`). The two types of cancer are having drastically different outcomes.

Summary

In this chapter, we explored different ways of performing exploratory data analysis, specifically focusing on population health information. With all the code provided in this book, the readers can definitely combine more datasets and explore the hidden characteristics. For instance, one can explore whether illegal drug usage is correlated with suicide, or whether exercise is anti-correlated with heart disease across the USA. One key message is that the readers should not mix up association and causality, which is a frequent mistake even made by experienced data scientists. Hopefully, by now, the readers are getting more comfortable with data analysis using Python, and we, the authors, are looking forward to your contribution to the Python community.

Happy coding!

Index

D

E

F

G

H

I

J

K

L

M

N

O

P

Q

R

S

T

U

V

W

X

Made in the USA
Columbia, SC
19 September 2018